TEXAS

HOME LANDSCAPING

Including Oklahoma

Other titles available in the *Home Landscaping* series:

CALIFORNIA

MID-ATLANTIC

MIDWEST
including Southern Canada

NORTHEAST
including Southeast Canada

NORTHWEST
including Western British Columbia

SOUTHERN COASTAL

SOUTHEAST

WESTERN

TEXAS

HOME LANDSCAPING

Including Oklahoma

Fourth Edition

Greg Grant
Roger Holmes

CREATIVE HOMEOWNER®, Upper Saddle River, New Jersey

Technical Editor for this edition: Charles Sadler

CREATIVE
HOMEOWNER®

A Division of Federal Marketing Corp.
Upper Saddle River, NJ

TEXAS HOME LANDSCAPING

Fourth Edition

MANAGING EDITOR Gretchen Bacon
EDITOR Madeline DeLuca
TECHNICAL EDITOR Charles Sadler
DESIGNER Freire. Disseny+ Comunicacio

Printed in China
First Printing

Texas Home Landscaping, Fourth Edition
Library of Congress Control Number: 2010933378
ISBN:978-1-58011-589-6

CREATIVE HOMEOWNER®
is distributed by
Fox Chapel Publishing Company, Inc., 800-457-9112,
903 Square Street, Mount Joy, PA 17552.

About the Authors

Greg Grant is a horticulturist with the Stephen F. Austin State University Pineywoods Native Plant Center in Nacogdoches. He previously held positions with the Texas Agricultural Extension Service, Louisiana State University, Lone Star Growers, San Antonio Botanical Garden, and Mercer Arboretum. He is a regular contributor to *Texas Gardener, Neil Sperry's Gardens,* and *Ornamental Outlook* magazines and co-author of *The Southern Heirloom Garden*.

Roger Holmes is the founding editor of *Fine Gardening* magazine. He co-edited the monumental Taylor's *Master Guide to Gardening* and other highly regarded gardening books, and produced the landscaping series of which this book is part. He also co-wrote Creative Homeowner's *Creating Good Gardens*.

Planet Friendly Publishing
- ✓ Made in the United States
- ✓ Printed on Recycled Paper
  Text: 10% Cover: 10%

Learn more: www.greenedition.org

At Creative Homeowner we're committed to producing books in an earth-friendly manner and to helping our customers make greener choices.

Manufacturing books in the United States ensures compliance with strict environmental laws and eliminates the need for international freight shipping, a major contributor to global air pollution.

And printing on recycled paper helps minimize our consumption of trees, water, and fossil fuels. *Texas Home Landscaping* was printed on paper made with 10% post-consumer waste.
According to the Environmental Defense Fund Paper Calculator, by using this innovative paper instead of conventional papers we achieved the following environmental benefits:

Trees Saved: 25

Water Saved: 11,506 gallons

Solid Waste Eliminated: 729 pounds

Greenhouse Gas Emissions Eliminated: 2,552 pounds

Courier Corporation, the manufacturer of this book, owns the Green Edition Trademark.

Safety First

Though all concepts and methods in this book have been reviewed for safety, it is not possible to overstate the importance of using the safest working methods possible. What follows are reminders—dos and don'ts for yard work and landscaping. They are not substitutes for your own common sense.

- *Always* use caution, care, and good judgment when following the procedures described in this book.
- *Always* determine locations of underground utility lines before you dig, and then avoid them by a safe distance. Buried lines may be for gas, electricity, communications, or water. Start research by contacting your local building officials. Also contact local utility companies; they will often send a representative free of charge to help you map their lines. In addition, there are private utility locator firms that may be listed in your Yellow Pages. Note: previous owners may have installed underground drainage, sprinkler, and lighting lines without mapping them. National Call Before You Dig, Dial 811.
- *Always* inspect your work area before you begin a project. Check for trip hazards, overhead wires, loose rocks or branches, uneven ground, or holes. Check if hard surfaces are wet, such as paved areas, patios, and decks. If they are wet, it is best to postpone work until they are dry.
- *Always* read and heed the manufacturer's instructions for using a tool, especially the warnings.
- *Always* inspect tools before beginning work, check that they are sharpened and tightened, free of defects or rust, well-piled and sanitzed to reduce the risk of spreading disease or pests from previous work. Remember to oil after using. White lithium grease is beneficial to spray on tools to prevent rust. This is important to do when storing tools for a prolonged period.
- *Always* ensure that the electrical setup is safe; be sure that no circuit is overloaded and that all power tools and electrical outlets are properly grounded and protected by a ground-fault circuit interrupter (GFCI). Do not use power tools in wet locations.
- *Never* transport firewood since it can harbor pests or disease, spreading invasive pests. See *www.fs.usda.gov* for more info.
- *Always* wear eye protection when using chemicals, sawing wood, pruning trees and shrubs, using power tools, and striking metal onto metal or concrete.
- *Always* read labels on chemicals, solvents, and other products; provide ventilation; heed warnings.
- *Always* wear heavy rubber gloves rated for chemicals, not mere household rubber gloves, when handling toxins.
- *Always* wear a disposable face mask or a special filtering respirator when creating sawdust or working with toxic gardening substances.
- *Always* be aware of biosecurity. When purchasing plants or receiving as a gift make sure to inspect for pests or disease. It is also important to sanitize all your garden tools before and after pruning and between pruning of different plants to reduce risk of spreading pests or disease.
- *Always* wear garden gloves when sawing or pruning trees and shrubs. Remember to keep your hands and other body parts clear of the cutting blades and bits.
- *Always* obtain approval from local building officials before undertaking construction of permanent structures.
- *Never* work with power tools when you are tired or under the influence of alcohol or drugs.
- *Never* carry sharp or pointed tools, such as knives or saws, in your pockets. If you carry such tools, use special-purpose tool scabbards.

The Landscape Designers

John Ahrens, with Barry Landry, RLA, and Nena Scott, King's Creek Landscape Management, Austin, Texas. Their designs appear on pp. 36–39, 60–63, 70–73, and 88–91.
Mark Bowen, Living Art Landscapes, Houston, Texas. His designs appear on pp. 30–33, 80–83, and 84–87.
Michael Buccino, Michael Buccino Associates, Palm Desert, California. His designs appear on pp. 34–35 and 64–65.
Rosa Finsley, with Cheryl Bryant, King's Creek Gardens, Cedar Hill, Texas. Their designs appear on pp. 52–55, 94–97, and 112–115.
Michael Parkey, Dallas, Texas. His designs appear on pp. 20–23, 56–59, and 100–103.
Susan Romiti and Ross Holmquist, Mike Parker Landscape, Laguna Beach, California. Their design appears on pp. 28–29.
Carolyn Singer owns Foothill Cottage Gardens, Grass Valley, California. Her design appears on pp. 78–79.
John S. Troy, with Anne Solsbery, John S. Troy Landscape, San Antonio, Texas. Their designs appear on pp. 40–43, 48–51, and 66–69.

John Valentino and Bob Truxell, Truxell and Valentino Landscape Development, Inc., Clovis, California. Their designs appear on pp. 98–99, and 110–111.
Jenny Webber, Oakland, California. Her design appears on pp. 92–93.
Mary Wilhite and Sharon Lee Smith, Blue Moon Gardens, Tyler, Texas. Their designs appear on pp. 24–27, 44–47, 74–77, and 106–109.
Richard William Wogisch, Oasis Gardens, San Francisco, California. His design appears on pp. 104–105.

Contents

Plant Profiles 121

Guide to Installation 154

About This Book

Of all the home-improvement projects homeowners tackle, few offer greater rewards than landscaping. At the main entrance, an attractive brick walkway flanked by eye-catching shrubs and perennials provides a cheerful welcome. A carefully placed grouping of small trees, shrubs, and fence panels creates privacy on the patio or screens a nearby eyesore from view. An island bed divides the backyard into several areas for a variety of activities.

Planting and caring for shrubs, perennials, and other plants can afford years of enjoyment. For those who like to build things, outdoor construction projects can be especially satisfying.

While the installation and maintenance of plants and outdoor structures are within the means and abilities of most people, few of us are as comfortable determining exactly which plants or structures to use and how best to combine them. It's one thing to decide to dress up the front entrance or patio, another to come up with a design for doing so.

That's where this book comes in. Here, in the Portfolio of Designs, you'll find designs for more than 28 common home-landscaping situations, created by landscape professionals. Drawing on years of experience, these designers balance functional requirements including extreme weather and aesthetic possibilities, choosing the right plant or structure for the task, confident in its proven performance in similar landscaping situations.

The second section, Plant Profiles, gives information on all the plants used in the book. Complementing the Portfolio of Designs and Plant Profiles is the Guide to Installation, the book's third section, which will help you install and maintain the plants and structures called for in the designs. The discussions that follow take a closer look at each section; we've also printed representative pages of the sections on pp. 9-10 and pointed out their features.

Portfolio of Designs

This section is the heart of the book, providing examples of landscaping situations and solutions that are at once inspiring and accessible. Some are simple, others more complex, but each one can be installed in a few weekends by homeowners with no special training or experience.

For most situations, we present two designs, the second a variation of the first. As the sample pages on the facing page show, the first design is displayed on a two-page spread. A perspective illustration (called a "rendering") depicts what the design will look like several years after installation, when the perennials and many of the shrubs have reached mature size. To see how a landscape changes within a single year, see "Seasons in Your Landscape," pp. 12–15. For more on how plantings change as they age, refer to "As Your Landscape Grows," pp. 16–17. The rendering also shows the planting as it will appear at a particular time of year. A site plan indicates the positions of the plants and structures on a scaled grid. Text introduces the situation and the design and describes the plants and projects used.

The second design, presented on the second two-page spread, addresses the same situation as the first but differs in one or more important aspects. It might show a planting suited for a shady rather than a sunny site, or it might incorporate different structures or kinds of plants to create a different look. As in the first design, we present a rendering, site plan, and written information, but in briefer form. The second spread also includes photographs of a selection of the plants featured in the two designs. The photos showcase noteworthy qualities—lovely flowers, handsome foliage, or striking form—that these plants contribute to the designs.

Install plants exactly as shown here or rearrange groupings and substitute favorite ones to suit your taste.

The Texas State Flower

Arrival of the Bluebonnets is a magical time in Texas. This cherished state flower is an annual; it grows from seed dispersed the previous season. Because of this, they can be a challenge to get established, requiring certain conditions and taking several seasons to establish. October and November are the best months to sow the seeds. Learn more from www.wildflower.org.

PORTFOLIO OF DESIGNS

FIRST DESIGN OPTION

Plants & Projects
Noteworthy qualities of the plants and structures and their contributions to the design.

Concept Box
Summarizes an important aspect of the design; tells whether the site is sunny or shady and what season is depicted in the rendering.

Site Plan
Positions all plants and structures on a scaled grid.

Summary
An overview of the situation and the design.

Rendering
Shows how the design will look when plants are well established.

78 PORTFOLIO OF DESIGNS

A Beginning Border

FLOWERS AND A FENCE MAKE A CAREFREE DESIGN

SITE: Sunny
SEASON: Summer
CONCEPT: Use the fence as a backdrop for this gorgeous border.

Plants & Projects

A BEGINNING BORDER 79

SECOND DESIGN OPTION

Summary
Addressing the same situation as the first design, this variation may differ in design concept, site conditions, or plant selection.

Variations on a Theme
Photos of inspiring designs in similar situations.

Site Plan
Plants and structures on a scaled grid.

Concept Box
Site, season, and design summary.

Rendering
Depicts the design when plants are well established.

80 PORTFOLIO OF DESIGNS

Autumn blooms

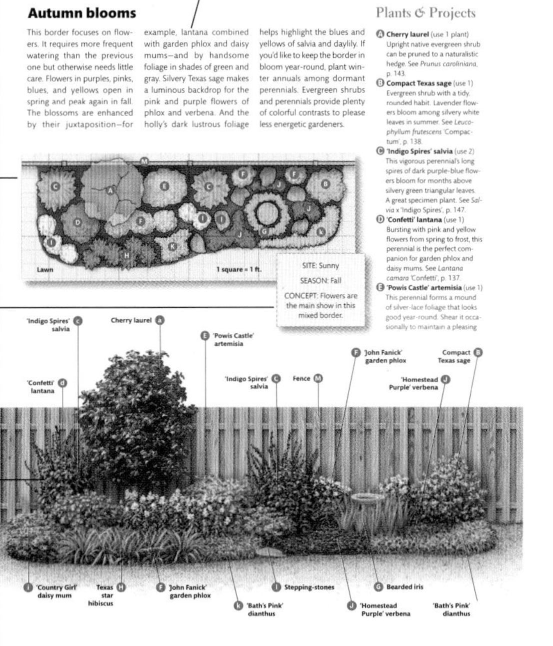

SITE: Sunny
SEASON: Fall
CONCEPT: Flowers are the main show in this mixed border.

Plants & Projects

A BEGINNING BORDER 81

PLANT PORTRAITS

These well-behaved, low-care shrubs, bulbs, and perennials bring form, texture, flowers, and scent to a formal garden.
● = First design, pp. 78–79
▲ = Second design, pp. 80–81

'Country Girl' daisy mum (*Chrysanthemum*, p. 129) ▲

Cherry laurel (*Prunus caroliniana*, p. 143) ▲

'John Fannick' garden phlox (*Phlox paniculata*, p. 141) ▲

Gray santolina (*Santolina chamaecyparissus*, p. 148) ●

PLANT PROFILES

Detailed Plant Information
Descriptions of each plant's noteworthy qualities and requirements for planting and care.

Plant Portraits
Photos of selected plants.

Choices
Selections here help you choose from the many varieties of certain popular plants.

126 PLANT PROFILES Recommended Bulbs

Recommended Bulbs

***Narcissus tazetta*, Narcissus**
This enduring perennial bulb blooms between late fall and early spring. Extremely fragrant white flowers open in dense clusters on 1 to 1½ ft. stalks and make great cut flowers. The dark-green foliage occurs in clumps 1 ft. wide and tall, emerging in the fall and going dormant during the summer. 'Avalanche' (p. 107, ***107***) has creamy-white flowers with lemon yellow cups. 'Grand Primo' (p. 91) is a southern heirloom with creamy white flowers and pale-yellow cups; if unavailable, use 'Avalanche' as a substitute. Paperwhite (*N. tazetta papyraceous*) has pure-white flowers and can be used as a substitute in the milder areas below Interstate 10. Tazetta narcissus are pest free and require no irrigation. Pages: 85, 117.

Narcissus pseudonarcissus 'Ice Follies'
DAFFODIL

Narcissus tazetta
NARCISSUS

***N. pseudonarcissus* 'Ice Follies', 'Ice Follies' daffodil**
Along with the golden yellow cultivars 'Carlton' and 'Fortune', this is one of the few daffodils that does well in Texas. A spring-blooming perennial bulb, it has wide, ruffled, yellow trumpets fading to creamy white. The extremely showy blooms rise 1 ft. among blue-green foliage and make great cut flowers for display in the home. Daffodils require full sun and good drainage. Divide them every 5 to 10 years to keep them blooming. Pages: 35, 52, **54**.

***N. jonquilla*, Jonquil**
This early spring bulb has heavenly scented small golden-yellow flowers above dark-green rushlike foliage. Goes dormant during the summer, re-emerging with fresh foliage in the winter. It has no pest problems and prefers dry summers. 'Trevithian' and 'Sweetness' are commonly available. Pages: 61, **63**.

***Leucojum aestivum*, Snowflake**
This dependable perennial bulb delights with clusters of tiny white bells on 1 ft. stalks in early spring. The healthy green foliage emerges in early winter and goes dormant in summer. Snowflakes are great for introducing bright patches of early bloom among ground covers and landscaped beds. They grow in sun or shade and in moist or dry conditions. This foolproof bulb is pest free and requires no supplemental watering. Pages: 31, 119.

***Zephyranthes candida*, White rainlily**
This hardy little bulb produces dark- green grasslike foliage during the cool months of the year. In late summer the leaves often die back in exchange for showy white crocuslike flowers in the fall. White rainlily grows less than a foot tall and wide. It will grow in full sun or partial shade and tolerates dry or boggy soil. It has no serious insect or disease problems and can be used to naturalize in beds or as a border substitute. Pages: 75, **77**.

Leucojum aestivum
SNOWFLAKE

Carpenteria californica 127

Callicarpa americana
AMERICAN BEAUTYBERRY. This native deciduous shrub has a lax habit, spreading 4 ft. wide and tall. Tapered dull green leaves line the slightly arching branches. In fall, they give way to profuse clusters of vivid violet-purple berries. Beautyberry is pest free and drought tolerant. Irrigation may be needed during periods of drought to maintain attractive foliage. Thin one-third of the older branches to the ground each spring to promote a denser appearance. Pages: 25, 55, 58, 86, 118.

Campanula
BELLFLOWER. A large group of useful flowering perennials (a few are annuals) that vary in plant habit and flower form. Plant them in flower beds, rock gardens, or containers. Spreading types are useful as small-scale ground covers. All grow best in partial shade but can take full sun near the coast.

***Campsis* x *tagliabuana* 'Mme. Galen'**
'MME. GALEN' TRUMPET CREEPER, OR VINE. This hummingbird favorite is a vigorous deciduous vine with a stout woody trunk, large compound leaves, and clusters of salmon-red flowers from summer until frost. Trumpet vine needs full sun, room to grow, and only occasional watering during summer droughts. Once established, it can climb and cover a trellis, fence, or wall with no further assistance or care. It grows at least 10 ft. tall and can reach 20 to 30 ft. Pages: 82, 92, **94**.

Carex planostachys
CEDAR SEDGE.
This species evolved to grow in the shade of Cedar trees and as an understory plant in tall grass prairies and meadows. It is drought tolerant and can grow in a variety of soil types. It prefers well-draining humus-rich soil, it will also grow in clay, caliche and limestone-based soils. Pages: 42-43, 47, 52, 55, 63, 66-67, 83, 99,

Carex texenis
TEXAS SEDGE. A common sedge in Texas, this sedge is a good turf substitute with a tufted, grass-like appearance. It is a suitable option for a ground cover with a similar aesthetic to grass. Pages: 55, 58, 67.

Carpenteria californica
BUSH ANEMONE. This evergreen shrub is grown for its lovely, lightly fragrant white flowers with yellow centers, which are displayed in late spring and early summer against handsome, glossy, dark-green leaves. Grows upright 4 to 6 ft. high and equally as wide. Plant in full sun except in the hottest areas, where partial shade is best. Page: 115.

Callicarpa americana
AMERICAN BEAUTYBERRY

Carex planostachys
CEDAR SEDGE

GUIDE TO INSTALLATION

Sidebars
Detailed information on special topics, set within ruled boxes.

Step-by-Step
Illustrations show process; steps are keyed by number to discussion in the main text.

168 GUIDE TO INSTALLATION

Laying the surface

Whether you're laying a loose or hard material, take time to plan your work. Provide access for delivery trucks, and have material deposited as close to the worksite as possible.

Loose materials
Install water-permeable landscape fabric over the gravel base to prevent gravel from mixing with the surface material. Spread bark or wood chips 2 to 4 in. deep. For a pine-needle surface, spread 2 in. of needles on top of several inches of bark or chips. Spread loose pea gravel about 2 in. deep. For a harder, more uniform surface, add ½ in. of fine crushed stone on top of the gravel. You can let traffic compact crushed-rock surfaces, or compact them by hand or with a machine.

Bricks and precast pavers
Take time to figure out the pattern and spacing of the bricks or pavers by laying them out on the lawn or driveway, rather than disturbing your carefully prepared sand base. When you're satisfied, begin in a corner, laying the bricks or pavers gently on the sand so the base remains even ❶. Lay full bricks first; then install cut bricks to fit as needed at the edges. To produce uniform joints, space bricks with a piece of wood cut to the exact joint width. You can also maintain alignment of the bricks with a straightedge or with a string stretched across the path between nails or stakes. Move the string as you proceed with the work.

As you complete a row or section, bed the bricks or pavers into the sand base with several firm raps of a rubber mallet or a hammer on a scrap 2x4. Check with a level or straightedge to make sure the surface is even ❷. (You'll have to do this by feel or eye across the width of a crowned path.) Lift low bricks or pavers carefully and fill beneath them with sand; then reset them. Don't stand on the walk until you've filled the joints.

When you've finished a section, sweep fine, dry mason's sand into the joints, working across the surface of the path in all directions ❸. Wet thoroughly with a fine spray, and let dry; then sweep in more sand if necessary. If you want a living walk, sweep a loam-sand mixture into the joints and plant small, tough, ground-hugging plants, such as dwarf mondo grass, in them.

Rare is the brick walk that can be laid without cutting something to fit. To cut brick, mark the line of the cut with a dark pencil all around the brick. With the brick resting firmly on sand or soil, score the entire line by rapping a wide mason's chisel called a "brickset" with a heavy wooden mallet or a soft-headed steel hammer as shown on the facing page. Place the brickset in the scored line across one face and give it a sharp blow with the hammer to cut the brick.

If you have a lot of bricks to cut, or if you want greater accuracy, consider renting a masonry saw. Whether you work by hand or machine, always wear safety glasses.

LOOSE MATERIALS

Cover gravel base with water-permeable landscape fabric and add 2 to 4 in. of bark or wood chips.

BRICKS AND PRECAST PAVERS

To turn square corners, align the edging board with a carpenter's square.

❶ Begin laying in a corner.

❷ Check the surface with a level or straightedge. Fill under low bricks; tamp down high ones. Use a plank to distribute your weight if you must work on the path.

❸ Sweep fine, dry sand into the joints to fix the bricks or pavers in place.

MAKING PATHS AND WALKWAYS 169

Stepping-stones

A stepping-stone walk set in turf creates a charming effect and is very simple to lay. You can use cut or irregular flagstones or fieldstone, which is irregular in thickness as well as in outline. Arrange the stones on the turf; then set them one by one. Cut into the turf around the stone with a sharp flat shovel or trowel, and remove the stone; then dig out the sod with the shovel. Placing stones at or below grade will keep them away from mower blades. Fill low spots beneath the stone with earth or sand so the stone doesn't move when stepped on.

Cut around stepping-stone with shovel or trowel.

Remove sod and soil.

Set in place, filling with sand or soil to bed stone firmly.

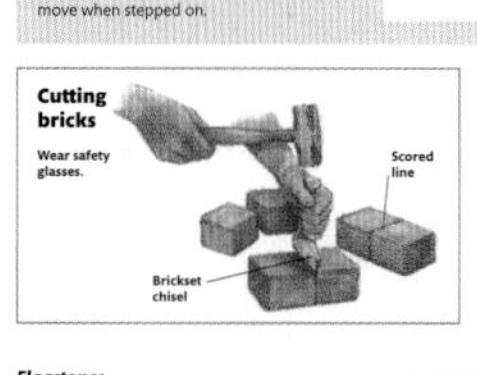

Cutting flagstones

Wear safety glasses.

Scored line

Brickset

Wood batten

Flagstones
Install cut stones of uniform thickness as described for bricks and pavers. Working out patterns beforehand is particularly important—stones are too heavy to move around more than necessary. To produce a level surface with cut or irregular stones of varying thickness, you'll need to add or remove sand for each stone. Set the stone carefully on sand; then move it back and forth to work it into place ❶. Lay a level or straightedge over three or four stones to check the surface's evenness ❷. When a section is complete, fill the joints with sand or with sand and loam as described for bricks and pavers.

You can cut flagstone with a technique similar to that used for bricks. Score the line of the cut on the top surface with a brickset and hammer. Prop the stone on a piece of scrap wood, positioning the line of the cut slightly beyond the edge of the wood. Securing the bottom edge of the stone with your foot, place the brickset on the scored line, and strike sharply to make the cut.

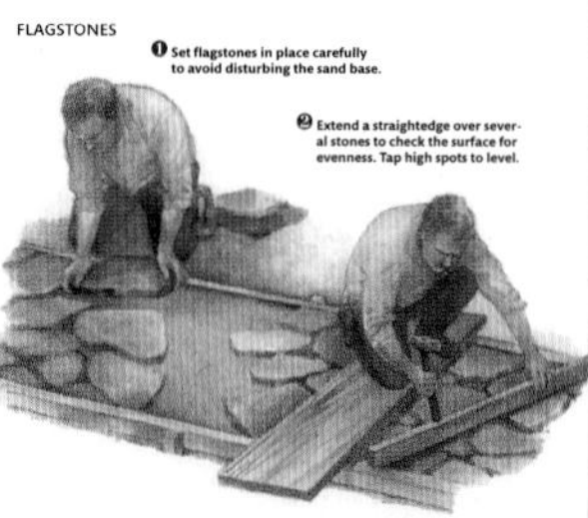

Plant Profiles

This section of the book includes a description of each of the plants featured in the Portfolio. These profiles outline the plants' basic preferences for environmental conditions—such as soil, moisture, and sun or shade—and provide advice about planting and ongoing care.

Working with plant experts in Texas, we selected plants carefully, following a few simple guidelines: every plant should be a proven performer in the state; once established, it should thrive without pampering. All plants should be available from a major local nursery or garden center. If they're not in stock, they could be ordered, or you could ask the nursery staff to recommend suitable substitutes.

In the Portfolio section, you'll note that plants are referred to by their common name but are cross-referenced to the Plant Profiles section by their Latinized scientific name. While common names are familiar to many people, they can be confusing. Distinctly different plants can share the same common name, or one plant can have several different common names. Scientific names, therefore, ensure greater accuracy and are more appropriate for a reference section such as this. Although you can confidently purchase most of the plants in this book from local nurseries using the common name, knowing the scientific name allows you to ensure that the plant you're ordering is the same one shown in our design.

Guide to Installation

In this section you'll find detailed instructions and illustrations covering all the techniques you'll need to install any design from start to finish. Here we explain how to think your way through a landscaping project and anticipate the various steps. Then you'll learn how to do each part of the job: readying the site; laying out the design; choosing materials; addressing basic irrigation needs; building paths, trellises, or other structures; preparing the soil for planting; buying the recommended plants and putting them in place; and caring for the plants to keep them healthy and attractive year after year.

We've taken care to make installation of built elements simple and straightforward. The paths, trellises, and arbors all use basic, readily available materials, and they can be assembled by people who have no special skills or tools beyond those commonly used for home maintenance. The designs can be adapted easily to meet specific needs or to fit with the style of your house or other landscaping features.

Installing different designs requires different techniques. You can find the techniques that you need by following the cross-references in the Portfolio to pages in the Guide to Installation, or by skimming the Guide. You'll find that many basic techniques are reused from one project to the next. You might want to start with one of the smaller, simpler designs. Gradually you'll develop the skills and confidence to do any project you choose.

Most of the designs in this book can be installed in several weekends; some will take a little longer. Digging planting beds and erecting fences and arbors can be strenuous work. If you lack energy for such tasks, consider hiring a neighborhood teenager to help out; local landscaping services can provide more comprehensive help.

TEXAS AND OKLAHOMA HARDINESS ZONES

This map is based on one developed by the U.S. Department of Agriculture. It divides Texas and its neighbors into "hardiness zones" based on minimum winter temperatures. While most of the plants in this book will survive the lowest temperatures in Zone 7, a few may not. These few are noted in the Plant Profiles descriptions, where we have usually suggested alternatives. When you buy plants, most will have "hardiness" designations corresponding to a USDA hardiness zone on the map. A Zone 7 plant, for example, can be expected to survive winter temperatures as low as 0°F, and it can be used with confidence in Zones 7 and 8, but not in the colder Zone 6. It is useful to know your zone and the zone designation of any plants that you wish to add to those in this book.

This is not an official USDA Plant Hardiness Zone Map.

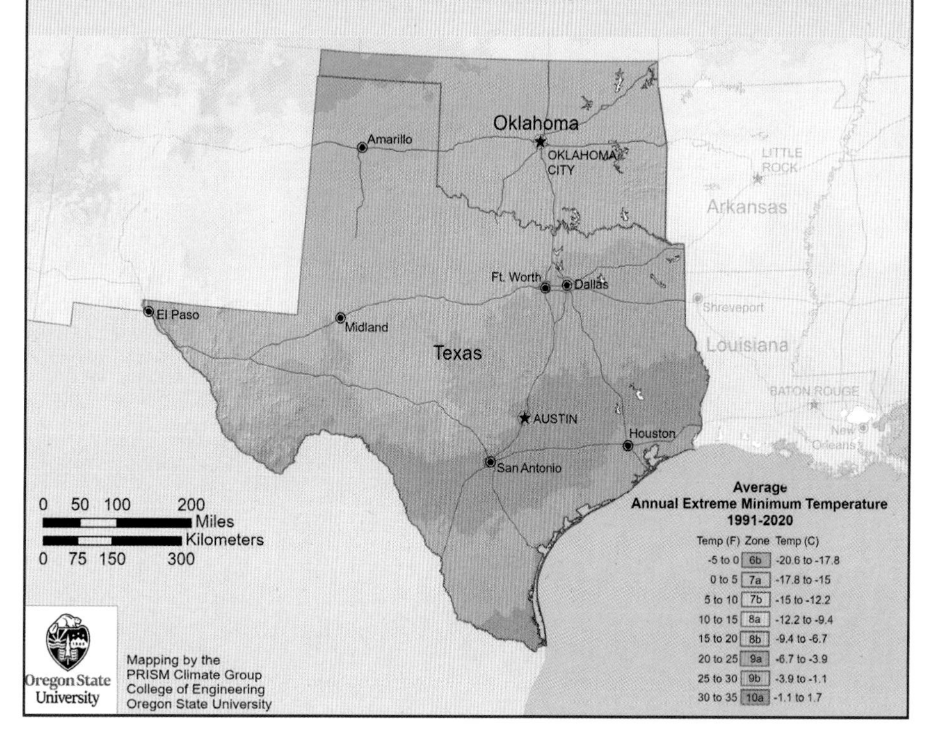

Seasons in Your Landscape

One of the rewards of landscaping is watching how plants change through the seasons. During the winter months, you look forward to the bright, fresh flowers of spring. Then the lush green foliage of summer is transformed into the blazing colors of fall. Perennials that rest underground in winter can grow chest-high by midsummer, and hence a flower bed that looks flat and bare in December becomes a jungle in July.

To illustrate typical seasonal changes, we've chosen one of the designs from this book (see pp. 78-81) and shown here how it would look in spring, summer, fall, and winter. As you can see, this planting looks different from one season to the next, but it always remains interesting. Try to remember this example of transformation as you look at the other designs in this book. There we show how the planting will appear in one season and call attention to any plants that will stand out at other times of year.

The task of tending a landscape also changes with the seasons. So we've noted the most important seasonal jobs in the annual work cycle.

SPRING

Spring

The spring flower season begins in March in much of Texas and peaks in April when the lawns turn green and the trees leaf out. In this garden, spring offers a refreshing display of new growth. Grasses and perennials are greening up, and a thick profusion of new shoots sprout from the cut-back crown of the desert willow. A sprinkling of miniature blue flowers on the rosemary and the gaura's pinkish-white flower buds garnish the greenery. Do a thorough cleanup in early spring. Remove last year's perennial flower stalks and foliage, cut ornamental grasses to the ground, prune shrubs and trees, renew the mulch, lightly fertilize, and neaten the edges between flower beds and lawn.

Summer

The summer garden is an explosion of color. Nearly every plant is in bloom. The nodding lily-like flowers of the soft-tip yucca, the purple spikes of the desert willow, and the coral red spikes of the red yucca make a big show. The diminutive blue, white, and yellow flowers of the Russian sage, gaura, and santolina shout less for attention but are no less pleasing. Despite its name, autumn sage produces a fine show of tubular red flowers. White plumes wave in the breeze above clumps of Indian grass. Water new plantings at least once a week during dry spells, and water older plants, too, if the soil gets so dry that they wilt. Pull any weeds that sprout up through the mulch; this is easiest when the soil is moist.

Fall

Fall brings changes in the garden as well as mercifully cooler temperatures. New for the season are the small lavender-purple flowers that almost smother the pale-gray foliage of the fall aster. Deadheading has produced a full second bloom on the desert willow, while distinctive seedpods have replaced bright flowers on the soft-tip and red yuccas. Gaura and autumn sage continue to bloom. The Russian sage has lost most of its tiny blossoms, but its foliage is an attractive, wispy presence. The santolina has been sheared to keep it tidy. You can leave grasses and perennial stalks standing all winter, if you choose, or clear them away whenever hard frosts turn them brown or knock them down. Toss the stems on the compost pile, along with any leaves that you rake up.

Winter

In winter, when much of the landscape turns tan and brown, you'll appreciate evergreen plants such as the red and soft-tip yuccas, trailing rosemary, and santolina. After a hard frost, the Russian sage, fall aster, and gaura have been cut back to ground-hugging crowns. The narrow leaves and plumes of the Indian grass remain a pleasing sight throughout the winter, as do the branching forms of the desert willow and autumn sage. In late winter, cut back these two plants in preparation for vigorous new growth in the spring.

As Your Landscape Grows

Landscapes change over the years. As plants grow, the overall look evolves from sparse to lush. Trees cast cool shade where the sun used to shine. Shrubs and hedges grow tall and dense enough to provide privacy. Perennials and ground covers spread to form colorful patches of foliage and flowers. Meanwhile, paths, arbors, fences, and other structures gain the comfortable patina of age.

Continuing change over the years—sometimes rapid and dramatic, sometimes slow and subtle—is one of the joys of landscaping. It is also one of the challenges. Anticipating how fast plants will grow and how big they will eventually become is difficult, even for professional designers, and it was a major concern in formulating the designs for this book.

To illustrate the kinds of changes to expect in a planting, these pages show one of the designs at three different "ages." Even though a new planting may look sparse at first, it will soon fill in. And because of careful spacing, the planting will look as good in ten to fifteen years as it does after three to five. It will, of course, look different, but that's part of the fun.

AT PLANTING

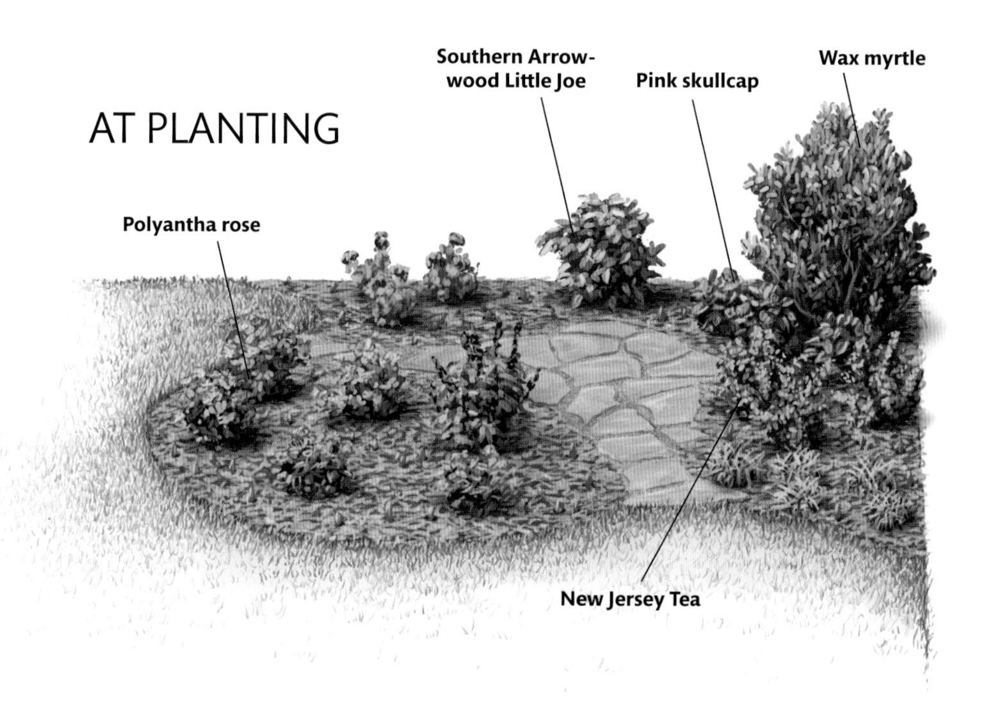

THREE TO FIVE YEARS

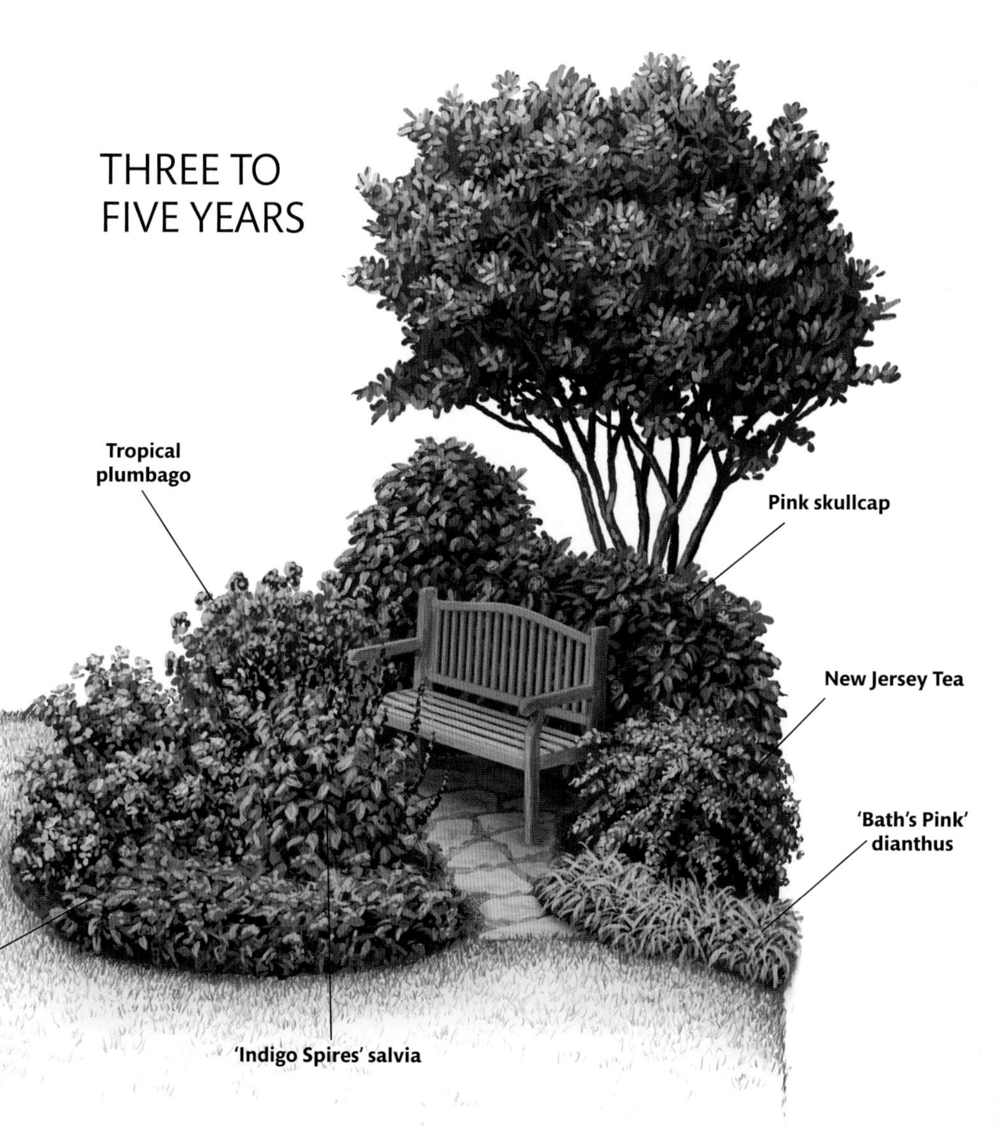

At Planting—Here's how the backyard hideaway (pp. 88-91) might appear immediately after a fall planting. The plants, of course, are small, though their size may vary from what we show here if you want to spend more for more mature trees and shrubs. The multitrunked wax myrtle looks like a bush rather than the small tree it will become. The viburnum, New Jersey Tea, and polyantha rose are several years from filling out their spaces or your expectations. With a good fall start and spring awakening, the perennials will make a creditable show next summer. The first year after planting, be sure to water during dry spells and to pull weeds that pop up through the mulch.

Three to Five Years—As shown here in fall, the planting has filled out nicely. Limbed up to about 5 ft., the wax myrtle provides shade for the bench, while the nearby shrubs have grown to make a comfy enclosure. The now well-established perennials join the shrubs in producing the blue and pink floral scene. Evergreen foliage of the wax myrtle, camellia, viburnum, and New Jersey Tea make this an attractive spot through the winter as well.

Ten to Fifteen Years—Shown again in fall, the planting has become even more of a hideaway with the passing years. The wax myrtle envelopes the site with its presence and its shade. The shrubs are fuller and larger, though kept in bounds by judicious pruning. The perennials have been divided several times since planting to keep them healthy and tidy looking. Their offspring may feature in parts of the landscape elsewhere on the property.

TEN TO FIFTEEN YEARS

Eco-Friendly Plants

Have you enjoyed the shade and cooling effects of a mature oak on a hot summer day? The many oaks native to Texas are up to the challenges of twenty-first century weather extremes. There is a sublime harmony experienced from native plants in your home garden, a well-timed orchestra ebbing and flowing with seasonal wonders and delights, something to enjoy in each season.

Many popular garden plants originate from Asia, such as azaleas, boxwood, camellias, crape myrtle, heavenly bamboo, roses, Asian jessamine, cast iron plant, and many others. To survive in your garden, these non-native species often require irrigation, fertilization, and the application of pesticides and other chemicals. Plus, they are likely to be affected by the increased extreme freezes and droughts now common in Texas.

Some of the plants you purchase at your local garden center are known to "escape," seeding in the surrounding landscape. A key problem with some non-native species is how they can spread uncontrolled, becoming an invasive pest, crowding out beneficial native plants. In addition, popular non-native species seem to be more susceptible to failure from drought, temperature extremes, and common garden pests.

A native plant like Texas sage, shown here, is well suited to its local climate and has a higher chance of thriving than a non-native plant.

So, what exactly is a native plant and why do they matter? The benefits of native plants start with being suited to their local climate and conditions without much assistance once established. In this author's experience, "low maintenance" is a top landscape request; native plants are known to be lower maintenance.

Native plants are suited to the local soil types, annual rainfall, wind conditions, and more. In addition, the local birds, insects, and other wildlife have developed over millennia to coexist and benefit from these species and use them as food, shelter, reproductive sites, and more. Plus, these local creatures perpetuate the plants' success by pollinating them, dispersing their seeds, and helping plants decompose.

As climate extremes increase, it is more important than ever to be mindful of which plants are best suited to thrive in your home landscape. Texas has experienced epic droughts, including the drought from 2011 through 2014 in which many non-native species perished. This was particularly true in Houston's Memorial Park, a 1,500-acre urban green space treasured by Houstonians. Memorial Park lost more than half of its mature trees, many of which were non-native species. Its subsequent redevelopment included returning large areas to drought tolerant coastal savannahs with native plants.

Texas and the rest of the Southern U.S. have experienced savagely cold winters and extended freezes. This author has witnessed the high mortality rate and damage to non-native plants following prolonged below-freezing temperatures. Some non-native plants may not appear to succumb initially but decline and die over a period of months or even a year. Conversely, this author has been pleasantly surprised to see the incredible resilience of native species through freezing temperatures and even snowfall. Following the severe winter freezes it is uncommon to see the failure of native species.

In addition to being well suited to your climate, native species are full of surprises: offering flowers and fruit to attract birds, bees, butterflies, and other attractive pollinators. Your native plant additions can provide sustenance or even a temporary home for migrating birds or seasonally active pollinators. Unfortunately, commonly used non-native plants did not evolve to coexist with your local birds and other fauna. Therefore, local creatures are generally not interested in non-native plants. These same non-native species often repel local fauna and may even be poisonous to them, as well as being poisonous to you, your family, and your household pets.

So, does this mean to jettison all your non-native plants? Many of which may have sentimental meaning, certainly not. While a completely native home landscape is admirable, beautiful, and ecologically beneficial it is not necessary to create a 100% native garden to reap the benefits and enjoyment of their seasonal wonder.

In his publication *Bringing Nature Home: How Native Plants Sustain Wildlife in Our Gardens,* author and University of Delaware scientist Doug Tallamy, PhD suggests limiting your use of non-native plants to about 30%. If some of your favorite plants happen to be non-native, consider locating those near your home where you can enjoy them most. It is suggested you work toward planting 70% of your property with resilient native plants, proven to thrive in your region.

Once established, native plants succeed without irrigation, fertilizers, or pesticides. Of course, during the first year or two during the establishment period plantings require supplemental watering as well as during prolonged droughts. Native plants can be the workhorses that provide beauty and a wide range of benefits your property. Placing native species on the perimeter of your property, also called an eco-tone, is where local birds, insects, and other fauna can enjoy the fruits, flowers, habitat, and security that shrubs and trees provide.

If you had to plant one tree for the most ecological impact and beauty while providing food and shelter for native creatures, what would it be? Ecologists explain that the majestic oak supports more biodiversity than about any other tree species, hosting insects being born, developing, and becoming a food source for birds and other fauna.

As you now know, native plants require less attention once established than non-native plants. With all the time you save, you can enjoy your garden more and spend less time and money, watering, weeding, fertilizing, and applying pesticides.

A native plant like Texas oak supports biodiversity and is a food source for birds like the Carolina chickadee, shown here.

Climate Change Impact

You have likely witnessed the effects and costs of climate change, with the increase in extreme weather events which can disrupt life as you know it. Such as longer, hotter summers, power outages, extended drought, followed by more concentrated rainfall, with possible flooding and erosion, increased storms, high winds, and extreme freezing winter temperatures. This volatility stresses the power grid, can deplete water supplies, and the deep freezes can even burst pipes in your home.

The changes in climate of course also affect plants in your landscape which are limited in their ability to quickly adapt to sudden environmental changes. The USDA Plant Hardiness Zone Map latest data was released in 2023. With this new Hardiness Zone Map, changes in climate were reflected. For instance, some U.S. regions are getting warmer, some drier, and some wetter. Texas is generally getting hotter and dryer in some locations.

Selecting the right plant for the right location has the added benefit of reducing maintenance and increasing the plant survival rate, saving you money. The benefit of selecting an appropriate plant is that it will reach its desired size and shape without much pruning. This reduces time, money, and the emissions or pollution often required to trim oversized plantings. Not to mention a reduction of all the debris created.

As you have likely noticed, Texas is experiencing both higher temperatures and longer summers. This change is coupled with increased intervals between rainfall. Overall, precipitation is staying about the same (in some regions) but being concentrated in fewer storms. Species requiring wetland conditions (obligate wetlands) or favoring moist conditions (facultative wetlands) may not survive prolonged drought. Especially when the drought is repeated year after year. The same is true for species suited to dryer upland conditions. These plant varieties can also succumb to prolonged drought and experience drought stress, dieback, and even failure. Drought stress increases a plant's susceptibility to pests and other diseases.

Deciduous trees and shrubs can shed their leaves during a drought and, if already established, will likely recover. Evergreens, such as pines, if established, will generally survive a drought. However, smaller evergreen trees (less than 5–10 feet tall) and those recently planted may not survive a prolonged drought. A long period without precipitation may not

Blue fescue grass, shown here, is a plant that can survive drought.

kill mature evergreens, but the moisture stress caused by the drought can weaken the tree. This can lead to their eventual decline and failure.

In Texas, native pine trees weakened by drought are likely to be attacked by a variety of pine bark beetles, which only attack weakened trees. So, during a typical weather season the pines are relatively safe. The problem is that drought and hotter summers seem to be the norm now.

An existing landscape or garden can be adapted to be more climate resilient. Adaptations, such as leaving leaf litter below the trees, can help retain soil and moisture. In autumn, leaves falling on lawn areas can be mulched with your home lawn mower. By repeatedly passing over the leaves with a mower, they will become small, mulched bits. These leaf particles add needed organic matter which becomes soil. This process helps lawn areas retain more moisture and stay cooler during hot weather. This creates a cooler more welcoming landscape for you, your landscape, and local fauna. Overall, mulching your leaves back into your lawn creates a healthier, greener, and more vigorous lawn, requiring less water and more resilient against drought. The same is true for mulching planting beds of ground covers, perennials, grasses, and shrubs.

A landscape element loved by many is a water hog. Of course, there is no substitute for a grassy area to picnic or play sports. Consider how much of your lawn area you use for recreation and as play areas for children and pets. If you don't use your lawn this way, you might consider reducing the volume of lawn requiring regular mowing. Of course, there are more ecologically friendly turf grasses which require less water and even some that stay low with minimal mowing, such as Zoysia grass, and low growing drought tolerant fescue and sedge varieties.

If it is feasible to reduce your lawn area. The next step toward a more ecologically friendly landscape and lower maintenance is to retire your gas-powered garden implements (mowers and trimmers). There is now high-quality long-lasting battery powered tools for the home gardener. These products continue to be more affordable with longer battery lives as the technology increases along with their popularity.

Areas where a mown lawn is not required are perfect for a wildflower meadow area, ornamental grasses, native low-growing plants, or spreading ground covers. Additional resources for plant selection are available at the Lady Bird Johnson Wildflower Center, The University of Texas at Austin (*www.wildflower.org*).

A soil test is a good tool to learn the makeup of your soil, and if you compost, soil amendments or fertilizers are needed. Synthetic fertilizers are not needed for the home landscape. In fact, compost and mulched leaves is likely to be all your plants ever need to reach their full potential. Remember to use fertilizers wisely. If you do a soil test and fertilizers are needed, aim to use organic fertilizers—these are milder and not likely to cause harm to your plants if overused or spilled. Research *(www.fws.gov)* shows that synthetic nitrogen fertilizers greatly contribute to greenhouse gas emissions, contributing to climate change.

A simple means to conserve home energy use is to plant deciduous shade trees on the east and west sides of your home. Make sure to allow ample space for the trees to develop. These shade trees will provide cooling shade and the cooling effects of the tree's transpiration in summer. Shading your HVAC air handlers is also an important step to help reduce energy use to cool your home during the warm months of the year. The use of deciduous trees to shade of your home has the added benefit of allowing sunlight to brighten and warm your home once the leaves fall in autumn.

Mulching leaves with a lawn mower helps your lawn retain moisture in hot weather. Put mulched leaf litter underneath trees in the autumn.

Portfolio *of* Designs

As you peruse the following pages, you will find 48 home landscape designs by 19 notable landscape designers who have devised ways to enhance entrances, decks, and patios; create gardens of colorful perennials and shrubs as well as structures and plantings for shady hideaways; dress up nondescript walls; and even make a centerpiece of a lowly recycling area. Plant selections have been carefully chosen with weather extremes in mind, with an aim to create resilient landscapes. Large color illustrations show what the designs will look like, and site plans delineate the layout and planting scheme. Each design is accompanied by text that describes the plants and projects appearing in them. Installed as shown or adapted to meet your site and personal preferences, these designs can make your property more attractive, more useful, and—most important—more enjoyable for you, your family, and your friends.

Up Front Informal

TURN A SMALL FRONT YARD INTO A WELCOMING GARDEN

With a little imagination and a host of pleasing plants, front yards can be transformed into inviting front gardens. Replacing the existing lawn and concrete walkways with colorful plantings and decorative paving will not only reduce mowing and watering, it will also provide a pleasant setting for welcoming guests or watching the world go by.

The transformation from yard to garden begins here with an oversized front walk that widens into a space for sitting. The front walk and patio are tightly laid flagstone to accommodate foot traffic and furniture. A more casual path to the drive is set with wide joints that are planted with a grasslike ground cover.

Bordering the seating area is an informal planting of trees and shrubs. The small oak and two large hollies will create a cozy atmosphere around the entry, and the tree will provide shade as it matures. Beneath these taller plants are colorful shrubs, grasses, perennials, and a durable carpet of evergreen ground covers. While the ground covers won't stand up to much traffic, they will look good year-round with less water and maintenance than a turfgrass lawn.

The planting is illustrated here at its showiest—during the cooler months of fall—when the weather invites lingering outdoors. But each season holds attractions. An abundance of emerging foliage will give the garden a fresh look in spring, the Turk's cap blooms will invite hummingbirds in summer, and evergreen foliage and purple and red berries will keep color in the garden through winter.

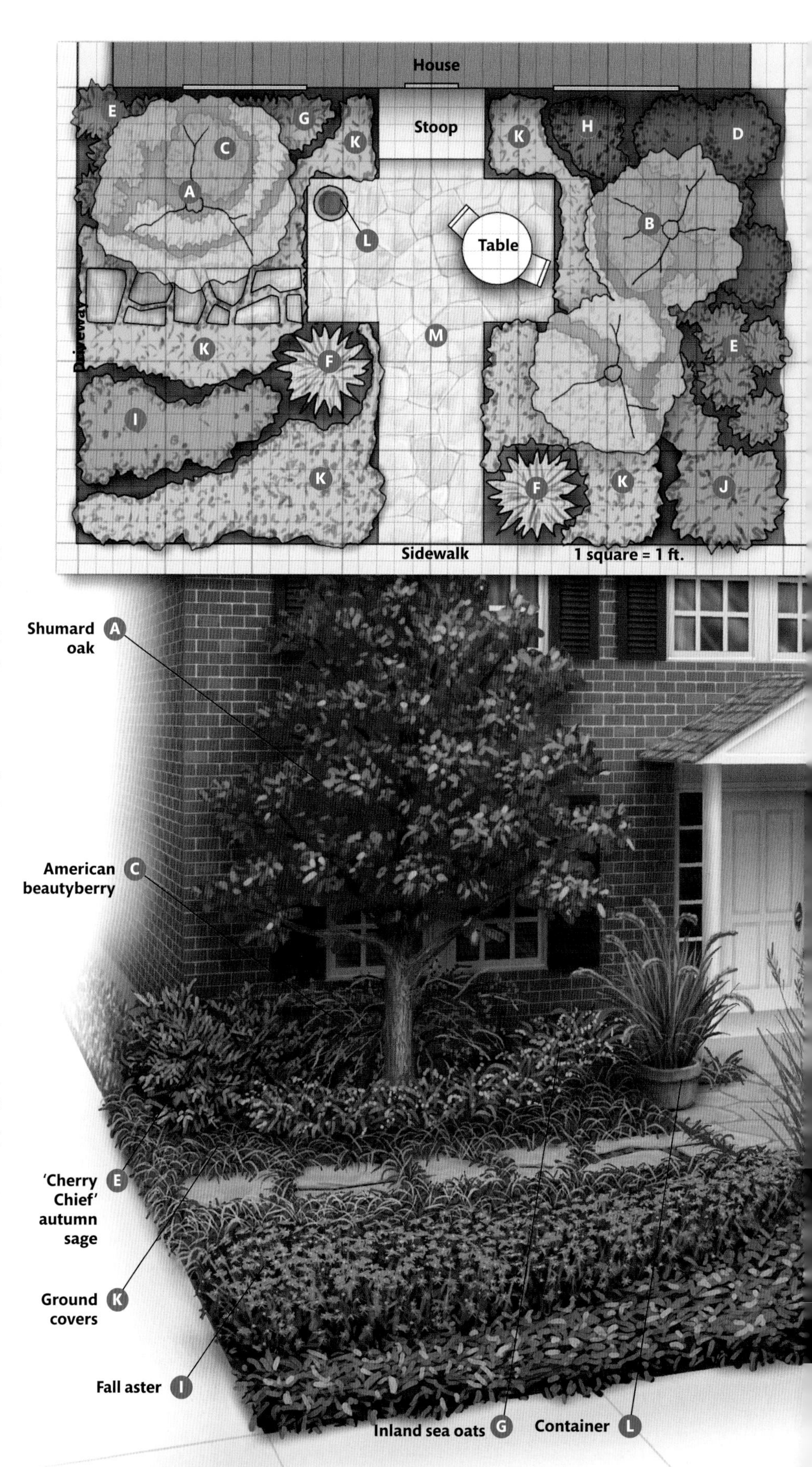

Plants & Projects

Once established, the plants in this design are not particularly demanding. Prune trees and shrubs as needed to maintain size and shape. Seasonal cleanup will keep the planting tidy.

SITE: Sunny

SEASON: Fall

CONCEPT: Well-chosen plants and paving create an entry garden of comfortable informality.

A Shumard oak (use 1 plant)
A handsome shade tree with leavs turning red in the fall and thick, smooth bark. See *Quercus shumardii*, p. 143.

B 'Warren's Red' possumhaw holly (use 2)
These multitrunked deciduous hollies have small lustrous dark-green leaves. They bear countless showy red berries in fall that persist on bare silver-gray branches in the winter. See *Ilex decidua* 'Warren's Red', p. 135.

C American beautyberry (use 1)
Prized for its bright clusters of violet berries that hang on through winter, this deciduous shrub spreads into a loose thicket of green leaves under the oak. See *Callicarpa americana*, p. 127.

D Dwarf yaupon holly (use 4)
These evergreen shrubs form neat mounds of tiny, oval, olive-green leaves. They can be sheared into a low hedge for an even more formal appearance. See *Ilex vomitoria* 'Nana', p. 135.

E 'Cherry Chief' autumn sage (use 9)
This bushy perennial's small oval leaves echo the holly's foliage, but are softer and paler. Small red flowers bloom heavily in spring and lightly in summer and fall. See *Salvia greggii* 'Cherry Chief', p. 147.

F Switchgrass (use 2)
This grass grows 3–5 ft. tall, producing fine-textured lacey seedheads in late summer which persist throughout winter. See *Panicum virgatum*, p. 140.

G Inland sea oats (use 12)
A clump-forming grass grown for long, dangling, oatlike seedheads that dance above the foliage in late summer, turning from light green to bronze and then to tan. See *Chasmanthium latifolium*, pp. 128-129.

H Turk's cap (use 8)
Cousin to hibiscus, these bushy perennials make an attractive flowering hedge near the patio. Deep-green foliage is speckled from late spring to fall with red blossoms resembling small Turkish turbans. See *Malvaviscus arboreus drummondii*, p. 139.

I Fall aster (use 16)
These carefree perennials form a solid mass of fine-textured foliage completely covered in autumn with lavender-purple daisylike blossoms. See *Aster oblongifolius*, p. 124.

J Mexican bush sage (use 7)
From late summer to frost, this grayish green bushy perennial bristles with long spikes of purple-and-white flowers. See *Salvia leucantha*, p. 147.

K Ground covers (as needed)
Two low-growing evergreen perennials make durable "welcome mats" along the paths and around the patio. Mondo grass (*Ophiopogon japonicus*, p. 140) has fine dark-green foliage that adds grassy texture around the patio and between the flagstones on the narrow walk to the driveway.

L Container
Plant a patio pot with purple fountain grass for a fountain of foliage topped with foxtail-like flowers. See Annuals, p. 123.

M Paving
A wide front walk of flagstone handles heavy foot traffic and outdoor furniture. A more casual flagstone path to the drive has wide joints filled with prepared soil and planted with mondo grass. See pp. 168-169.

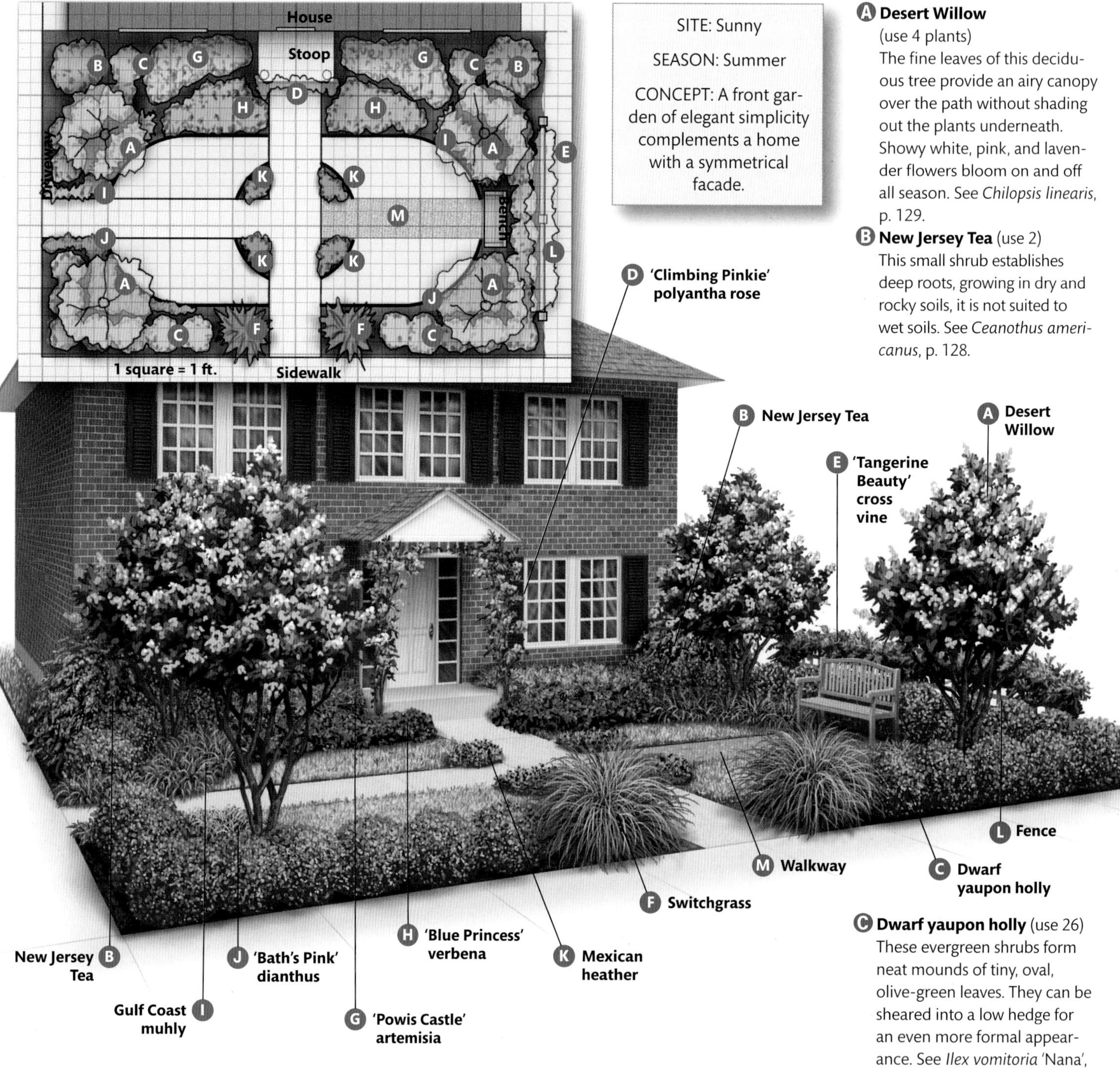

Plants & Projects

A Desert Willow
(use 4 plants)
The fine leaves of this deciduous tree provide an airy canopy over the path without shading out the plants underneath. Showy white, pink, and lavender flowers bloom on and off all season. See *Chilopsis linearis*, p. 129.

B New Jersey Tea (use 2)
This small shrub establishes deep roots, growing in dry and rocky soils, it is not suited to wet soils. See *Ceanothus americanus*, p. 128.

C Dwarf yaupon holly (use 26)
These evergreen shrubs form neat mounds of tiny, oval, olive-green leaves. They can be sheared into a low hedge for an even more formal appearance. See *Ilex vomitoria* 'Nana', p. 135.

D 'Climbing Pinkie' polyantha rose (use 2)
A mannerly, thornless, climbing rose that bears loose clusters of pink, semidouble flowers from April through November. See *Rosa* x *polyantha* 'Climbing Pinkie', p. 145.

E 'Tangerine Beauty' cross vine
(use 3)
This twining vine will cover the fence with lustrous, dark-green

Up front formal

Homes that have a symmetrical facade are especially suited for a formal garden makeover, one that complements and accents the geometry of the architecture. This design offers a simpler makeover than the first by retaining existing concrete walks. The symmetrical layout features a central oval of lawn flanked by almost mirror image plantings on each side of the main walk. A loose-surface path extends the cross walk to a garden bench, a perfect perch for enjoying the view.

Whether approaching from the street or the drive, visitors get an attractive welcome. Small flowering trees and a hedge of low-growing shrubs give the garden its structure. A variety of contrasting foliage textures and colors provide interest year-round. And there are flowers in spring and summer.

leaves all year. Bears orange or red trumpet-shaped flowers in late spring and again in fall. See *Bignonia capreolata* 'Tangerine Beauty', p. 125.

F **Switchgrass** (use 2)
This grass grows 3–5 ft. tall, producing fine-textured lacey seedheads in late summer which persist throughout winter. See *Panicum virgatum*, p. 140.

G **'Powis Castle' artemisia** (use 14)
Silvery mounds of lacy foliage make this evergreen perennial an outstanding choice next to the lavender-blue verbena and the pink-blooming climbing rose. See *Artemisia* x 'Powis Castle', p. 124.

H **'Blue Princess' verbena** (use 16)
This perennial forms a fine mat of deep-green leaves topped with masses of tiny lavender-blue flowers. Especially showy in spring. See *Verbena* x *hybrida* 'Blue Princess', p. 151.

I **Gulf coast muhly** (use 50) A 1–3 ft perennial grass with with fine, arching leaves that create an ornamental grass appeal. See *Muhlenbergia capillaris*, p. 137.

J **'Bath's Pink' dianthus** (use 44)
A fine-textured perennial that forms a mat of silver-gray foliage all year. Topped in spring with pretty pink flowers. See *Dianthus* 'Bath's Pink', p. 130.

K **Mexican heather** (use 12)
For texture as well as color, plant in the circular bed where the walks intersect. This tender perennial forms a low bush of tiny leaves in fernlike fans and delicate lavender-pink flowers. See *Cuphea hyssopifolia*, p. 123.

L **Fence**
Interlaced with flowering vines, the lattice-panel fence behind the bench creates a sense of privacy, as well as a focal point for the garden. See p. 187.

M **Walkway**
A loose surface of decomposed granite extends the existing walkway to the bench and provides a level surface beneath it. See p. 163.

PLANT PORTRAITS

These well-behaved plants require little care while garnering lots of attention.

● = First design, pp. 24-25

▲ = Second design, pp. 26-27

'Climbing Pinkie' polyantha rose
(*Rosa* x *polyantha*, p. 145) ▲

Desert willow
(*Chilopsis linearis*, p. 129) ▲

'Warren's Red' possumhaw holly
(*Ilex decidua*, p. 135) ●

A Foundation with Flair

FLOWERS AND FOLIAGE CREATE A FRONT GARDEN

Rare is the home without foundation plantings. These simple skirtings of greenery hide unattractive underpinnings and help integrate a house with its surroundings. Useful as these plantings are, they are too often monochromatic expanses of clipped evergreens, dull as dishwater. But as this design shows, a low-maintenance planting can be more varied, more colorful, and more fun.

By adding smaller plants in front of the taller shrubs near the house and including a small flowering tree, a mix of shrubs and perennials, and a flowering vine along the railing, the design transforms a foundation planting into a small garden. Here, there's something for everyone to enjoy, from porch sitters to passersby.

Starting in early spring with fragrant jessamine and rosemary and the eye-catching flowers of the esperanza and verbena, the garden reaches full exhuberance in summer, with bright flowers in yellows, purples, blues, and oranges. Foliage in a mixture of greens and grays and a variety of textures showcases the flowers, several of which attract butterflies and hummingbirds. And the evergreen leaves of many plants extend the planting's appeal through the winter.

SITE: Sunny

SEASON: Midsummer

CONCEPT: Mixing small trees, vines, shrubs, and perennials makes a colorful foundation planting.

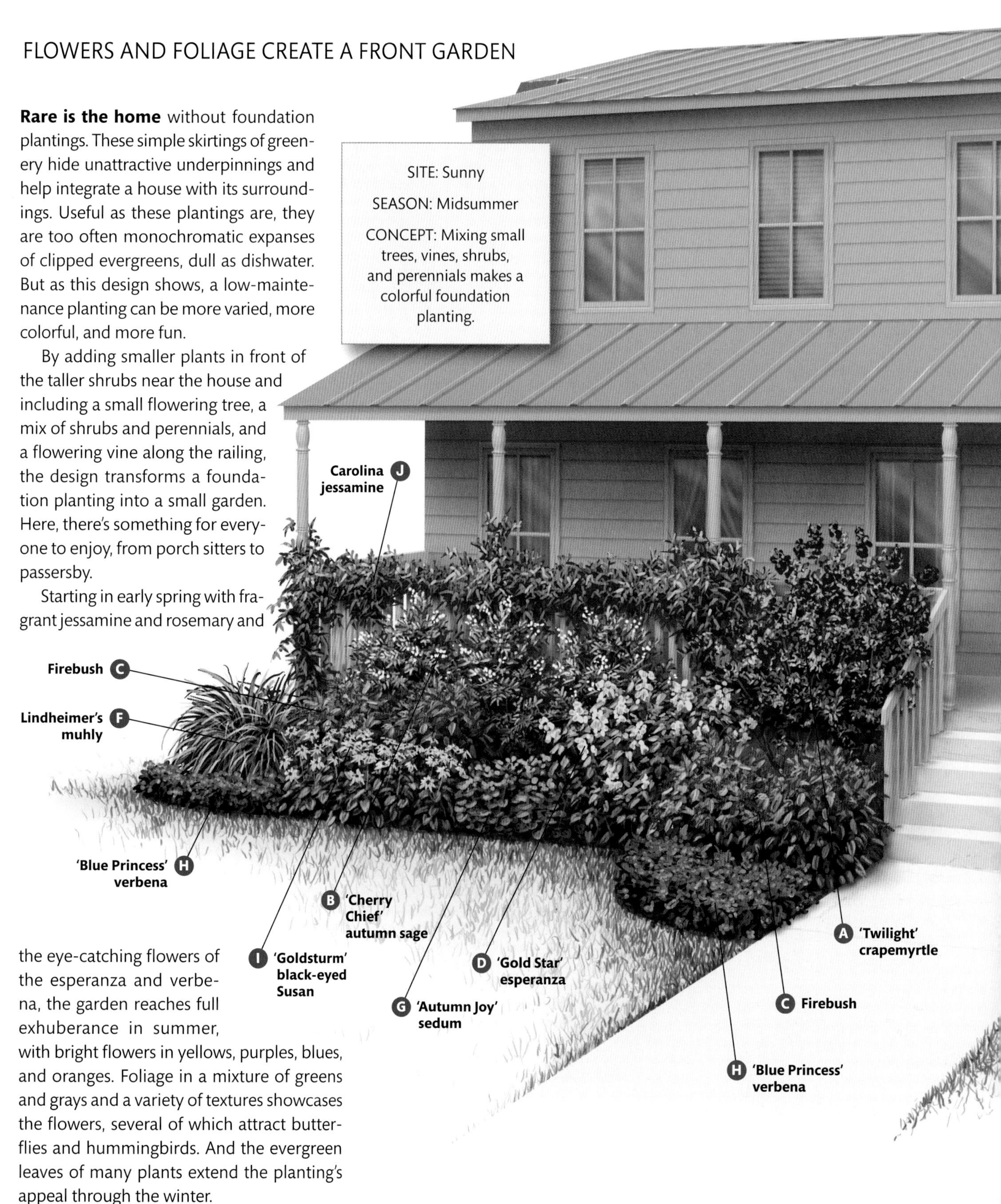

Plants & Projects

This is a low-care planting that offers a dazzling display of color in summer and fall. In addition to routine seasonal pruning, cut the firebush back in midsummer to keep it in check. If the verbena quits blooming, shear it back to about one-third to encourage new bloom. Train the jessamine up porch columns by attaching the vines to wires with twist ties. Add trellising if you want additional shade on the porch. For winter color in the beds, consider planting pansies or snapdragons when perennials fade.

A 'Twilight' crapemyrtle (use 1 plant)
This tree has deep-purple flowers and grows to 10–15 ft. It is drought resistant, low maintenance, and blooms all summer long. See *Lagerstroemia indica* 'Twilight', p. 136.

B 'Cherry Chief' autumn sage (use 5)
This bushy perennial's small oval leaves echo the holly's foliage, but are softer and paler. Small red flowers bloom heavily in spring and lightly in summer and fall. See *Salvia greggii* 'Cherry Chief', p. 147.

C Firebush (use 6)
Small red-orange flowers light up this bushy tropical shrub in summer, attracting butterflies and hummingbirds as well as human admirers. See *Hamelia patens*, p. 133.

D 'Gold Star' esperanza (use 6)
Known also as Texas yellow bells, this shrub bears big bright clusters of yellow flowers from spring to fall, creating a colorful contrast with the crapemyrtle and firebush beside it. See *Tecoma stans* 'Gold Star', p. 150.

E Rosemary (use 2)
This shrubby perennial herb forms a tight bouquet of branches clad in small needle-like leaves and topped with small blue flowers in early spring. It makes a fragrant edging next to the steps, within easy reach to snip a few leaves for cooking. See *Rosmarinus officinalis*, p. 146.

F Lindheimer's muhly (use 3)
A beautiful, fine-textured ornamental grass. Blue-green leaves and soft texture makes this grass popular for screening. See *Muhlenbergia lindheimeri*, p. 139.

G 'Autumn Joy' sedum (use 3)
This bold-textured perennial grows in neat mounds of grayish green succulent leaves. Dense clusters of tiny burnt-orange flowers appear in fall, turn pink, and gradually fade to tan. See *Sedum* 'Autumn Joy', p. 149.

H 'Blue Princess' verbena (use 8)
Butterflies can't resist this perennial's lavender-blue flowers, which bloom continuously from spring to fall in clusters the size of silver dollars. See *Verbena* x *hybrida* 'Blue Princess', p. 151.

I 'Goldsturm' black-eyed Susan (use 4)
In early summer golden dark-eyed daisylike flowers rise above this perennial's deep-green heart-shaped foliage. See *Rudbeckia fulgida* 'Goldsturm', p. 146.

J Carolina jessamine (use 3)
Shiny neat evergreen leaves and a show of fragrant yellow flowers in spring make this vigorous vine ideal for training up porch columns or along a railing. See *Gelsemium sempervirens*, p. 133.

PLANT PORTRAITS

This mix of shrubs and perennials will dress up the most nondescript foundation, while requiring little care.
● = First design, pp. 28-29
▲ = Second design, pp. 30-31

White autumn sage
(*Salvia greggii* 'Alba', p. 147) ▲

'Twilight' crapemyrtle
(*Lagerstroemia indica*, p. 136) ●

Dwarf wax myrtle
(*Morella cerifera var. pumila*, p. 139) ▲

In a shady setting

This foundation planting graces a house with a shady entry. The mix of evergreen foliage and cool white flowers not only brightens up the shade, but also makes it even more welcome on a hot summer's day.

Foliage is the key here. The delicately cut fronds of the wavy cloak fern are striking accents. The less dramatic foliage of the evergreen is a highly effective backdrop for displaying the lovely flowers of these plants.

Lower-growing perennials and bulbs also contribute attractive foliage, and their flowers reinforce the planting's flowering color scheme of cool whites and pinks. With its mix of bold foliage and lovely flowers, this planting can be enjoyed from the windows as well as the street.

Plants & Projects

A Magnolia 'Little Gem' (use 1 plant)
A dwarf southern magnolia with small, dark-green foliage and a compact form. Large, white blooms. See *Magnolia grandiflora*, p. 138.

B Turk's Cap (use 4)
A Texas favorite, this perennial forms a low bush of large leaves and red turbanlike flowers in summer. Hummingbirds attracted to the flowers will hover near the bench. Other birds may stop by for the cherrylike berries. See *Malvaviscus arboreus drummondii*, p. 139.

C White autumn sage (use 8)
This perennial forms a mat of small oval leaves that usually stay green all winter. A profusion of pure-white flowers greets visitors at the steps from spring to fall. See *Salvia greggii* 'Alba', p. 147.

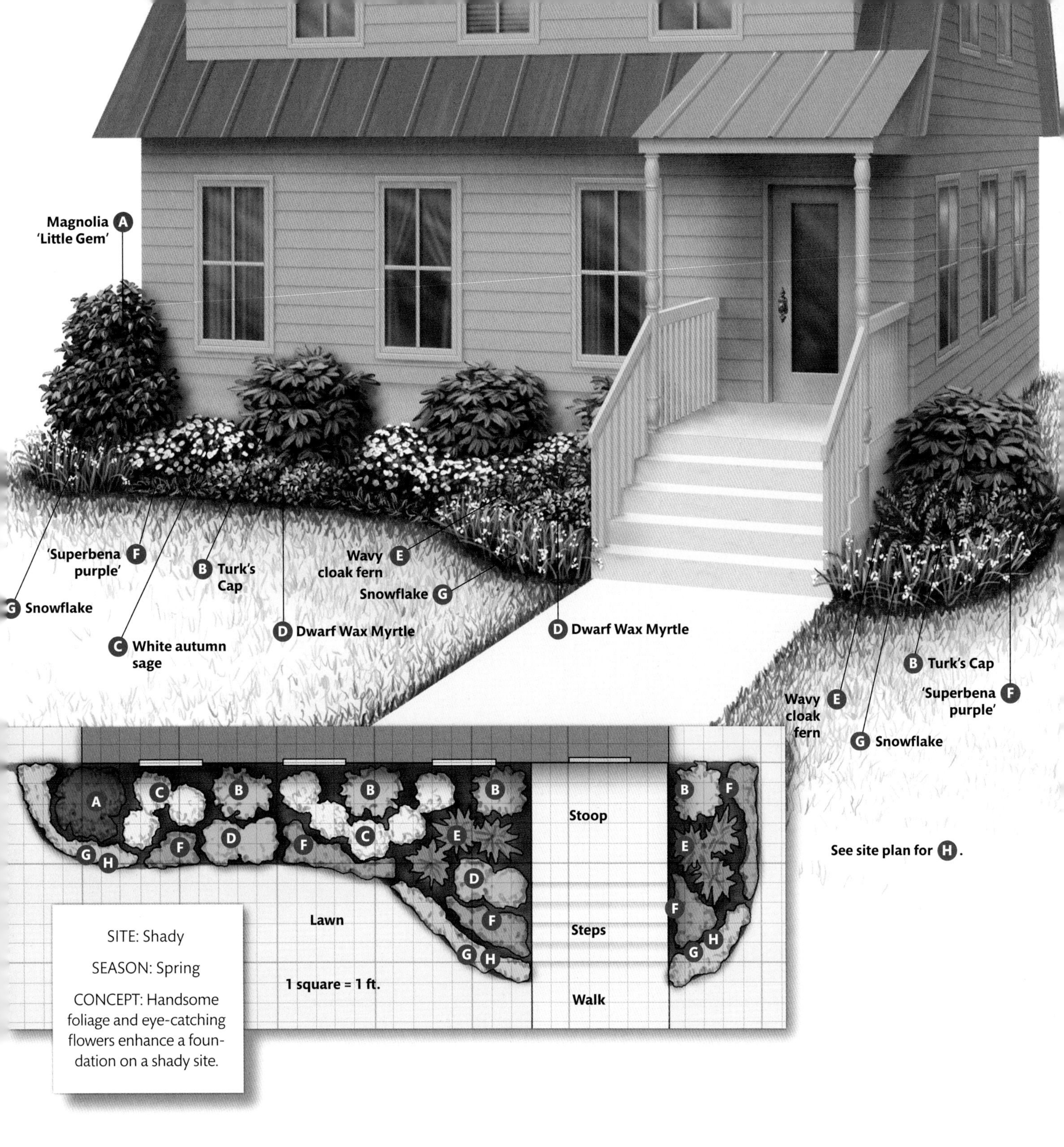

D Dwarf Wax Myrtle (use 4)
Useful for foundation plantings, this native can be used for underplanting with larger woody plants or can create a midsized hedge. See *Morella cerifera var. pumila*, p. 139.

E Wavy cloak fern (use 6)
This semi-evergreen fern produces clumps of attractive rich green foliage, with a contrasting cinnamon underside. It is uniquely drought tolerant and suited to poor rocky soils, preferring sun or part shade. It is clump forming and slowly spreads via rhizomes. See *Astrolepsis sinuata*, p. 124.

F 'Superbena purple' (use 11)
This spreading native blooms all summer, growing in full sun, it is heat and drought tolerant. See *Verbena* hybrid, p. 151.

G Snowflake (use 60)
Planted among the Mexican petunias, these spring bulbs produce grassy leaves and numerous flower stems topped with small clusters of tiny white flower bells. See Bulbs: *Leucojum aestivum*, p. 126.

H Dwarf Mexican petunia
(use 20)
Picking up where the spring bulbs leave off, this perennial's elegant white blooms and dark leaves are on display from summer through fall. See *Ruellia brittoniana* 'Katie', p. 148.

Fancy Foundation

CREATE A STRIKING ENTRY GARDEN

There's something to enjoy in all four seasons in this foundation planting, which has been transformed into a small garden to welcome visitors. All the plants bear eye-catching flowers in pinks, purples, or blues for long seasons, some almost year-round. They are sure to attract hummingbirds and butterflies for your enjoyment. Foliage in a mixture of greens and grays and a variety of textures showcases the flowers and is handsome in its own right. In front of the bed, the airy chitalpa casts a light shade on the front windows and provides a measure of privacy without blocking the street entirely.

Plants & Projects

This is a low-care, low-water-use planting. In addition to routine seasonal pruning, you can promote flowering of the summersweet by cutting older stems to 1 ft. long in late winter. Shear the sweet-pea shrub to maintain the variation in height with the neighboring Cape mallows and, if necessary, below window height, as shown here.

A 'Pink Dawn' chitalpa (use 1 plant)
This small but fast-growing deciduous tree provides airy shade near the house. Spectacular clusters of ruffled, trumpet-shaped pink flowers bloom in early summer. See x *Chitalpa tashkentensis*, p. 129.

B 'Ruby Spice' summersweet (use 1)
This deciduous shrub bears long spikes of fragrant rose-pink flowers from midsummer through fall. Butterflies and hummingbirds love them. See *Clethra alnifolia*, p. 130.

C Texas bluebell (use 1)
Showy, bell-shaped flowers with 1–3 ft stems. Waxy perennial bloom. See *Eustoma exaltum ssp. russellianum*, p. 131.

D Mexican bush sage (use 1)
This shrubby perennial is prized for its long, arching purple-and-white flower spikes and attractive gray-green foliage. See *Salvia leucantha*, p. 147.

E Cape mallow (use 2)
Pink, hollyhocklike flowers blanket this fast-growing evergreen shrub almost year-round. (Its bloom season is more restricted in cooler areas.) See *Anisodontea* x *hypomandarum*, p. 123.

F Sweet-pea shrub (use 3)
This evergreen shrub's light-textured foliage is covered for months with small purple flowers. See *Polygala* x *dalmaisiana*, p. 142.

G 'Goodwin Creek Gray' lavender (use 3)
Fragrant gray foliage and short spikes of blue flowers recommend this mounding evergreen shrub. Blooms in early summer and for much of the year where winters are mild. See *Lavandula*, p. 136.

H Garden penstemon (use 3)
This perennial's striking flower spikes are right at the front of the planting. Blooms in late spring and summer. Choose one with pink or purple flowers. See *Penstemon gloxinioides*, p. 141.

I Pincushion flower (use 3)
Showcased at the center of the planting, this perennial bears light-blue flowers above airy foliage for much of the summer. See *Scabiosa caucasica*, p. 149.

J 'Peter Pan' agapanthus (use 7)
A dwarf variety of a perennial, its blue pom-pom-like flowers float above green foliage by the front steps in late spring and summer. See *Agapanthus*, p. 122.

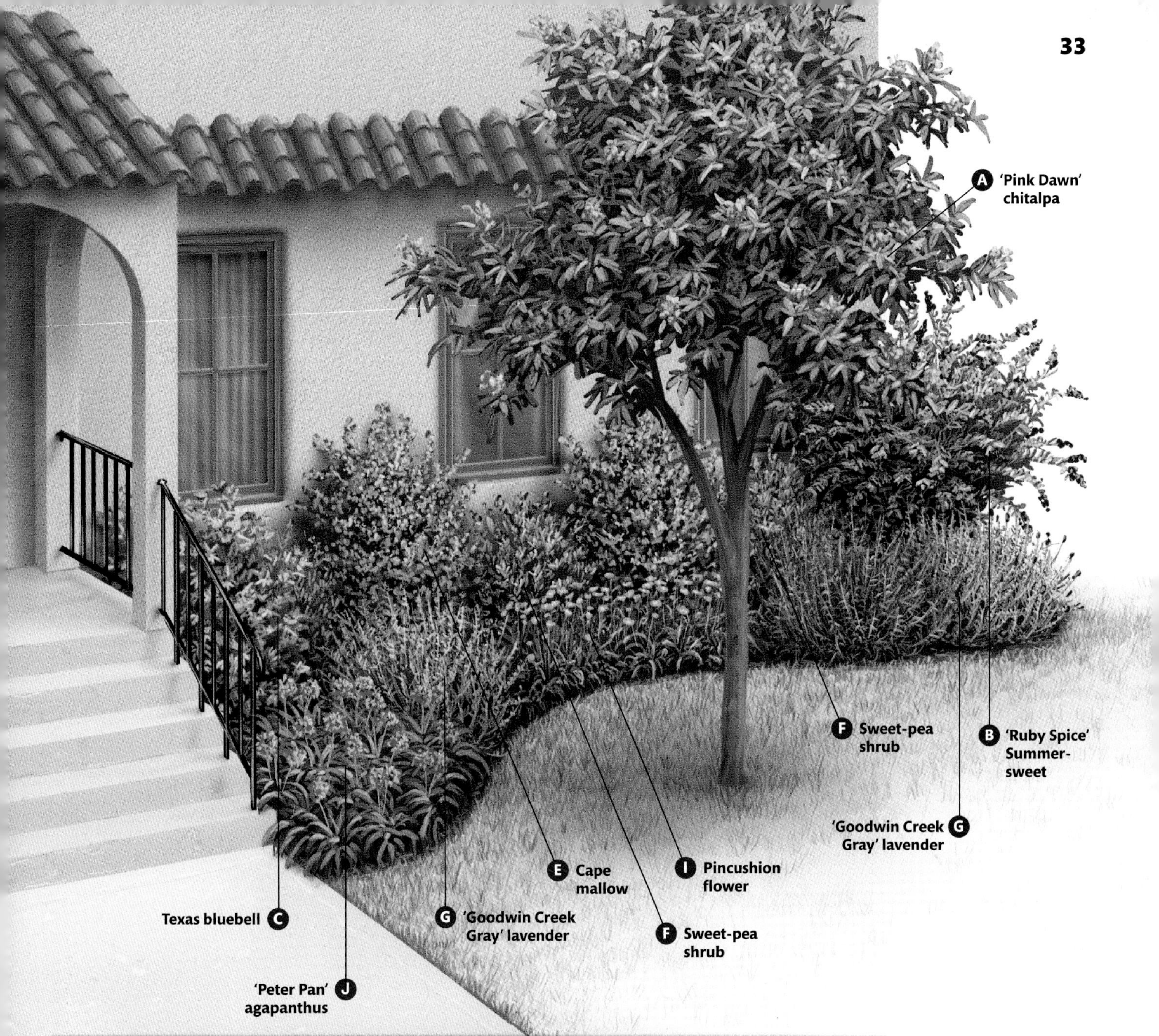

A 'Pink Dawn' chitalpa

B 'Ruby Spice' Summer-sweet

F Sweet-pea shrub

G 'Goodwin Creek Gray' lavender

E Cape mallow

I Pincushion flower

F Sweet-pea shrub

G 'Goodwin Creek Gray' lavender

Texas bluebell C

'Peter Pan' J agapanthus

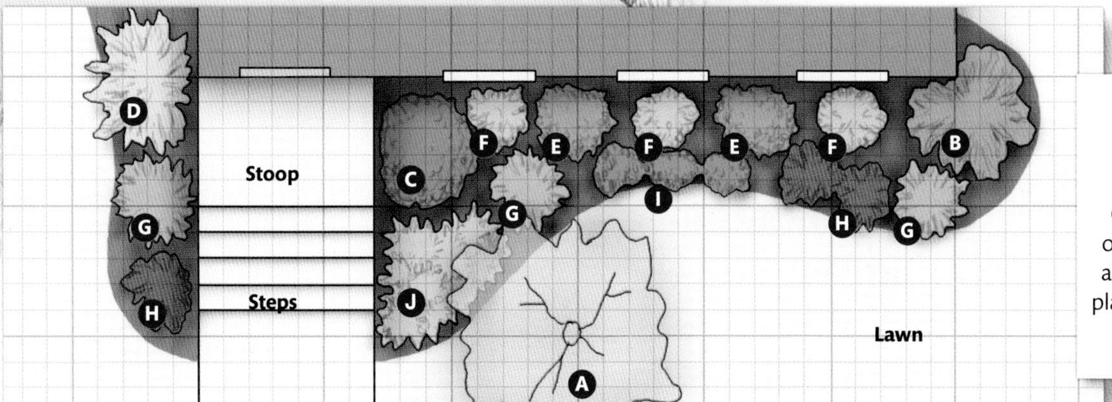

D
Stoop
G
Steps
H
Walk
C
F
E
F
E
F
B
G
I
H
G
J
A
Lawn
1 square = 1 ft.

SITE: Sunny

SEASON: Summer

CONCEPT: A mixture of shrubs and perennials makes a foundation planting with year-round color.

First Impressions

MAKE A PLEASANT PASSAGE TO YOUR FRONT DOOR

Why wait until a visitor reaches the front door to extend a cordial greeting? An entryway landscape of well-chosen plants and a revamped walkway not only make the short journey a pleasant one, they can also enhance your home's most public face and help settle it comfortably in its surroundings.

In this design, a flagstone walkway curves gracefully to the front door, creating a roomy planting bed near the house. Extending along the driveway, the paving makes it easier for passengers to get in and out of a car. Where the paving widens out at the front stoop, there's room for a welcoming bench sheltered by a small tree. Fragrant flowers and eye-catching foliage make the stroll to the door inviting, while providing interest to viewers inside the house and on the street.

The plants here are selected for a shady entry, one that gets less than six hours of sun a day. Flowers and foliage will keep the entry colorful and fragrant throughout the year. Redbud blossoms will join the daffodils and dianthus in the early spring, followed by columbine, plumbago, Mexican petunia, and gardenia. All continue to bloom well into fall. White daffodils and red camellias arrive in November just in time for the winter holidays.

SITE: Shady

SEASON: Spring

CONCEPT: Easy-care plantings and a distinctive walkway enhance a home's main entrance.

Plants & Projects

Preparing the planting beds and laying the flagstone walkway are the main tasks in this design. Once plants are established, only seasonal cleanup and pruning are required.

A Redbud (use 1 plant) With a splurge of pink blossoms in early spring, this small deciduous tree is an eye-catching accent. Heart-shaped leaves are light green in summer and yellow in fall. See *Cercis canadensis*, p. 128.

B White autumn sage (use 2) This perennial forms a mat of small oval leaves that usually stay green all winter. A profusion of pure-white flowers greets visitors at the steps from spring to fall. See *Salvia greggii* 'Alba', p. 147.

C Magnolia 'Little Gem' (use 1) A dwarf southern magnolia with small, dark-green foliage and a compact form. Large, white blooms. See *Magnolia grandiflora*, p. 139.

D Dwarf yaupon holly (use 5) These shrubs form neat low mounds of tiny, oval, evergreen leaves in front of the windows. Clusters of red berries decorate the foliage in winter. See *Ilex vomitoria* 'Nana', p. 135.

E Dwarf Mexican petunia (use 22) The large lush leaves of this low-growing perennial emerge just in time to cover fading spring bulbs. Purple flowers bloom from the center of each plant all season. See *Ruellia brittoniana* 'Katie', p. 147.

F Texas gold columbine (use 3) This perennial forms neat mounds of lacy foliage. Slender stalks bear delicate golden flowers in spring and summer. See *Aquilegia chrysantha hinckleyana*, p. 123.

G Wavy cloak fern (use 16) This semi-evergreen fern produces clumps of attractive rich green foliage, with a contrasting cinnamon underside. See *Astrolepis sinuata*, p. 124.

H Tropical plumbago (use 5) Ideal as a ground cover beside the drive, this trouble-free perennial creates compact tufts of small, pointed, pale-green leaves. Its clear blue flowers look cool and inviting next to the pavement, especially in summer heat. See *Plumbago auriculata*, p. 142.

I 'Bath's Pink' dianthus (use 9) This perennial creates a pretty border of fine-textured blue-green foliage topped in spring with masses of delicate and fragrant pink flowers. Leaves look fresh all year. See *Dianthus* 'Bath's Pink', p. 131.

J 'Ice Follies' daffodil (use 27) Scatter these bulbs on both sides of the walk for white flowers in spring. The spiky leaves are a nice blue-green. See Bulbs: *Narcissus pseudonarcissus* 'Ice Follies', p. 126.

K Walkway Flagstones of random size and shape are perfect for the curved walk and for the stepping-stones into the front lawn. See p. 169.

L Bench Extend your welcome beyond the front door with a comfortable bench next to the stoop.

PLANT PORTRAITS

These perennials and shrubs enhance a blank wall and narrow entry walk with handsome foliage and pretty flowers all year.

● = First design, pp. 35-36

▲ = Second design, pp. 37-38

'Apple Blossom' yarrow (*Achillea millefolium*, p. 122) ▲

White autumn sage (*Salvia greggii* 'Alba', p. 147) ●

Magonlia 'Little Gem' (*Magnolis grandiflora*, p. 138) ●

A sunny welcome

If your entrance is sunny, consider this design. Here, flagstone walkways invite visitors to stroll from the driveway to the front door along a choice of paths lined with eye-catching flowers and equally attractive foliage.

Many of these perennials bloom nonstop from spring to frost. The lavender blossoms of aster appear in the fall, extending an already long season of bloom well into November. Handsome foliage, much of it evergreen, ensures interest all year. Like the planting in the previous design, this one needs only seasonal care.

Plants & Projects

Ⓐ **Desert willow** (use 1 plant)
The fine leaves of this deciduous tree provide an airy canopy over the path without shading out the plants underneath. Showy white, pink, and lavender flowers bloom on and off all season. See *Chilopsis linearis*, p. 129.

Ⓑ **Southern Arrowwood Little John** (use 2)
This hybrid stays a manageable size growing 4–5 feet tall and wide and developing dark blue berries enjoyed by the birds. See *Viburnum dentatum*, page 152.

Ⓒ **'Belinda's Dream' rose** (use 1)
This rose forms a lovely vase of glossy leaves and exquisite pink flowers. See *Rosa* x 'Belinda's Dream', p. 145.

Ⓓ **New Jersey Tea** (use 3)
This small shrub establishes deep roots, growing in dry and rocky soils, it is not suited to wet soils. See *Ceanothus americanus*, p. 128.

Ⓔ **Rosemary** (use 3)
This low-growing evergreen shrub produces tiny pungent gray-green leaves. Whorls of equally aromatic blue flowers dot the shrub in late winter and early spring. See *Rosmarinus officinalis*, p. 146.

Ⓕ **Texas star hibiscus** (use 16)
This perennial forms a large airy clump of slender, deeply divided, glossy leaves borne on red-tinged stems. Brilliant red five-petaled flowers open daily during the summer and fall. See *Hibiscus coccineus*, p. 134.

Ⓖ **Fall aster** (use 1)
Just one of these perennials will fill the space near the walkway with a dense stand of gray-green leaves, blanketed all fall with small lavender daisylike flowers. See *Aster oblongifolius*, p. 124.

Ⓗ **'Apple Blossom' yarrow** (use 7)
Fine feathery leaves and a lacework of tiny pink flowers that bloom for months makes this perennial an especially lovely companion for pink roses. See *Achillea millefolium* 'Apple Blossom', p. 122.

Ⓘ **'Homestead Purple' verbena** (use 3)
This perennial forms a bright green mat of foliage that is covered from spring through fall with clusters of violet-purple flowers. See *Verbena* x *hybrida* 'Homestead Purple', p. 151.

Ⓙ **'Confetti' lantana** (use 3)
A bushy perennial, it offers a festive mix of pink and yellow flowers throughout the growing season. Shear after bloom cycles. See *Lantana camara* 'Confetti', p. 137.

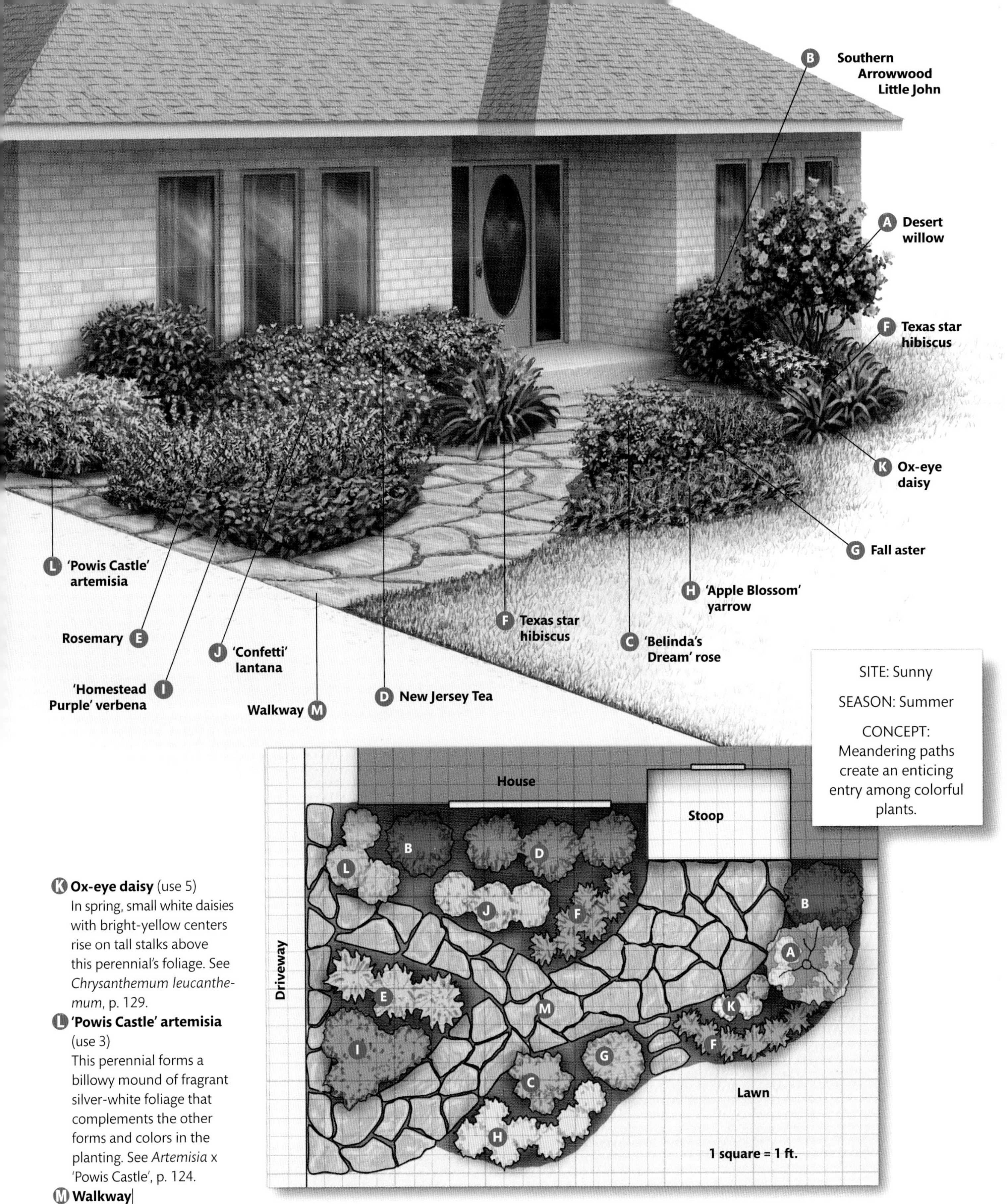

K Ox-eye daisy (use 5)
In spring, small white daisies with bright-yellow centers rise on tall stalks above this perennial's foliage. See *Chrysanthemum leucanthemum*, p. 129.

L 'Powis Castle' artemisia (use 3)
This perennial forms a billowy mound of fragrant silver-white foliage that complements the other forms and colors in the planting. See *Artemisia* x 'Powis Castle', p. 124.

M Walkway
Paving of irregular flagstones curves around the planting beds and widen out gracefully to the stoop. See p. 169.

An Entry Oasis

EXTEND A FRIENDLY DESERT WELCOME

A trend in new suburban developments is to crowd larger homes onto smaller and smaller lots. As a consequence, homeowners enjoy spaciousness inside the house but not outside. Making the most of limited space for outdoor living requires expanding the uses of some traditional areas.

This design transforms the entrance of a desert home from a corridor linking the front door and the driveway into a courtyard garden that invites gathering or relaxing outdoors. Shaded by the canopy of a small tree, enclosed by a wall low enough to allow breezes in, and soothed by the trickle of a small fountain, the courtyard can be enjoyed by family and friends year-round.

The design celebrates the desert environment and low-maintenance, low-water use principles. Local materials such as gravel, granite, and boulders provide natural surfaces to showcase striking desert plants. To fully integrate the design with the yard and house, you may want to cover the entire yard in gravel as we've shown here. It makes a water-efficient surface that is comfortable for both plants and people. Note the mounded undulating surface around the wall, indicated on the plan by broken lines.

The desert-loving plants featured here contribute distinctive forms, textures, and colors. Grouped together they create a dramatic composition. Spiky agave and ocotillo are boldly paired with the loosely arching honeysuckle and low-spreading lantana. The flowers in the planting bloom in spring, and they are a spectacular sight.

See site plan for E I K N

SITE: Sunny

SEASON: Spring

CONCEPT: A host of desert plants and a shady courtyard make an inviting entry to a desert home.

Plants & Projects

Installing the paving, wall, and fountain are the biggest jobs here, though not beyond the means of a resourceful do-it-yourselfer. Once established, the plants will thrive with occasional watering and just seasonal care.

A Desert willow (use 1)
From spring to fall this tree's willowy gray-green leaves are decorated with orchidlike flowers in shades of red, purple, pink, and white. The flowers are followed by long dangling seedpods. Leaves drop in winter, exposing

attractive twisting branches. See *Chilopsis linearis*, p. 129.

B Twin-flower agave (use 4)
An unusually fine-textured agave, with narrow succulent leaves that form a perfect rosette 2 to 3 ft. in diameter. In spring, it sends up double spikes of large, pale-yellow, bell-shaped flowers. See *Agave geminiflora*, p. 122.

C 'Gold Star' Esperanza (use 1)
Known also as Texas yellow bells, this shrub bears big bright clusters of yellow flowers from spring to fall. See *Tecoma stans* 'Gold Star', p. 150.

D Coral honeysuckle (use 2)
Unlike the more invasive honeysuckles, this native vine is mannerly, climbing up the fence in neat tiers of rounded bluegreen leaves. Clusters of coral-colored flowers radiate from the foliage in summer and sometimes fall. See *Lonicera sempervirens*, p. 138.

E Damianita (use 2
Fragrant yellow daisies blanket this small shrub in spring and fall. Needlelike leaves have a pungent but pleasant aroma. Evergreen. See *Chrysactinia mexicana*, p. 129.

F Mexican grass tree (use 1)
This unusual shrub creates a fountain of succulent evergreen foliage. As it matures it forms a central trunk capable of reaching 10 ft. tall and produces long dense clusters of bell-shaped white flowers in summer. See *Dasylirion longissima*, p. 131.

G Euphorbia hybrid (use 2)
Euphorbias have been hybridized into dozens of varieties. Pick a compact one for this entry. Shown here is crown of thorns (*E. milii*), which has bright red flowers all year. See *Euphorbia* hybrids, p. 131.

H Ocotillo (use 1)
This desert shrub is noted for its burst of brilliant orange-red blossoms in spring. Leaves are small, gray-green, and deciduous in dry spells. See *Fouquieria splendens*, p. 132.

I Sabal palm (use 1)
This robust palm generally grows to 30 to 40 feet tall. It sinks its roots deep, down to 15–20 feet and is drought tolerant once established. See *Sabal palmetto*, p. 148.

J Lantana (use 2)
Small lavender flowers brighten this low-spreading perennial's dark-green leaves. Evergreen and ever-blooming where winters are mild. See *Lantana montevidensis*, p. 136.

K Annuals (as needed)
A collection of colorful pansies and snapdragons adds a festive look to this desert entry.

L Paving
Flagstones in muted desert tones provide an attractive surface for the patio. See p. 170.

M Stone wall
Choose your favorite stone. Shown here is a colorfully veined granite.

N Water feature
Water is a wonderful focal point for a courtyard. Incorporate a small fountain or pool into the landscape. See p. 168.

O Gravel
Gravel emulates a desert surface. Shown here is desert tan bird's-eye gravel.

A No-Mow Slope

A TERRACED GARDEN TRANSFORMS A STEEP SITE

SITE: Sunny

SEASON: Fall

CONCEPT: Retaining walls, steps, and plants tame this slope and enhance the home's public face.

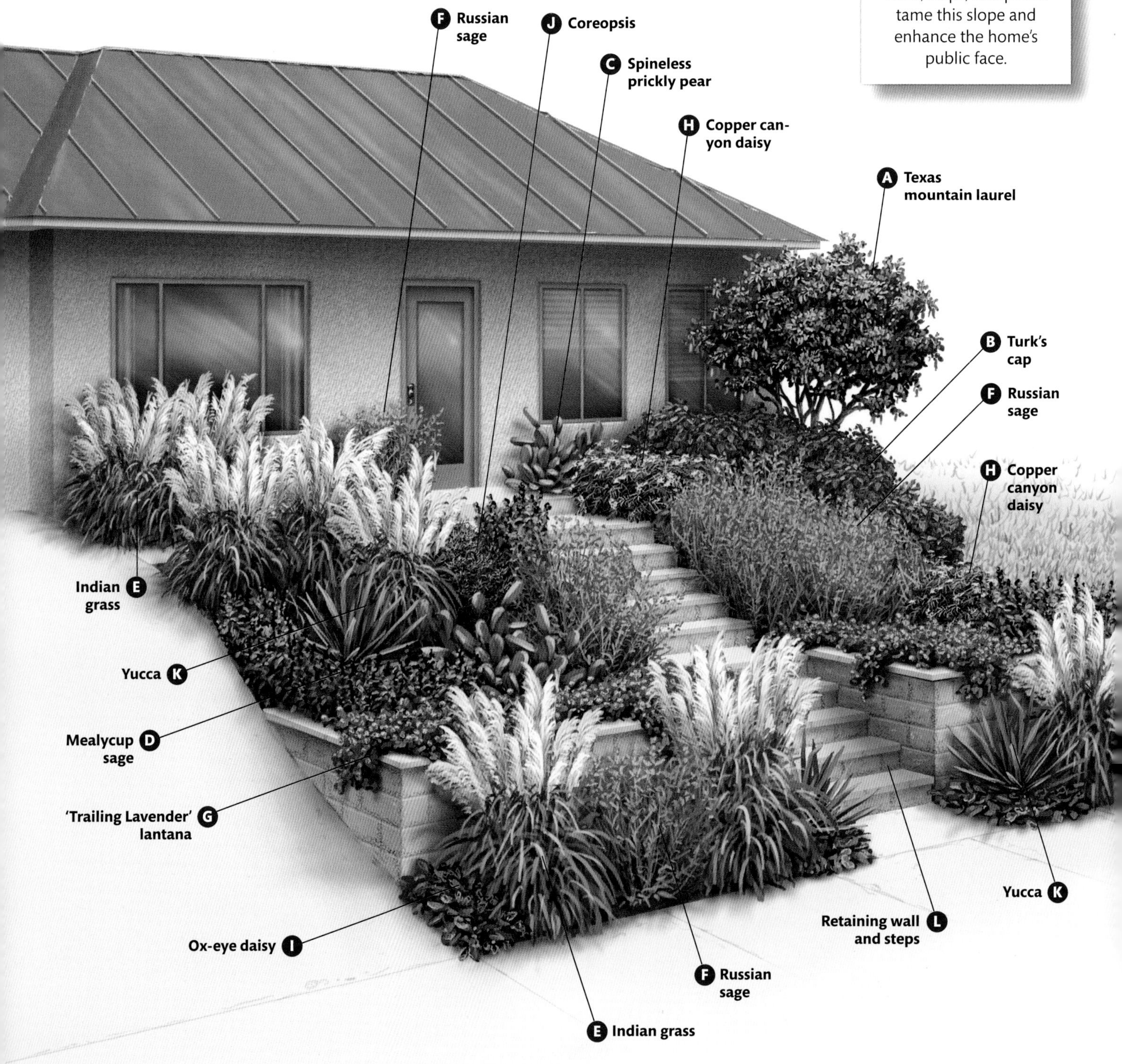

F Russian sage
J Coreopsis
C Spineless prickly pear
H Copper canyon daisy
A Texas mountain laurel
B Turk's cap
F Russian sage
H Copper canyon daisy
E Indian grass
K Yucca
D Mealycup sage
G 'Trailing Lavender' lantana
I Ox-eye daisy
E Indian grass
F Russian sage
L Retaining wall and steps
K Yucca

Steep slopes can be a landscaping headache. Planted with lawn grass, they're a chore to mow, and they can present problems of erosion and maintenance if you try to establish other ground covers or plantings. One solution to this dilemma is shown here—tame the slope by building a low retaining wall and steps. Then plant the resulting flat (or flatter) beds with an assortment of interesting low-care trees, shrubs, and perennials.

Steep slopes near the house are common in some areas of Texas. Here, a narrow steeply sloping front yard has been terraced and walled and the lawn replaced by plantings. The result transforms the home's public face and creates an enticing walk to the front door. You can extend the planting, or leave some lawn for kids to enjoy.

Visitors approaching from the sidewalk pass through colorful shrubs and perennials. A small landing on the steps, introduced at wall height, offers the opportunity to pause and enjoy nearby plants. The walk from the drive is no less pleasant. Visitors from both directions will be met with a profusion of blooms in nearly every season, and a few surprises as well: the sweet scent of Texas mountain laurel in spring, the spectacle of large white yucca blossoms in summer, and purple cactus fruit in fall.

Plants & Projects

Reshaping the slope and building the hardscape (retaining walls, steps, and walkways) is a big job. Even if you plan to do much of the work yourself, it is prudent to consult a landscape contractor for advice. Once the plants are established, this design requires little more than seasonal pruning and cleanup.

A Texas mountain laurel (use 1 plant)
A Texas native evergreen tree with gnarly branches and attractive bark. Wisteria-like clusters of grape-scented flowers in spring are followed by fat bean pods that eventually reveal shiny red seeds. See *Dermatophyllum secundiflorum*, p. 131.

B Turk's cap (use 9)
This tough perennial makes a velvety patch of foliage that showcases small red flowers all season. See *Malvaviscus arboreus drummondii*, p. 139.

C Spineless prickly pear (use 2)
A bold "sculpture" for the entry, this cactus forms an interesting patchwork of coarse succulent leaf pads. In some years, it may produce yellow flowers in summer and purple fruits in the fall. See *Opuntia lindheimeri*, p. 140.

D Mealycup sage (use 11)
The fringe of bright-blue flowers borne on this perennial makes a pretty edge around plants and lawn. Shear a few times during the season to refresh their bloom. See *Salvia farinacea*, p. 147.

E Indian grass (use 11)
A perennial grass with upright blue-green foliage that turns orange and yellow in fall and hints of those colors through winter. See *Sorghastrum nutans*, p. 149.

F Russian sage (use 14)
This erect perennial forms an airy vase of slender, silver-leaved stems tipped with tiny pale-blue flowers. Blooms nonstop from midsummer to fall. Cut plant back after frost. See *Perovskia atriplicifolia*, p. 141.

G 'Trailing Lavender' lantana (use 4)
This perennial spreads into a wide mound of fuzzy leaves covered with small domes of lavender-purple flowers. See *Lantana montevidensis* 'Trailing Lavender', p. 137.

H Copper canyon daisy (use 8)
A pretty, lace-leafed perennial marigold bearing bright-gold flowers in autumn. See *Tagetes lemmonii*, p. 150.

I Ox-eye daisy (use 8)
White daisies with yellow centers will cheer visitors in spring. The rest of the season this perennial offers a mound of curly green leaves. See *Chrysanthemum leucanthemum*, p. 129.

J Coreopsis (use 15)
A mounding perennial with linear leaves and many slender stalks of single flower heads with sunlike rays. See *Coreopsis lanceolata*, p. 130.

K Yucca (use 3)
These spiky evergreen shrubs make striking accents. Spectacular stalks of nodding white flowers rise as high as lampposts in late spring and last through midsummer. See *Yucca filamentosa*, p. 153.

L Retaining wall and steps
The walls and steps are made with a precast concrete retaining-wall system available at garden centers. See p. 176.

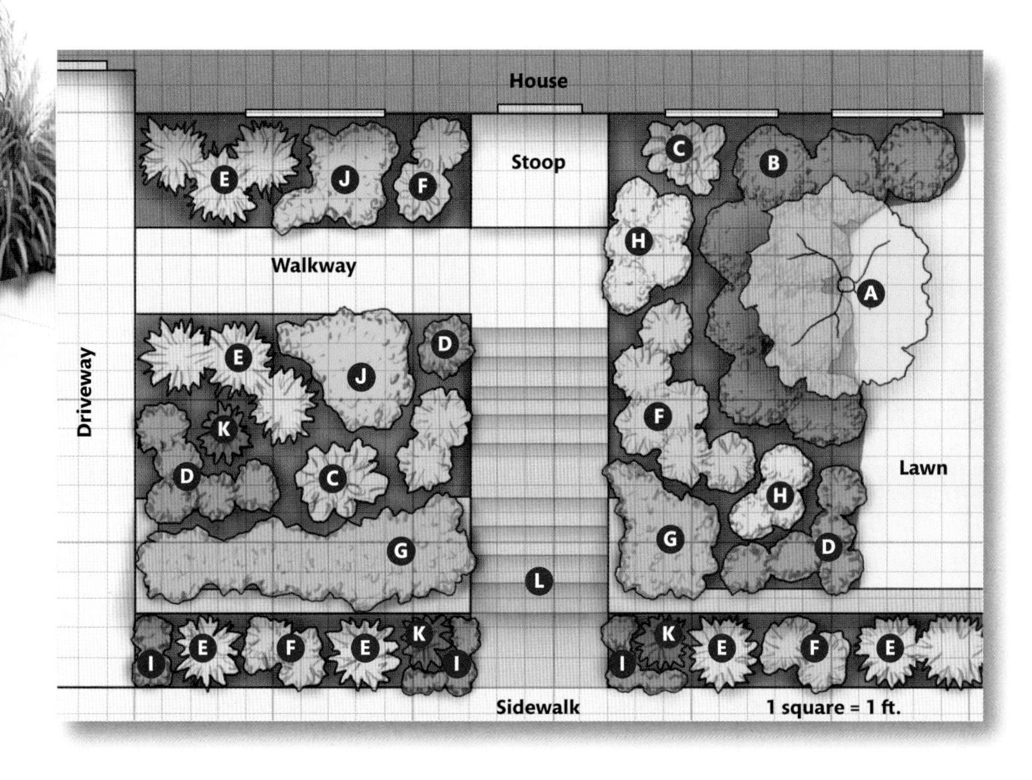

PLANT PORTRAITS

These durable, low-care plants will help transform difficult hillsides.

● = First design, pp. 41-42

▲ = Second design, pp. 43-44

Partridgeberry
(*Mitchella repens*, p. 139) ▲

Yucca (*Yucca filamentosa*, p. 153) ●

'Trailing Lavender' lantana
(*Lantana montevidensis*, p. 137) ●

Turk's cap (*Malvaviscus arboreus drummondii*, p. 139) ▲

Victoria regina agave
(*Agave victoriae-reginae*, p. 122) ▲

Working with a hillside

If terracing a slope with retaining walls and steps does not appeal to you, or is beyond your budget, consider this design. Here we've worked with the existing hillside, replacing turfgrass with tough, easy-care ground covers. A small tree provides a colorful accent as well as a modest level of privacy from street and sidewalk traffic.

These plants thrive in the poor, dry soil and the heat often found on slopes. Their tenacious root systems, particularly those of partridgeberry and cedar sedge, will hold the soil in place. With no exception, these plants require infrequent watering once they're established.

The planting is as attractive as it is durable. There are flowers blooming nearly all season. And the varied textures and colors of the foliage are pleasing year-round.

Plants & Projects

A Desert willow (use 1 plant)
The fine leaves of this deciduous tree provide an airy canopy over the path without shading out the plants underneath. Showy white, pink, and lavender flowers bloom on and off all season. See *Chilopsis linearis*, p. 129.

B Turk's cap (use 6)
A Texas favorite, this perennialforms a low bush of large heartshaped leaves and red turbanlike flowers in summer. Hummingbirds attracted to the flowers will hover near the bench. Other birds may stop by for the cherrylike berries. See *Malvaviscus arboreus drummondii*, p. 139.

C Partridgeberry (as needed)
An evergreen creeping groundcover with small leaves, it produces small white flowers followed by scarlet berries enjoyed by birds and mammals. See *Mitchella repens*, p. 139.

D Red yucca (use 3)
Spiky foliage gives this shrub a strik-

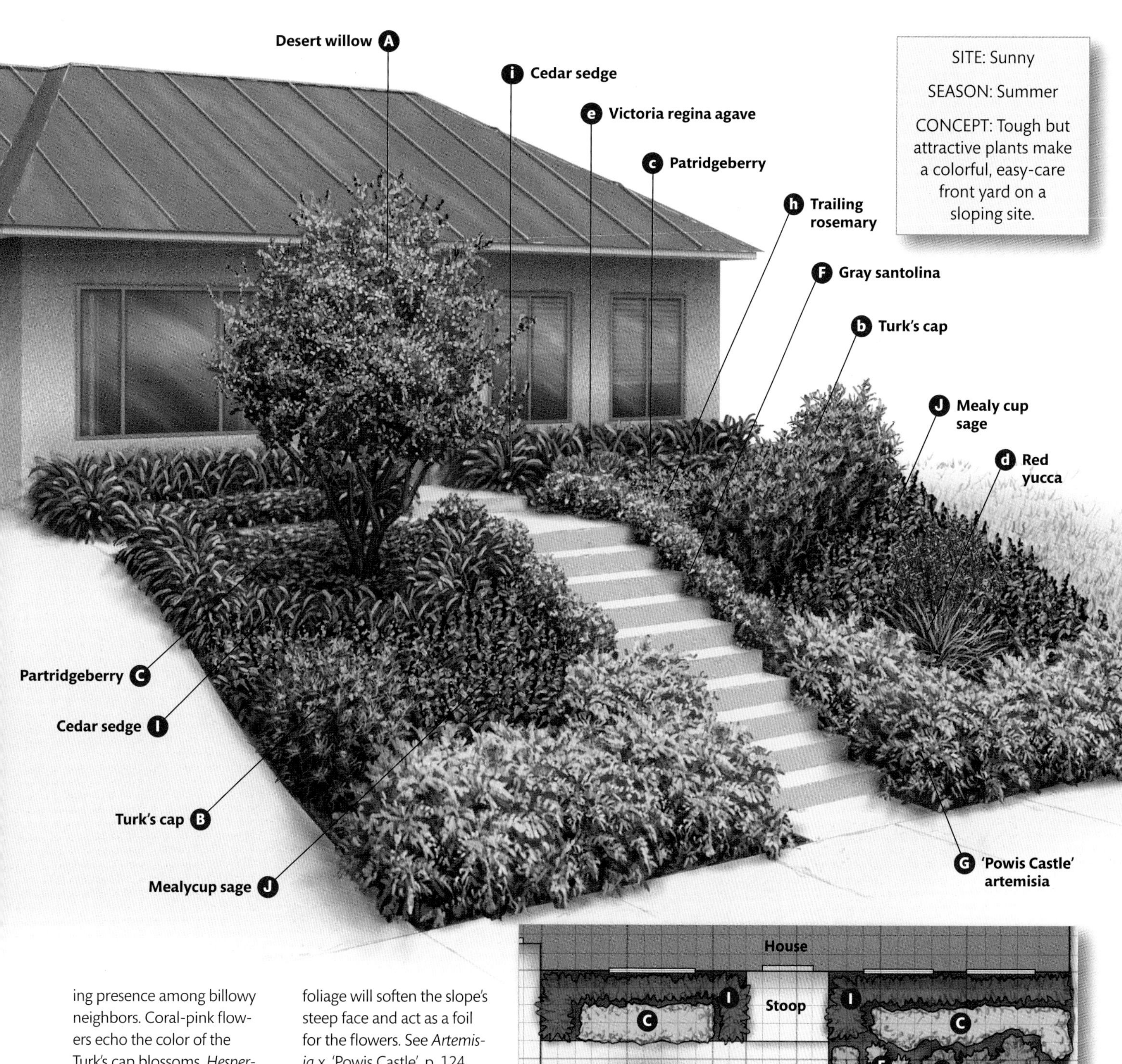

SITE: Sunny

SEASON: Summer

CONCEPT: Tough but attractive plants make a colorful, easy-care front yard on a sloping site.

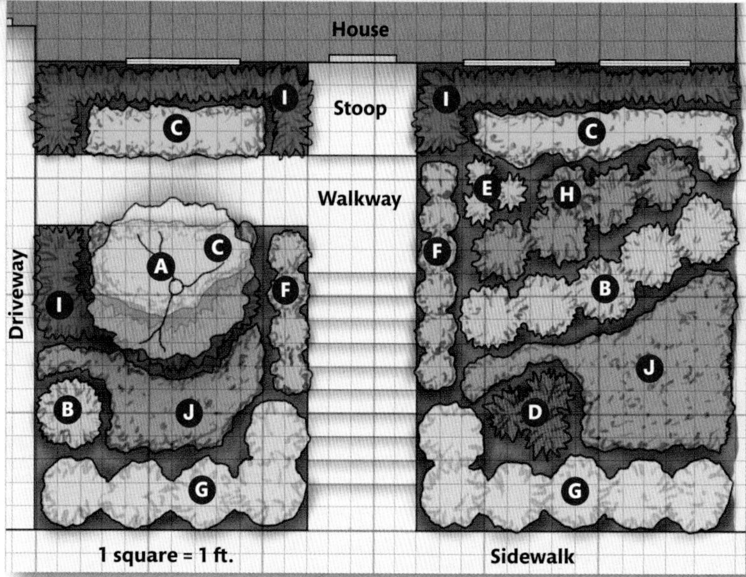

ing presence among billowy neighbors. Coral-pink flowers echo the color of the Turk's cap blossoms. *Hesperaloe parviflora*, p. 134.

E Victoria regina agave (use 3) A small but bold succulent perennial, it resembles an artichoke bud. See *Agave victoriae-reginae*, p. 122.

F Gray santolina (use 10) Ideal for edges, this evergreen shrub's low mounds of thick leaves bear countless flowers in summer. See *Santolina chamaecyparissus*, p. 148.

G 'Powis Castle' artemisia (use 11) A billowy perennial whose foliage will soften the slope's steep face and act as a foil for the flowers. See *Artemisia* x 'Powis Castle', p. 124.

H Trailing rosemary (use 5) A low, spreading evergreen shrub bearing tiny fragrant quill-like leaves and equally fragrant blue blossoms. See *Rosmarinus officinalis* 'Prostratus', p. 146.

I Cedar sedge (as needed) This is an understory plant in tall grass prairies and meadows. It is drought tolerant and can grow in a variety of soil types. See Carex planostachys, p. 127.

See p. 41 for the following:

J Mealycup sage (use 30)

An Eye-Catching Corner

BEAUTIFY A BOUNDARY WITH EASY-CARE PLANTS

The corner where your property meets your neighbor's and the sidewalk is often a kind of grassy no-man's-land. This design defines that boundary with a planting that can be enjoyed by property owners, as well as passersby. Good gardens make good neighbors, so we've used well-behaved, low-maintenance plants that take the heat and won't make extra work for the person next door—or for you.

Because of its exposed location, remote from the house and close to the street, this is a less personal planting than those in more private and frequently used parts of your property. It is meant to be appreciated from a distance. Dramatic foliage and flowers are the key to its success. At the center is the strikingly bold century plant. Playing off its coarse texture and gray tones are the gray-green foliage of the Mexican bush sage, gaura, and yucca. A patchwork blanket of blooms in yellow, orange, red, and purple offers cheery contrast to the foliage all season long.

Plants & Projects

As befits a planting that is some distance from the house, these durable, reliable plants are heat and drought tolerant, requiring little care beyond seasonal pruning and cleanup.

A Century plant (use 1 plant)
This regal perennial makes a striking centerpiece with its wide silvery blue leaves ending in single dark-purple spines. See *Agave americana*, p. 122.

B 'Gold Star' esperanza (use 1)
Clusters of yellow bell-shaped flowers adorn every branch of this bushy tropical shrub from summer to frost. Attractive bright green leaves. See *Tecoma stans* 'Gold Star', p. 150.

C Mexican bush sage (use 2)
This big bushy perennial fills the space behind the century plant with fine green-gray foliage. In fall the plant is topped with long spikes of lavender and white flowers. See *Salvia leucantha*, p. 147.

D Red yucca (use 3)
This evergreen perennial bears 3-ft. stalks of coral-red, trumpet-shaped flowers all season. They bloom above clumps of succulent gray-green foliage. See *Hesperaloe parviflora*, p. 134.

E 'Radiation' lantana (use 1)
Round clusters of tiny bright-orange and yellow flowers blanket this spreading perennial throughout the growing season. See *Lantana camara* 'Radiation', p. 137.

F 'New Gold' lantana (use 3)
This lantana cultivar boasts masses of tiny golden yellow flowers covering dark-green foliage. See *Lantana* x *hybrida* 'New Gold', p. 137.

G Gaura (use 3)
An outstanding Texas native, this fine-textured perennial softens the planting with airy masses of small pink and white flowers. See *Gaura lindheimeri*, p. 132.

H 'Homestead Purple' verbena (use 3)
Vibrant purple flowers top this perennial's clump of bright-green foliage, forming a colorful mat in front of the century plant. See *Verbena* x *hybrida* 'Homestead Purple', p. 151.

I Edging
This decorative border of weathered-gray stones harmonizes with the colors of the foliage and flowers. See p. 166.

Lawn

Sidewalk

1 square = 1 ft.

SITE: Sunny

SEASON: Fall

CONCEPT: A colorful planting that looks good year-round marks the property line in a neighborly fashion.

See site plan for C.

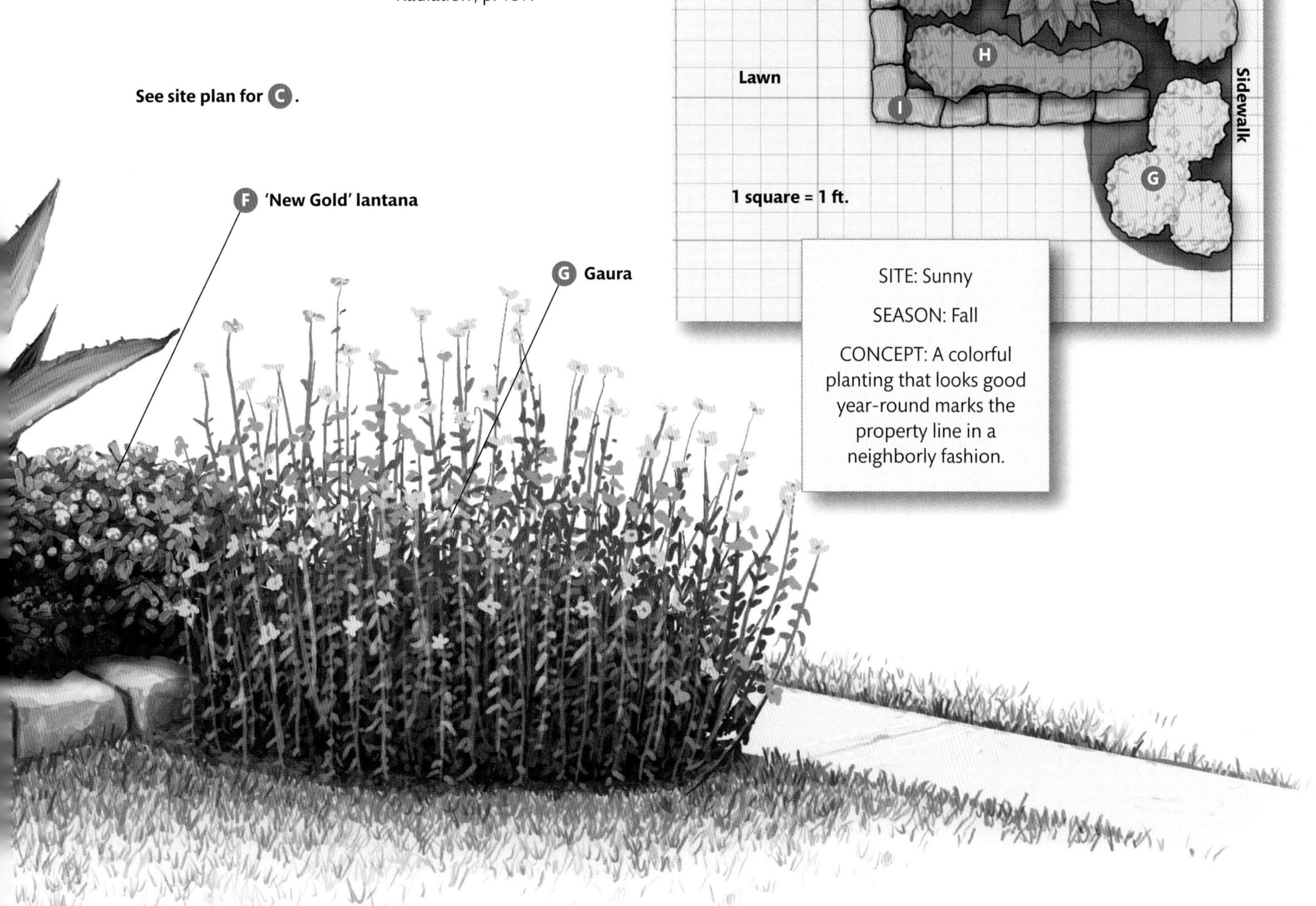

A comfortable corner

Why not make the most of a shady corner with a welcoming garden bench under a small tree? Framed by evergreen shrubs and perennials, the design offers a cozy corner for conversing with the neighbors, reading a book, or just sitting and relaxing. A small mound, or "berm," next to the walk helps nestle the bench into the garden setting. (Planted with sedum and daisies, this berm is about 12 in. above grade.) Two or three steppingstones edge the bench.

Viewed up close or from a distance, the planting offers color in every season: spring blossoms in a palette of pastels; vivid blue, gold, and red flowers in summer; fall foliage and flowers in yellows, pinks, and bronzes; and for winter, evergreens and plenty of cheerful red berries.

Plants & Projects

A Texas redbud (use 1 plant)
This lovely small tree provides a pleasant canopy for bench-sitters in every season. Small pink blossoms line bare branches in early spring, giving way to shiny heart-shaped green leaves scattered with light-green bean pods in summer, and bright-yellow leaves in fall. Hints of violet-purple on the gray bark brighten up the branches in dull winter months. See *Cercis texensis*, p. 128.

B 'Cherry Chief' autumn sage (use 3)
This bushy perennial's small oval leaves echo the holly's foliage, but are softer and paler. Small red flowers bloom heavily in spring and lightly in summer and fall. See *Salvia greggii* 'Cherry Chief', p. 147.

C Turk's cap (use 1)
A Texas favorite, this perennial forms a low bush of large heart-shaped leaves and red turbanlike flowers in summer.

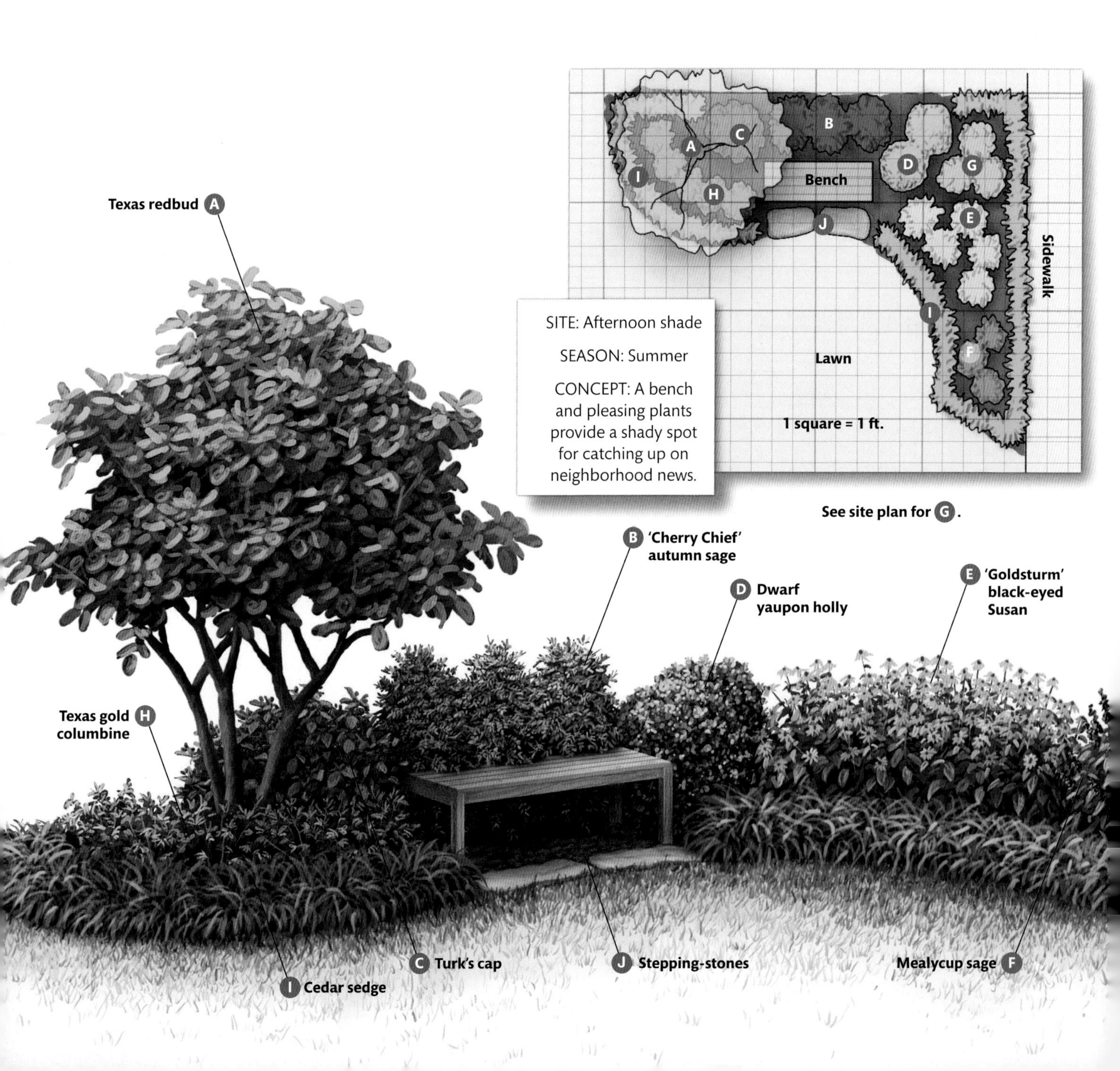

Hummingbirds attracted to the flowers will hover near the bench. Other birds may stop by for the cherrylike berries. See *Malvaviscus arboreus drummondii*, p. 139.

D Dwarf yaupon holly (use 2)
This compact evergreen shrub forms a fine-textured globe of olive-green leaves that are free of spines. See *Ilex vomitoria* 'Nana', p. 135.

E 'Goldsturm' black-eyed Susan (use 5)
Masses of golden "daisies" with dark eyes cover the coarse leaves of this sturdy perennial in early summer. See *Rudbeckia fulgida* 'Goldsturm', p. 146.

F Mealycup sage (use 3)
An erect bushy perennial with narrow gray-green leaves. Its many flower spikes are lined with small deep-blue blossoms from spring to fall. See *Salvia farinacea*, p. 147.

G 'Autumn Joy' sedum (use 3)
A bold-textured perennial that grows in mounds of dull-gray succulent leaves. Tight clusters of tiny buds open pink and fade to tan. See *Sedum* 'Autumn Joy', p. 149.

H Texas gold columbine (use 5)
This perennial's lacy leaves form dainty mounds. Yellow-gold flowers nod above the foliage from late spring through summer. See *Aquilegia chrysantha hinckleyana*, p. 123.

I Cedar sedge (use 46)
This clump-forming perennial grass, prefers some shade and can be combined with other woodland and meadow natives. See *Carex planostachys*, p. 127.

J Stepping-stones
Gray flagstones provide a place to rest your feet. See p. 169.

PLANT PORTRAITS

These tough plants provide a splash of color for many months in exchange for just a minimum of care.

● = First design, pp. 44-45
▲ = Second design, pp. 46-47

Century plant
(*Agave americana*, p. 122) ●

Dwarf yaupon holly
(*Ilex vomitoria* 'Nana', p. 135) ▲

Texas redbud
(*Cercis texensis*, p. 128) ▲

Mexican bush sage (*Salvia leucantha*, p. 147) ●

Streetwise and Stylish

GIVE YOUR CURBSIDE STRIP A NEW LOOK

SITE: Sunny

SEASON: Fall

CONCEPT: Plants with striking foliage and flowers transform an often-neglected area and treat visitors and passersby to a colorful display.

Homeowners seldom give a thought to the part of their property adjacent to the street. Often bounded by a sidewalk, this area is at best a tidy patch of lawn and at worst a weed-choked eyesore. Yet this is one of the most public parts of many properties. Filling this strip with attractive plants and paths from street to sidewalk can give pleasure to passersby and visitors who park next to the curb, as well as enhancing the streetscape you view from the house. (Curbside strips are usually city-owned, so check local ordinances for restrictions before you start a remake.)

This can be a difficult site, subject to summer heat and drought, pedestrian and car traffic, and errant dogs. Plants need to be tough and drought-tolerant to perform well here. (Many towns and cities encourage water-conserving plantings in curbside areas.)

The plants in this design meet both criteria. And they look good, too. There are flowers from late winter to frost in the fall. Foliage in a variety of complementary shades and texture, much of it evergreen, keeps the curbside looking attractive through winter. The 4-ft.-wide path allows ample room for passengers getting in and out of a car.

If your curbside property doesn't include a sidewalk, you can extend the planting farther into the yard and connect the path to the walkway leading to your front door.

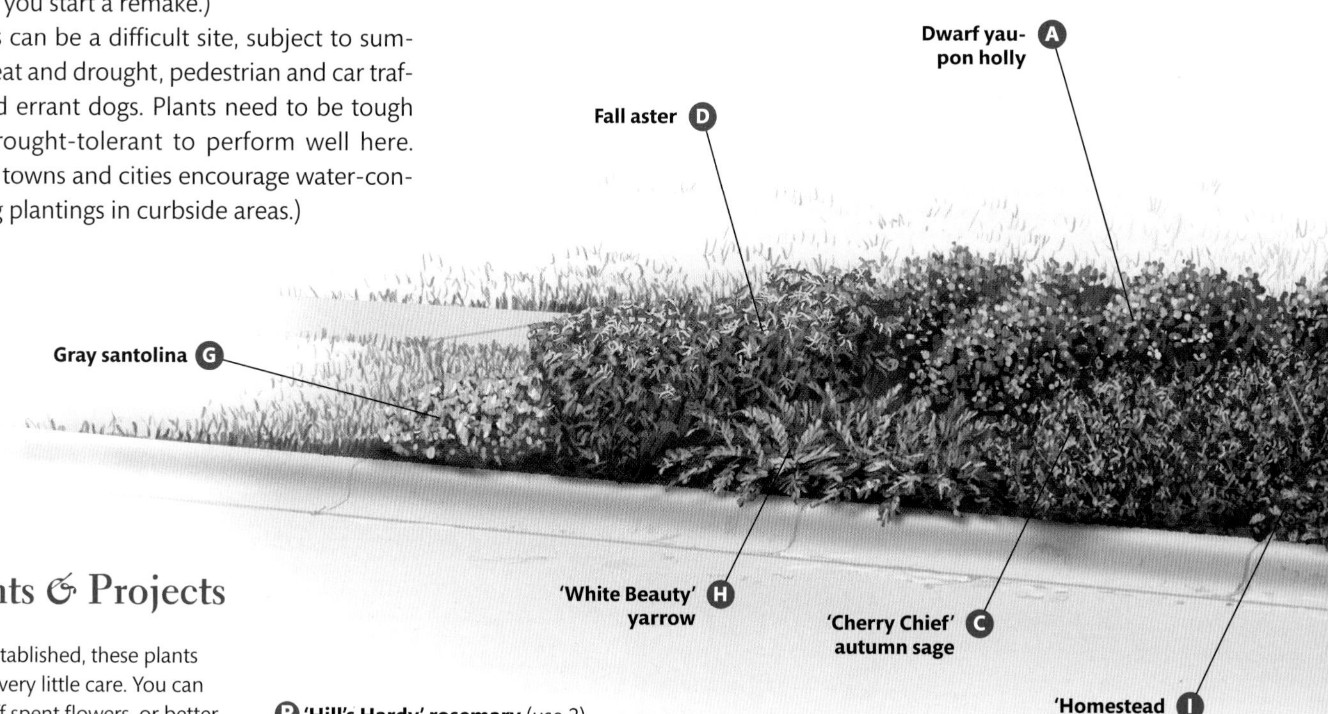

Plants & Projects

Once established, these plants require very little care. You can shear off spent flowers, or better yet, cut and dry the sage, santolina, and rosemary flowers for long-lasting arrangements. An occasional trim will keep the artemisia tidy. Prune the gaura to the ground after a freeze. Cut back the old stems of santolina in early spring.

A Dwarf yaupon holly
(use 5 plants)
This evergreen shrub forms a dense, rounded globe of tiny, spineless, oval leaves that never need shearing. See *Ilex vomitoria* 'Nana', p. 135.

B 'Hill's Hardy' rosemary (use 2)
Fine texture and fragrance distinguish both the foliage and flowers of this upright evergreen shrub. Blue flowers arrive in early spring. See *Rosmarinus officinalis*, p. 146.

C 'Cherry Chief' autumn sage
(use 3)
This bushy perennial's small oval leaves echo the holly's foliage, but are softer and paler. Small red flowers bloom heavily in spring and lightly in summer and fall. See *Salvia greggii* 'Cherry Chief', p. 147.

D Fall aster (use 3)
Lavender-purple daisies literally blanket this carefree perennial's small dull-green leaves in early summer. See *Aster oblongifolius*, p. 124.

E 'Dauphin' gaura (use 3)
With straight stems rising from a base of small pale-green leaves and delicate pink and white flowers, this tall perennial adds an airy presence to the planting. See *Gaura lindheimeri* 'Dauphin', p. 132.

F 'Powis Castle' artemisia
(use 4)
Prized for its foliage, this perennial forms a dense billowing mound of very fine silvery leaves. See *Artemisia* x 'Powis Castle', p. 124.

G Gray santolina (use 8)
This perennial spreads to form a low, dense cushion of fragrant gray leaves along the

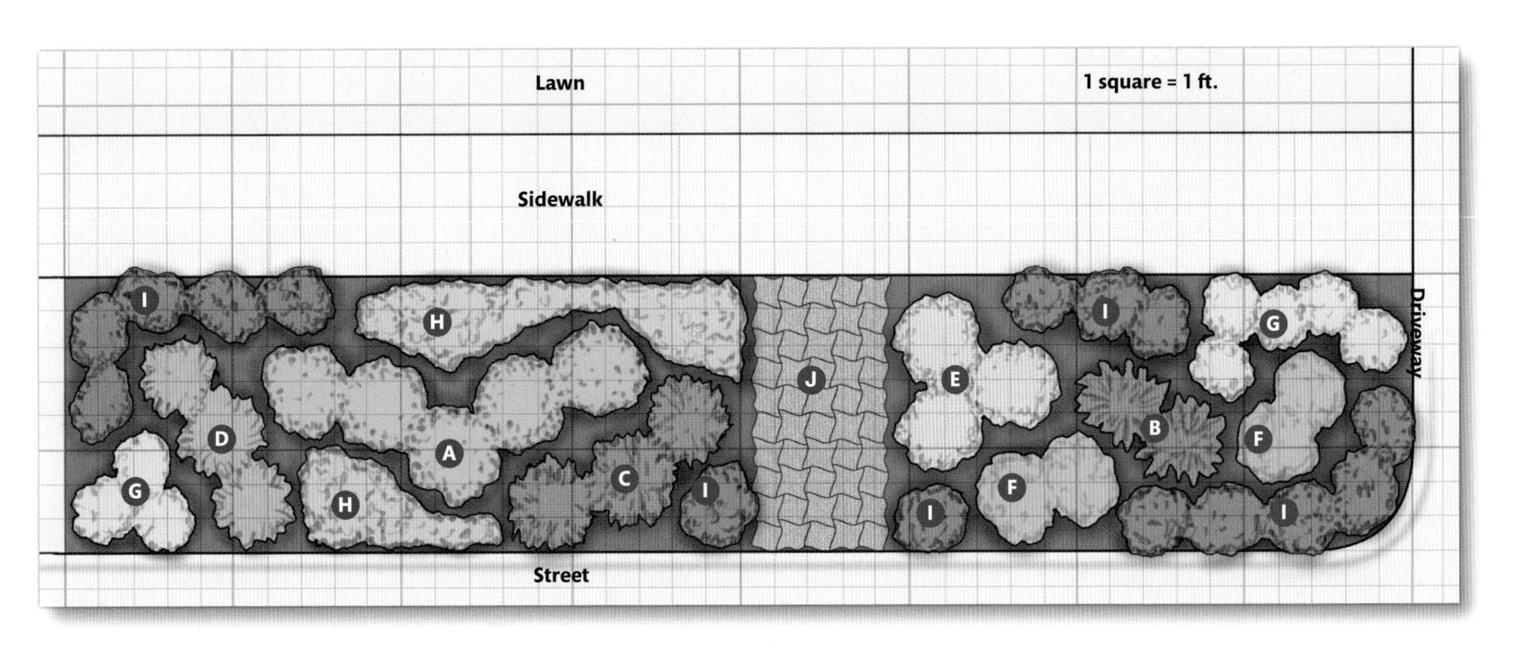

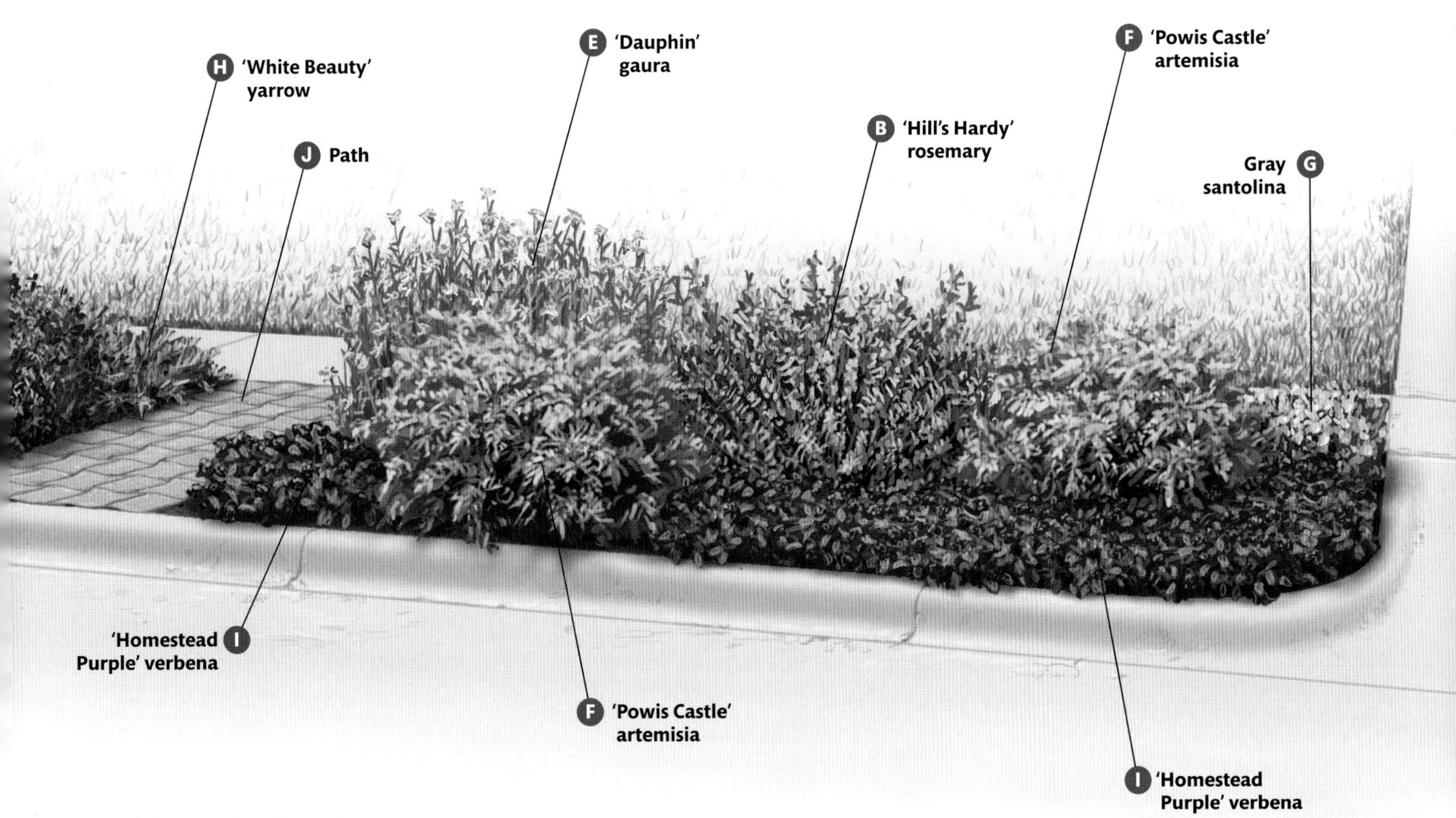

curb. Bears yellow flowers in summer. See *Santolina chamaecyparissus*, p. 148.

H 'White Beauty' yarrow
(use 13)
The white flowers of this mat-forming perennial edge the walk in spring. Ferny leaves are green all year. See *Achillea millefolium* 'White Beauty', p. 122.

I 'Homestead Purple' verbena
(use 15)
This perennial's deeply cut bright-green leaves and masses of purple flowers will enliven the curbside from spring to frost. See *Verbena* x *hybrida* 'Homestead Purple', p. 151.

J Path
Interlocking pavers create an attractive, durable, and easily maintained surface. The gray paver shown here ties in with the sidewalk, street, and planting. See p. 163.

Branching out

A small tree and a branching path distinguish this design and give it an informal appeal. The long-lasting deciduous foliage of the evergreen shrubs and perennials is colorful year-round, mixing shades of green, gray, red, and purple. Flowers in white, pink, and yellow complement the foliage and are pretty in their own right.

Like the previous design, this one is a low-maintenance, low-water-use planting. It requires little more than shearing off spent flowers, trimming back the lantana after a freeze, and lightly pruning the spirea and barberry to maintain their size and shape.

Plants & Projects

A Wax myrtle (use 1 plant)
A graceful shrub that can be pruned into a shapely multi-trunked tree. In most parts of Texas, foliage stays green through the winter. See *Myrica cerifera*, p. 138.

B 'Pink' autumn sage (use 1)
Massed on both sides of the entry, these fine-textured perennials help tie the planting together. 'Pink' is a large and dependable cultivar with bright pink blooms from spring to fall. Use this or any pink cultivar. Evergreen in warm winters. See *Salvia greggii* 'Pink', p. 147.

C 'Cherry Chief' autumn sage (use 6)
This bushy perennial's small oval leaves echo the holly's foliage, but are softer and paler. Small red flowers bloom heavily in spring and lightly in summer and fall. See *Salvia greggii* 'Cherry Chief', p. 147.

D Partridgeberry (use 4)
An evergreen creeping groundcover with small leaves, it produces small white flowers followed by scarlet berries enjoyed by birds and mammals. See *Mitchella repens*, page 139.

E 'Weeping White' trailing lantana (use 13)
Clusters of pure white flowers cover this vigorous low-growing perennial from spring to fall. In mild-winter areas plant sometimes blooms all year. See *Lantana montevidensis* 'Weeping White', p. 137.

F St.-John's-wort (use 13)
Under the wax myrtle, this evergreen shrub creates a dense, fine-textured carpet, dotted in summer with bright yellow periwinkle-like flowers. Small oval leaves turn reddish purple in winter. See *Hypericum calycinum*, p. 134.

G 'Bath's Pink' dianthus (use 7)
Delightfully fragrant pink flowers greet visitors in spring. The rest of the year this perennial's fine blue-green foliage attracts all the attention. See *Dianthus* 'Bath's Pink', p. 131.

See p. 49 for the following:

H Path

SITE: Sunny

SEASON: Summer

CONCEPT: Two streetside paths join up with colorful plantings to welcome visitors.

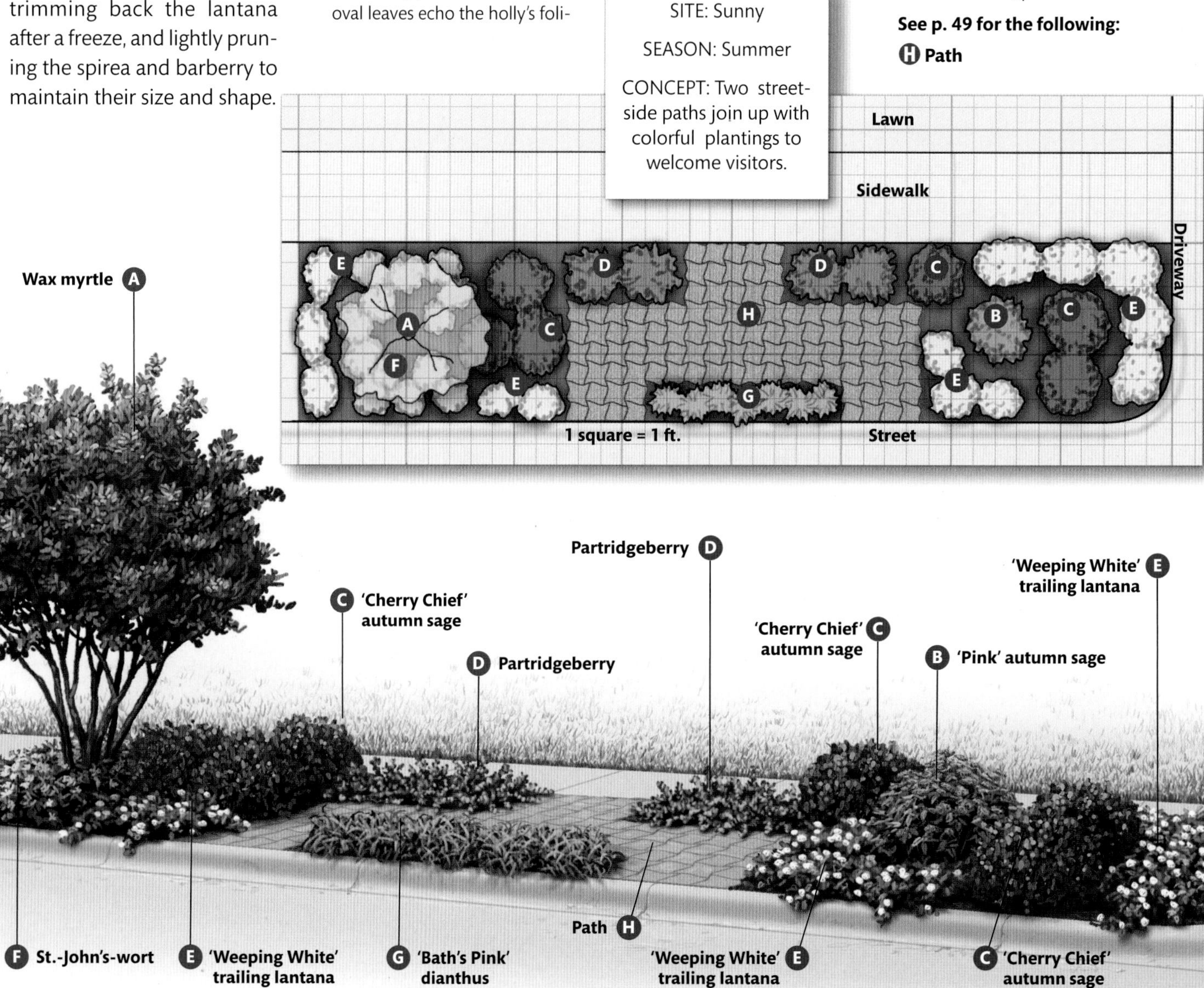

PLANT PORTRAITS

These low-maintenance plants will improve any curbside area, while withstanding the rigors of life by the street.

● = First design, pp. 48-49
▲ = Second design, p. 50

'Dauphin' gaura
(*Gaura lindheimeri*, p. 132) ●

'Weeping White' trailing lantana
(*Lantana montevidensis*, p. 137) ▲

'Pink' autumn sage
(*Salvia greggii* 'Pink', p. 147) ▲

'Bath's Pink' dianthus
(*Dianthus*, p. 131) ▲

'Powis Castle' artemisia
(*Artemisia*, p. 124) ●

Fall aster
(*Aster oblongifolius*, p. 124) ●

A Garden Path

RECLAIM A NARROW SIDE YARD FOR A STROLL GARDEN

Many residential lots include a slim strip of land between the house and a property line. Usually overlooked by everyone except children and dogs racing between the front yard and the back, this neglected passageway can become a valued addition to the landscape. In this design, a delightful little stroll garden invites adults, and even children, to linger as they move from one part of the property to another.

The wall of the house and a tall fence at the property line create a cozy "room," one that is enhanced by trees, vines, shrubs, and ground covers. Like furnishings in a room, the plantings make the small space seem bigger than it is. A gently curving flagstone path widens the passage visually and lengthens the stroll through it.

In spring, scented blossoms of daffodil, wisteria, and Texas mountain laurel will perfume the entire passage. As these flowers fade, the red crapemyrtle will begin its long season of bloom, joined by purple verbena along the fence, bushy mounds of baby blue plumbago where the daffodils had been, and a continuous row of pretty pink salvia. As the trees grow, their boughs will arch over the path, creating a bower heavy with blossoms for much of the year.

Plants & Projects

Install the fence and flagstone path. Then prepare and plant the beds. You'll need to add sturdy trellises or other strong supports for the vines. As the trees grow, prune them so they arch over the path, yet provide headroom for strollers. Once established, the plants require seasonal care as well as pruning to maintain size and shape.

A 'Dynamite' crapemyrtle (use 2 plants)
A beautiful addition to any landscape, this tree requires full sun. It flowers in the spring and summertime, catching the eye of passers by. See *Lagerstroemia* x *fauriei* 'Dynamite,' p. 136.

B Texas mountain laurel (use 1)
Clusters of purple flowers hang from this small glossy evergreen tree in early spring. Passersby on both sides of the fence will appreciate the delightful perfume. Bean pods with bright-red seeds follow the flowers. See *Dermatophyllum secundiflorum*, p. 131.

C Compact Texas sage (use 4)
A native evergreen shrub with small woolly leaves and a billowy shape. It bears masses of orchid-pink flowers after summer rains. See *Leucophyllum frutescens* 'Compactum', p. 138.

D Tropical plumbago (use 3)
After the daffodils fade, this perennial emerges apple green and bushy. In summer it spills over with big clusters of clear-blue flowers. See *Plumbago auriculata*, p. 142.

E 'Pink' autumn sage (use 6)
These low, bushy mounds of tiny oval leaves bristle with spires of bright-pink flowers all season. Plant this or any pink cultivar. See *Salvia greggii* 'Pink', p. 147.

F American wisteria (use 2)
This is a vigorous deciduous vine with spectacular clusters of fragrant pea-like purple or blue flowers in summer. Prune in spring to control its size and to stimulate abundant bloom. See *Wisteria frutescens*, p. 153.

G Purple verbena (use 2)
Countless bright clusters of purple flowers rise airily from this perennial's base of dull green leaves. Blooms from midsummer to frost. See *Verbena bonariensis*, p. 151.

H Cedar sedge (use 24)
This clump-forming perennial grass, prefers some shade and can be combined with other woodland and meadow natives. See *Carex planostachys*, p. 127.

I 'Ice Follies' daffodil (as needed)
Fresh-looking white daffodil flowers with pale yellow centers line the path in early spring. See Bulbs: *Narcissus pseudonarcissus* 'Ice Follies', p. 126.

J Fence
Easy to build, this fence provides privacy and an attractive framework for plants. See pp. 196-197.

K Path
Flagstones in random shapes and sizes trace a graceful curve through the planting. A neutral gray would complement any house. See p. 163.

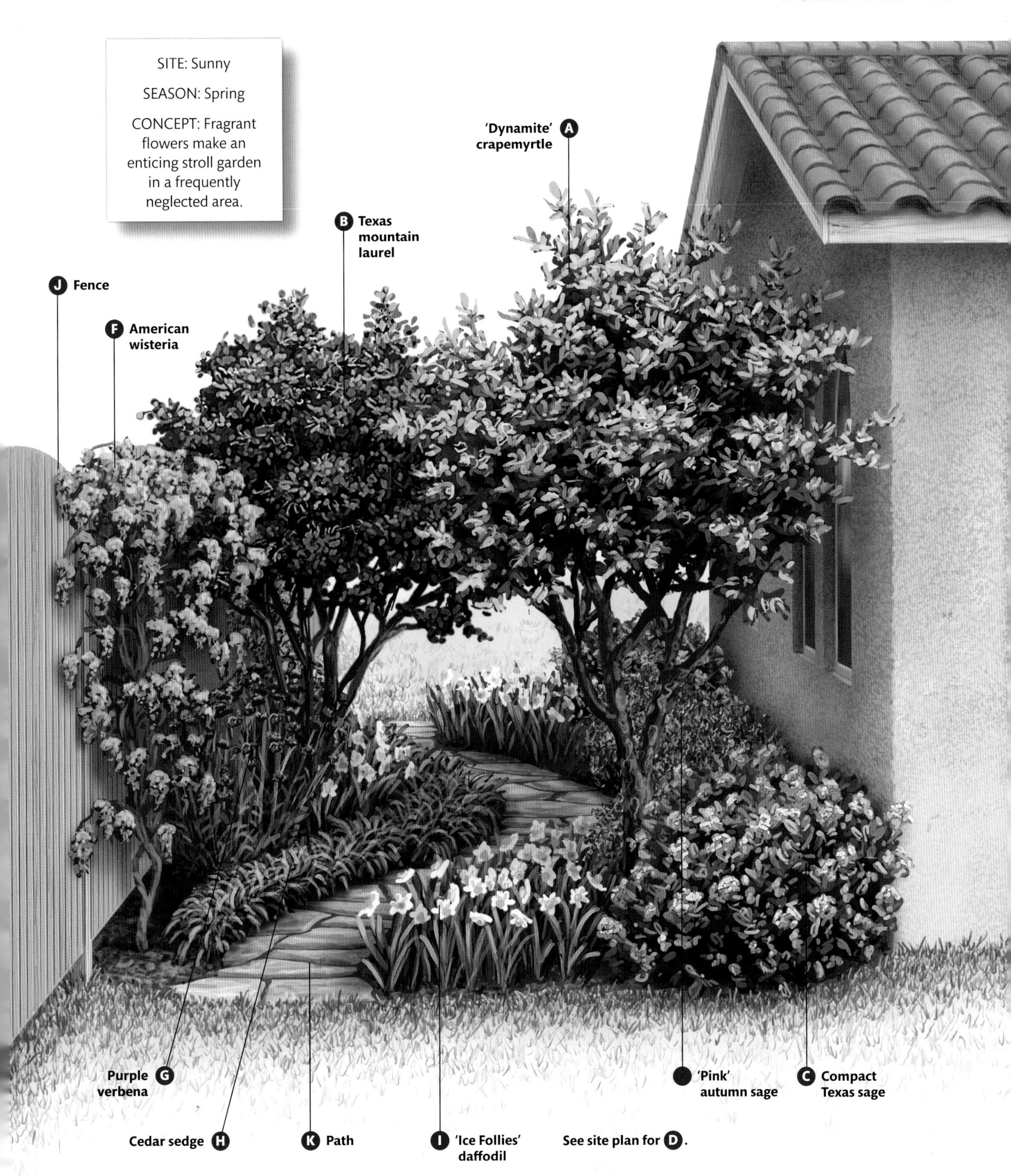
SITE: Sunny
SEASON: Spring
CONCEPT: Fragrant flowers make an enticing stroll garden in a frequently neglected area.
'Dynamite' crapemyrtle A
B Texas mountain laurel
J Fence
F American wisteria
Purple verbena G
'Pink' autumn sage
C Compact Texas sage
Cedar sedge H
K Path
I 'Ice Follies' daffodil
See site plan for D.

PLANT PORTRAITS

Eye-catching plants for an overlooked spot, here are flowers, foliage, and fragrance to make your side-yard stroll garden a favorite.

● = First design, pp. 52-53

▲ = Second design, p. 55

'Ice Follies' daffodil
(Bulbs: *Narcissus pseudonarcissus*, p. 126) ●

Compact Texas sage
(*Leucophyllum frutescens* 'Compactum', p. 138) ●

'Pink' autumn sage
(*Salvia greggii*, p. 147) ●

'Dynamite' crapemyrtle (*Lagerstroemia* x *fauriei*, p. 136) ●

American wisteria (*Wisteria frutescens*, p. 153) ●

A shady corridor

If the side of your house has a shady exposure, try this design. Shade-loving shrubs and ground covers are arrayed in colorful layers along the passage. These "furnishings" are selected primarily for their foliage, ranging from light green to purple-black, fine-textured to coarse, dull to glossy, and low-growing to large and bold. The big leaves of the turk's cap and wax myrtle combine well with ground covers, soft fern fronds, and stiff, swordlike aspidistra. In this evergreen garden, flowers and berries are added enticements. Fragrant jessamine scents the air in spring and purple berries brighten a winter stroll.

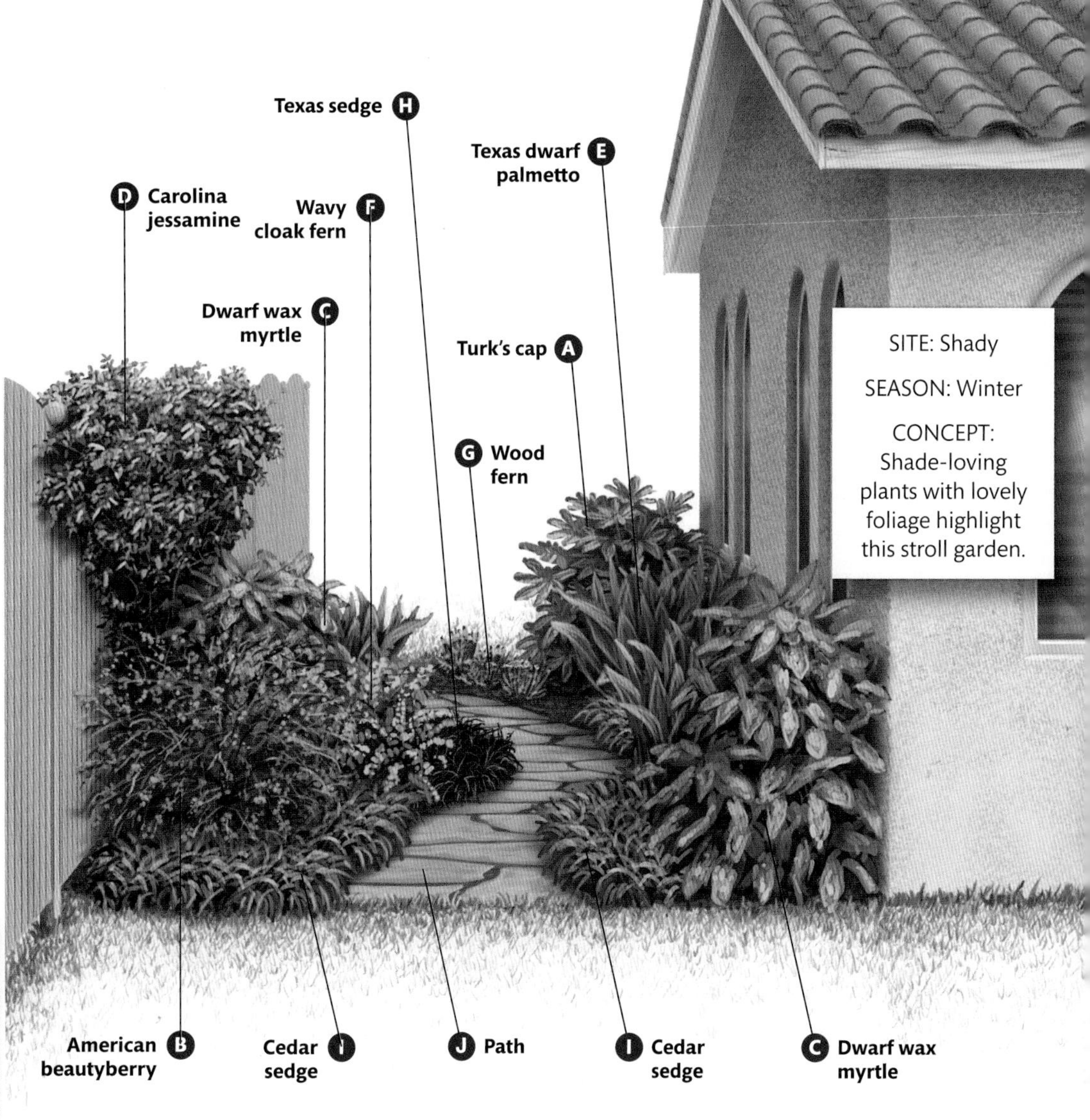

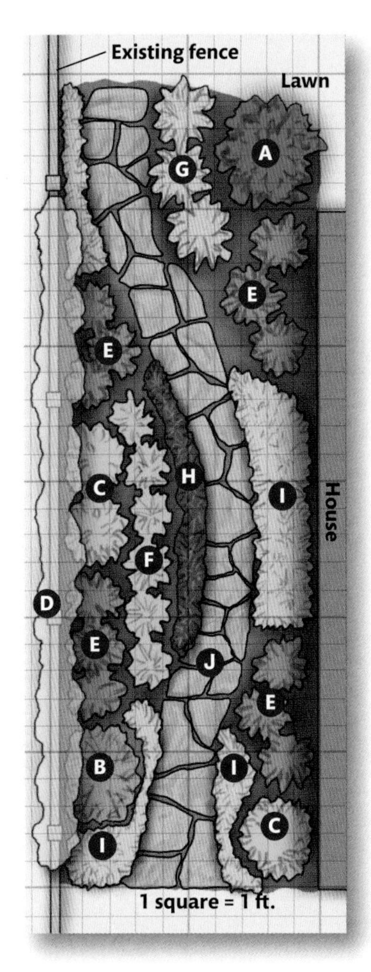

Plants & Projects

A Turk's cap (use 1 plant)
A Texas favorite, this perennial forms a low bush of large leaves and red turbanlike flowers in summer. Hummingbirds attracted to the flowers will hover near the bench. Other birds may stop by for the cherrylike berries. See *Malvaviscus arboreus drummondii*, p. 139.

B American beautyberry (use 1)
This shrub has an open, slightly sprawling habit. Purple berries are showy on bare branches in fall and winter. See *Callicarpa americana*, p. 127.

C Dwarf wax myrtle (use 3)
This small evergreen tree offers a fragrant and shady canopy for bench sitters. Leaves are smooth and slender. See *Myrica cerifera*, p. 139.

D Carolina jessamine (use 3)
Shiny neat evergreen leaves and a show of fragrant yellow flowers in spring make this vigorous vine ideal for training up porch columns or along a railing. See *Gelsemium sempervirens*, p. 133.

E Texas dwarf palmetto (use 12)
This slow-growing shrub has pale-green fan-like leaves and spineless stems. See *Sabal minor*, p. 148.

F Wavy cloak fern (use 6)
This semi-evergreen fern produces clumps of attractive rich green foliage, with a contrasting cinnamon underside. It is uniquely drought tolerant and suited to poor rocky soils, preferring sun or part shade. It is clump forming and slowly spreads via rhizomes. See *Astrolepsis sinuata*, p. 124.

G Wood fern (use 3)
This is a deciduous fern with a soft shaggy look. Cut back after frost for an attractive brown flat-top. See Ferns: *Thelypteris kunthii*, p. 132.

H Texas sedge (use 12) A common sedge in Texas, this sedge is a good turf substitute with a tufted, grass-like appearance. See *Carex texensis*, p. 127.

See p. 52 for the following:

I Cedar sedge (use 24)

J Path

Landscape a Low Wall

A TWO-TIERED GARDEN REPLACES A BLAND SLOPE

Some things may not love a wall, but plants and gardeners do. For plants, walls offer warmth for an early start in spring and good drainage for roots. Gardeners appreciate the rich visual potential of composing a garden on two levels, as well as the practical advantage of working on two relatively flat surfaces instead of a single sloping one.

This design places complementary plantings above and below a wall bounded at one end by a set of steps. While each bed is relatively narrow, when viewed from the lower level the two combine to form a border more than 10 ft. deep. Two other design features add depth to the display. A jog in the wall creates a niche for a splashy fountain grass, and the beds are rounded rather than linear. Together with a selection of billowy plants, these features soften the face of the wall and offer pleasing views from many vantage points.

Building the wall that makes this impressive sight possible doesn't require the time or skill it once did. Nor is it necessary to scour the countryside for tons of fieldstone or to hire an expensive contractor. Thanks to precast retaining-wall systems, anyone with a healthy back (or access to energetic teenagers) can install a knee-high do-it-yourself wall in as little as a weekend or two.

Plants & Projects

This planting showcases colorful flowers against curtains of soft silvery green foliage. All the plants tolerate heat and drought and need only a little care to keep them performing at their best. Trim the autumn and mealycup sages lightly through summer to encourage new bloom. The Mexican bush sage and mint marigold will benefit from pruning in late spring and again in midsummer to make them dense and full by showtime in fall.

A Lindheimer's muhly (use 1 plant)
A beautiful, fine-textured ornamental grass. Blue-green leaves and soft texture makes this grass popular for screening. See *Muhlenbergia lindheimeri*, p. 139.

B Compact Texas sage (use 3)
A native evergreen shrub with small woolly leaves and a billowy shape. It bears masses of orchid-pink flowers after summer rains. See *Leucophyllum frutescens* 'Compactum', p. 138.

C Mexican bush sage (use 1)
This big bushy perennial anchors the end of the border and echoes the arching habit of the fountain grass. Slender branches bear gray-green foliage. In autumn, long wands of small purple and white flowers bloom from branch tips. See *Salvia leucantha*, p. 147.

D White autumn sage (use 3)
This perennial forms a mat of small oval leaves that usually stay green all winter. A profusion of pure-white flowers greets visitors at the steps from spring to fall. See *Salvia greggii* 'Alba', p. 147.

E Mealycup sage (use 6)
A fringe of blue flower spikes top the narrow grayish leaves of this compact bushy perennial throughout the growing season. Bumblebees will buzz among the blooms. See *Salvia farinacea*, p. 147.

F Soft-tip yucca (use 1)
This perennial forms an attractive rosette of succulent gray-blue leaves. It puts on a dazzling display of bloom in summer, when clusters of large creamy white bells rise from the center on sturdy stalks. See *Yucca gloriosa*, p. 153.

G Mexican mint marigold (use 1)
This compact perennial has narrow, emerald green leaves topped with a profusion of small gold flowers. See *Tagetes lucida*, p. 150.

H Fall aster (use 3)
In autumn, a solid mass of purple daisylike flowers makes this perennial a knockout in front of the gray foliage and white flowers of the sage. See *Aster oblongifolius*, p. 124.

I 'Blue Princess' verbena (use 2)
Lavender-blue flowers blanket this low-growing perennial from spring through fall. It will spread wide enough to surround the yucca in a sea of bloom. See *Verbena* x *hybrida* 'Blue Princess', p. 151.

J Retaining wall and steps
Prefabricated wall systems make this project easy to install. See p. 176.

K Path
We've shown gravel here, but use any materials that complement the wall. See p. 163.

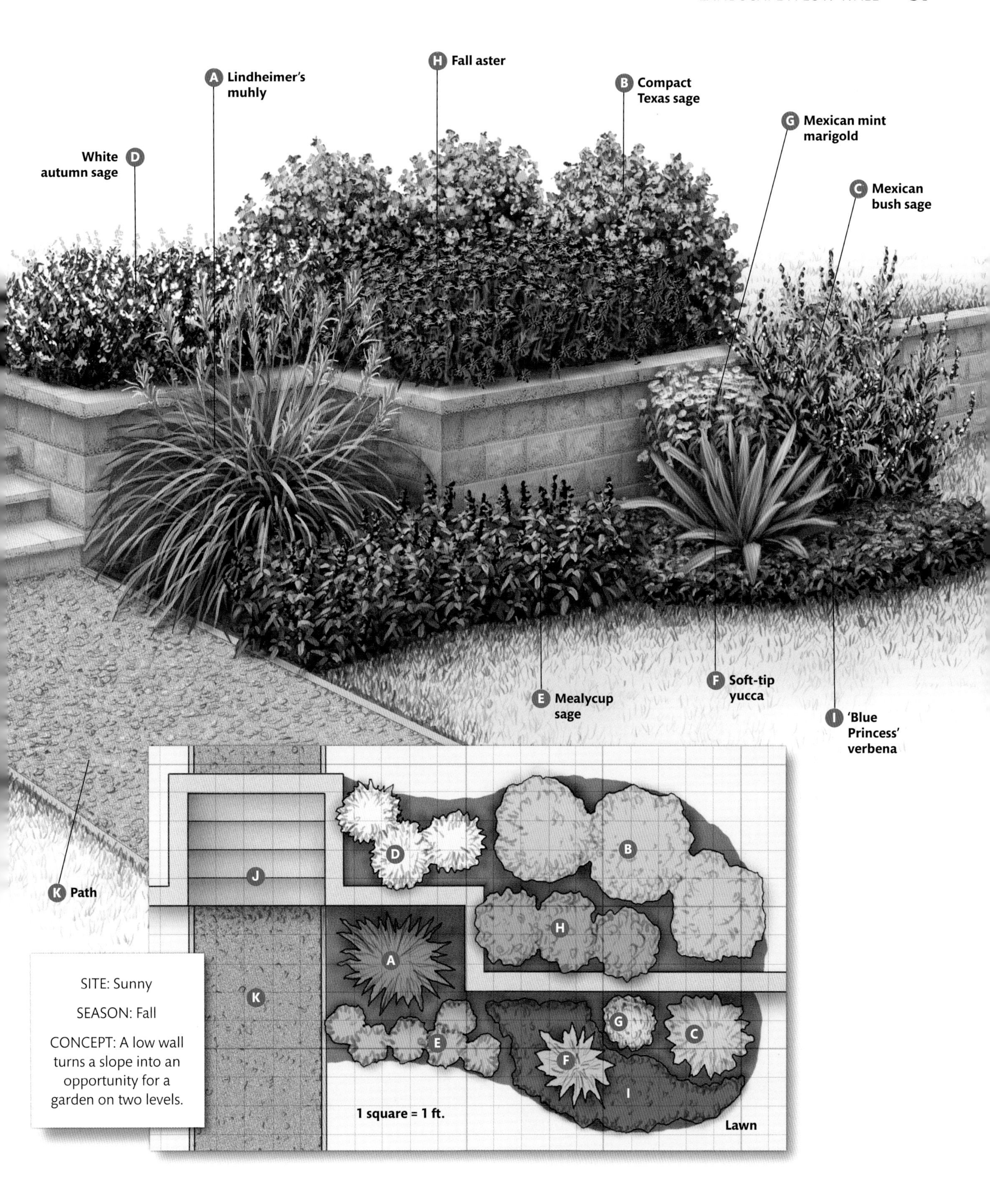

SITE: Sunny

SEASON: Fall

CONCEPT: A low wall turns a slope into an opportunity for a garden on two levels.

PLANT PORTRAITS

These plants double the pleasure of a retaining wall with eye-catching flowers and handsome foliage.
● = First design, pp. 56-57
▲ = Second design, pp. 58-59

Lindheimer's muhly (*Muhlenbergia lindheimeri*, p. 139) ●

Soft-tip yucca (*Yucca gloriosa*, p. 153) ●

White autumn sage (*Salvia greggii* 'Alba', p. 147) ●

Two tiers in the shade

A retaining-wall planting can be equally alluring in a shady yard. This design uses the same wall-and-step system but keeps the wall straight and nestles the steps into the lawn. Bold shrubs on both levels break up the retaining wall's horizontal plane while bringing the garden together as a whole. These shade-loving plants are chosen for their colorful foliage and flowers in a contrasting palette of rosy purples, cool blues, and cheerful yellows.

Plants & Projects

A Flame acanthus (use 1 plant)
This spreading deciduous shrub has red-orange tubular flowers and light-green leaves. It attracts hummingbirds and takes well to shearing. See *Anisacanthus quadrifidus var. wrightii*, p. 122.

B Turk's cap (use 1)
A Texas favorite, this perennial forms a low bush of large leaves and red turbanlike flowers in summer. Hummingbirds attracted to the flowers will hover near the bench. Other birds may stop by for the cherrylike berries. See *Malvaviscus arboreus drummondii*, p. 139.

C American beautyberry (use 1)
This shrub wears a thick coat of pale green foliage most of the year. Clusters of eye-popping purple berries line the branches in late summer. See *Callicarpia americana*, p. 127.

D Texas dwarf palmetto (use 3)
This slow-growing shrub has pale-green fan-like leaves and spineless stems. See *Sabal minor*, p. 148.

E Wavy cloak fern (use 9)
This semi-evergreen fern produces clumps of attractive rich green foliage, with a contrasting cinnamon underside. It is uniquely drought tolerant and suited to poor rocky soils, preferring sun or part shade. It is clump forming and slowly spreads via rhizomes. See *Astrolepsis sinuata*, p. 124.

F Carolina jessamine (use 1)
In no time at all this vine will twine under the redbud and trail over the wall. Tiny lancelike evergreen leaves are almost hidden in spring by sweet-scented yellow flower bells. See *Gelsemium sempervirens*, p. 133.

G Louisiana iris (use 3)
This perennial forms an erect clump of narrow arching leaves. Large flowers rise above the foliage in spring. Choose a blue or lavender variety to complement the color scheme. See *Iris x Louisiana* hybrids, p. 152.

H Texas gold columbine (use 3)
Plant this evergreen perennial at the front of the border to show off the neat mounds of attractive ferny foliage. Delicate yellow flowers with long spurs rise above the plant in spring. See *Aquilegia chrysantha hinckleyana*, p. 123.

I St.-John's-wort (use 3)
This semi-evergreen perennial makes a thick mat of miniature leaves along the wall and cascading over it. Small yellow flowers decorate the plant in summer. Foliage is reddish purple in autumn. See *Hypericum calycinum*, p. 134.

J Texas sedge (use 15)
A common sedge in Texas, this sedge is a good turf substitute with a tufted, grass-like appearance. See *Carex texenis*, p. 127.

K Dwarf Mexican petunia (use 6)
This low-growing perennial produces tufts of narrow, long, dark-green leaves that are ideal for an informal edging. Slow to emerge in spring, this plant makes up time with a long season of purple bloom. The flowers are funnel-shaped and light purple. See *Ruellia brittoniana* 'Katie', p. 148.

L 'Superbena purple' (use 1)
This spreading native blooms all summer, growing in full sun, it is heat and drought tolerant. See *Verbena hybrid*, p. 151.

See p. 56 for the following:

M Retaining wall and steps

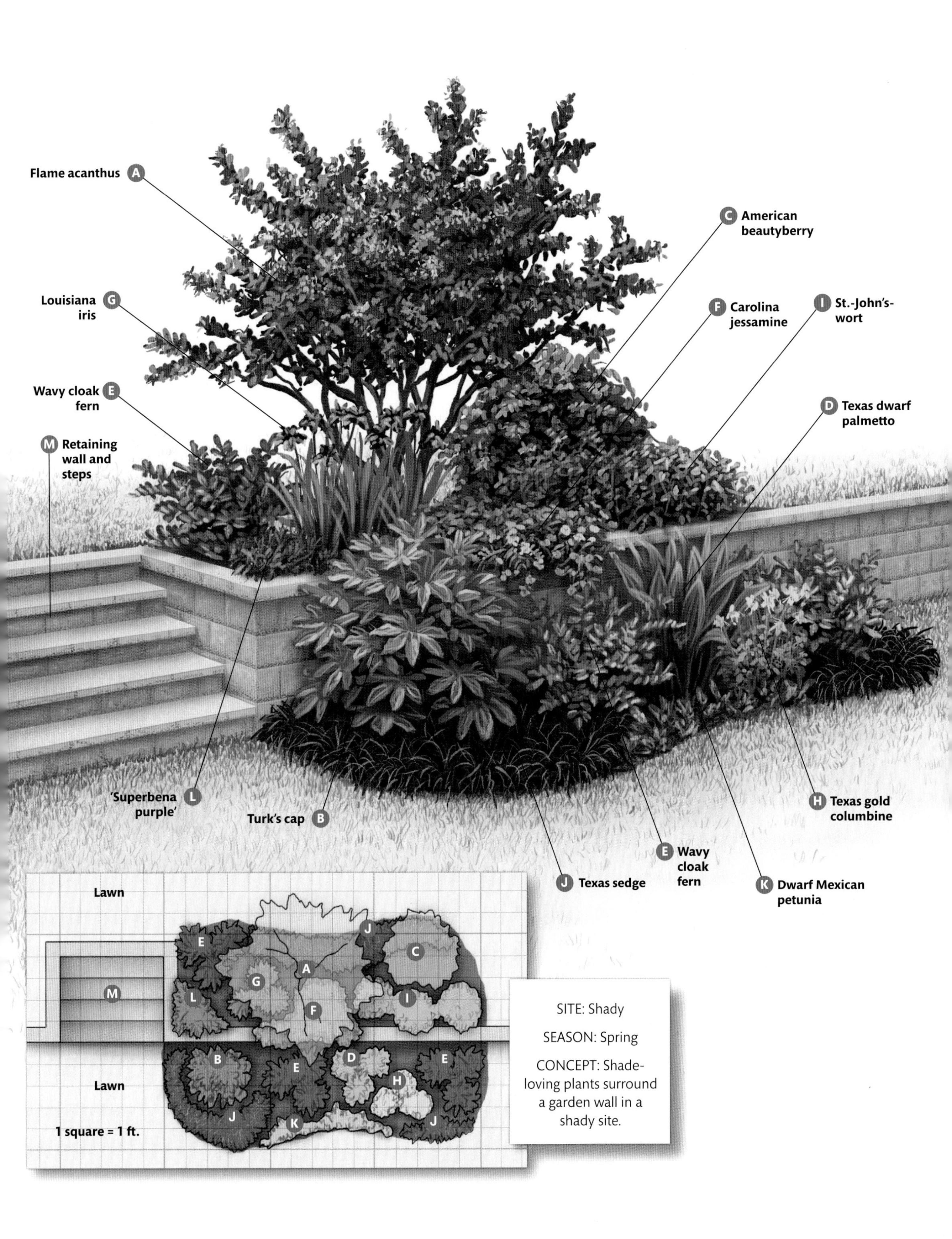

SITE: Shady

SEASON: Spring

CONCEPT: Shade-loving plants surround a garden wall in a shady site.

Angle of Repose

MAKE A BACK-DOOR GARDEN IN A SHELTERED NICHE

Many homes offer the opportunity to tuck a garden into a protected corner. In the front yard, such spots are ideal for an entry garden or a landscaping display that enhances the view of the house from the sidewalk or the street. If the corner is in the backyard, like the site shown here, it can be more intimate, part of a comfortable outdoor "room" you can stroll through at leisure or enjoy from a nearby terrace or window.

This planting introduces shrubs and perennials with a distinctive Southwestern flare. Though not all of them are desert natives, they have the spiky forms and gray-green foliage of desert plants—without the accompanying thorns or spines. Tolerant of heat and drought, they'll do well with good drainage and plenty of sun.

Enjoyable year-round, this garden features the bold, cactuslike foliage of yuccas and prickly pears as well as the softer tones and finer textures of sage and rosemary. The evergreen foliage enhances the garden all year, but particularly before the "desert" begins to bloom in spring. At the first hints of warmth, jonquils and dianthus will entice viewers outdoors with their springtime fragrance. By May the planting will be brimming with flowers in vibrant pinks and yellows, purples and blues. Flowers peak again in fall, after a summer kept colorful by consistent bright clusters of yellow lantana, long-lasting spikes of coral-red yucca, and repeated bursts of pink from the Texas sage bush.

Plants & Projects

Once established, these plants will provide years of pleasure. Heat and drought tolerant in summer, they will do best if their roots are kept dry in winter.

Ⓐ Desert willow (use 3 plants)
The fine leaves of this deciduous tree provide an airy canopy over the path without shading out the plants underneath. Showy white, pink, and lavender flowers bloom on and off all season. See *Chilopsis linearis*, p. 129.

Ⓑ Spineless prickly pear (use 3)
A bold cactuslike accent with tiny hidden prickles. This evergreen shrub forms an interesting erect clump of succulent leaf pads, occasionally bearing yellow flowers in summer and showy purple fruit in fall. See *Opuntia lindheimeri*, p. 140.

Ⓒ Compact Texas sage (use 4)
An evergreen shrub that forms a billowy mound of small fuzzy gray leaves on pale stems. This cultivar is a denser, bushier version of the popular Texas sage and has orchid-pink flowers. See *Leucophyllum frutescens* 'Compactum', p. 138.

Ⓓ 'Hill's Hardy' rosemary (use 2)
Both foliage and flowers of this handsome evergreen shrub are fragrant. Most cold tolerant of all the rosemary cultivars. See *Rosmarinus officinalis* 'Hill's Hardy', p. 146.

Ⓔ Red yucca (use 15)
Slow-growing but worth it, these evergreen perennials create a low, striking hedge. Spikes of coral-pink flowers rise from the narrow succulent leaves and bloom from May to frost. See *Hesperaloe parviflora*, p. 134.

Ⓕ 'Pink' autumn sage (use 7)
Massed on both sides of the entry, these fine-textured perennials help tie the planting together. 'Pink' is a large and dependable cultivar with bright pink blooms from spring to fall. Use this or any pink cultivar. Evergreen in warm winters. See *Salvia greggii* 'Pink', p. 147.

Ⓖ Mexican bush sage (use 7)
These bushy perennials will fill the space under the tree with downy gray leaves and stems. The nectar of the white and purple flowers in autumn draws hummingbirds. See *Salvia leucantha*, p. 147.

Ⓗ Mealycup sage (use 4)
For a touch of bright blue, plant this perennial among the pinks and yellows of autumn sage and lantana. See *Salvia farinacea*, p. 147.

Ⓘ 'New Gold' lantana (use 7)
These vigorous perennials will spread to form a continuous border of gold flowers atop small green elliptical leaves. A butterfly favorite. See *Lantana* x *hybrida*, p. 137.

Ⓙ 'Bath's Pink' dianthus (use 18)
This perennial is grown for its thick mat of tiny blue-green leaves and its fragrant pink flowers in early spring. See *Dianthus* 'Bath's Pink', p. 131.

Ⓚ Jonquil (as needed)
Plant these bulbs for fresh grassy foliage and yellow trumpets that announce the arrival of early spring. Sprinkle them throughout, and particularly around plants that are dormant in winter, such as the salvias and lantana. See Bulbs: *Narcissus jonquilla*, p. 127.

Ⓛ Stepping-stones
Flagstones provide access from the slab through the planting to the side yard. See p. 169.

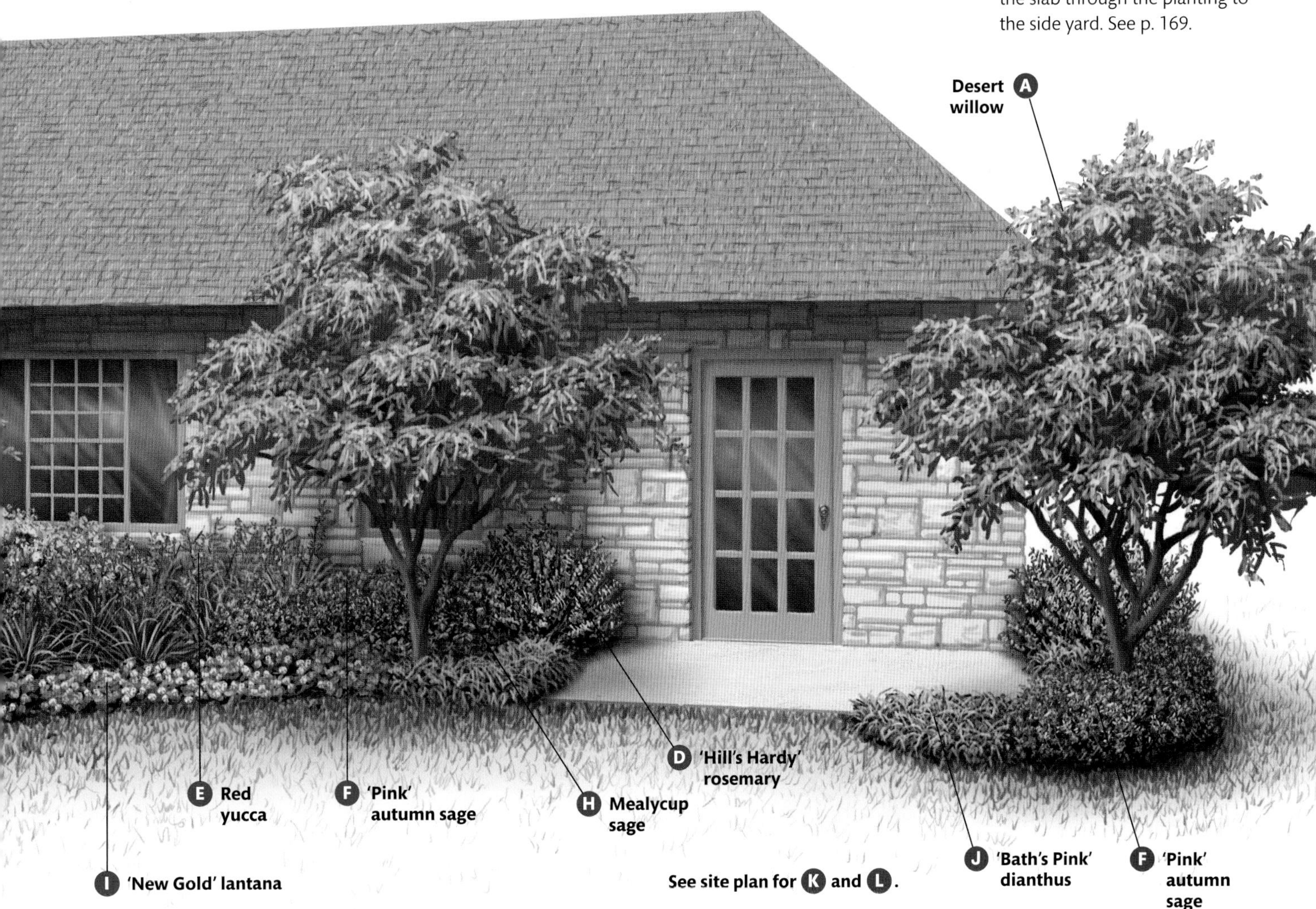

A touch of the tropics

Chosen for a niche in shade, these plants provide the look of a balmy Pacific island. Almost entirely evergreen, the planting will change little from season to season; the interest comes from the many contrasts in plant forms and in foliage texture and color.

Five sabal palms set a dramatic tone across the front of the planting. Their hairy trunks frame views of the plants behind. From front to back, the foliage progresses from fine-textured to coarse and alternates between light and dark colors, finishing with the very bold, very dark foliage of the turk's cap. The pattern is repeated on a smaller scale and with some variation on the other side of the entry.

This planting is most effective in late winter, the season shown here.

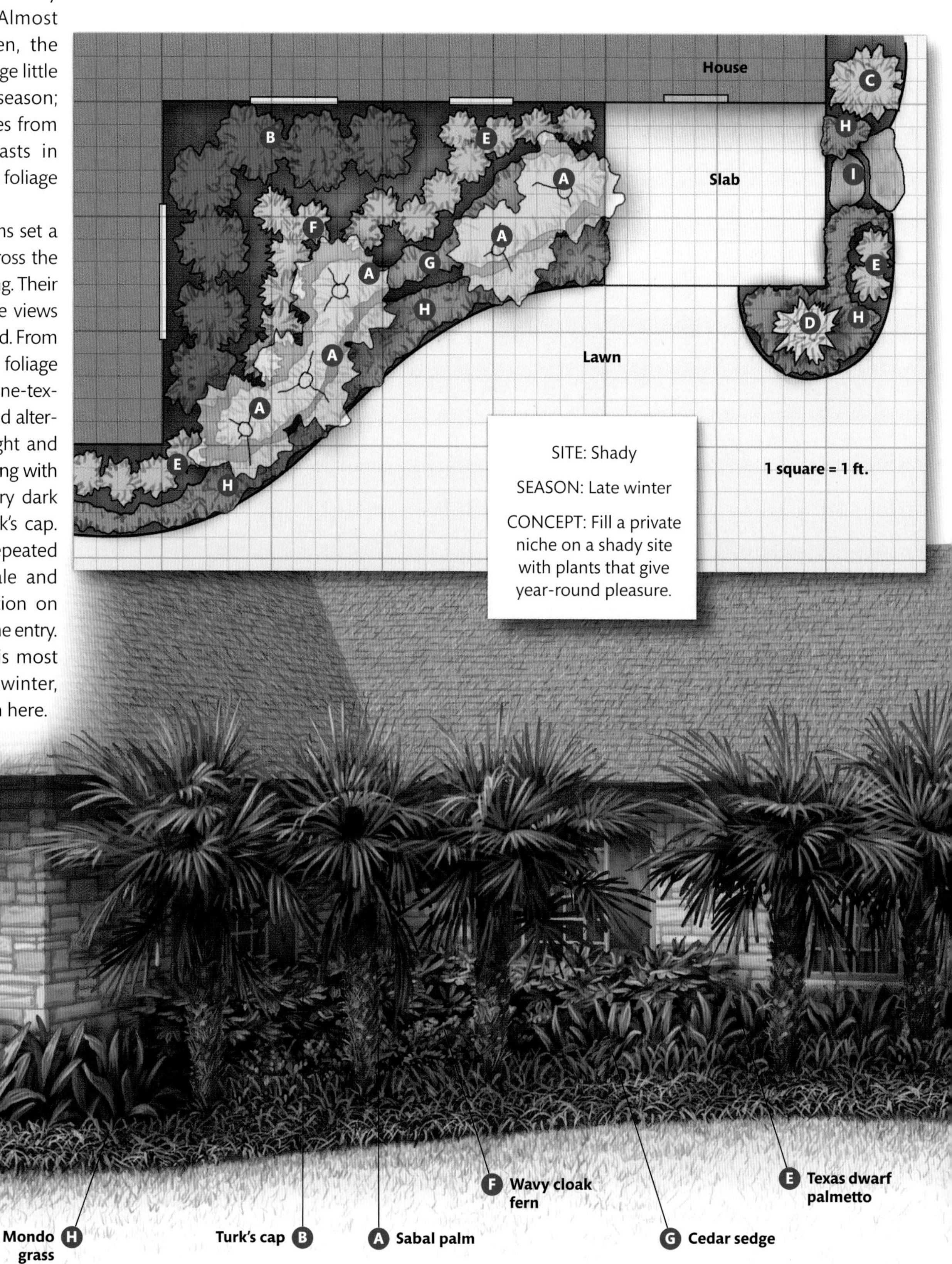

Plants & Projects

A Sabal palm (use 5 plants)
This robust palm generally grows to 30 to 40 feet tall. It sinks its roots deep, down to 15–20 feet and is drought tolerant once established. See *Sabal palmetto*, p. 148.

B Turk's cap (use 7)
A Texas favorite, this perennial forms a low bush of large leaves and red turbanlike flowers in summer. Hummingbirds attracted to the flowers will hover near the bench. Other birds may stop by for the cherrylike berries. See *Malvaviscus arboreus drummondii*, p. 139.

C Dwarf wax myrtle (use 1 or more)
This small evergreen tree offers a fragrant and shady canopy for bench sitters. Leaves are smooth and slender. See *Myrica cerifera*, p. 139.

D Soft rush (use 1)
Plant this bold grasslike wetland perennial for its yellow-green flowers and low maintenance requirements. Can survive in up to 4 inches of water. See *Juncus effusus*. p. 136.

E Texas dwarf palmetto (use 15)
This slow-growing shrub has pale-green fan-like leaves and spineless stems. See *Sabal minor*, p. 148.

F Wavy cloak fern (use 6)
This semi-evergreen fern produces clumps of attractive rich green foliage, with a contrasting cinnamon underside. It is uniquely drought tolerant and suited to poor rocky soils, preferring sun or part shade. It is clump forming and slowly spreads via rhizomes. See *Astrolepsis sinuata*, p. 124.

G Cedar sedge (use 40)
This clump-forming perennial grass, prefers some shade and can be combined with other woodland and meadow natives. See *Carex planostachys*, p. 127.

H Mondo grass (use 60)
Another, darker band of grassy perennials for the front of the palms. See *Ophiopogon japonicus*, p. 140.

See p. 61 for the following:

I Stepping-stones

PLANT PORTRAITS

Tropical or desertlike, these exotic looking plants provide interest all year.

● = First design, pp. 60-61

▲ = Second design, pp. 62-63

Jonquil (Bulbs: *Narcissus jonquilla*, p. 127) ●

Desert willow (*Chilopsis linearis*, p. 129) ●

Mondo grass (*Ophiopogon japonicus*, p. 140) ▲

Beautify a Blank Wall

A VERTICAL GARDEN MAKES THE MOST OF A NARROW SITE

Just as a painting enhances a wall in your home, a blank wall outdoors can be decorated with plants. The design shown on these pages transforms a nondescript front entrance by showcasing perennials, vines, and a flowering shrub against an adjacent garage wall. Such entrances are common in suburban homes, but a vertical garden like this is ideal for other spots where yard space is limited.

Selected for a sunny site, these plants offer something in every season. Many are evergreen with foliage that looks fresh year-round. From March to December, flowers enhance the entrance with color and fragrance. In fall, the pomegranate will decorate the wall with large, cream-colored fruits.

The garden has two flowering peaks: spring and autumn. Fragrant white flowers of jessamine greet visitors to the front door early in spring. Chiming in later are the bold blossoms of the pomegranate, iris, and hibiscus and the more delicate blooms of dianthus and sage. Hibiscus and sages continue to flower through the heat of summer, joined by santolina's bright-yellow buttonlike blooms. Expect another round of bloom that covers much of the color wheel when the weather turns cool in fall.

SITE: Sunny

SEASON: Spring

CONCEPT: Handsome plants arrayed against a blank wall make a picture that pleases year-round.

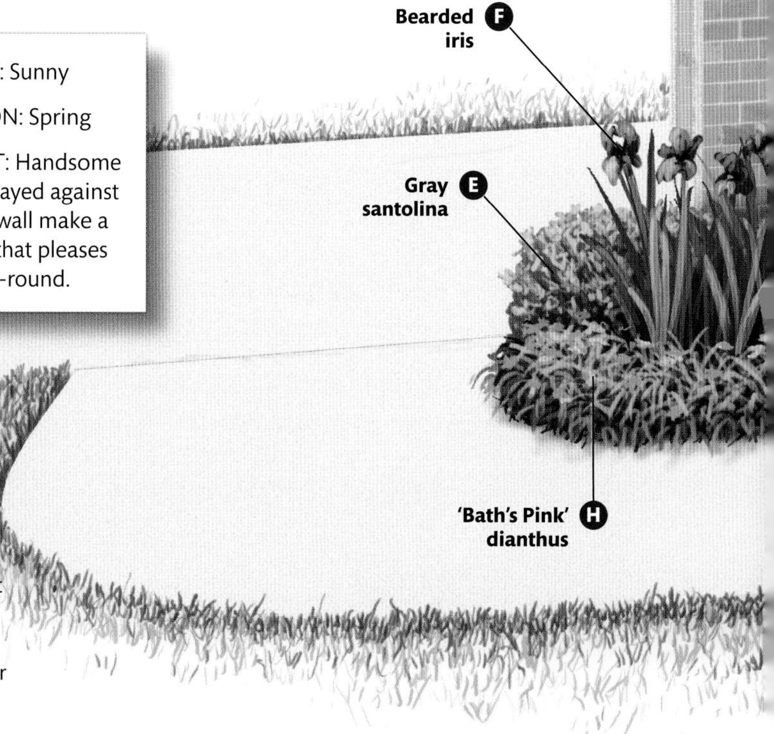

Bearded iris (F)

Gray santolina (E)

'Bath's Pink' dianthus (H)

Plants & Projects

Training the pomegranate and the jessamine are the most demanding aspects of this planting. As the pomegranate grows, select horizontal branches that grow parallel with the wall and fasten them to wires attached to the wall. Prune to restrict growth to the wires. Train the jessamine vines by securing the runners to the trellises. The perennials are generally carefree.

A 'Wonderful' pomegranate (use 1 plant)
This upright deciduous shrub is easily trained against a wall. It bears bright-green glossy foliage and dazzling orange-red flowers in spring. A bounty of sweet, juicy pomegranates follows. Leaves are colorful in fall. See *Punica granatum* 'Wonderful', p. 143.

B Carolina jessamine (use 2)
Shiny neat evergreen leaves and a show of fragrant yellow flowers in spring make this vigorous vine ideal for training up porch columns or along a railing. See *Gelsemium sempervirens*, p. 133.

C Mealycup sage (use 5)
From spring to fall, this upright perennial produces showy blue flower spikes that rise in clusters from clumps of slender gray-green leaves. See *Salvia farinacea*, p. 147.

D Autumn sage (use 3)
This bushy perennial has tiny oval leaves that contrast with the strappy foliage of the daylilies nearby. Colorful flower spikes surround the plant all season. We've shown a purple variety, but pink, white, or red are also available. See *Salvia greggii*, p. 147.

E Gray santolina (use 4)
This evergreen perennial forms a tight mound of narrow silver-gray foliage, just right for borders and tucked into corners. Small yellow flowers top the foliage in summer. See *Santolina chamaecyparissus*, p. 148.

F Bearded iris (use 3)
Prized for handsome swordlike foliage as well as large lavender blossoms, this perennial is a standout against the daintier dianthus. It often blooms again in autumn. See *Iris* x *germanica*, p. 135.

G Texas star hibiscus (use 5)
This perennial forms a large airy clump of slender, deeply divided, glossy leaves borne on red-tinged stems. Brilliant red five-petaled flowers open daily during the summer and fall. See *Hibiscus coccineus*, p. 134.

H 'Bath's Pink' dianthus (use 15)
Sprinkled with small pink flowers in spring, this perennial trims the walk the rest of the year with a fringe of fine silvery foliage. See *Dianthus* 'Bath's Pink', p. 131.

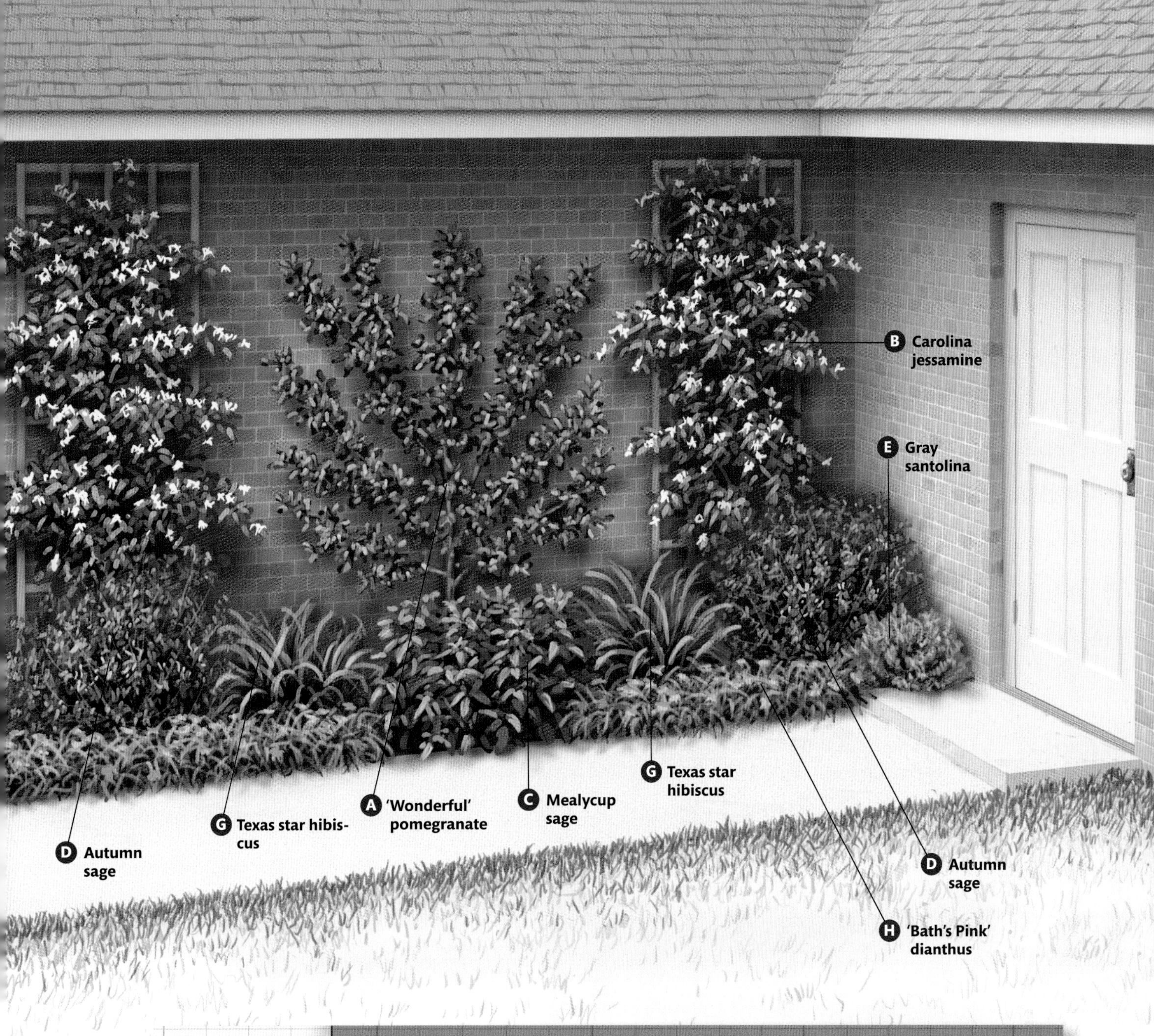
B Carolina jessamine
E Gray santolina
G Texas star hibiscus
A 'Wonderful' pomegranate
C Mealycup sage
G Texas star hibis-cus
D Autumn sage
D Autumn sage
H 'Bath's Pink' dianthus

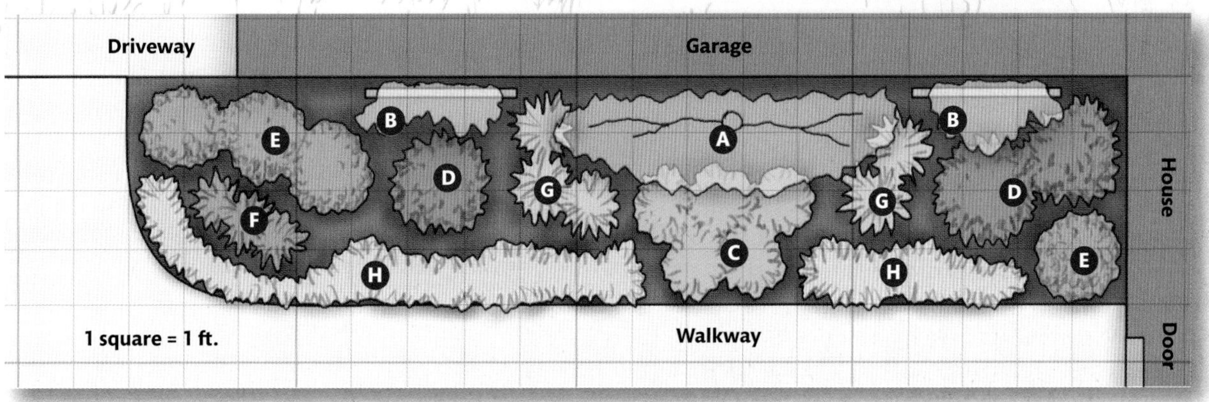
Driveway
Garage
House
Door
Walkway
1 square = 1 ft.
A
B
B
C
D
D
E
E
F
G
G
H
H

PLANT PORTRAITS

These perennials and shrubs fill a blank wall with handsome foliage and pretty flowers for many months of the year.

● = First design, pp. 64-65

▲ = Second design, pp. 66-67

River cane (*Arundinaria gigantea*, p. 124) ▲

Texas star hibiscus (*Hibiscus coccineus*, p. 134) ●

'Kyoto Dwarf' mondo grass (*Ophiopogon japonicus*, p. 140) ▲

Dressing up a shady wall

A shadier site calls for a different palette of plants. The basic idea of this design remains the same as the previous one—incorporate wall space to make the best use of a narrow plot.

Here the focus is on foliage. All the plants are evergreen or nearly so, and they offer a continuous array of colors, textures, and architectural qualities that brighten a dark space and deepen a narrow one. The result is a planting as bright and attractive in winter as it is the rest of the year.

Impressive canes of river cane fill the corner with color, while dark-leaved ivy along a trellis provides a ruffled backdrop for two bold-leaved shrubs, the variegated wax myrtle and the tropical-looking turk's cap. The border is trimmed in grassy ground covers of differing textures and colors. Summer flowers of the turk's cap and cedar sedge are seasonal treats.

Plants & Projects

Ⓐ River cane (use 1 plant)
A perennial grass with a round, hollow stem that can grow up to 33 ft high. See *Arundinaria gigantea*, p. 124.

Ⓑ Turk's cap (use 1)
A Texas favorite, this perennial forms a low bush of large leaves and red turbanlike flowers in summer. Hummingbirds attracted to the flowers will hover near the bench. Other birds may stop by for the cherrylike berries. See *Malvaviscus arboreus drummondii*, p. 139.

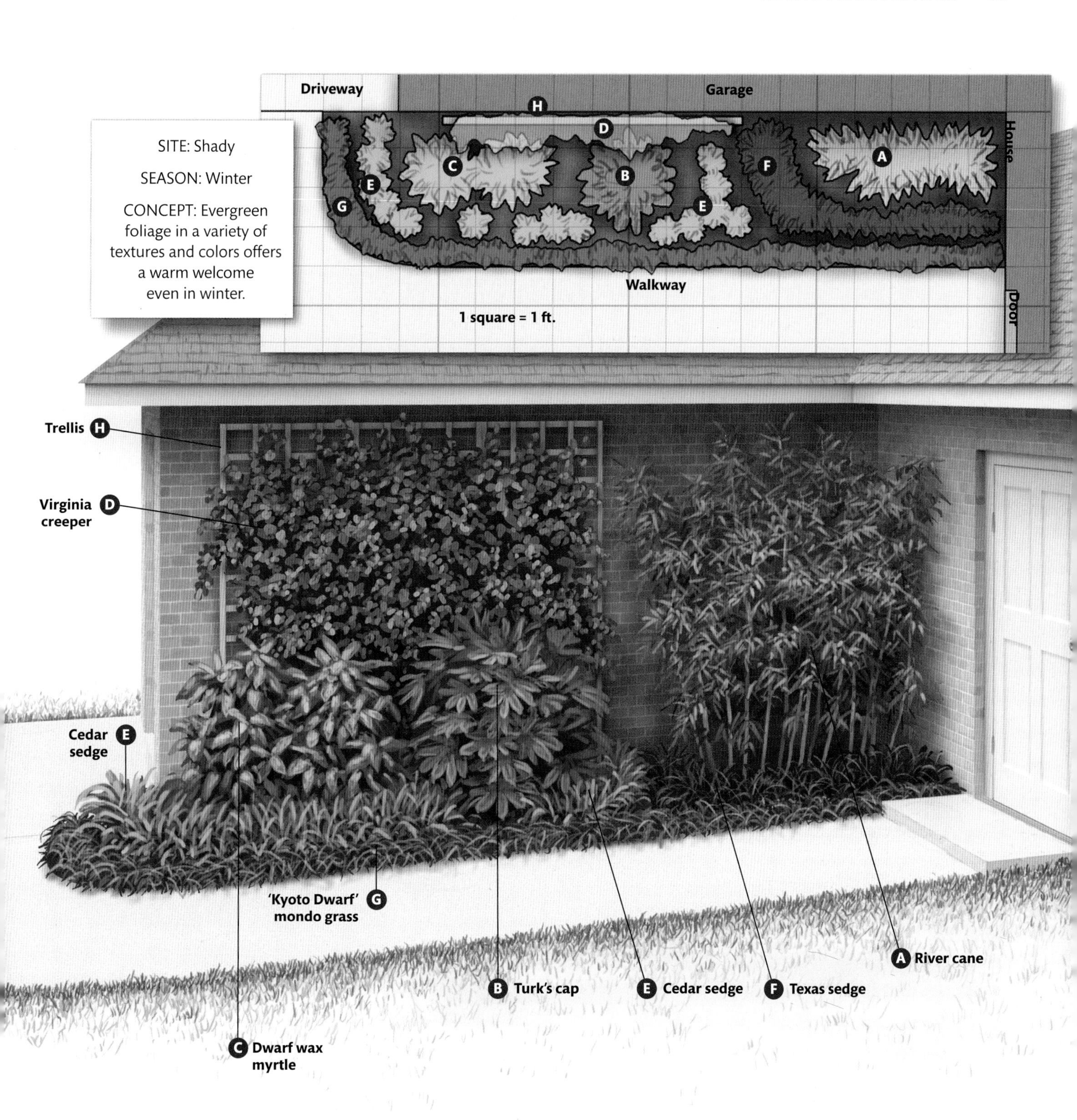

C Dwarf wax myrtle (use 2)
This small evergreen tree offers a fragrant and shady canopy for bench sitters. Leaves are smooth and slender. See *Myrica cerifera*, p. 139.

D Virginia creeper (use 6)
This native deciduous vine has a climbing habitat similar to ivy and can provide a similar effect in landscaping. Leaves turn red and purple in early fall. See *Parthenocissus quinquefolia*, p. 140.

E Cedar sedge (use 15)
This species evolved to grow in the shade of Cedar trees and as an understory plant in tall grass prairies and meadows. See *Carex planostachys*, p. 127.

F Texas sedge (use 14)
A common sedge in Texas, this sedge is a good turf substitute with a tufted, grass-like appearance. See *Carex texenis*, p. 127.

G 'Kyoto Dwarf' mondo grass (use 50)
Dark green and very low growing, this evergreen plant adds a fine finish to the planting along the walk. See *Ophiopogon japonicus* 'Kyoto Dwarf', p. 140.

H Trellis
You can support the Virginia creeper with the sturdy homemade trellis shown here, or buy one ready-made at a garden center. See p. 186.

Backyard Makeover

GET A LOT OUT OF A SMALL, TROPICAL GARDEN

Space is at a premium on many suburban lots, but this needn't cramp your outdoor living style. The design shown here makes use of the entire area in a small backyard to provide opportunities for open-air gatherings as well as family relaxation and play. (The rendering is shown as if viewed from the house, which is indicated on the plan.)

At the center is a large flagstone patio bordered by grassy verges where children can play or adults can kick off their shoes and recline. A continuous garden bed meanders along a privacy fence enclosing the lot. As the shade tree matures, its generous canopy will accommodate a table or recliners. To cater outdoor feasts, there's a barbecue. A small pool and fountain provide a cooling presence and the music of bubbling water.

Curving gently around the perimeter, the plantings comprise a pleasing array of trees, shrubs, and trellised vines. Several "boulders" add to the natural composition and provide a few extra places to sit.

The native plants of Texas, Mexico, and the Gulf Coast are chosen for their proven performance in heat, drought, and freezing temperatures.

SITE: Sunny

SEASON: Spring

CONCEPT: A large patio and gorgeous plants make the most of a small backyard.

Plants & Projects

Ambitious do-it-yourselfers can install the entire design. If you're less energetic, have a landscaping service put in the hardscape and do the planting yourself. A layer of small river-washed rocks mulches the beds, complementing the look of the plants and helping to conserve water.

A **Tipu tree** (use 1 plant)
Long clusters of yellow-to apricot-colored blossoms dangle among this small evergreen tree's fine-textured leaves in spring and early summer. Long seedpods add interest in autumn and winter. See *Tipuana tipu*, p. 151.

B **Mediterranean fan palm** (use 1)
This compact palm fits nicely under the tree and thrives in its shade. It forms a clump of trunks crowned with coarse blue-gray fronds, each looking like a giant handheld fan. See *Chamaerops humilis*, p. 128.

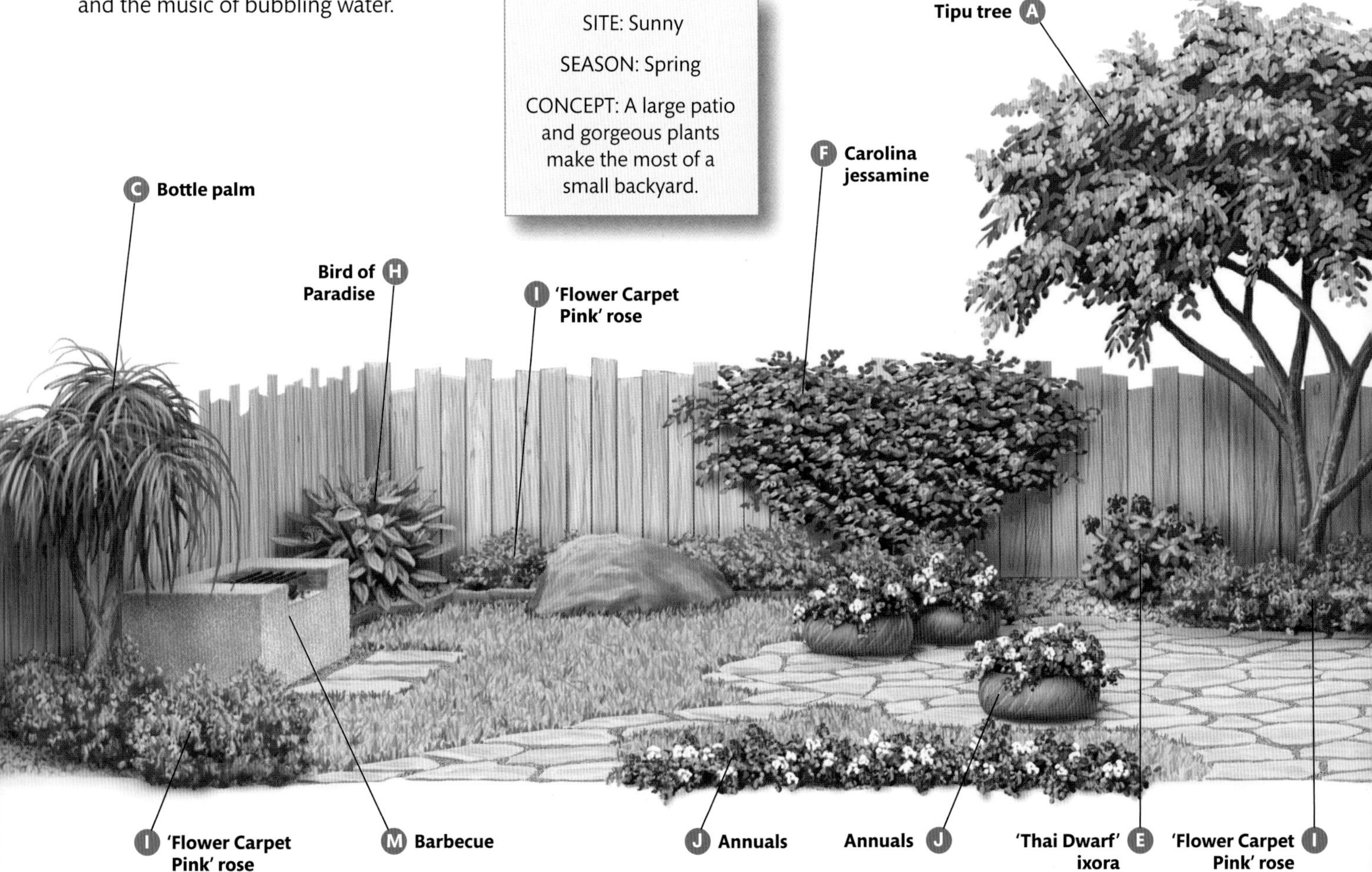

C Bottle palm (use 1)
Another palm with great structural appeal. The trunk starts swollen and then narrows before branching into a shaggy bright green crown. See *Nolina recurvata*, p. 139.

D Coral honeysuckle (use 1)
Unlike the more invasive honeysuckles, this native vine is mannerly, climbing up the fence in neat tiers of rounded bluegreen leaves. Clusters of coral-colored flowers radiate from the foliage in summer and sometimes fall. See *Lonicera sempervirens*, p. 138.

E 'Thai Dwarf' ixora (use 2)
In a sheltered spot, this beautiful shrub promises a bounty of large colorful flowers. Evergreen foliage. See *Ixora* 'Thai Dwarf', p. 135.

F Carolina jessamine (use 2)
Shiny neat evergreen leaves and a show of fragrant yellow flowers in spring make this vigorous vine ideal for training up porch columns or along a railing. See *Gelsemium sempervirens*, p. 133.

G Sabal palm (use 1)
This robust palm generally grows to 30 to 40 feet tall. It sinks its roots deep, down to 15–20 feet and is drought tolerant once established. See *Sabal palmetto*, p. 148.

H Bird of Paradise (use 2)
This evergreen perennial forms a wide clump of long-stemmed bluish green leaves and an abundance of large and unusual orange flowers. See *Strelitzia reginea*, p. 150.

I 'Flower Carpet Pink' rose (use 13)
Shear this ground cover rose once in winter to keep it compact and blooming vigorously. Forms a nearly continuous mass of pink. See *Rosa*, p. 145.

J Annuals
Grow your favorites in large pots and narrow beds next to the house to enliven the patio. Ivy geranium is shown here.

K Paving
Choose a flagstone that complements the color of your home. See p. 163.

L Water feature
A small fiberglass pool and a simple fountain add interest at a modest cost. See p. 172.

M Barbecue
You can install a custom grill of stone or adobe as shown here or use a movable gas unit.

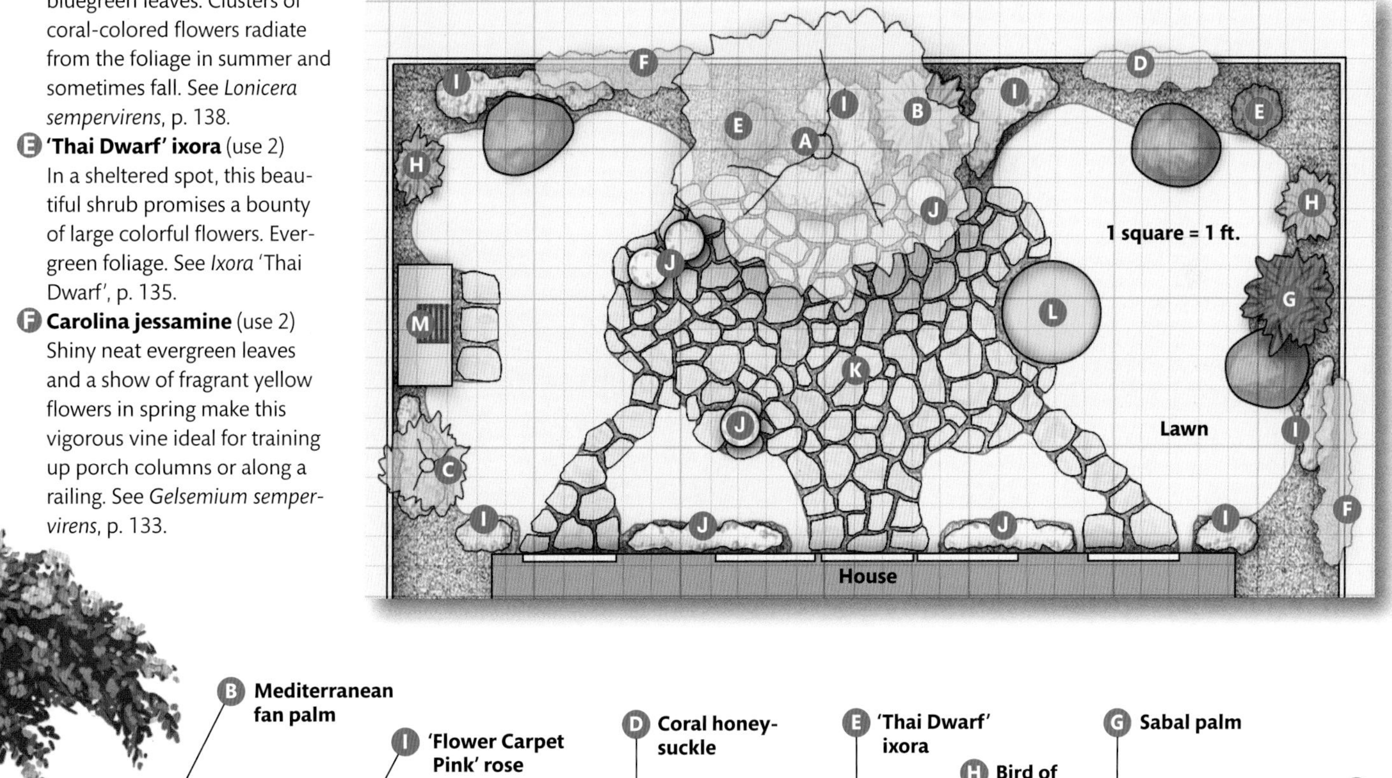

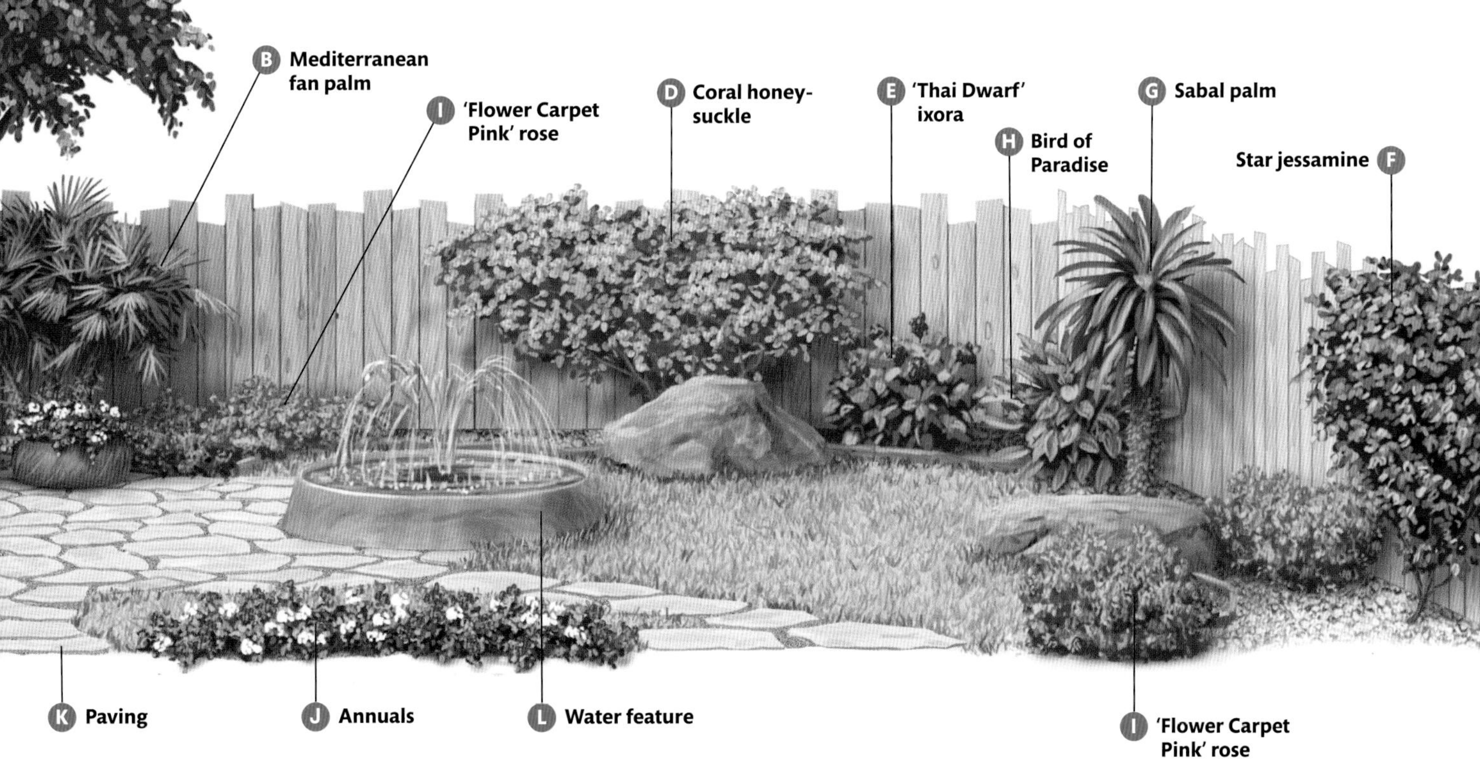

Gateway Garden

ARBOR, FENCE, AND PLANTINGS MAKE AN INVITING ENTRY

Entrances are an important part of any landscape. They can welcome visitors onto your property; highlight a special feature, such as a rose garden; or mark the passage between two areas with different character or function. The design shown here can serve in any of these situations.

A picket fence set amid shrubs and perennials creates a friendly and attractive barrier, just enough to signal the boundary of the front yard. The simple vine-covered arbor provides welcoming access.

Uncomplicated elements are combined imaginatively in this design, creating interesting details to catch the eye and an informal, happy-to-see-you overall effect. The arbor will be covered with cheerful yellow flowers in spring, and the fence with fragrant honeysuckle blossoms in summer. For winter color, both offer evergreen foliage. A multilayered planting in front of the fence offers contrasts in foliage texture as well as pretty flowers, and enough structure to be inviting after the blossoms fade.

Plants & Projects

For many people, a picket fence and vine-covered arbor represent old-fashioned neighborly virtues. The structures and plantings are easy to install. You can extend the fence and plantings as needed.

A Carolina jessamine (use 2 plants)
A lovely evergreen vine for the arbor. Sweetly fragrant clear-yellow flowers bloom among the masses of shiny leaves in early spring. See *Gelsemium sempervirens*, p. 133.

B Firebush (use 1)
Summers set this perennial ablaze with orange-red flowers. New clusters keep coming until frost. It is planted near the arbor so you can catch a glimpse of hummingbirds as you come and go. See *Hamelia patens*, p. 133.

C Lindheimer's muhly (use 1)
A beautiful, fine-textured ornamental grass. Blue-green leaves and soft texture makes this grass popular for screening. See *Muhlenbergia lindheimeri*, p. 139.

D 'Radiation' lantana (use 1)
This perennial spreads to form a 3-ft. mound of coarse green leaves topped with many small, round clusters of orange and yellow flowers. Blooms prolifically all season. See *Lantana camara* 'Radiation', p. 137.

E Coral honeysuckle (use 4)
Unlike the more invasive honeysuckles, this native vine is mannerly, climbing up the fence in neat tiers of rounded blue-green leaves. Clusters of coral-colored flowers radiate from the foliage in summer and sometimes fall. See *Lonicera sempervirens*, p. 138.

F Russian sage (use 4)
These perennials make a big splash when planted together. They offer silvery foliage and blue flowers to cool down the border's many hot colors. See *Perovskia atriplicifolia*, p. 141.

G 'Goldsturm' black-eyed Susan (use 1)
A popular perennial companion of ornamental grasses. It forms a robust stand of dark leaves that are blanketed in summertime with bright-gold flowers. See *Rudbeckia fulgida* 'Goldsturm', p. 146.

H Cigar plant (use 2)
An upright perennial with the look of a dwarf oleander. It forms a dense bush bearing multiple branches of narrow foliage that terminate in small tubelike orange and yellow flowers in autumn. See *Cuphea micropetala*, p. 130.

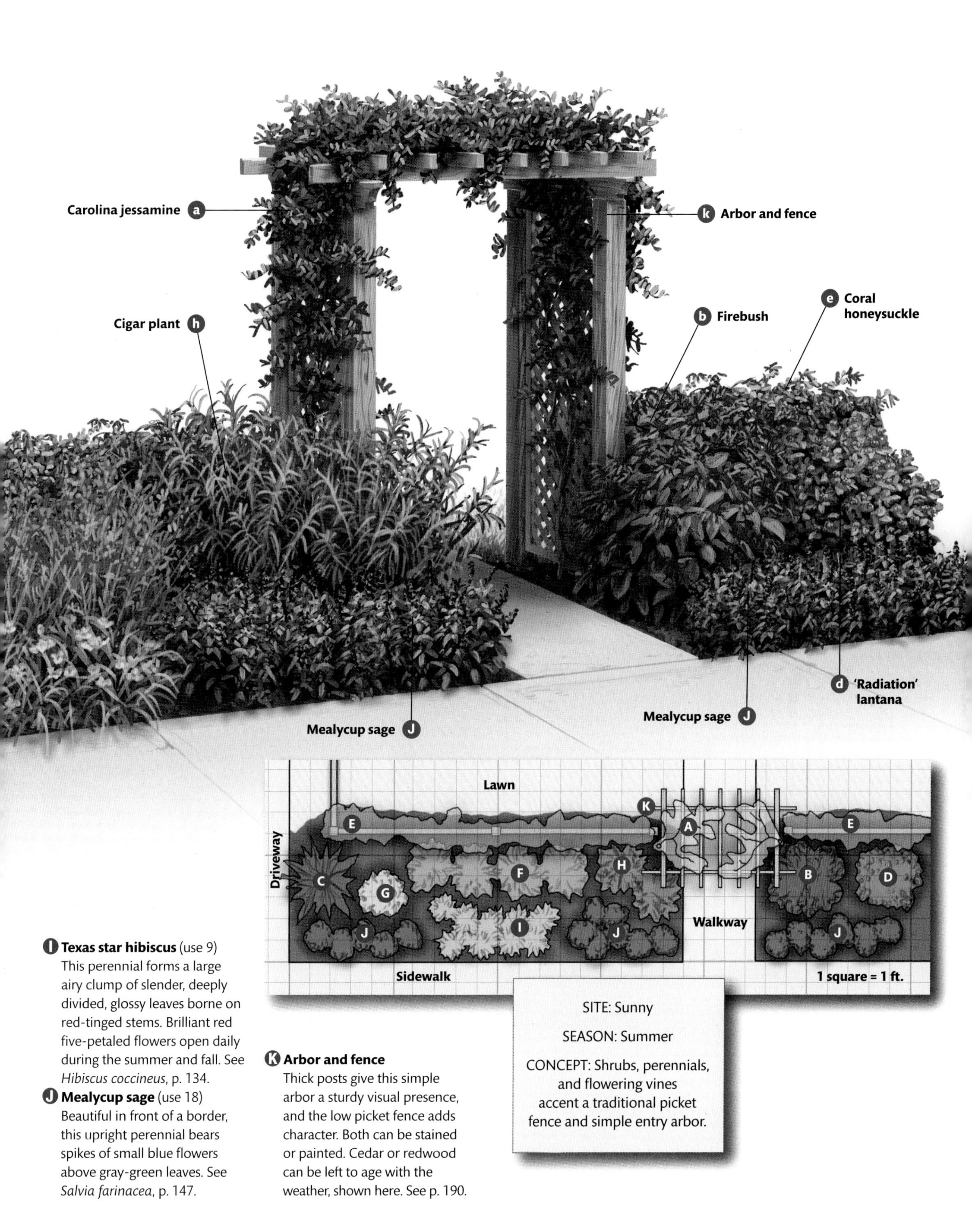

I Texas star hibiscus (use 9)
This perennial forms a large airy clump of slender, deeply divided, glossy leaves borne on red-tinged stems. Brilliant red five-petaled flowers open daily during the summer and fall. See *Hibiscus coccineus*, p. 134.

J Mealycup sage (use 18)
Beautiful in front of a border, this upright perennial bears spikes of small blue flowers above gray-green leaves. See *Salvia farinacea*, p. 147.

K Arbor and fence
Thick posts give this simple arbor a sturdy visual presence, and the low picket fence adds character. Both can be stained or painted. Cedar or redwood can be left to age with the weather, shown here. See p. 190.

SITE: Sunny

SEASON: Summer

CONCEPT: Shrubs, perennials, and flowering vines accent a traditional picket fence and simple entry arbor.

Say hello with roses

Not every entry calls for a fence. This design offers a traditional welcome with a rose garden. A border of tea roses and other flowering shrubs and perennials serves as a fragrant and colorful barrier on each side of a rose-covered entry arbor. The formal symmetry (an element often associated with rose gardens) is enhanced by hollies trimmed into pyramids at the foot of the arbor. The roses will bloom for many months. In spring they're joined by pink dianthus and blue iris and in late summer and fall by purple asters and sage. The holly's evergreen foliage provides green in winter.

Tea roses are less difficult than many people fear, but they require regular attention.

SITE: Sunny

SEASON: Fall

CONCEPT: Fragrant roses and other flowers provide a sweet welcome.

Plants & Projects

A 'Climbing Old Blush' China rose (use 2 plants)
This delicate-looking rose is nonetheless a vigorous climber. It bears apple-green foliage and a steady bloom of baby-pink semidouble flowers, especially in spring. See *Rosa chinensis* 'Climbing Old Blush', p. 145.

B 'Gilbert Nabonnand' tea rose (use 2)
The silky flowers of this bushy rose are pale pink and very fragrant all season. Petals are semidouble. See *Rosa* x *odorata* 'Gilbert Nabonnand', p. 145.

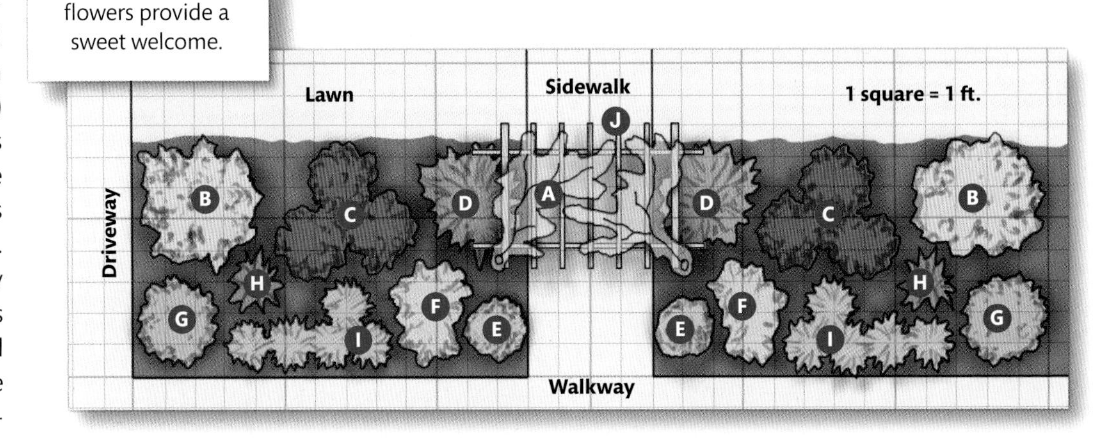

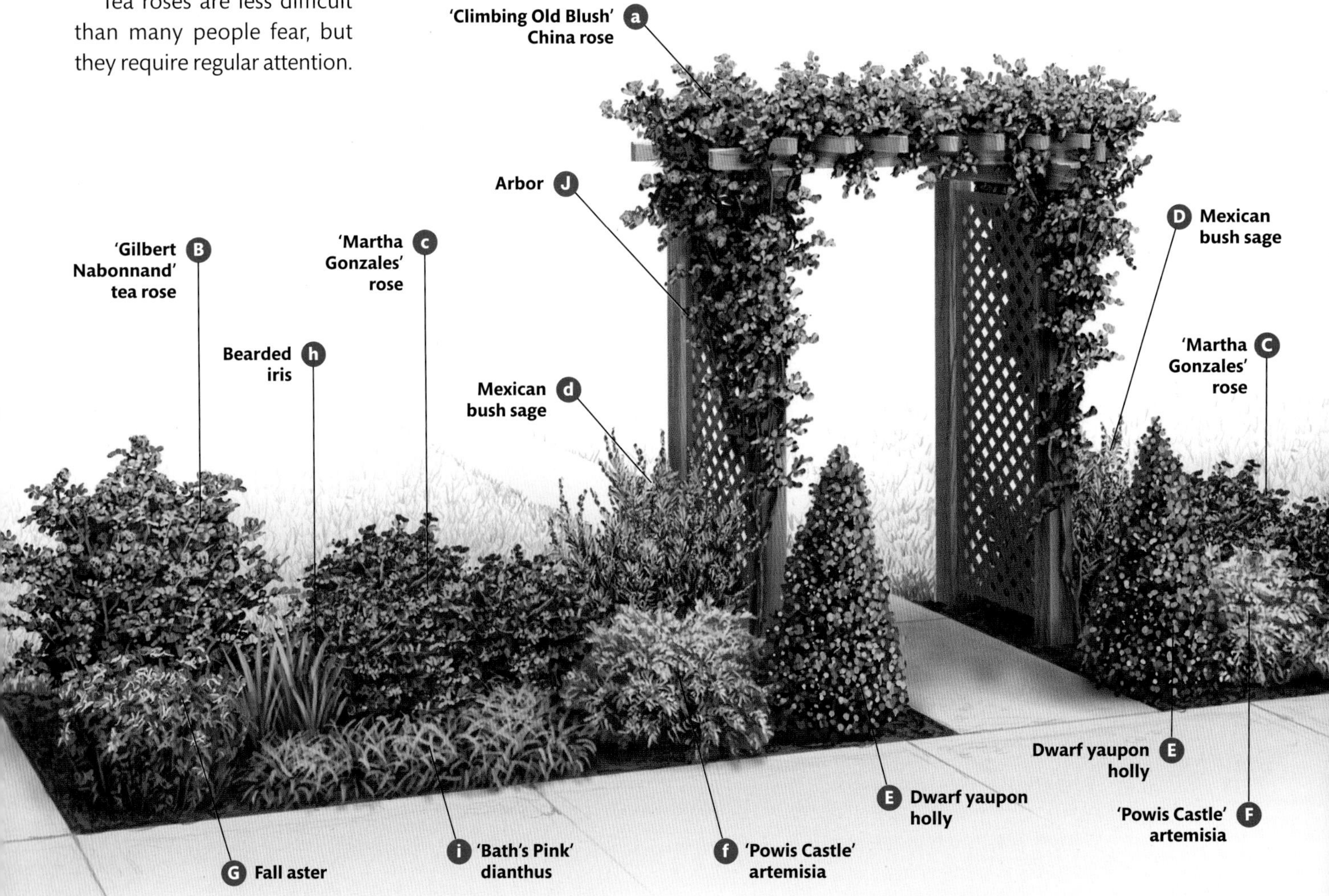

C 'Martha Gonzales' rose (use 6)
Wine red flowers cover this reliable dwarf rose in spring and fall. New shoots and leaves are also red. See *Rosa chinensis* 'Martha Gonzales', p. 145.

D Mexican bush sage (use 2)
This tall perennial adds height at the trellis. Bears spikes of purple-and-white flowers in fall. See *Salvia leucantha*, p. 147.

E Dwarf yaupon holly (use 2)
A dwarf version that reaches only 3 ft. tall and wide. Commonly used as a substitute for boxwood in Texas and the South. See *I. vomitoria*, p. 135.

F 'Powis Castle' artemisia (use 2)
Prized for its foliage texture and color, this perennial forms silvery pillows beside the boxwoods. See *Artemisia* x 'Powis Castle', p. 124.

G Fall aster (use 2)
Another fine-textured gray-green perennial to complement the hollies. For many weeks in fall it bursts into eye-catching lavender-purple bloom. See *Aster oblongifolius*, p. 124.

H Bearded iris (use 2)
This perennial's foliage adds a spiky presence to the planting as well as showy blue flowers in spring. See *Iris* x *germanica*, p. 132.

I 'Bath's Pink' dianthus (use 10)
This perennial spreads to form low, wide tufts of very fine-textured foliage. Delicate pink flowers blanket the gray-green leaves in spring. See *Dianthus* 'Bath's Pink', p. 131.

See p. 71 for the following:

J Arbor

PLANT PORTRAITS

Combining compelling fragrance, lovely flowers, and handsome foliage, these plants create a distinctive entry.

● = First design, pp. 70-71

▲ = Second design, pp. 72-73

'Martha Gonzales' rose
(*Rosa chinensis*, p. 145) ▲

'Climbing Old Blush' China rose
(*Rosa chinensis*, p. 145) ▲

'Gilbert Nabonnand' tea rose
(*Rosa* x *odorata*, p. 145) ▲

Elegant Symmetry

MAKE A FORMAL GARDEN FOR YOUR BACKYARD

Formal landscaping often lends dignity to the public areas around a home. (See pp. 28–29.) Formality can also be rewarding in a more private setting. There, the groomed plants, geometric lines, and symmetrical layout of a formal garden can help to organize the surrounding landscaping, provide an elegant area for entertaining, or simply be enjoyed for their own sake.

Formal need not mean elaborate. This elegant design is no more than a circle inside a square. Concentric low hedges of clipped hollies define the circle; a gravel path around the perimeter defines the square. The path continues through the center, opening into a small square decorated with a terra-cotta planter set on a grassy carpet.

The tallest elements in the design are four white-flowering trees interplanted with pyramidal evergreens. Enclosed in semicircular hedges and surrounded by grassy ground covers, white roses, and stately purple and gold perennials, these trees and shrubs create the effect of an enchanted *bosque*, a French word for a small, formal wood.

Even more than other types of landscaping, formal gardens work well only when carefully correlated with other elements in the landscape, including structures and plants. A round garden can be difficult to integrate. Relate it to rectilinear elements, such as a fence or hedges. And repeat plants used in the design elsewhere in your landscape to tie things together.

Plants & Projects

Of all gardens, a formal garden most obviously reflects the efforts of its makers. After the hedge has filled in, this garden requires attention mostly to keep it looking neat—shearing the hedges, pruning, deadheading the perennials, and seasonal cleanup.

A Desert willow (use 4 plants)
The fine leaves of this deciduous tree provide an airy canopy over the path without shading out the plants underneath. Showy white, pink, and lavender flowers bloom on and off all season. See *Chilopsis linearis*, p. 129.

B Compact Carolina cherry laurel (use 4)
A native evergreen shrub, it offers shiny green leaves and spikes of scented white flowers in spring. Shear to maintain a formal shape. See *Prunus caroliniana* 'Compacta', p. 142.

C 'Marie Pavie' polyantha rose (use 4)
Clusters of small white roses cover this shrub rose from spring to frost.

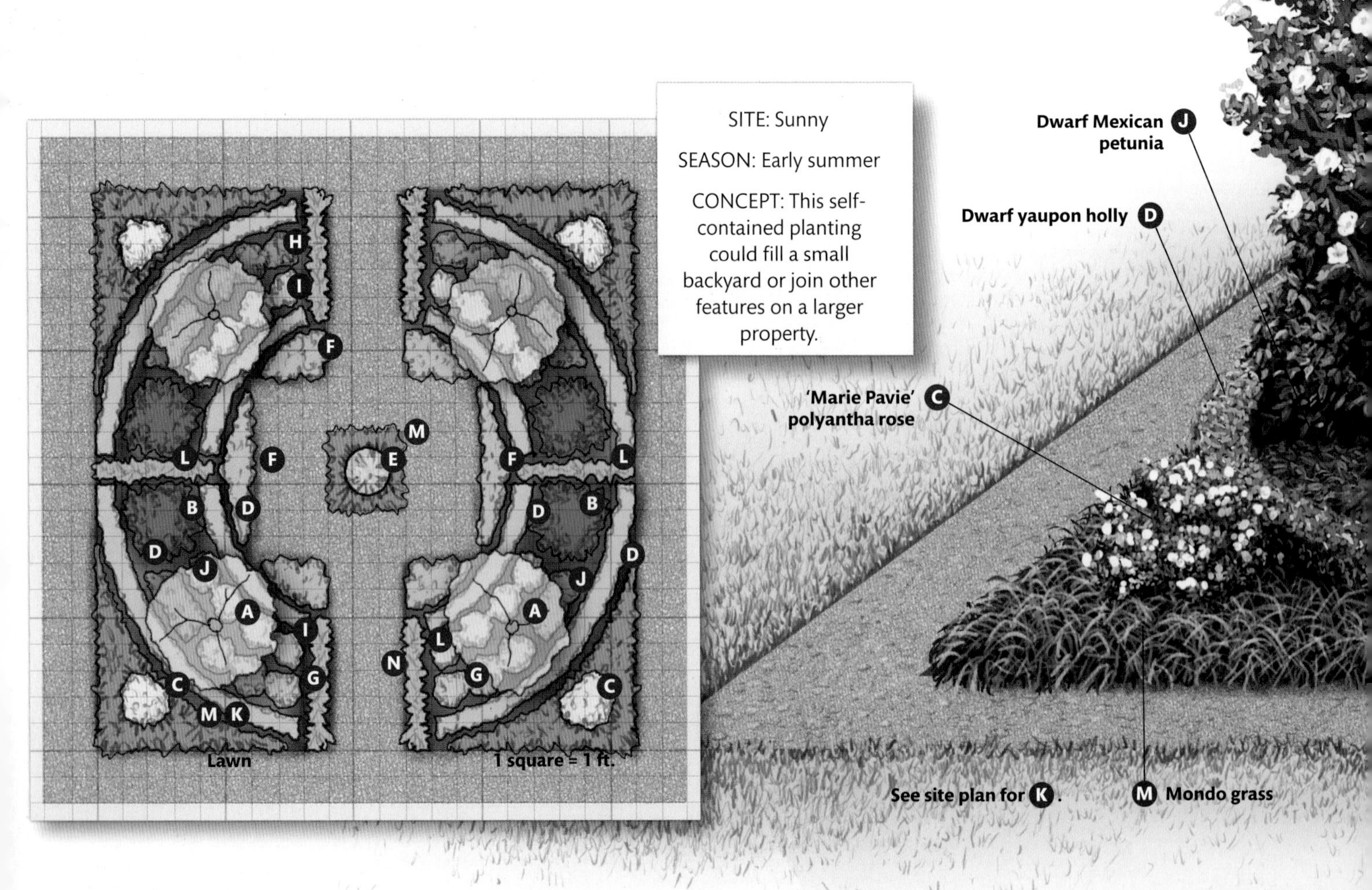

SITE: Sunny

SEASON: Early summer

CONCEPT: This self-contained planting could fill a small backyard or join other features on a larger property.

Buds have a pink cast. If this cultivar isn't available, consider 'White Pet' or 'Marie Daly'. See *Rosa* x *polyantha* 'Marie Pavie', p. 145.

D Dwarf yaupon holly (use 68)
A dwarf version that reaches only 3 ft. tall and wide. Commonly used as a substitute for boxwood in Texas and the South. See *I. vomitoria*, p. 135.

E Yellow variegated agave (use 1)
Similar to yucca but shorter, this shrub creates a bold centerpiece above a planting of fine-leafed grass. See *Agave americana* 'Marginata', p. 122.

F 'Trailing Lavender' lantana (use 6)
Lantanas are prized for their continuous and lavish bloom. This cultivar frames the central walkway with lacy clusters of lavender-purple flowers from spring to frost. See *Lantana montevidensis* 'Trailing Lavender', p. 137.

G Texas gold columbine (use 6)
This perennial's bright yellow flowers float above soft mounds of fernlike foliage in spring. Blooms are abundant and long lasting. See *Aquilegia chrysantha hinckleyana*, p. 123.

H Purple verbena (use 6)
Masses of wispy purple flowers wave above low clumps of foliage. This perennial complements the gold columbine. See *Verbena bonariensis*, p. 151.

I St.-John's-wort (use 16)
This mounding semievergreen shrub forms a dense mass of medium-green foliage that turns colorful in fall. Yellow flowers appear in summer. See *Hypericum calycinum*, p. 134.

J Dwarf Mexican petunia (use 20)
A beautiful and durable perennial ground cover. Clusters of purple petunialike blooms appear at the center of neat leafy mounds. See *Ruellia brittoniana* 'Katie', p. 148.

K White rainlily (use 48)
Planted among the blue-eyed grass, this bulb makes white flowers after late summer rains. See Bulbs: *Zephyranthes candida*, p. 126.

L Blue-eyed grass (use 30)
This native perennial has narrow, grass-like light-green leaves with blue flowers. See *Sisyrinchium angustifolium*, p. 149.

M Mondo grass (use 100)
This perennial will gradually grow into a continuous mat of very fine leaves. See *Ophiopogon japonicus*, p. 140.

N Walkway
Crushed stone is easy to install and suits the simple lines of this design. The pink granite we've shown here weathers to a terra-cotta pink. See p. 163.

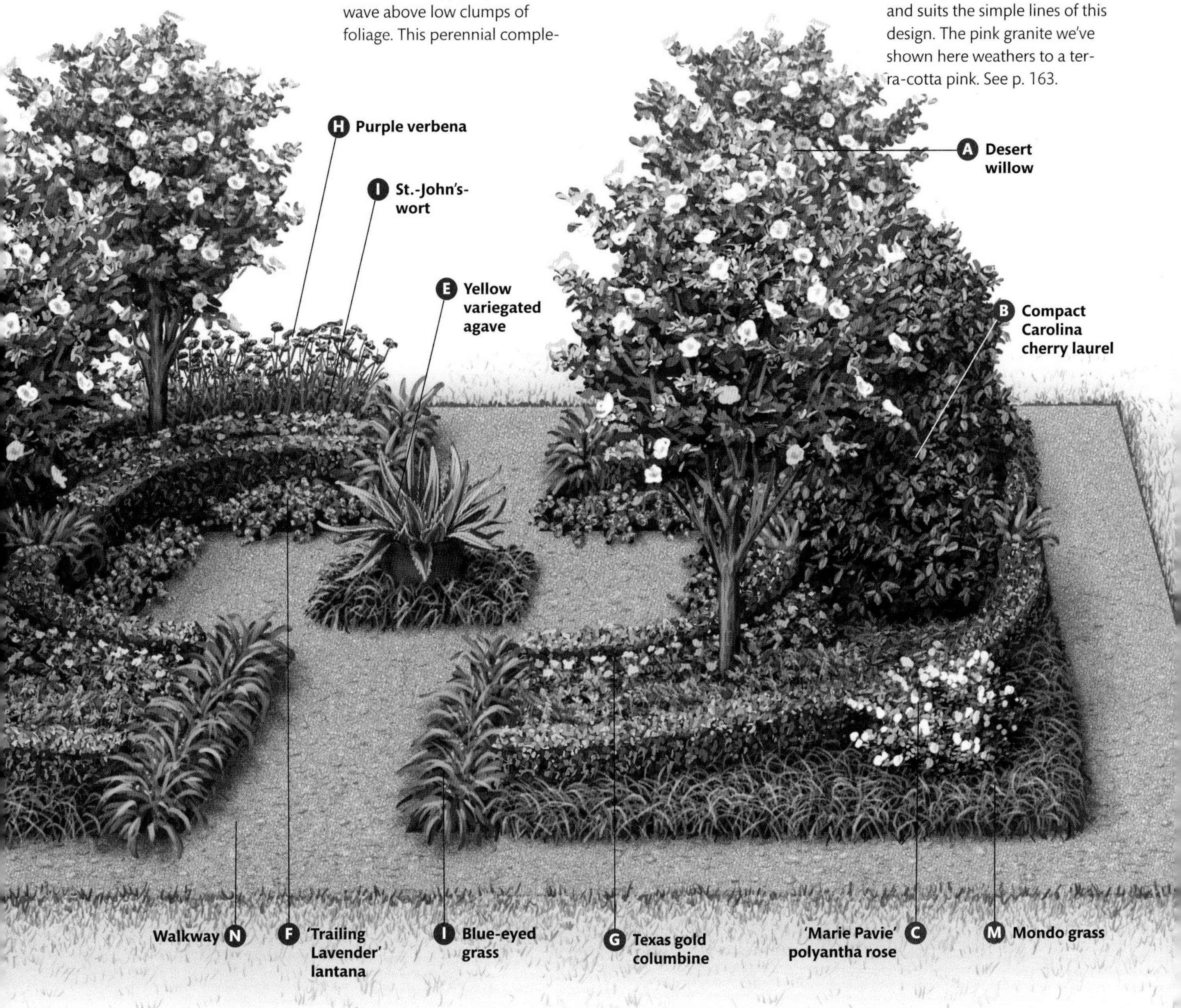

Garden oasis

Palms and a pool give this garden a tropical look. The layout takes its inspiration from a compass or sundial. Four columnar palm trees planted outside the peri-meter path mark the four directions of the compass. Interior paths lead from the living "columns" to a small lily pond at the center.

The planting beds are designed with the sun's path in mind. Two beds on the side of the afternoon sun are planted with bold shrubs and perennials that look cool even in the heat. The beds receiving morning light feature delicate roses and fine-textured grasses. Added water will produce more foliage and flowers.

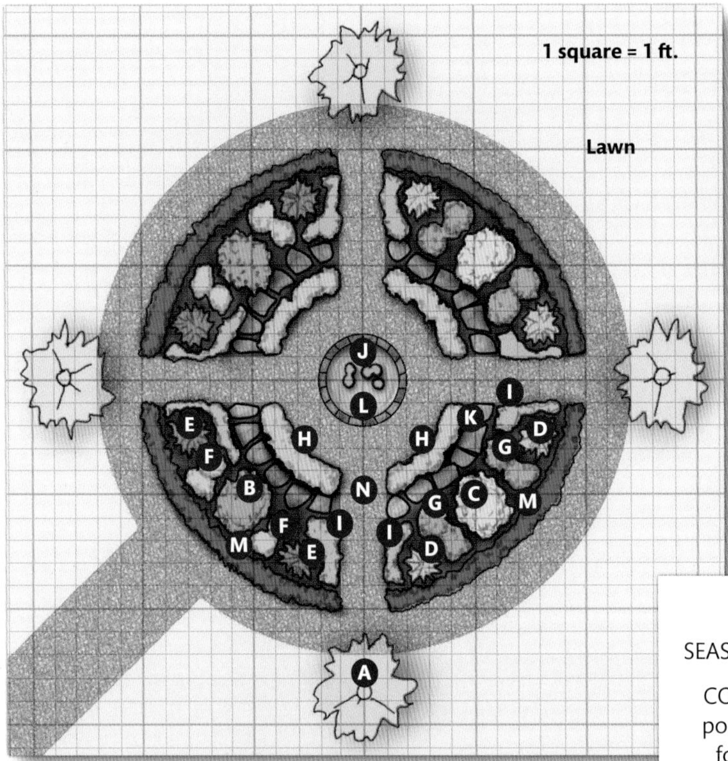

SITE: Sunny

SEASON: Late summer

CONCEPT: A small pond becomes the focal point for a formal setting.

Plants & Projects

A Sabal palm (use 4 plants)
This robust palm generally grows to 30 to 40 feet tall. It sinks its roots deep, down to 15–20 feet and is drought tolerant once established. See *Sabal palmetto*, p. 148.

B 'Mutabilis' China rose (use 2)
This rose forms a 4-ft. bush of dark-green leaves and red shoots. The flowers are single, five-petaled, and change from pale yellow to orange to pink. See *Rosa chinensis* 'Mutabilis', p. 145.

C 'Gold Star' esperanza (use 2)
A very showy tropical-looking shrub. The foliage is bright green and has a crisp look. Golden bell-like flowers

bloom in clusters from May to November. Deciduous in most parts of Texas. See *Tecoma stans* 'Gold Star', p. 150.

D **Soft-tip yucca** (use 4)
A bold accent plant, this perennial bears long pointed swordlike leaves with bent tips. It sends up branched stalks of large white flowers in summer. See *Yucca gloriosa*, p. 153.

E **Switchgrass** (use 4)
This grass grows 3–5 ft. tall, producing fine-textured lacey seedheads in late summer which persist throughout winter. See *Panicum virgatum*, p. 140.

F **Tropical plumbago** (use 8)
This perennial will fill the space with small, oval, bright-green leaves. Bears tight clusters of cool blue flowers in the heat of summer. See *Plumbago auriculata*, p. 142.

G **'Superbena purple'** (use 8)
This spreading native blooms all summer, growing in full sun, it is heat and drought tolerant. See *Verbena hybrid*, p. 151.

H **Gray santolina** (use 20)
A handsome low-growing shrub. Thick gray foliage looks like lavender. Yellow flowers in the summer. See *Santolina chamaecyparissus*, p. 148.

I **'Bath's Pink' dianthus** (use 32)
Another excellent edging, this perennial forms a year-round mat of short, very narrow silver foliage. Spring flowers are pink and fragrant. See *Dianthus* 'Bath's Pink', p. 131.

J **Dauben water lily** (use 1)
A small plant for a small-scale pond. Lavender flowers bloom among floating leaves nonstop in summer heat. See p. 152.

K **Stepping-stones**
Gray limestone makes a decorative edging around the santolina. See p. 169.

L **Pond**
Use a round fiberglass shell for this small pool. See p. 172.

See p. 75 for the following:

M **Blue-eyed grass** (use 30)

N **Path**

PLANT PORTRAITS

These well-behaved, low-care shrubs, bulbs, and perennials bring form, texture, flowers, and scent to a formal garden.

● = First design, pp. 74-75

▲ = Second design, pp. 76-77

'Marie Pavie' polyantha rose
(*Rosa* x *polyantha*, p. 145) ●

Dauben water lily
(Water plants: *Nymphaea*, p. 152) ▲

Yellow variegated agave
(*Agave americana* 'Marginata', p. 122) ●

White rainlily
(Bulbs: *Zephyranthes candida*, p. 126) ●

A Beginning Border

FLOWERS AND A FENCE MAKE A CAREFREE DESIGN

A mixed border can be one of the most delightful of all gardens. Indeed, that's usually its sole purpose. Unlike many other types of landscape plantings, a traditional border is seldom yoked to any function beyond that of providing as much visual pleasure as possible.

This border is designed for a beginning or busy gardener. In parts of Texas, watering is one of the most formidable garden tasks. To reduce the time and cost associated with this chore, we've selected low-water-use plants for this border. Durable and carefree, they'll maximize the time you spend enjoying the garden.

Behind the planting, a simple fence screens out distractions and provides a unifying frame for the display. The border is meant to be viewed from the front, so taller plants go in back. A small flowering tree in the center serves as a colorful focal point.

The planting offers a selection of flowers in blues, reds, pinks, yellows, and creamy whites. Blooming over many months, there are flowers borne in spiky clusters as well as large feathery plumes, pendent bells, and bright cheerful "daisies."

The garden's foliage is at least as compelling as its flowers. A range of textures and colors contrast with and complement one another. At the back of the planting, the striking spiky yucca contrasts with the bushy green mounds of autumn sage and fall aster. These plants in turn are framed by airy masses of silvery green and blue foliage. Similar juxtapositions of color and texture are repeated on a smaller scale at the front of the planting.

If you want a larger border, just plant more of each plant to fit the space, or repeat parts of the design.

SITE: Sunny

SEASON: Summer

CONCEPT: Use the fence as a backdrop for this gorgeous border.

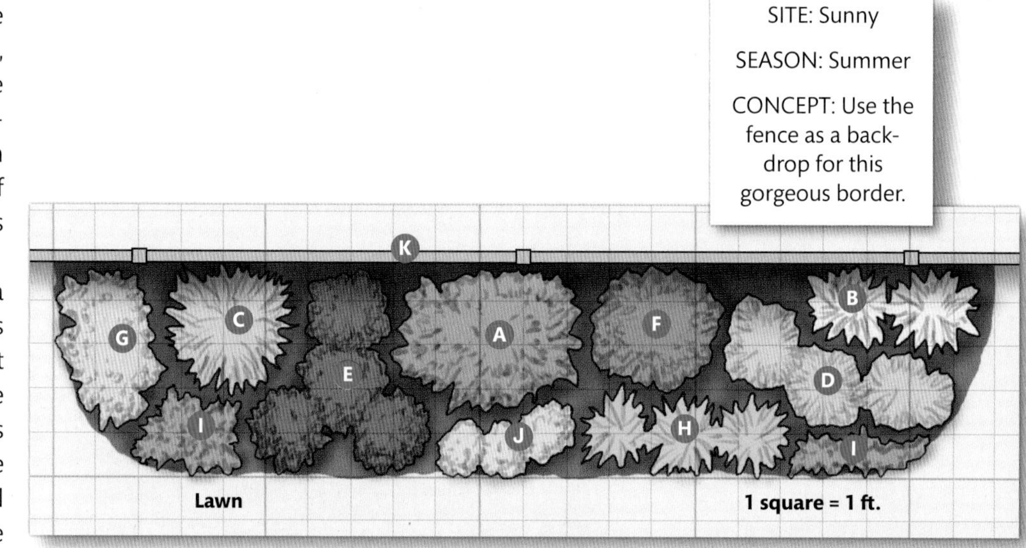

Plants & Projects

Once established, this planting will require almost no supplemental water and little other care. The only maintenance will be removing spent flowers during the summer and annual pruning of the desert willow, fall aster, and santolina.

A Desert willow (use 1 plant)
The fine leaves of this deciduous tree provide an airy canopy over the path without shading out the plants underneath. Showy white, pink, and lavender flowers bloom on and off all season. See *Chilopsis linearis*, p. 129.

B Soft-tip yucca (use 2)
This evergreen shrub forms a mound of attractive blue-gray swordlike foliage terminating in soft, rather than stiff, tips. In summer and fall, it sends up very tall stalks of nodding, lilylike white flowers. See *Yucca gloriosa*, p. 153.

C Indian grass (use 1)
A perennial grass with upright blue-green foliage that turns orange and yellow in fall and hints of those colors through winter. See *Sorghastrum nutans*, p. 149.

D Russian sage (use 3)
This bushy perennial's small silvery leaves and slender blue flower stalks are a nice contrast to the surrounding greens. See *Perovskia atriplicifolia*, p. 141.

E Autumn sage (use 4)
These perennials form rounded mounds of bright foliage and flowers. Choose red or coral blooms for best effect. Evergreen in most of the state. See *Salvia greggii*, p. 147.

F Fall aster (use 1)
Another round shape for an otherwise spiky garden, this native perennial sports a dense growth of pale-gray foliage on wiry stems. Lavender-purple flowers in fall echo the color of the desert willow and Russian sage blooms. Looks best when trimmed a couple of times during the growing season. See *Aster oblongifolius*, p. 124.

G Gaura (use 1)
A tough heat-tolerant Texas native, it produces surprisingly delicate masses of pink and white flowers above slender swaying stems. See *Gaura lindheimeri*, p. 132.

H Red yucca (use 3)
This mini yucca has slender gray-green leaves adorned with many stalks of small, coral-pink trumpet-shaped flowers. See *Hesperaloe parviflora*, p. 134.

I Trailing rosemary (use 2)
An evergreen shrub forming a low clump of sinuous branches lined with tiny pinelike leaves. Blooms mostly in early spring but the small blue flowers may appear sporadically throughout the year. See *Rosmarinus officinalis* 'Prostratus', p. 146.

J Gray santolina (use 3)
This compact shrub reinforces the silver-gray theme. Small, fragrant, toothed leaves grow in low mounds. In summer they sport bright-yellow button flowers. Cut back to about 6 in. in early spring to maintain a nice round shape. See *Santolina chamaecyparissus*, p. 148.

K Fence
A tall fence provides a backdrop for the border and privacy for you. See p. 194.

Autumn blooms

This border focuses on flowers. It requires more frequent watering than the previous one but otherwise needs little care. Flowers in purples, pinks, blues, and yellows open in spring and peak again in fall. The blossoms are enhanced by their juxtaposition—for example, lantana combined with garden phlox and daisy mums—and by handsome foliage in shades of green and gray. Silvery Texas sage makes a luminous backdrop for the pink and purple flowers of phlox and verbena. And the holly's dark lustrous foliage helps highlight the blues and yellows of salvia and daylily. If you'd like to keep the border in bloom year-round, plant winter annuals among dormant perennials. Evergreen shrubs and perennials provide plenty of colorful contrasts to please less energetic gardeners.

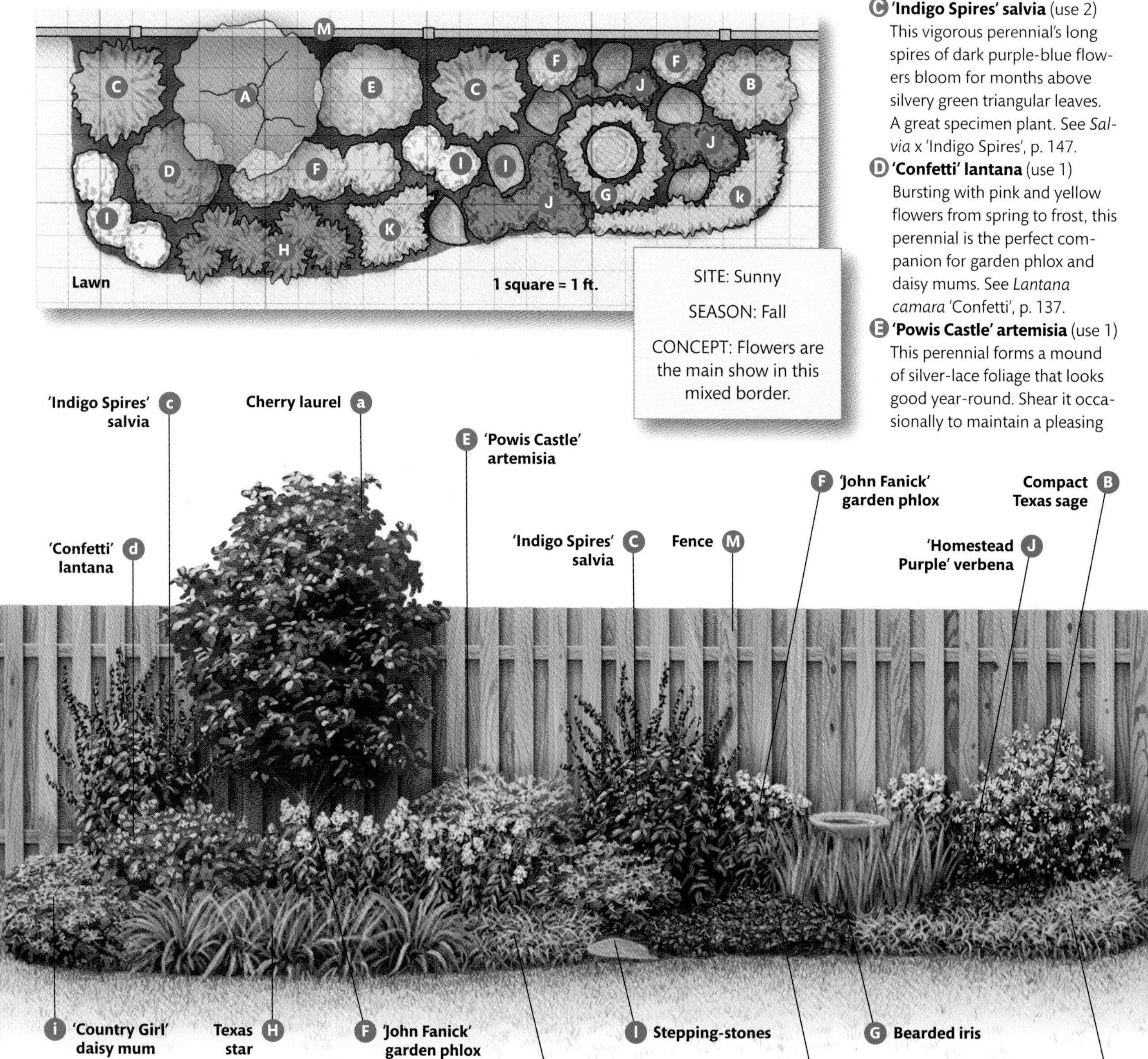

Plants & Projects

A Cherry laurel (use 1 plant) Upright native evergreen shrub can be pruned to a naturalistic hedge. See *Prunus caroliniana*, p. 143.

B Compact Texas sage (use 1) Evergreen shrub with a tidy, rounded habit. Lavender flowers bloom among silvery white leaves in summer. See *Leucophyllum frutescens* 'Compactum', p. 138.

C 'Indigo Spires' salvia (use 2) This vigorous perennial's long spires of dark purple-blue flowers bloom for months above silvery green triangular leaves. A great specimen plant. See *Salvia* x 'Indigo Spires', p. 147.

D 'Confetti' lantana (use 1) Bursting with pink and yellow flowers from spring to frost, this perennial is the perfect companion for garden phlox and daisy mums. See *Lantana camara* 'Confetti', p. 137.

E 'Powis Castle' artemisia (use 1) This perennial forms a mound of silver-lace foliage that looks good year-round. Shear it occasionally to maintain a pleasing round shape. See *Artemisia* x 'Powis Castle', p. 124.

F 'John Fanick' garden phlox (use 5)
A floriferous perennial, it produces long-lasting clusters of small pink flowers with dark-pink eyes from spring through fall. See *Phlox paniculata* 'John Fanick,' p. 141.

G Bearded iris (use 9)
Spectacular flowers and striking foliage make this perennial a must for the flower border. It blooms in spring and may repeat in fall. Shop for a reblooming cultivar in yellow or white for this garden. See *Iris* x *germanica*, p. 135.

H Texas star hibiscus (use 6)
This perennial forms a large airy clump of slender, deeply divided, glossy leaves borne on red-tinged stems. Brilliant red five-petaled flowers open daily during the summer and fall. See *Hibiscus coccineus*, p. 134.

I 'Country Girl' daisy mum (use 5)
This perennial's pretty pink flowers add color to the border in the fall. Prune halfway in spring and again in early summer to keep the clump compact. See *Chrysanthemum* x 'Country Girl', p. 129.

J 'Homestead Purple' verbena (use 5)
Plant this perennial among the stepping-stones for a thick carpet of vibrant purple flowers. A trim twice a year keeps it tidy. See *Verbena* x *hybrida* 'Homestead Purple', p. 151.

K 'Bath's Pink' dianthus (use 11)
This fine-textured evergreen perennial for the front of the border forms a low dense mat of silvery needlelike foliage topped with fragrant pink flowers in spring. See *Dianthus* 'Bath's Pink', p. 131.

L Stepping-stones
Flagstones placed around the birdbath provide access for cleaning and filling. See p. 169.

See p. 79 for the following:

M Fence

PLANT PORTRAITS

These well-behaved, low-care shrubs, bulbs, and perennials bring form, texture, flowers, and scent to a formal garden.

● = First design, pp. 78-79

▲ = Second design, pp. 80-81

'Country Girl' daisy mum (*Chrysanthemum*, p. 129) ▲

Cherry laurel
(*Prunus caroliniana*, p. 143) ▲

'John Fannick' garden phlox
(*Phlox paniculata*, p. 141) ▲

Gray santolina (*Santolina chamaecyparissus*, p. 148) ●

Year-In-Year-Out Border

PERENNIALS AND A WALL MAKE A TRADITIONAL DESIGN

Using durable plants that are easy to establish and maintain, this border is intended for a beginning or busy gardener. Behind the planting, providing a solid backdrop, is a simple wall. The border is meant to be viewed from the front, so taller plants go at the back. Draped over the wall, a trumpet vine adds a swath of dark-green leaves to the backdrop, dappled for weeks in late summer with lovely deep-pink flowers.

The planting offers a selection of flowers in blues, reds, pinks, and purples. Blooming over many months, there are small flowers borne in spiky clusters as well as bright cheerful daisies.

The garden's foliage is at least as compelling as its flowers. A range of textures and colors contrast with and complement one another. At the back of the planting, the striking spiky purple leaves of New Zealand flax contrast with the bushy green mound of the autumn sage. These plants are in turn framed by lacy masses of silver-gray foliage. Similar juxtapositions of color and texture are repeated on a smaller scale at the front of the planting.

If you want a larger border, just plant more of each plant to fit the space, or repeat parts of the design.

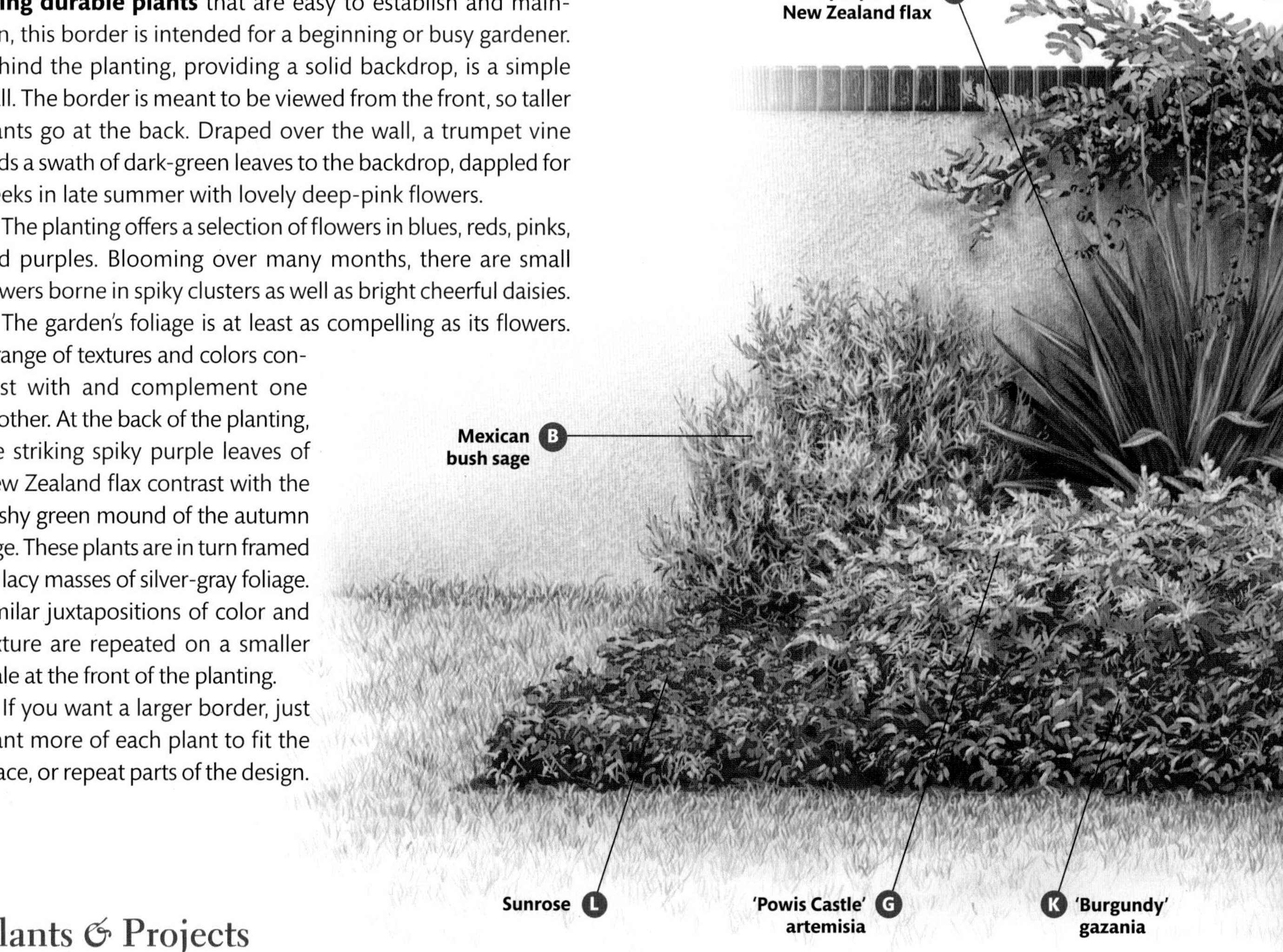

Plants & Projects

Removing spent flowers and seasonal pruning are the main chores in this garden. (To allow for maintenance, leave a space between the plants at the front of the border and those at the back, as shown on the site plan.) In winter, cut the gaura and Russian sage almost to the ground, cut the germander sage back by one-third, and prune the trumpet vine to control its size. Once established, the plants require little supplemental water.

A 'Atropurpureum' New Zealand flax (use 1 plant)
A bold, colorful accent, this perennial offers long, reddish purple, straplike leaves. From late spring to midsummer, branched stalks of reddish flowers rise above the foliage. See *Phormium tenax*, p. 141.

B Mexican bush sage (use 1)
This perennial has silver-gray foliage. It bears purple-and-white flowers from midsummer into fall. See *Salvia leucantha*, p. 147.

C Gaura (use 1)
Another wispy perennial, its graceful arching stems bear small leaves and spikes of small pink-and-white flowers from spring through fall. See *Gaura lindheimeri*, p. 132.

D Autumn sage (use 5)
This bushy perennial's green foliage bristles with striking spikes of red flowers from spring into fall. See *Salvia greggii*, p. 147.

E Russian sage (use 1)
From early summer into fall, small lavender-blue flowers seem to float amidst this perennial's stiff gray-green stems and silvery foliage. See *Perovskia atriplicifolia*, p. 141.

F 'Mme. Galen' trumpet vine (use 1)
This deciduous vine bears large compound leaves on thick stems. Clusters of salmon flowers bloom in late summer. Stake it the first year; after that its aerial rootlets will cling to the wall. See *Campsis* x *tagliabuana*, p. 127.

G 'Powis Castle' artemisia (use 3)
This perennial makes a mound of lacy silver foliage that looks good year-round. It is an excellent companion for the colorful gazania and New Zealand flax. See *Artemisia*, p. 124.

H Germander sage (use 1)
Forming a low, spreading mass of small silvery leaves, this perennial bears wispy spikes of bright-blue flowers from summer into fall. See *Salvia chamaedryoides*, p. 147.

SITE: Sunny

SEASON: Early summer

CONCEPT: Easy-care perennials with colorful flowers and foliage make this border ideal for beginning and busy gardeners alike.

I Cedar sedge (use 3)
This clump-forming perennial grass, prefers some shade and can be combined with other woodland and meadow natives. See *Carex planostachys*, p. 127.

J Blue marguerite (use 3)
Blue daisies nod above the spreading foliage throughout the year (if you deadhead them). See *Felicia amelloides*, p. 131.

K 'Burgundy' gazania (use 4)
This perennial flower produces large reddish purple daisies during late spring and in early summer. Dark-green foliage remains attractive for months. See *Gazania*, p. 133.

L Sunrose (use 3)
Small, bright-colored flowers sparkle in spring and early summer on the evergreen foliage of this small shrub. See *Helianthemum nummularium*, p. 132.

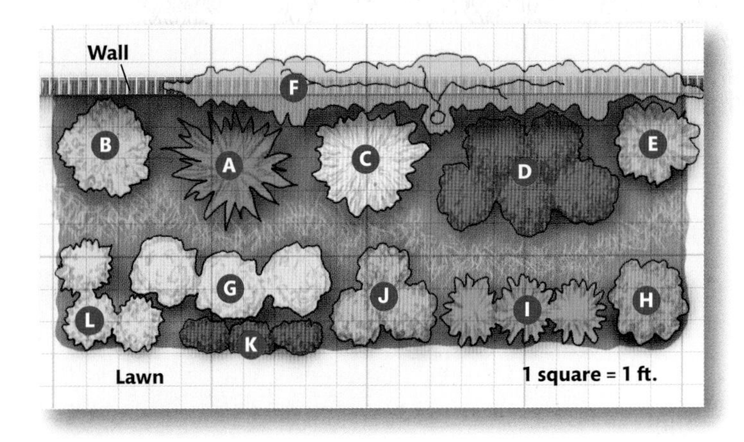

Garden in the Round

CREATE A PLANTING WITH SEVERAL ATTRACTIVE FACES

SITE: Sunny

SEASON: Summer

CONCEPT: A free-floating garden offers beauty all around, and a bonus of butterflies.

In domestic landscapes, plantings are often meant to be viewed from the front, similar to a wall-mounted sculpture in raised relief. However, the planting shown here forms an island bed that you can stroll around. Plants displayed in the round present different scenes from several vantage points. This is an excellent option for those who want to squeeze more gardening space from a small lot, add interest to a rectangular plot, or divide a large area into smaller outdoor "rooms."

A bed that floats free of any anchors requires a sensitivity to scale. To be successful, the bed must neither dominate its surroundings nor be lost in them. The plants here, with their bold textures and bright colors, have presence when viewed from a distance, while also offering a visual feast on close inspection. A festive parade of flowers begins in spring and continues through November. First up are the red Texas star hibiscus, followed closely by the showy purples of the desert willow, salvia, and verbena. Joining them are vivid yellows of lantana, esperanza and rudbeckia, and the calmer pinks of roses, yarrows, and gaura.

Among the garden's delights will be countless butterflies, attracted to the flowers of almost all plants here, in particular those of the desert willow, verbena, and lantana. Position a small decorative birdbath among the blooms, and let it double as a butterfly basin.

See site plan for I and K.

A Desert willow

D Mexican bush sage

E Gaura

H 'Goldsturm' black-eyed Susan

Plants & Projects

This planting offers flowers and foliage that look good with a minimum of care. Prune the desert willow into a tree form to allow space and light for nearby plants. To keep the gaura looking fresh, remove stems that have played out their blooms. Cut back the Mexican bush sage by a third in late spring to keep it from getting floppy in fall due to the weight of the flower spikes.

A Desert willow (use 1 plant)
The fine leaves of this deciduous tree provide an airy canopy over the path without shading out the plants underneath. Showy white, pink, and lavender flowers bloom on and off all season. See *Chilopsis linearis*, p. 129.

B 'Gold Star' esperanza (use 1)
Big, bright-yellow, bell-like flowers dangle from the tips of this bushy perennial's many branches from summer to frost. Flowers have a pleasant, light fragrance. See *Tecoma stans* 'Gold Star', p. 150.

C 'Belinda's Dream' rose (use 3)
These bushy roses will fill the space behind the Texas star hibiscus with luxuriant dark-green foliage and abundant fragrant pink blossoms from early spring to hard frost. See *Rosa* x 'Belinda's Dream', p. 145.

D Mexican bush sage (use 5)
These bushy perennials skirt the desert willow with slender gray-green leaves. Spikes of lavender flowers will echo the blossoms just above them in fall. See *Salvia leucantha*, p. 147.

E Gaura (use 3)
A favorite of butterflies, this fine-textured perennial forms a base of small pale-green leaves from which numerous slender stems rise, bearing pink-and-white flowers that appear to float above the plant. See *Gaura lindheimeri*, p. 132.

F 'Confetti' lantana (use 1)
Festive clusters of bicolored flowers in pink and yellow cover this bushy perennial from spring to frost. See *Lantana camara* 'Confetti', p. 137.

G Texas star hibiscus (use 11)
This perennial forms a large airy clump of slender, deeply divided, glossy leaves borne on red-tinged stems. Brilliant red five-petaled flowers open daily during the summer and fall. See *Hibiscus coccineus*, p. 134.

H 'Goldsturm' black-eyed Susan (use 5)
A golden blanket of dark-eyed "daisies" covers this perennial in early summer. See *Rudbeckia fulgida* 'Goldsturm', p. 146.

I 'Fire King' yarrow (use 7)
This perennial forms a mat of fine fernlike foliage topped with flat, lacy flowerheads in shades of hot pink. See *Achillea millefolium* 'Fire King', p. 122.

J Homestead Purple' verbena (use 4)
Masses of purple flowers and the butterflies they attract hover among the bright-green leaves of this perennial all season. See *Verbena x hybrida* 'Homestead Purple', p. 151.

K Narcissus (use as needed)
Small trumpet-shaped flowers open in clusters on stalks that rise above dark-green leaves. Each stalk may produce as many as 20 flowers. Common cultivars have white petals and a yellow cup. Plant throughout the bed for a carpet of bloom in spring. See Bulbs: *Narcissus tazetta*, p. 126.

L Butterfly basin
A small birdbath can also serve up food and drink for butterflies. Fill it with water, or leave bits of fruit to ferment for a sugary treat.

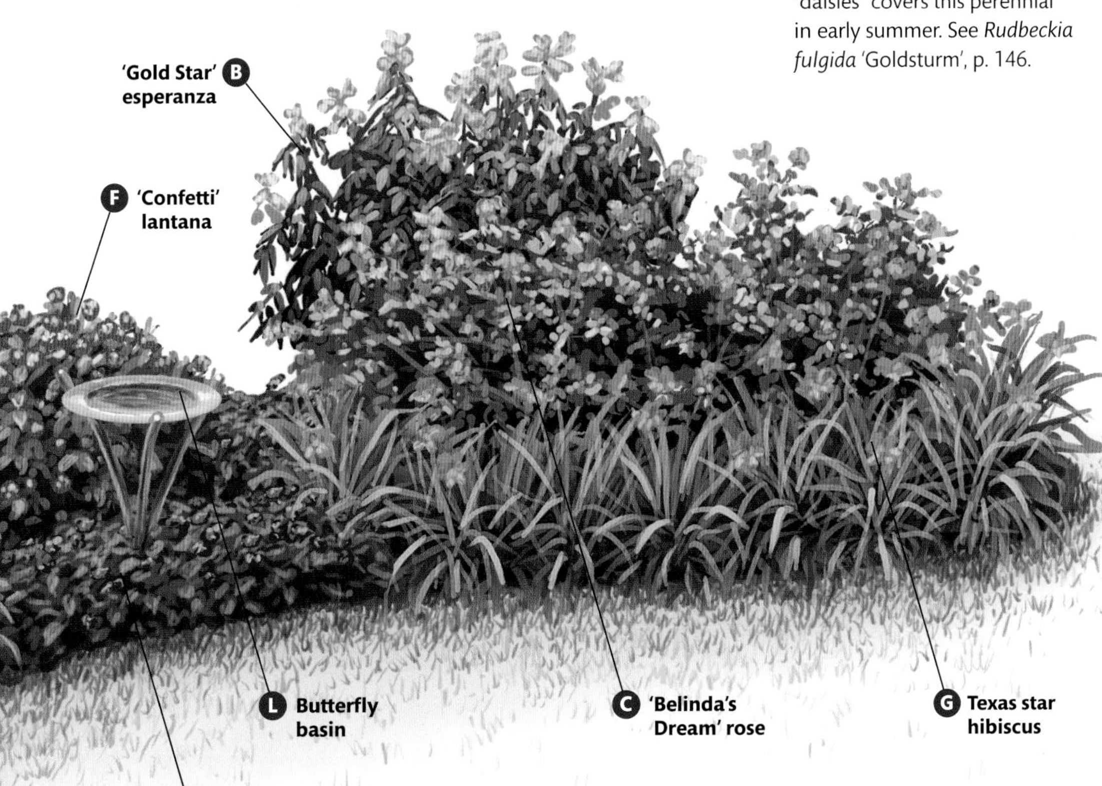

An island garden for the birds

This design uses an existing shade tree as an anchor for a free-floating island bed and adds a smaller tree at its opposite end for balance. The trees are underplanted with shrubs and mid-height perennials. Lower-growing perennials fill the rest of the gently curved bed in repeating waves of contrasting foliage and flower. Like the previous design, this one affords attractive views from all sides.

Plants are chosen not only for their lush woodsy look but also for the birdlife they'll attract. The redbud offers flowers in early spring, attractive seasonal foliage, and a welcome perch for songbirds year-round. The unusual flowers of the Turk's cap open just in time for migrating hummingbirds. And the decorative seeds of beautyberry and inland sea oats keep groundfeeding birds feasting in autumn and winter.

This garden requires little maintenance beyond annual pruning. The columbines and ferns naturally shed their stems and can be thinned out as needed. To maintain its bushy shape and encourage more flowers, the Turk's cap can be cut back by about a third after each flowering spurt.

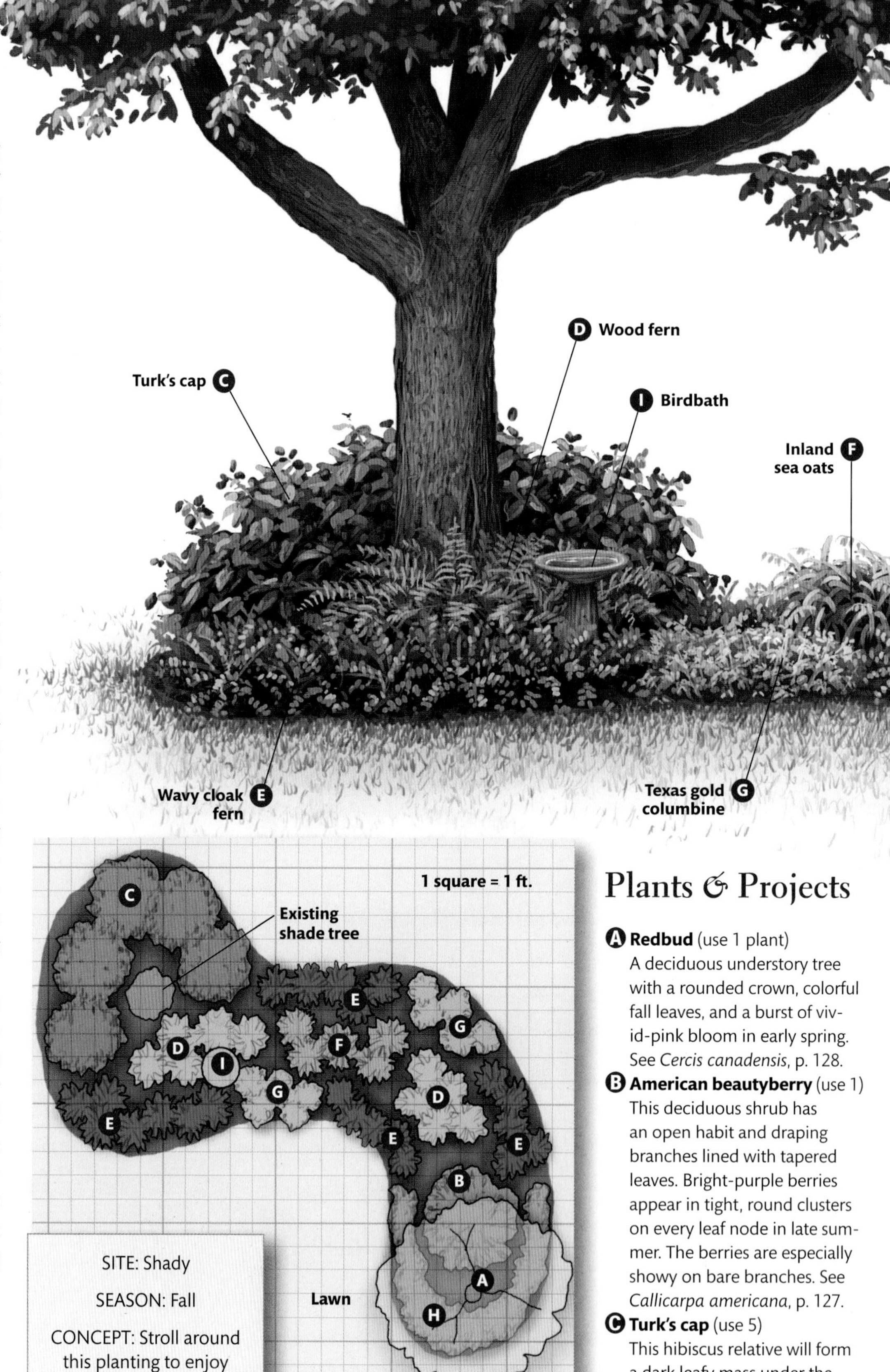

Plants & Projects

A Redbud (use 1 plant)
A deciduous understory tree with a rounded crown, colorful fall leaves, and a burst of vivid-pink bloom in early spring. See *Cercis canadensis*, p. 128.

B American beautyberry (use 1)
This deciduous shrub has an open habit and draping branches lined with tapered leaves. Bright-purple berries appear in tight, round clusters on every leaf node in late summer. The berries are especially showy on bare branches. See *Callicarpa americana*, p. 127.

C Turk's cap (use 5)
This hibiscus relative will form a dark leafy mass under the shade tree. Small red-orange flowers resembling a Turkish fez decorate the shrub all season. See *Malvaviscus arboreus drummondii*, p. 139.

D Wood fern (use 10)
Light-green fronds add a cool fresh look to the garden from spring through fall. See Ferns: *Thelypteris kunthii*, p. 132.

E Wavy cloak fern (use 22)
This semi-evergreen fern produces clumps of attractive rich green foliage, with a contrasting cinnamon underside. It is uniquely drought tolerant and suited to poor rocky soils, preferring sun or part shade. It is clump forming and slowly spreads via rhizomes. See *Astrolepsis sinuata*, p. 124.

F Inland sea oats (use 5)
Forming a small patch of prairie between the trees, this grass is most interesting in late summer, when long oatlike seedheads dangle on arching stalks among the foliage. See *Chasmanthium latifolium*, p. 128.

G Texas gold columbine (use 10)
Yellow flowers nod in spring above this perennial's dainty mounds of fernlike foliage. See *Aquilegia chrysantha hinckleyana*, p. 123.

H Dwarf Mexican petunia (use 18)
A tough perennial gound cover, its dark-green leaves create an informal fringe around the redbud, with clusters of small, petunialike purple flowers opening in the center of each plant. See *Ruellia brittoniana* 'Katie', p. 148.

I Birdbath
This island bed will attract lots of birdlife, so place a favorite birdbath under the tree for their refreshment.

PLANT PORTRAITS

These distinctive plants will bring color and texture to any garden in the round.

● = First design, pp. 84-85

▲ = Second design, pp. 86-87

'Belinda's Dream' rose (*Rosa*, p. 145) ●

'Fire King' yarrow (*Achillea millefolium*, p. 122) ●

A Shady Hideaway

BUILD A COZY RETREAT IN A CORNER OF YOUR YARD

One of life's pleasures is sitting in a shady spot reading or just looking out onto your garden. If your property is long on lawn and short on shade, a chair under an arbor can provide a cool respite from the heat or the cares of the day. Tucked into a corner of the yard and set among attractive shrubs, vines, and perennials, the arbor shown here is a desirable destination even when the day isn't sizzling.

A small tree and an overhead vine create a cozy enclosure, affording privacy as well as shade. Plantings in front of the arbor and extending along the property lines integrate the hideaway with the lawn and make a handsome scene when viewed from the house. The design is also effective in an open corner or backed by a property-line fence. The arbor is small; it's easy to make it wider and longer by extending the plantings.

Flowers contribute warm colors. Festive yellows, pinks, and reds start the year off and continue until the first frost. Along with a canopy of honeysuckle blossoms, there will be showy hibiscus flowers and lantanas by the bench. Masses of black-eyed Susans and red pomegranate flowers join up in summer. And in fall, deciduous foliage adds to the colorful mix. This is primarily a warm-season planting, but pomegranate fruits and holly berries will make the hideaway well worth a winter visit.

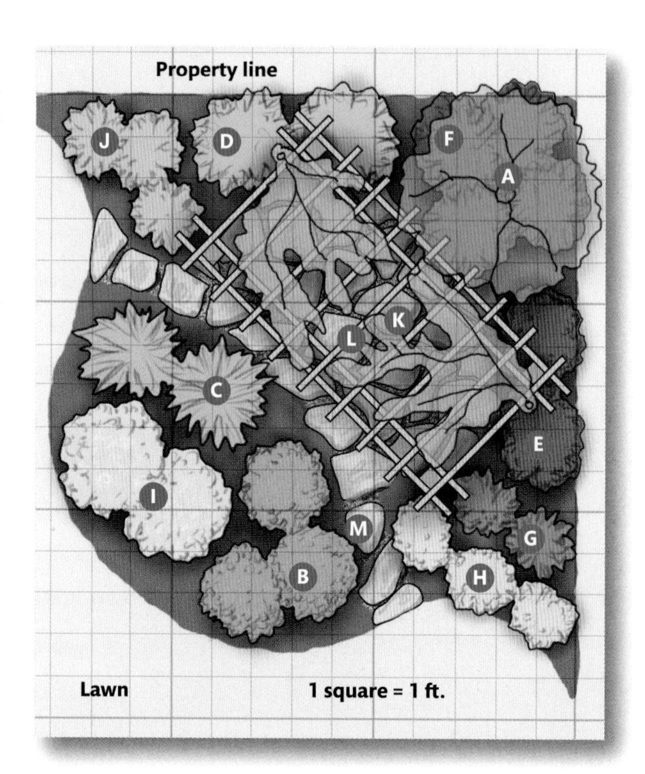

Plants & Projects

The arbor and plants can be installed in a few weekends. Once the plants are established, seasonal pruning and cleanup should keep this durable planting looking good year-round.

A Possumhaw holly (use 1 plant)
This fast-growing deciduous tree makes a handsome screen for the hideaway. Smooth oval leaves turn yellow in fall. When they drop, they expose silvery branches with bright red, orange, or yellow berries, the color depending on the cultivar. See *Ilex decidua*, p. 135.

B Compact pomegranate (use 3)
A low-growing form of a popular deciduous shrub. Lustrous foliage showcases red carnationlike flowers in summer and small ornamental fruits in fall. See *Punica granatum* 'Nana', p. 143.

C Lindheimer's muhly (use 2)
A beautiful, fine-textured ornamental grass. Blue-green leaves and soft texture makes this grass popular for screening. See *Muhlenbergia lindheimeri*, p. 139.

D Texas star hibiscus (use 2)
This perennial forms a large airy clump of slender, deeply divided, glossy leaves borne on red-tinged stems. Brilliant red five-petaled flowers open daily during the summer and fall. See *Hibiscus coccineus*, p. 134.

E Firebush (use 2)
Small slender flowers dangle at the ends of this perennial's many branches from summer to frost. Dull green leaves turn red in fall. See *Hamelia patens*, p. 133.

F Turk's cap (use 4)
This shrubby perennial will tolerate the eventual shade under the tree canopy, providing a lush screen of dark-green leaves studded with small red turbanlike flowers. See *Malvaviscus arboreus drummondii*, p. 139.

G Cigar plant (use 2)
Adding a vertical element to the planting, this perennial spreads to form a patch of upright stems topped with long narrow leaves. Thin orange and yellow flowers complement the firebush blossoms in summer. See *Cuphea micropetala*, p. 130.

H 'Goldstrum' black-eyed Susan (use 3)
This popular perennial's abundant, golden, dark-eyed daisies bloom abundantly in summer, with plenty to spare for flower arrangements. See *Rudbeckia fulgida* 'Goldsturm', p. 146.

I 'New Gold' lantana (use 2)
Tiny golden flowers in tight round clusters cover the foliage of this spreading perennial from late spring to frost. See *Lantana x hybrida* 'New Gold', p. 137.

J Mexican mint marigold (use 3)
Plant this perennial next to the bench for fragrant foliage and a fall display of rich yellow flowers. On your way into the house snip a few anise-flavored leaves for cooking and a handful of flowers for fall bouquets. See *Tagetes lucida*, p. 150.

K Coral honeysuckle (use 2)
Whorls of scarlet flowers decorate this popular vine from late spring to fall. Attractive blue-green foliage is evergreen. See *Lonicera sempervirens*, p. 138.

L Arbor
This simple structure can be built in a weekend or two. See p. 193.

M Paving
Flat fieldstones in tones of gray complement the arbor and the planting. See p. 163.

SITE: Sunny
SEASON: Summer
CONCEPT: Enjoy a colorful array of plants while you relax under a shady arbor.
Possumhaw holly A
Coral honeysuckle K
Arbor L
Texas star hibiscus D
See site plan for F.
Mexican mint marigold J
Lindheimer's muhly C
'New Gold' lantana I
Compact pomegranate B
Paving M
Firebush E
Cigar plant G
'Goldsturm' black-eyed Susan H

PLANT PORTRAITS

Privacy, shade, flowers, foliage, and fragrance—these plants provide all the necessities for a relaxing backyard retreat.
● = First design, pp. 88-89
▲ = Second design, pp. 90-91

Compact pomegranate (*Punica granatum* 'Nana', p. 143) ●

Narcissus (Bulbs: *Narcissus tazetta* 'Grand Primo', p. 126) ▲

Mexican mint marigold (*Tagetes lucida*, p. 150) ●

Polyantha rose (*Rosa* x *polyantha* 'Marie Daly', p. 145) ▲

Homegrown hideaway

Instead of building your garden retreat, you can grow it. A small tree and midsize shrubs replace the arbor in the previous design. Their lush greenery provides a sense of enclosure and privacy year-round, and the cool flower colors (blues, pinks, and whites) will soothe the senses even as the temperature rises.

Reliably evergreen, the wax myrtle's deliciously scented leaves will cast dappled shade over the bench all year. The camellias, viburnums, and abelias are evergreen too, their dark glossy foliage a perfect foil for pink and white blossoms. There will be flowers in every season: sweet-scented viburnum in early spring, roses from May to October, camellias in November, and narcissus for snow-white blooms in winter.

Plants & Projects

A Wax myrtle (use 1 plant)
This small evergreen tree offers a fragrant and shady canopy for bench sitters. Leaves are smooth and slender. See *Myrica cerifera*, p. 139.

B Pink skullcap (use 3)
A low-growing deciduous mound with pink flowers that requires full sun and low water. See *Scutellaria sufftutescens*, p. 149.

C Southern Arrowwood Little John (use 1)
This hybrid stays a manageable size growing 4–5 feet tall and wide and developing dark blue berries enjoyed by the birds. See *Viburnum dentatum*, page 153.

D New Jersey Tea (use 3)
This small shrub establishes deep roots, growing in dry and rocky soils, it is not suited to wet soils. See *Ceanothus americanus*, p. 128.

E Polyantha rose (use 3)
Apple-green foliage topped with pale-pink semidouble flowers make this dwarf rose a standout

next to the path. See *Rosa* x *polyantha* 'Marie Daly', p. 145.

F Tropical plumbago (use 4)
The clear blue flowers of this shrubby perennial add cool color to the planting in hot summer months. See *Plumbago auriculata*, p. 142.

G 'Indigo Spires' salvia (use 1)
This lush, vigorous perennial makes a bushy mound of triangular leaves topped all season with long spikes of blue-purple flowers. See *Salvia* x 'Indigo Spires,', p. 147.

H 'Blue Princess' verbena (use 2)
Plant this low-growing perennial up front for a season-long border of lavender-blue flowers. See *Verbena* x *hybrida* 'Blue Princess', p. 151.

I 'Bath's Pink' dianthus (use 5)
This evergreen perennial's pincushion-like blue-gray foliage adds texture and color to the border. Masses of small pink flowers blanket the plant in spring. See *Dianthus* 'Bath's Pink', p. 130.

J 'Grand Primo' narcissus (use 40)
Scatter bulbs of this small daffodil around the planting, especially the plumbago and salvia, for grassy foliage and white flowers after the perennials freeze back. See Bulbs: *Narcissus tazetta* 'Grand Primo', p. 126

See p. 89 for the following:

K Paving

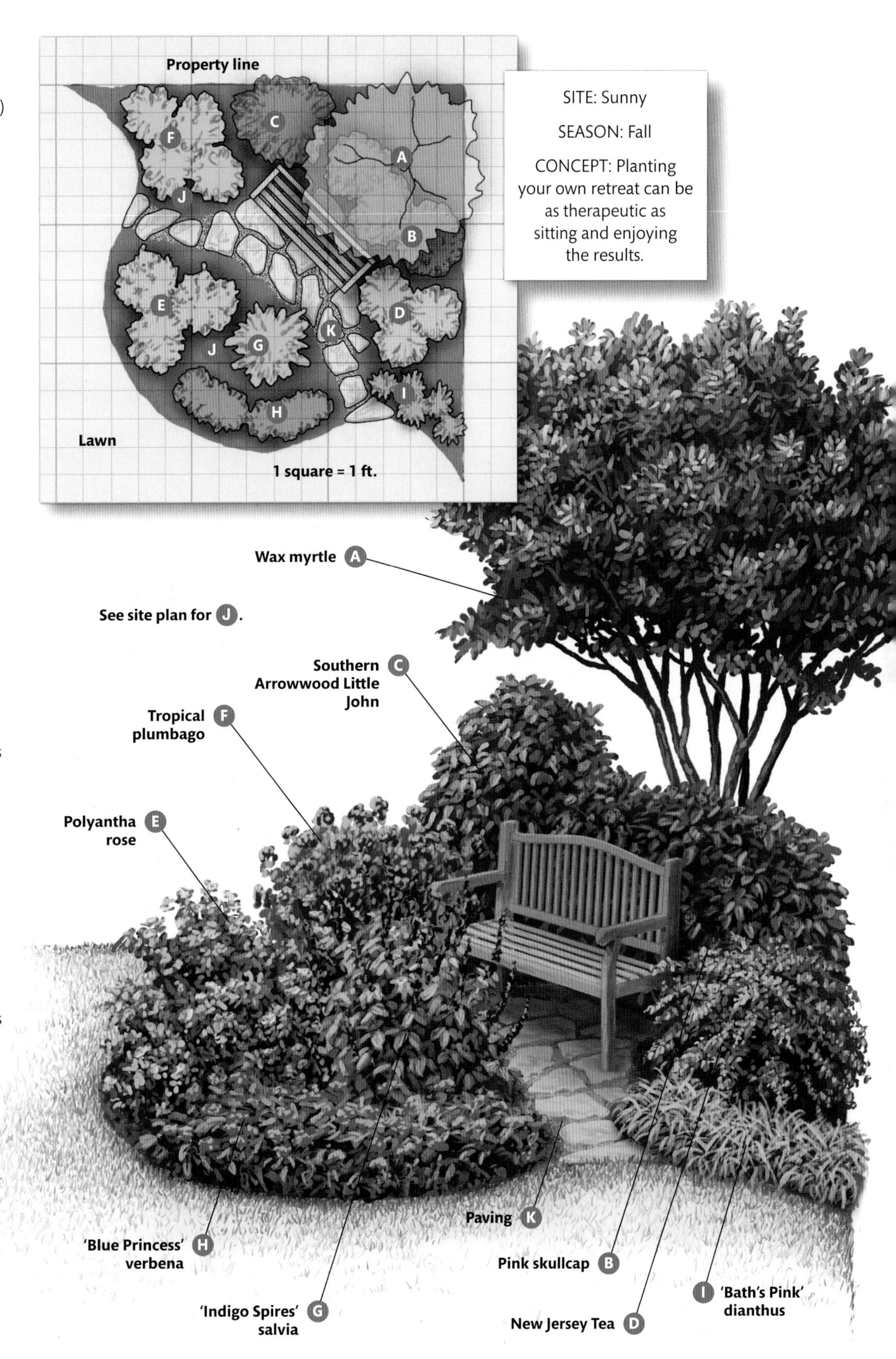

SITE: Sunny

SEASON: Fall

CONCEPT: Planting your own retreat can be as therapeutic as sitting and enjoying the results.

An Outdoor "Living" Room

PATIO AND SHADY ARBOR PROVIDE OPEN-AIR OPPORTUNITIES

In Texas, opportunities for outdoor living abound. This design demonstrates how a patio next to the house can become a true extension of your living space with the addition of an arbor, a fence, and plants that create an attractive setting—and attract hummingbirds as well.

At one end of an informal patio, a vine-covered arbor, anchored by a small tree, provides a cool shady spot for dining or relaxing. At the opposite end, a wooden fence bordered by flowers offers privacy as well as a colorful display to be enjoyed from the patio or the house. Together the fence, arbor, patio, and plants nicely mingle the indoors with the outdoors.

From early spring to late fall, the plantings will provide colorful accompaniments to your patio activities. Blossoms of fragrant jessamine open first. By May, the patio will boast long-lasting flowers and nectar-seeking hummingbirds.

Scale is particularly important when you're landscaping near the house. This design can be adapted to suit houses and properties in a range of sizes. The flagstone patio can be altered by adding or removing irregular pavers. And the plantings can be extended or reduced along the edges.

SITE: Sunny

SEASON: Summer

CONCEPT: Arbor, paving, and plants provide a pleasant ambiance for outdoor relaxation and entertaining.

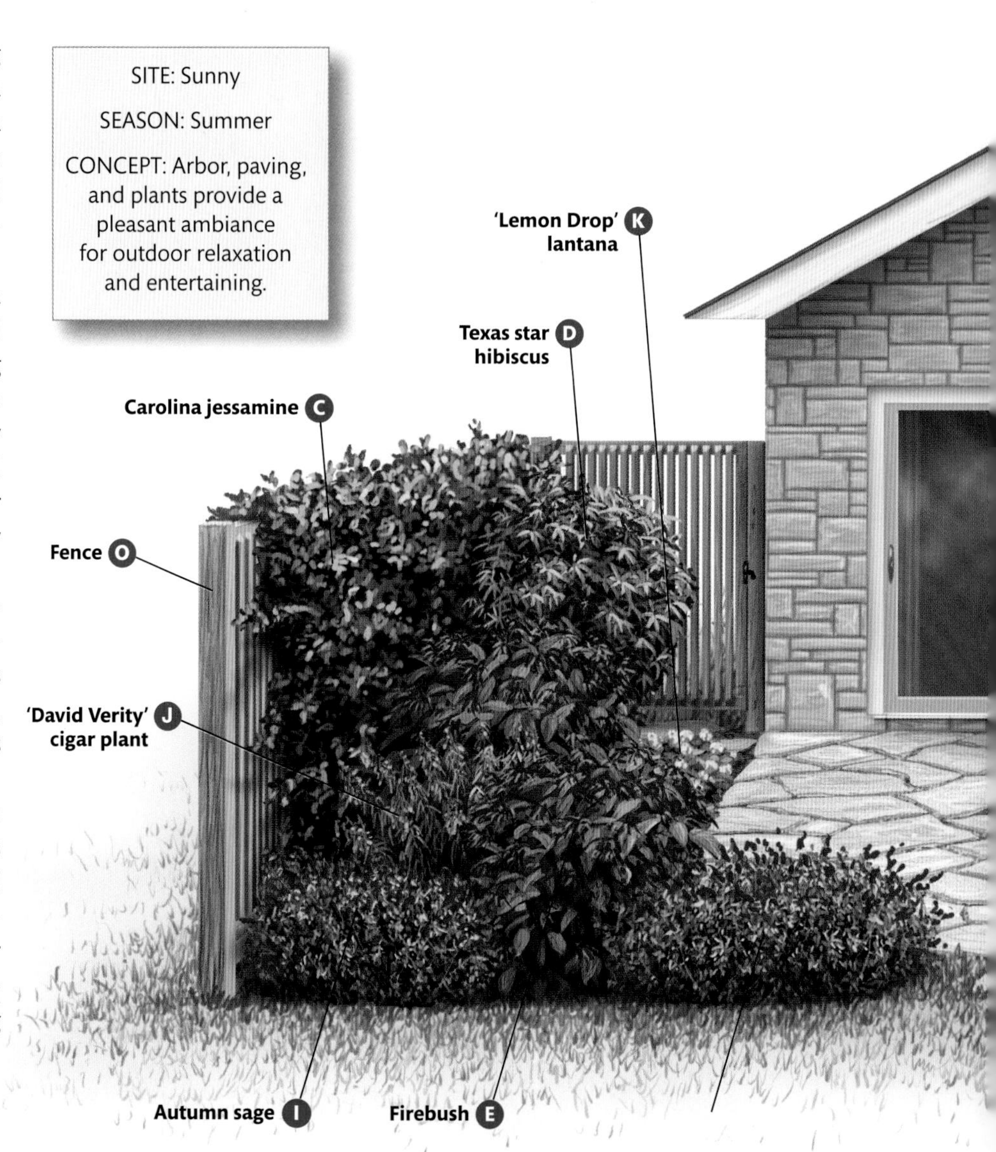

Plants & Projects

This design will keep your yard busy with winged creatures. Hummingbirds are drawn to the trumpet creeper, Texas star hibiscus, firebush, red yucca, Turk's cap, autumn sage, and the cigar plant. Butterflies are fond of Turk's cap and the two lantanas. The planting is also carefree.

A 'Bubba' desert willow (use 1 plant)
The willowy foliage of this small deciduous tree showcases orchidlike purple flowers on and off throughout the summer. See *Chilopsis linearis* 'Bubba', p. 129.

B 'Mme. Galen' trumpet creeper (use 1)
A vigorous, leafy, deciduous vine laden from summer to fall with clusters of showy salmon red flowers. A dense canopy of foliage provides shade for the patio in warm months. See *Campsis* x *tagliabuana* 'Mme. Galen', p. 127.

C Carolina jessamine (use 6)
Shiny neat evergreen leaves and a show of fragrant yellow flowers in spring make this vigorous vine ideal for training up porch columns or along a railing. See *Gelsemium sempervirens*, p. 133.

D Texas star hibiscus (use 1)
Dazzling star-shaped red flowers bloom at the tips of this bushy perennial's leafy green branches all season long. See *Hibiscus coccineus*, p. 134.

E Firebush (use 3)
This perennial forms a neat mound of dark-green foliage. Numerous small firecracker red flowers bloom from summer to frost. Stems and new growth are tinged red. See *Hamelia patens*, p. 133.

F 'Dallas Red' lantana (use 3)
Swirls of tight-knit tiny red-and-orange blossoms create a fine-textured backdrop for the wavy cloak fern. New flower clusters are yellowish orange inside and red outside. See *Lantana camara* 'Dallas Red', p. 137.

G Red yucca (use 1)
A bold year-round accent, this yucca relative forms a large clump of narrow succulent leaves. It is especially striking

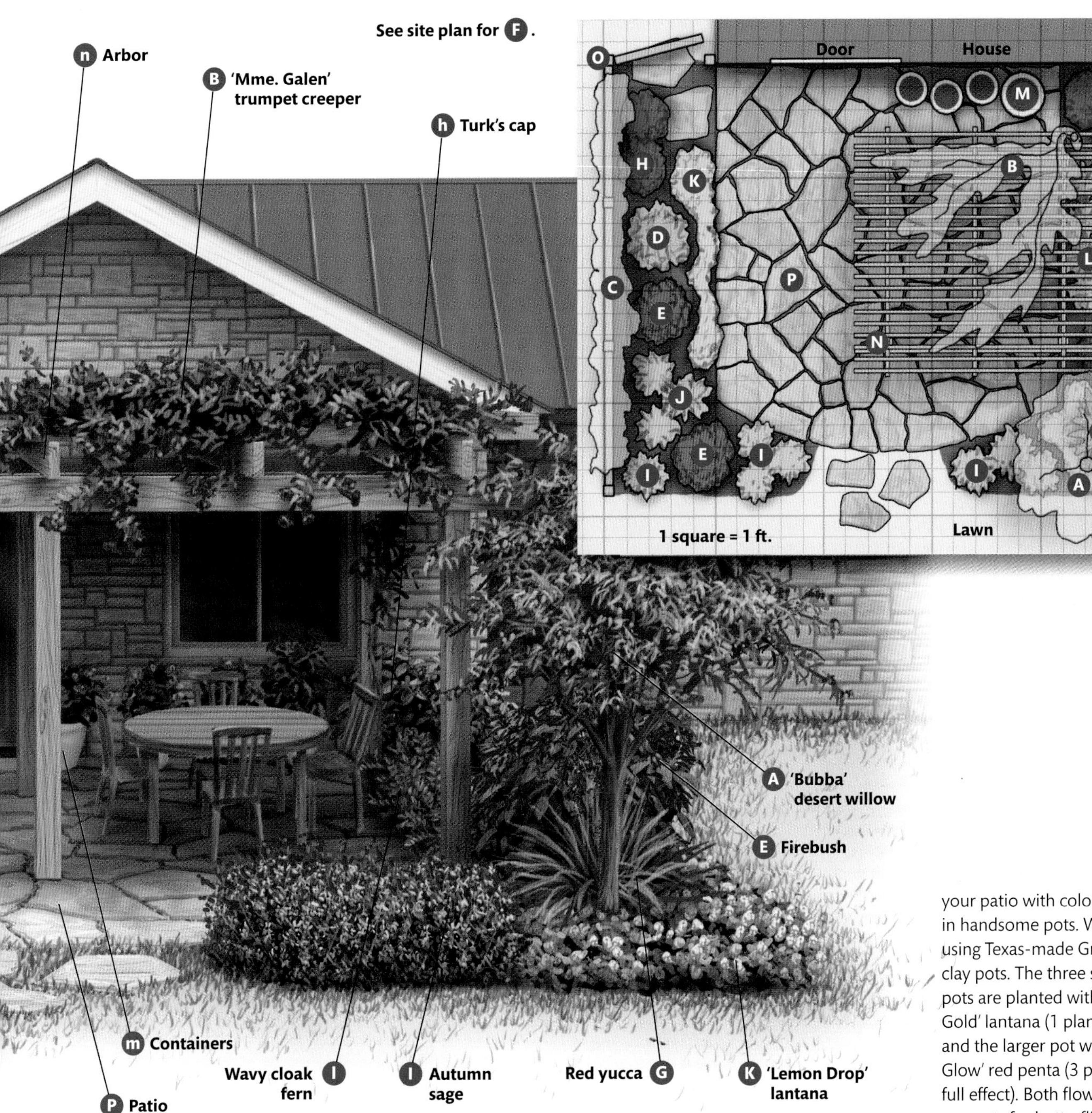

when in summer and fall bloom under the desert willow. Flowers are coral pink. See *Hesperaloe parviflora*, p. 134.

H Turk's cap (use 4)
Plant this perennial near the patio to enjoy its summer-to-frost display of unusual red flowers. Dense and upright, it will fill the corner with handsome dark green palmate leaves. See *Malvaviscus arboreus drummondii*, p. 139.

I Autumn sage (use 7)
Plant this perennial by the flagstones. Branch tips bear red blooms the size and shape of lipsticks. Flowers are especially abundant in spring and fall. See *Salvia greggii*, p. 147.

J 'David Verity' cigar plant (use 3)
A perfect companion for sage and firebush. Upright stems are topped with narrow leaves and a profusion of orange flowery "cigars" all summer long. See *Cuphea* x 'David Verity', p. 130.

K 'Lemon Drop' lantana (use 6)
This vigorous spreading perennial lays out a thick carpet of cheery yellow flowers next to the patio from late spring to late fall. See *Lantana* x *hybrida* 'Lemon Drop', p. 137.

L Wavy cloak fern (use 4)
This semi-evergreen fern produces clumps of attractive rich green foliage, with a contrasting cinnamon underside. It is uniquely drought tolerant and suited to poor rocky soils, preferring sun or part shade. It is clump forming and slowly spreads via rhizomes. See *Astrolepsis sinuata*, p. 124.

M Containers (as needed)
Bring butterflies right on to your patio with colorful plants in handsome pots. We suggest using Texas-made Grub's white-clay pots. The three smaller pots are planted with 'New Gold' lantana (1 plant in each) and the larger pot with 'Ruby Glow' red penta (3 plants for full effect). Both flowers are magnets for butterflies.

N Arbor
This large arbor will serve as a sunscreen for the patio even before the trumpet vine fills in. See p. 188.

O Fence
A simple structure creates an attractive screen for flowers as well as for privacy. See p. 196.

P Patio
Flagstones set on a sand-and-gravel base make a durable informal patio. See p. 170.

PLANT PORTRAITS

While lending privacy, shade, color, and fragrance to your outdoor room, this selection of plants attracts butterflies and other wildlife on the wing.

● = First design, pp. 92-93
▲ = Second design, pp. 94-95

'Dallas Red' lantana
(*Lantana camara*, p. 137) ●

'David Verity' cigar plant
(*Cuphea*, p. 130) ●

'Bubba' desert willow
(*Chilopsis linearis*, p. 129) ●

'Mme. Galen' trumpet creeper
(*Campsis* x *tagliabuana*, p. 127) ●

'Whirling Butterflies' gaura
(*Gaura lindheimeri*, p. 132) ▲

Butterfly viewing

This design creates an outdoor room that beckons butterflies along with friends and family. The live oak will provide pleasant shade for a portion of the patio, while playing host to duskywings, hairstreaks, and many other butterfly species. Long-blooming flowers are a feast for the eye and for skippers, swallowtails, and roving monarchs. Other plants play their part too. Texas sage and wavy cloak fern shelter butterflies from storms and pots of leafy edibles, such as dill, parsley, and fennel, give the pupa (caterpillars) something to munch.

Here are a few tips to increase your butterfly population once they discover your patio. Place decorative rocks or logs in the flower beds for them to rest on and spread their wings. Butterflies need to soak up warmth from the sun to become active. Protect their life stages, eggs, larva, and pupa by avoiding the use of pesticides on plants. And remember, some leaf eating is desirable and beneficial in a butterfly garden.

Plants & Projects

A **Live oak** (use 1 plant)
This large native tree forms a thick canopy of small hollylike evergreen leaves that will eventually shade the whole patio. If you'd like less shade, plant a smaller oak such as lacey oak. See *Quercus virginiana*, p. 143.

B **Butterfly rose** (use 1)
This delicate bush rose flowers all season. The profusion of single silky blossoms change color as yellow to orange to pink. New shoots and leaves are flushed

purple; mature leaves are dark green. See *Rosa chinensis* 'Mutabilis', p. 145.

C Compact Texas sage (use 3)
This native evergreen shrub is grown for striking purple bell-shaped flowers that open after summer rains. Woolly silver-gray leaves make a handsome informal year-round screen. See *Leucophyllum frutescens* 'Compactum', p. 138.

D Lindheimer's muhly (use 3)
A beautiful, fine-textured ornamental grass. Blue-green leaves and soft texture makes this grass popular for screening. See *Muhlenbergia lindheimeri*, p. 139.

E 'Whirling Butterflies' gaura (use 4)
From spring through fall, this graceful perennial sends up many slender stems of delicate "floating" flowers. They both resemble and attract butterflies. See *Gaura lindheimeri* 'Whirling Butterflies', p. 132.

F Fall aster (use 2)
This carefree native perennial puts on a dazzling show of lavender-purple "daisies" from early fall to frost. Their nectar draws roving monarchs. See *Aster oblongifolius*, p. 124.

G 'Homestead Purple' verbena (use 1)
This sprawling perennial forms a lacy mat of evergreen leaves and bright-purple flowers. It blooms nonstop from spring to fall if deadheaded regularly. See *Verbena* x *hybrida* 'Homestead Purple', p. 151.

H Purple verbena (use 3)
This perennial's lavender-purple flowers are borne aloft tall, stiff stems. A magnet for butterflies from spring to frost. See *Verbena bonariensis*, p. 151.

I Coreopsis (use 5)
Plant these perennials to weave a gold "daisy" chain through the border in spring. See *Coreopsis lanceolata*, p. 130.

J 'Trailing Lavender' lantana (use 5)
This evergreen shrub's weeping branches are laden with clusters of small lavender-purple flowers in summer. See *Lantana montevidensis* 'Trailing Lavender', p. 137.

K Containers (as needed)
Plant dill, parsley, carrots, fennel, and anise to attract swallowtail butterflies; abutilons, hibiscus, and mallows for skipper butterflies.

L Water basin
A shallow dish makes an ideal birdbath for butterflies. Place some sand in the bottom; add a few pebbles for butterflies to land on; fill it with water; and watch what happens.

M Paving
Shown here is a brick patio laid in a simple basketweave pattern. See p. 163.

See p. 93 for the following:

N Wavy cloak fern (use 20)

O Autumn sage (use 4)

SITE: Sunny

SEASON: Spring

CONCEPT: A butterfly garden brings this outdoor room to life.

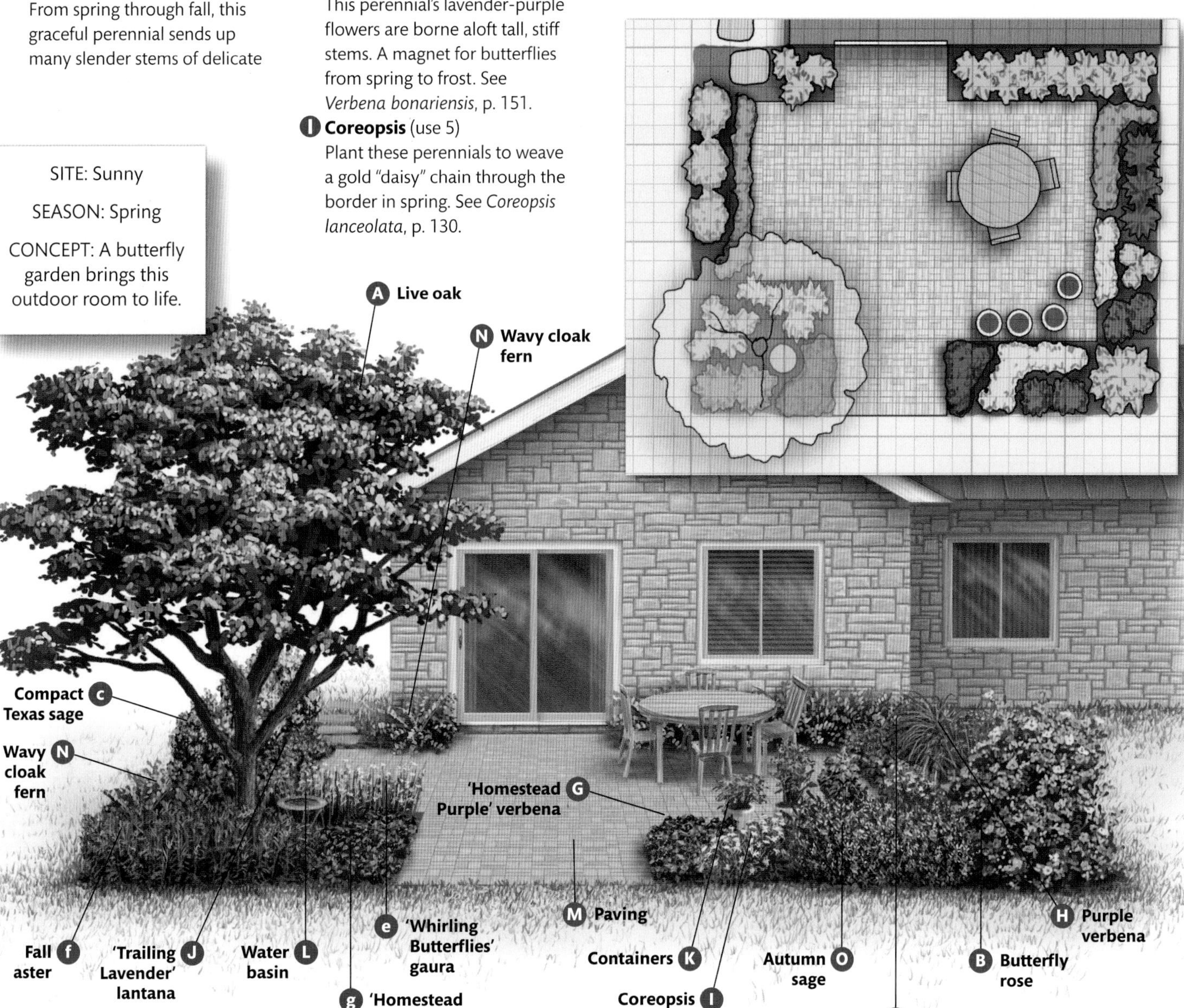

Formal Outdoor Living

CREATE SHADY ENTERTAINING SPACE ON THIS FORMAL PATIO

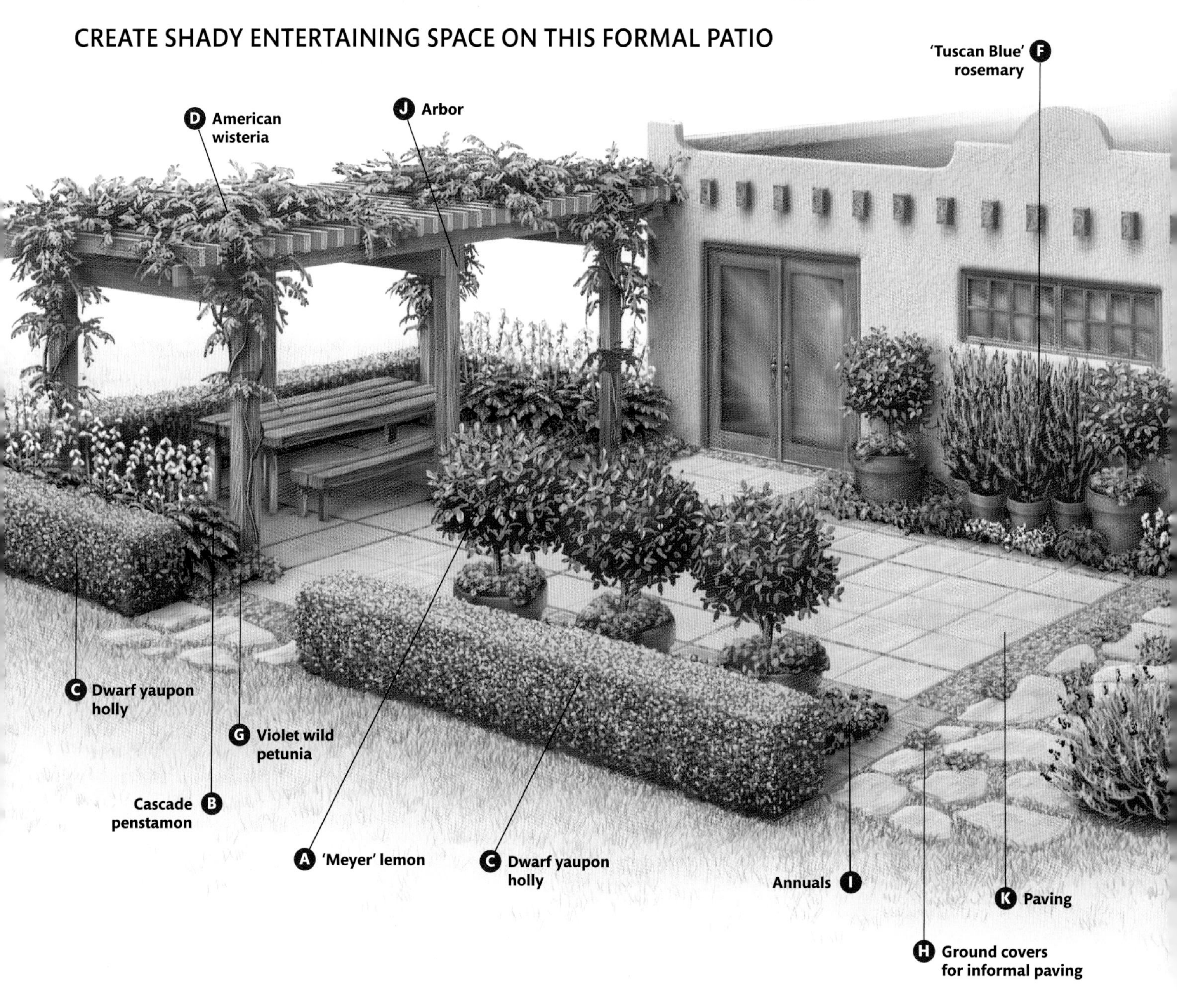

In Texas, opportunities for year-round outdoor living abound. This design demonstrates how a patio next to the house can become a true extension of your living space with the addition of an arbor and plants that create an attractive outdoor setting.

At one end of a formal patio, a vine-covered arbor provides a shady, cool spot for dining or relaxing. At the opposite end, random paving and a seat-height curved stone wall invite informal gatherings when the heat of the day has passed.

A neatly trimmed holly hedge, clipped trees, and shrubs in terra-cotta pots reinforce the formality of the gridwork paving, while annuals and ground covers spilling onto the pavement soften the effect. Backing the curved seating wall, a loose hedge of rosemary is an informal echo of its holly counterpart. Easily accessed and viewed from the house, the arbor, patio, and plants nicely mingle the indoors with the outdoors.

Scale is particularly important when you're landscaping near the house. This design can be adapted to suit houses and properties in a range of sizes. The gridwork patio can be altered by adding or removing rows of pavers. And the plantings can be extended or reduced along the edges.

SITE: Sunny

SEASON: Summer

CONCEPT: Arbor, paving, and plants provide shade and a pleasant ambiance for outdoor relaxation and entertaining.

Door

House

Lawn

1 square = 1 ft.

Plants & Projects

The patio and arbor are sizable projects, but their rewards are large, too. Grow the lemon trees in 3-ft.-diameter terra-cotta pots, the rosemary in deep pots, 12 in. in diameter. Prune these plants to emphasize their natural shapes: a loose ball for the lemons, a narrow column for the rosemary. Keep the holly hedge neatly clipped. Train a single stem of each wisteria to twist up its arbor post.

A 'Meyer' lemon (use 5 plants)
The evergreen foliage of these small trees showcases fragrant white flowers and tangy yellow fruits borne on and off all year. Bellflowers planted in the pots provide additional interest. See *Citrus*, p. 130.

B Cascade penstemon (use 6)
This shade-tolerant native perennial has showy tubular dark purple-and-blue flowers on 1- to 2-ft. stalks summer through early fall. See *Penstemon serrulatus*, p. 141.

C Dwarf yaupon holly (use 20)
A dwarf version that reaches only 3 ft. tall and wide. Commonly used as a substitute for boxwood in Texas and the South. See *I. vomitoria*, p. 135.

D American wisteria (use 4)
This is a vigorous deciduous vine with spectacular clusters of fragrant pea-like purple or blue flowers in summer. Prune in spring to control its size and to stimulate abundant bloom. See *Wisteria frutescens*, p. 153.

E 'Goodwin Creek Gray' lavender (use 9)
This evergreen shrub's mounding gray foliage makes an attractive informal hedge. Bears spikes of blue flowers in early summer. See *Lavandula*, p. 136.

F 'Tuscan Blue' rosemary (use 4)
Trim this evergreen shrub to a tall, narrow column. Foliage is aromatic; light-blue flowers bloom in winter and spring, sometimes in fall. See *Rosmarinus officinalis*, p. 146.

G Violet wild petunia (use 31)
This versatile wildflower has modest water needs, making it well suited to Texas' droughts once well established. See *Ruellia nudiflora*, p. 148.

H Ground covers for informal paving (as needed)
Planted in the gaps between the flagstones, these perennials accent the informality of this end of the design. Snow-in-summer (*Cerastium tomentosum*, p. 128) has silver leaves and bears white flowers in early spring. Coralbells (*Heuchera*, p. 134) features neat tufts of round leaves topped from spring to late summer by red flowers. Creeping thyme (*Thymus praecox* ssp. *arcticus*, p. 151) withstands light traffic and smells good when you step on it.

I Annuals (as needed)
Change the plantings of annuals in the beds around the potted trees and shrubs for seasonal interest. In summer (the season shown here), try phlox, snapdragons, and purple basil.

J Arbor
This large arbor is designed to serve as a sunscreen for the area beneath even without a foliage canopy. See p. 188.

K Paving
Use flagstone pavers, 24 in. square, in the formal area. Press rounded pebbles into the gaps between pavers for added interest. Irregular flagstones pave the informal area. See p. 163.

L Seating wall
This low wall provides seating and should be constructed with mortared fieldstone. If your budget doesn't allow hiring a mason, buy commercially made curved wooden or precast concrete benches.

Splash Out

MAKE A HANDSOME WATER GARDEN IN A FEW WEEKENDS

SITE: Sunny

SEASON: Summer

CONCEPT: Water is a welcome presence in the landscape, especially when surrounded by lovely plants.

A water garden adds a new dimension to a home landscape. It can be the eye-catching focal point of the entire property or a quiet out-of-the-way retreat. A pond can be a hub of activity—a place to garden, watch birds and wildlife, raise ornamental fish, or stage an impromptu paper-boat race. It just as easily affords an opportunity for some therapeutic inactivity; a few minutes contemplating the ripples on the water's surface provides a welcome break in a busy day.

A pond can't be moved easily, so choose your site carefully. Practical considerations are outlined on pp. 168–171 (along with instructions on installation and on planting water plants). In addition to those considerations, think about how the pond and its plantings relate to the surroundings. Before plopping a pond down in the middle of the backyard, imagine how you might integrate it, visually if not physically, with nearby plantings and structures.

The plantings in this design are intended to settle the pond comfortably into an expanse of lawn. Flagstone paving invites visitors to stroll up to the pond's edge. Framing the pond and path are a small broadleaf evergreen tree and perennial ground covers planted in contrasting waves of color and texture. A full season of flowers in complementary blues, purples, and golds will draw hummingbirds and butterflies as surely as they delight the eye.

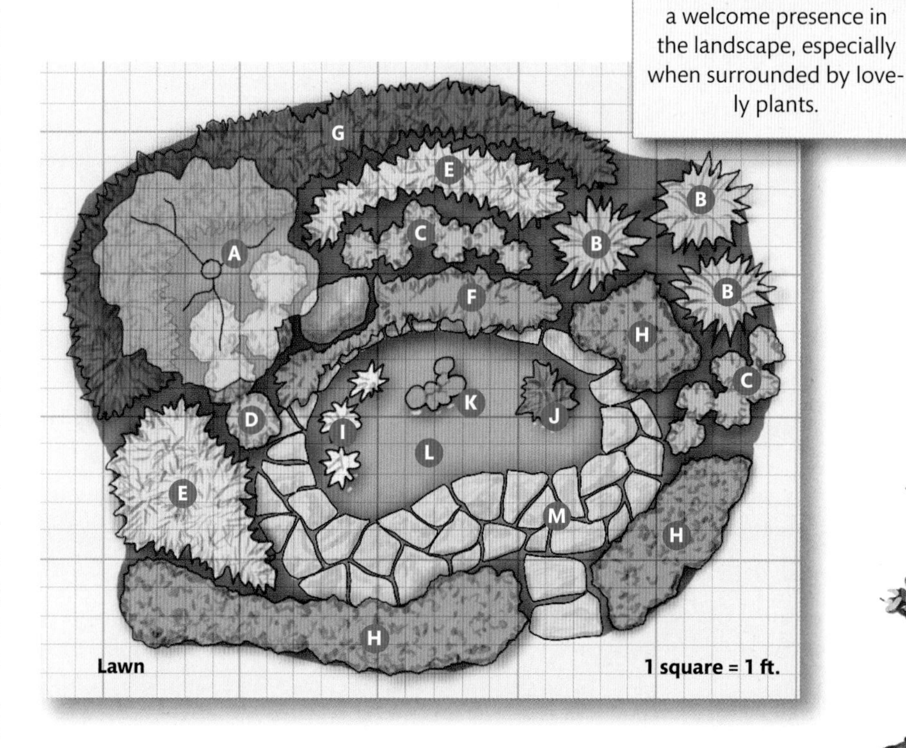

Plants & Projects

Installing a pond is arduous but simple work, requiring several weekends of energetic digging. Lay out and install the paving at the same time as the pond. Once established, the plants require only seasonal care. The pond will need regular attention to keep a healthy balance of water plants and fish (if you have them) in order to maintain oxygen levels and to keep algae in check. Consult local or mail-order suppliers to help you determine the right mix.

A Wax myrtle (use 1 plant)
This small tree adds graceful height to the pond planting. Fragrant leaves are fairly small, smooth, leathery, and evergreen; they won't litter the pond in fall. See *Myrica cerifera*, p. 139.

B Lindheimer's muhly (use 3)
A beautiful, fine-textured ornamental grass. Blue-green leaves and soft texture makes this grass popular for screening. See *Muhlenbergia lindheimeri*, p. 139.

C Mealycup sage (use 12)
This perennial's grayish green foliage is topped with many blue flower spikes visited by hummingbirds and butterflies. To keep it blooming all season, remove flowers as they fade. But don't discard them—they make wonderful dried flowers. See *Salvia farinacea*, p. 147.

D St.-John's-wort (use 5)
Bright-yellow flowers with showy stamens top this dense, mounding shrub in summer. Some will eventually cascade over the edge of the pond. The overlapping leaves are small and

oval, turning reddish purple in fall and last through winter. See *Hypericum calycinum*, p. 134.

E Texas gold columbine (use 20)
This native perennial forms a lacy clump of fernlike foliage topped with gold flowers in spring. See *Aquilegia chrysantha hinckleyana*, p. 123.

F 'Blue Pacific' shore juniper (use 3)
An evergreen shrub bearing bright blue-green trailing foliage that will fall softly over the flagstone edging and into the pond. See *Juniperus conferta* 'Blue Pacific', p. 136.

G Cedar sedge (use 30)
This clump-forming perennial grass, prefers some shade and can be combined with other woodland and meadow natives. See *Carex planostachys*, p. 127.

H 'Homestead Purple' verbena (use 6)
This perennial spreads out to form an edging of felty leaves interlaced with bright purple flowers. Cut back occasionally to encourage a new flush of bloom. See *Verbena* x *hybrida* 'Homestead Purple', p. 151.

I Louisiana iris (use 3)
This plant forms a tall clump of pale green swordlike leaves that can survive half-submerged in water. Bright yellow flowers rise a foot above the leaves in spring. Foliage is attractive year-round. See *Iris* x *Louisiana hybrids*, p. 152.

J Soft rush (use 2)
Plant this bold grasslike wetland perennial for its yellow-green flowers and low maintenance requirements. Can survive in up to 4 inches of water. See *Juncus effusus*. p. 136.

K Water lily (use 1)
No pond is complete without these lovely floating flowers. Pointed petals open in layers above saucer-shaped leaf pads. We've shown a pink-flowering cultivar here. See Water plants: *Nymphaea*, p. 152.

L Pond
You can make this pond with a commercially available flexible liner. See p. 172.

M Paving
A flagstone edge widens into a natural path around the front of the pond. See p. 163.

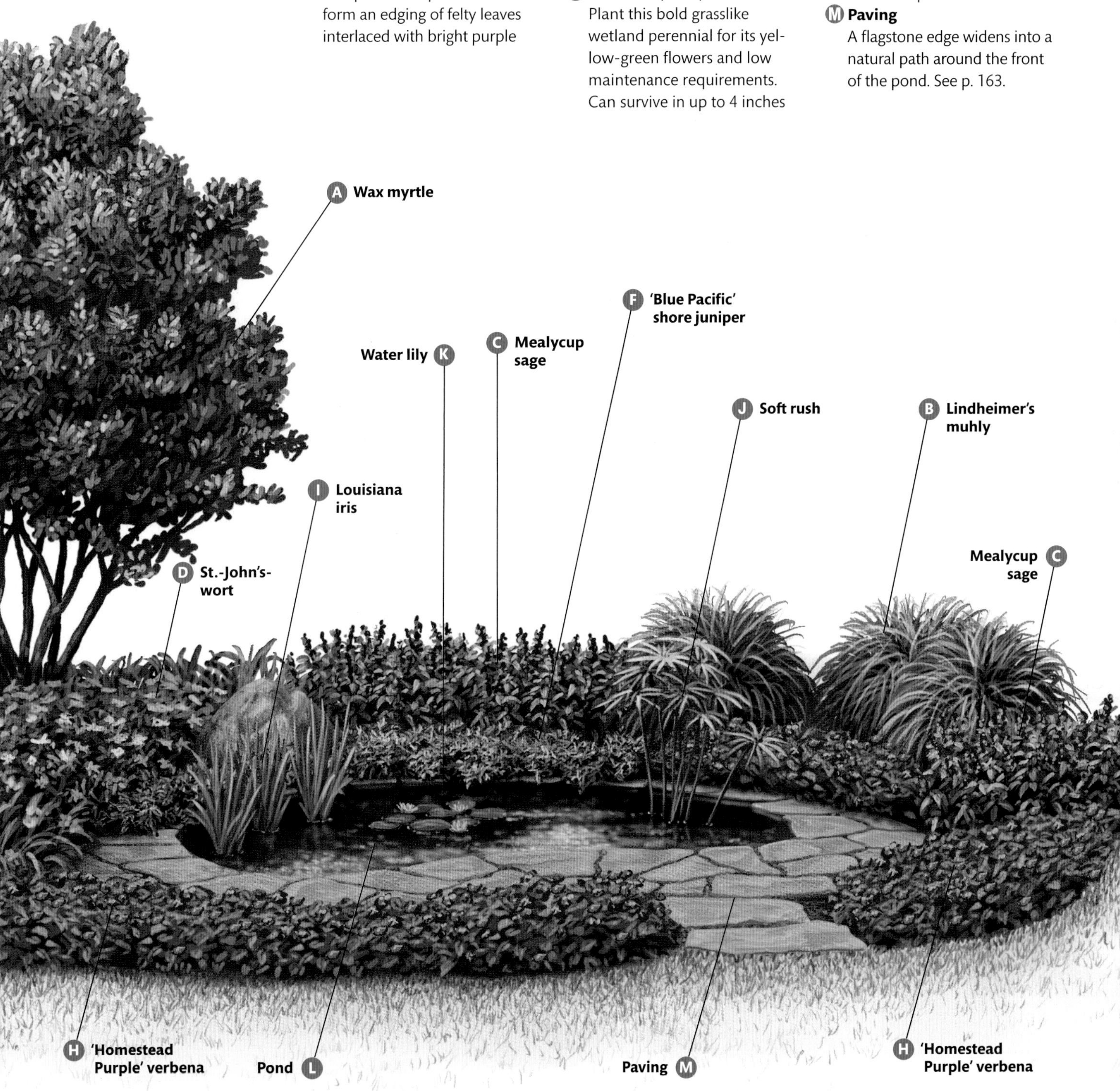

Patio pool

A little pond can make a big splash in a well-chosen setting. And it provides all the pleasures of water gardening without the energy or space required to install and maintain a larger pond. Within its confines you can enjoy water plants, fish, or even a small fountain.

The scale of this pond is just right for a small patio or as part of a larger patio planting. We've included a low fence along the per-im-eter of the patio, but the design would work just as well without it. The pond design is simple and inexpensive. We recommend using a 4-ft. diameter fiberglass tub sunk into the ground and planted all the way to the edge.

The planting displays an exuberant collection of foliage and flowers. We've selected plants that mound and arch, dangle and droop to create billowy, colorful contours around the small pool.

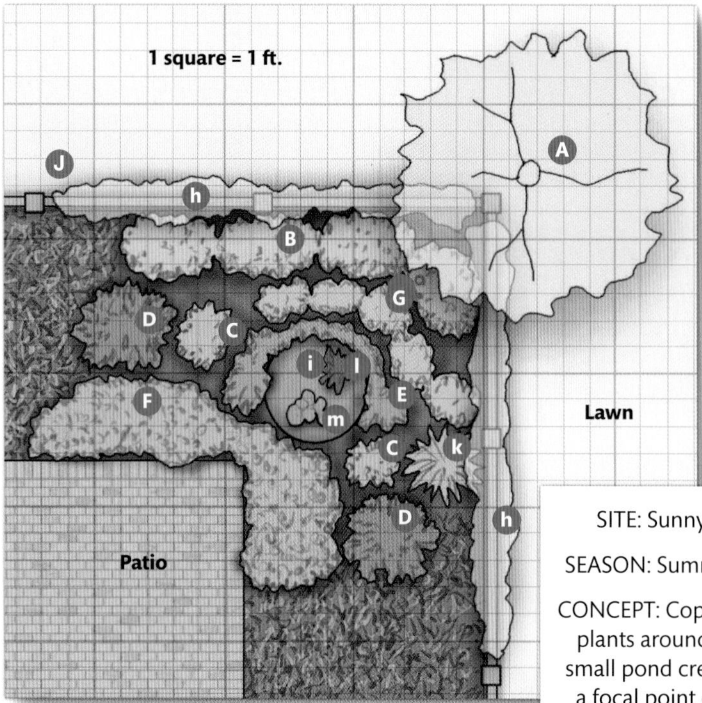

1 square = 1 ft.

Patio

Lawn

SITE: Sunny

SEASON: Summer

CONCEPT: Copious plants around a small pond create a focal point on a patio.

A 'Pink Dawn' chitalpa
B Compact Texas sage
C Autumn sage
G Tropical plumbago
H Coral vine
J Low fence
K Lindheimer's muhly
D Trailing rosemary
E Dwarf Japanese garden juniper
I Pond
M Water lily
L Soft rush
F 'Blue Princess' verbena

Plants & Projects

A 'Pink Dawn' chitalpa (use 1 plant)
This small fast-growing deciduous tree provides an open airy backdrop for the patio planting as well as decorative gray bark, attractive pale green leaves, and pink ruffled flowers. See x *Chitalpa tashkentensis* 'Pink Dawn', p. 129.

B Compact Texas sage (use 4)
Silver-gray foliage suffused with orchid pink blooms distinguish this evergreen shrub. It provides a soft background for the flower display in summer and a privacy screen during winter. See *Leucophyllum frutescens* 'Compactum', p. 138.

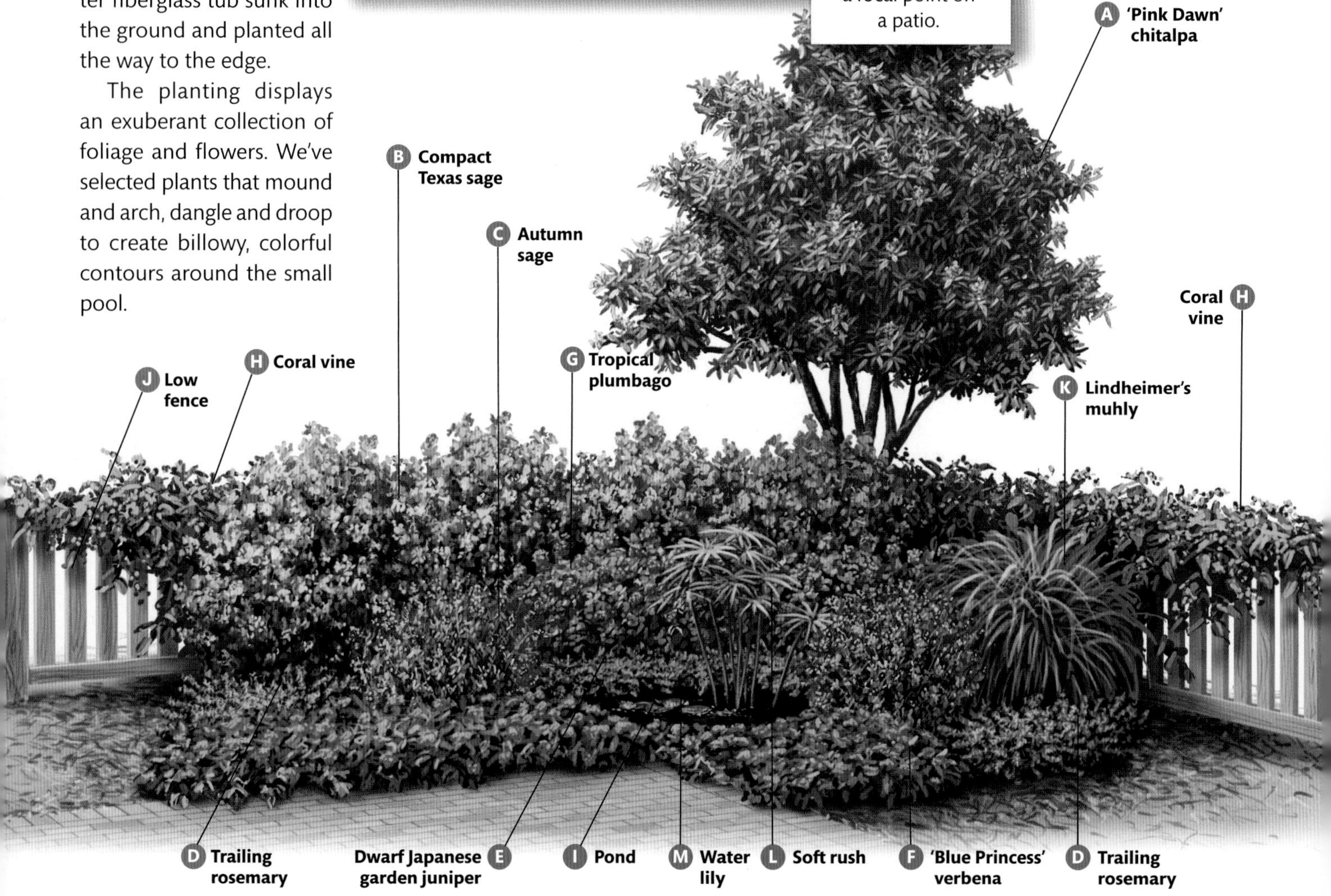

C Autumn sage (use 2)
Loose clusters of pretty flowers bloom at the tips of this bushy perennial's branches all season. Choose a cultivar with pink flowers for this planting. See *Salvia greggii*, p. 147.

D Trailing rosemary (use 2)
An attractive evergreen shrub, it forms a sprawling mound of needle-thin leaves that are both fragrant and tasty. Small blue flowers appear in spring and off and on through the year. See *Rosmarinus officinalis* 'Prostratus', p. 146.

E Dwarf Japanese garden juniper (use 3)
This beautiful compact shrub forms a blue-green mat of dense evergreen needles, layered sprays of which will eventually spill over the edge of the pond. See *Juniperus procubens* 'Nana', p. 136.

F 'Blue Princess' verbena (use 5)
This perennial produces clusters of small flowers from spring through fall (year-round in areas with mild winters). Its lavender-blue flowers complement the color scheme well. See *Verbena* x *hybrida* 'Blue Princess', p. 151.

G Tropical plumbago (use 5)
This perennial contributes baby blue flowers and fresh green foliage to the planting. See *Plumbago auriculata*, p. 142.

H Coral vine (use 2)
Grown for its showy panicles of tiny heart-shaped pink blossoms. Plant two of these vines and train them along the fence. They will cover it quickly. See *Antigonon leptopus*, p. 123.

I Pond
Bury a 4-ft.-diameter watertight tub and add water plants or a fountain, as you wish. See p. 170.

J Low fence
This variation on a picket fence frames the pond and patio nicely. See pp. 194-195.

See pp. 98-99 for the following:

K Lindheimer's muhly (use 1)

L Soft rush (use 1)

M Water lily (use 1)

PLANT PORTRAITS

Whether growing in the water or nearby, these plants combine fresh foliage and lovely flowers for your poolside pleasure.

● = First design, pp. 98-99

▲ = Second design, pp. 100-101

'Blue Pacific' shore juniper
(*Juniperus conferta*, p. 136) ●

Coral vine
(*Antigonon leptopus*, p. 123) ▲

Dwarf Japanese garden juniper
(*Juniperus procubens* 'Nana', p. 136) ▲

Water lily
(Water plants: *Nymphaea*, p. 152) ● ▲

'Pink Dawn' chitalpa
(x *Chitalpa tashkentensis*, p. 129) ▲

Poolside Pleasures

PLANTINGS ENHANCE YOUR SWIMMING POOL

Swimming pools are an increasingly common backyard amenity in many Texas communities. On a suburban lot, a pool is often the dominant backyard presence. Too often, however, the backyard pool is little more than an aquatic gym surrounded by a slab of concrete and lawn.

This design shows that a planting of trees, shrubs, and perennials and a little hardscaping can work magic to enhance all your outdoor activities, whether you're escaping with a good book, entertaining friends, working in the garden, or playing in the pool. (The rendering shows the design as seen from the house, which is indicated on the plan.)

Tall shrubs on the perimeter heighten the sense of enclosure and privacy provided by the fence, which building codes usually require around a pool. The paving surrounding the pool extends at each end to accommodate a table and chairs for entertaining and recliners for relaxing. An arbor creates a little niche along one side. Low-growing plants lining the surround add color and texture to the setting. And there's still ample lawn for playing games and lounging.

SITE: Sunny

SEASON: Spring

CONCEPT: A poolside filled with flowers and foliage lets you go for a swim in the garden.

Plants & Projects

The plants in this design are chosen not only for their year-round good looks, but also because they are well-behaved around a pool. All are low-maintenance evergreens that hold on to their foliage throughout the year, producing as little litter as possible. You won't be fishing leaves out of the water as you would with deciduous trees and shrubs.

A Wax myrtle (use 5)
This small tree adds graceful height to the pond planting. Fragrant leaves are fairly small, smooth, leathery, and evergreen; they won't litter the pond in fall. See *Myrica cerifera*, p. 139.

B Compact Texas sage (use 15)
Silver-gray foliage suffused with orchid pink blooms distinguish this evergreen shrub. It provides a soft background for the flower display in summer and a privacy screen during winter. See *Leucophyllum frutescens 'Compactum'*, p. 138.

C 'Cherry Chief' autumn sage (use 19)
This bushy perennial's small oval leaves echo the holly's foliage, but

are softer and paler. Small red flowers bloom heavily in spring and lightly in summer and fall. See *Salvia greggii 'Cherry Chief'*, p. 147.

D Oakleaf hydrangea (use 2)
A lobed shrub with oak-like foliage. Leathery green leaves turn purple, red, and bronze in the fall. See *Hydrangea quercifolia*, p. 134.

E Magnolia 'Little Gem' (use 3)
A dwarf southern magnolia with small, dark-green foliage and a compact form. Large, white blooms. See *Magnolia grandiflora*, p. 138.

F New Jersey Tea (use 7)
This small shrub establishes deep roots, growing in dry and rocky soils, it is not suited to wet soils. See *Ceanothus americanus*, p. 128.

G Texas star hibiscus (as needed)
This perennial forms a large airy clump of slender, deeply divided, glossy leaves borne on red-tinged stems. Brilliant red five-petaled flowers open daily during the summer and fall. See *Hibiscus coccineus*, p. 134.

H Winter-blooming bergenia (as needed)
Large round leaves with wavy margins distinguish this evergreen perennial. Pink flowers form on short thick spikes in winter. Plant the clumps 18 in. apart for a continuous border. See *Bergenia crassifolia*, p. 125.

I Carolina jessamine (as needed)
Shiny neat evergreen leaves and a show of fragrant yellow flowers in spring make this vigorous vine ideal for training up porch columns or along a railing. See *Gelsemium sempervirens*, p. 133.

J Arbor
Easily built, this attractive structure provides a central focal point and a welcome sun screen by the pool. See p. 188.

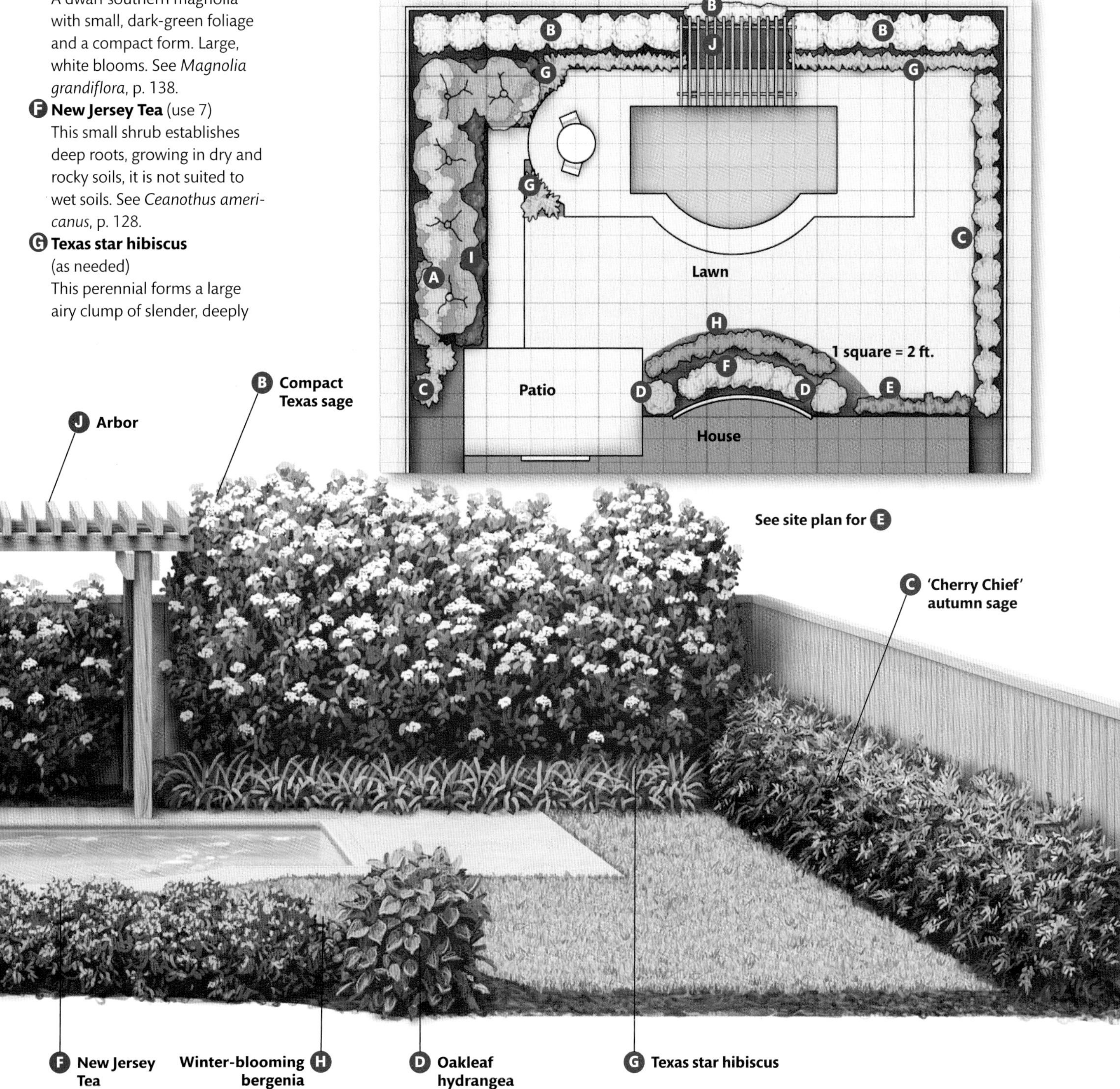

Down to Earth

HARMONIZE YOUR DECK WITH ITS SURROUNDINGS

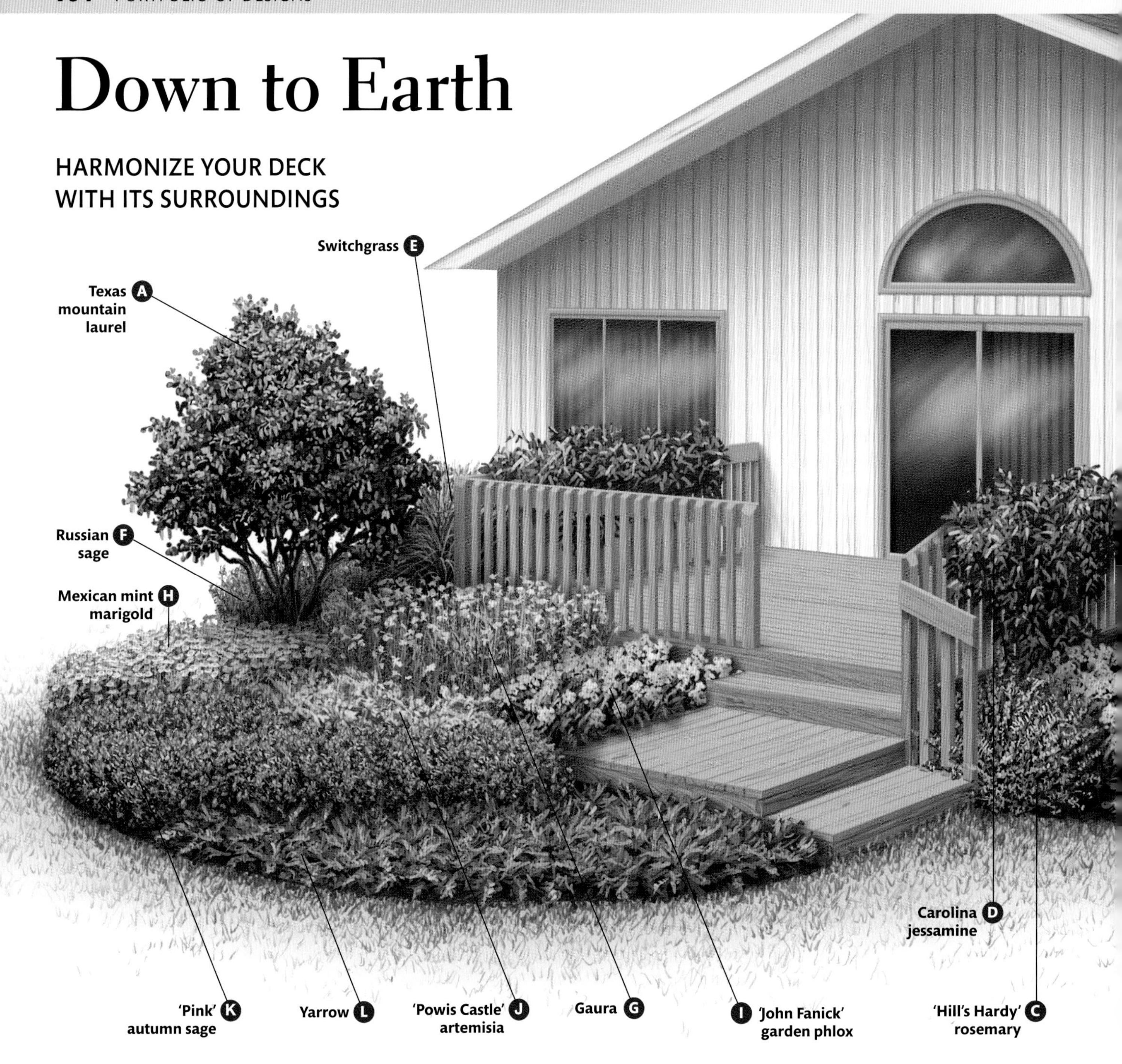

A backyard deck is a perfect spot for enjoying the garden. Too often, however, the deck offers little connection to its surroundings. Perched on bare posts above a patch of lawn, it is a lonely outpost rather than an inviting gateway to the world of plants and wildlife.

This design nestles the deck into its immediate surroundings while preserving the vista from the deck and the windows. The one exception to the low landscape of shrubs, vines, and ground covers is a small tree, whose fragrant spring flowers and attractive foliage will improve rather than screen the view.

Decreasing in height from the deck to the ground, the planting makes it easier for the eye to move between levels. Switchgrass and rosemary rise railing-high on one side of the deck, and New Jersey Teas fill in the other. Around the grasses is an airy border of Russian sage. A lower edging of fine-leaved yarrow frames the front of the deck.

Striking to look at, this deckside planting appeals to other senses as well. In March and April the large flower clusters of Texas mountain laurel will give off their distinctive fragrance. (Some liken it to grape soda.) The spring air will also carry the heady perfume of Carolina jessamine. Many of the plants also have fragrant leaves, releasing their pungence to the touch or on their own when days are hot. A few are flavorful too, adding zest to culinary dishes.

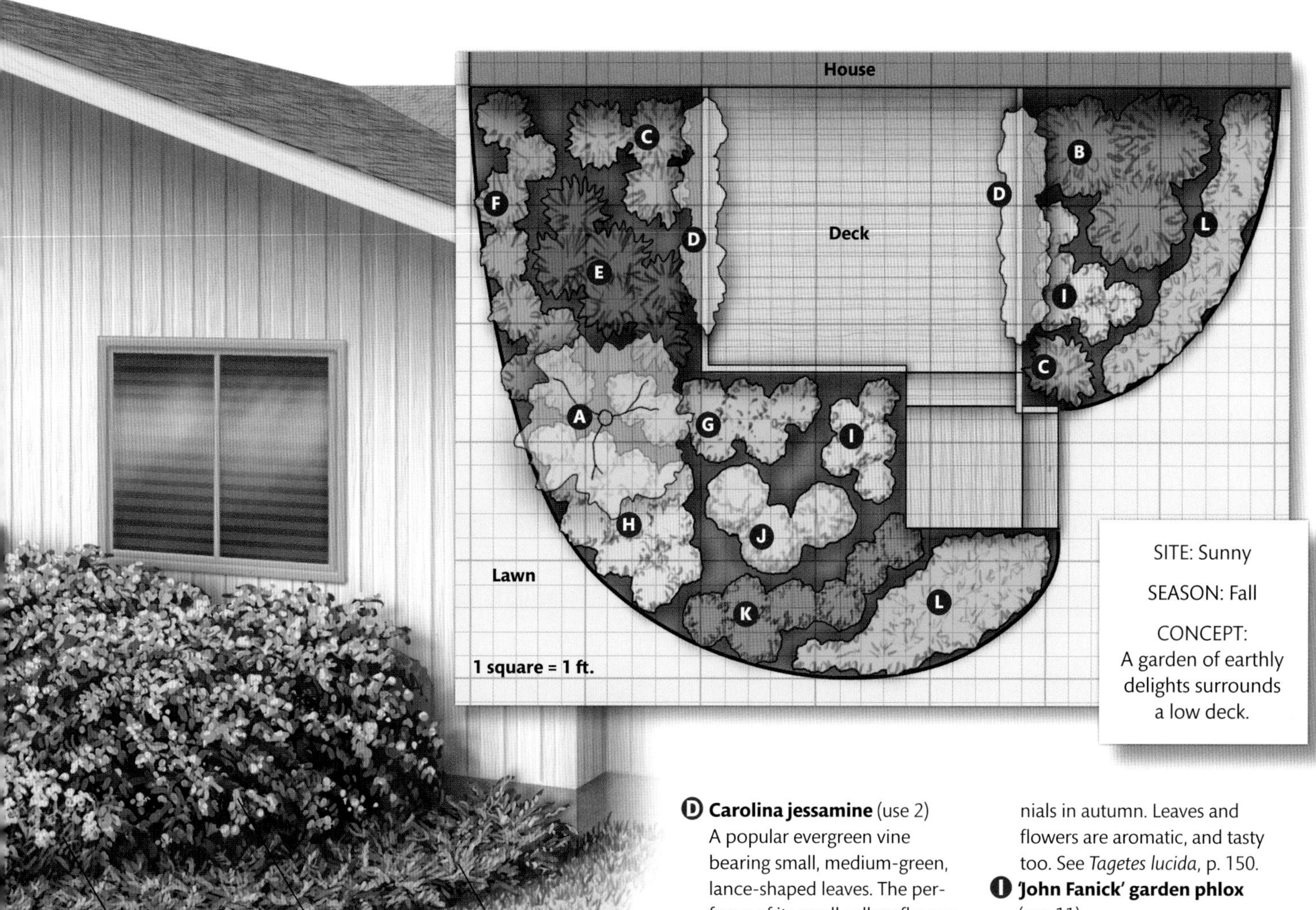

Plants & Projects

You'll need to water young plants to get them established. But after a year or two, these durable perennials and shrubs will require infrequent supplemental watering and little care beyond routine seasonal pruning and clean up.

A Texas mountain laurel
(use 1 plant)
Fragrant purple flowers will entice you outdoors in early spring. This native shrub or tree has interesting gnarled branches and shiny evergreen foliage. See *Dermatophyllum secundiflorum*, p. 131.

B New Jersey Tea (use 3)
This small shrub establishes deep roots, growing in dry and rocky soils, it is not suited to wet soils. See *Ceanothus americanus*, p. 128.

C 'Hill's Hardy' rosemary (use 4)
This attractive evergreen shrub deserves a spot by the steps. Crush a few leaves in your hand as you go by to release their pungent aroma. The piney branches are dotted with fragrant lavender-blue flowers in late winter and spring. See *Rosmarinus officinalis* 'Hills Hardy', p. 146.

D Carolina jessamine (use 2)
A popular evergreen vine bearing small, medium-green, lance-shaped leaves. The perfume of its small yellow flowers will intoxicate on early spring days. See *Gelsemium sempervirens*, p. 133.

E Switchgrass (use 6)
This grass grows 3–5 ft. tall, producing fine-textured lacey seedheads in late summer which persist throughout winter. See *Panicum virgatum*, p. 140.

F Russian sage (use 8)
This erect perennial forms a vase of silvery see-through stems and small aromatic gray leaves. Tiny pale-blue flowers bloom along stem tips from spring through summer. See *Perovskia atriplicifolia*, p. 141.

G Gaura (use 7)
Masses of delicate white to pink flowers float above low clumps of pale-green foliage from spring through summer. A favorite of butterflies. See *Gaura lindheimeri*, p. 132.

H Mexican mint marigold
(use 13)
Golden daisylike blossoms smother these upright perennials in autumn. Leaves and flowers are aromatic, and tasty too. See *Tagetes lucida*, p. 150.

I 'John Fanick' garden phlox
(use 11)
Big, fragrant clusters of long-blooming flowers make this perennial a great one to plant near patios and decks. This mildew-resistant cultivar bears pink flowers from spring to July. See *Phlox paniculata* 'John Fanick', p. 141.

J 'Powis Castle' artemisia (use 3)
This perennial's silvery foliage makes a beautiful foil for the pale-pink gaura flowers and the deeper pink of the autumn sage. See *Artemisia* x 'Powis Castle', p. 124.

K 'Pink' autumn sage (use 7)
Fine-textured bushy perennial with small oval medium-green leaves and spikes of bright-pink flowers. Blooms nonstop from March to October. See *Salvia greggii* 'Pink', p. 147.

L Yarrow (use 36)
The dense ferny foliage of this mounding perennial makes a fine edging. You can choose among many flower colors. Blooms in spring. See *Achillea millefolium*, p. 122.

Skirting a shady deck

This design also integrates the deck with its surroundings but does so in a shadier environment produced perhaps by large trees nearby. The layout is similar to the previous one, but the plants are shade-lovers from the forest understory.

This woodland garden of mostly deciduous platings offers a changing landscape throughout the year. A native redbud by the deck marks each of the seasons as it flowers, leafs out, turns gold, and bares its branches. For balance on the other side of the deck, a cherry laurel provides an evergreen presence. The railings are draped with cross vine and autumn clematis, two vines that bloom beautifully in shade. Wrapping around the deck is a collection of shrubs and ground covers for a woodland setting. Inland sea oats is one of the best ornamental grasses for a shaded area. And what woodland would be complete without some ferns? A leafy ground cover of Virginia creeper grows at their feet, underplanted with a host of narcissus for early spring color and fragrance.

Plants & Projects

A Redbud (use 1 plant)
This small native deciduous tree brings pink flowers to the deck in spring and a canopy of heart-shaped leaves in summer. Foliage turns yellow in fall. See *Cercis canadensis*, p. 128.

B Compact Carolina cherry laurel (use 1)
A glossy-leaved evergreen shrub with enough stature to balance the redbud. Trim to enhance the plant's natural conical shape. Inconspicuous but fragrant spring flowers are followed by black berries. See *Prunus caroliniana* 'Compacta', p. 142.

C American beautyberry (use 1)
This deciduous shrub creates a loose thicket of arching branches lined in fall with long-lasting purple berries. See *Callicarpa americana*, p. 127.

D 'Tangerine Beauty' cross vine (use 1)
An evergreen climber with lustrous deep-green foliage. It produces showy clusters

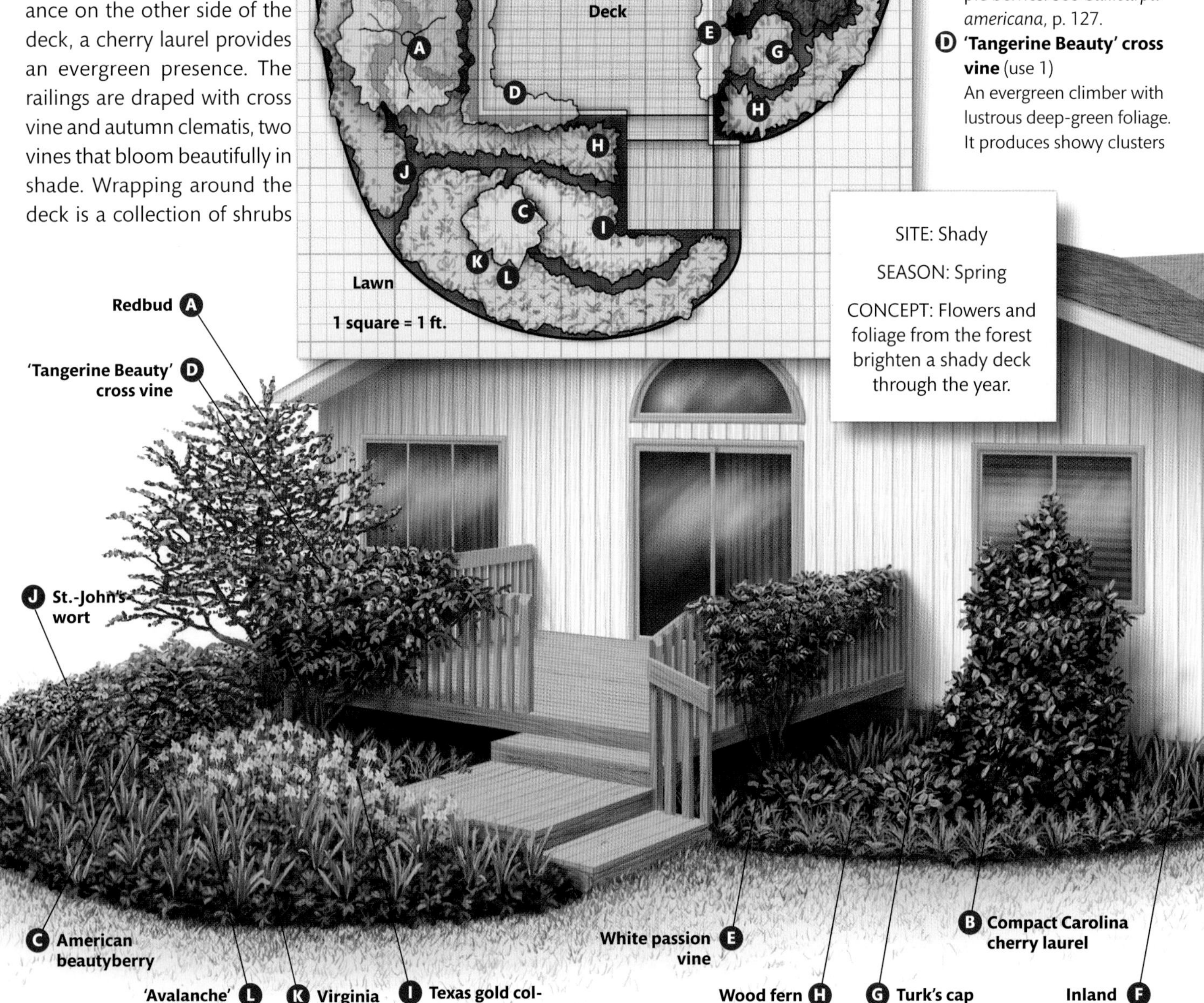

SITE: Shady

SEASON: Spring

CONCEPT: Flowers and foliage from the forest brighten a shady deck through the year.

of orange trumpet flowers in spring and occasionally afterwards. See *Bignonia capreolata*, p. 124.

E **White passion vine** (use 1)
This very striking deciduous vine grows in full sun to part shade, and it blooms from spring through fall. See *Passiflora incarnata 'Alba,'* page 141.

F **Inland sea oats** (use 30)
This grass grows in a dense upright clump that reaches knee height. In late summer, decorative seed heads unfurl among the leaves. See *Chasmanthium latifolium*, p. 128.

G **Turk's cap** (use 3)
After emerging from dormancy, this perennial will grow 2 ft. tall and 3 ft. wide by summer. It bears lobed leaves and curious red flowers. See *Malvaviscus arboreus drummondii*, p. 139.

H **Wood fern** (use 44)
Lacy, bright green fronds distinguish this woodland fern. See Ferns: *Thelypteris kunthii*, p. 132.

I **Texas gold columbine** (use 23)
A decorative screen for the space under the deck, this native perennial forms a lacy clump of fernlike foliage topped with gold flowers in spring. See *Aquilegia chrysantha hinckleyana*, p. 123.

J **St.-John's-wort** (use 18)
A low-growing semi-evergreen shrub that forms a fine-textured mound of small oval leaves, turning red and purple in fall. Bears five-petaled yellow flowers in summer. See *Hypericum calycinum*, p. 134.

K **Virginia creeper** (use 3)
Usually grown as a climber, this native deciduous vine is also useful as a ground cover. Compound leaves turn colorful in the autumn. See *Parthenocissus quinquefolia*, p. 141.

L **'Avalanche' narcissus** (use 35)
This bulb produces small white-and-yellow flowers in early spring. See Bulbs: *Narcissus tazetta* 'Avalanche', p. 126.

PLANT PORTRAITS

These plants can enhance a deck with lovely foliage textures, colors, and pretty flowers.
● = First design, pp. 105-106
▲ = Second design, pp. 107-108

'Tangerine Beauty' cross vine
(*Bignonia capreolata*, p. 124) ▲

Virginia creeper
(*Parthenocissus quinquefolia*, p. 141) ▲

'Avalanche' narcissus
(Bulbs: *Narcissus tazetta*, p. 126) ▲

Decked-out Deck

SITE: Sunny

SEASON: Early summer

CONCEPT: A pleasing mix of durable plants integrates a low deck with its hillside surroundings.

MAKE YOUR DECK AN INVITING GATEWAY TO THE OUTDOORS.

In the design shown here, a low deck nestles in a planting of trees, shrubs, and perennials. The plants provide shade and privacy as well as lovely flowers and foliage and the birds and other wildlife attracted to them. Conceived for a dry, hilly site with a backyard that slopes down from the deck, the planting makes effective use of terrain where play areas are impractical and a manicured lawn or traditional garden beds are difficult to maintain. (The planting can easily be adapted for sites that are steeper or more level than the gradual slope shown here.)

The plants are chosen for their ability to thrive in the hot, dry conditions found in many parts of Texas. Western redbud, manzanita, and ceanothus are joined by tough plants that are ideal for semiarid regions. There are flowers for much of the year, and a mixture of evergreen and deciduous foliage provides delightful colors and textures year-round. The planting makes a seamless transition to the surrounding cover of native grasses and wildflowers that naturally colonize such hillsides. Mow a path through this "volunteer" ground cover and extend the planting as far as you wish down the hill.

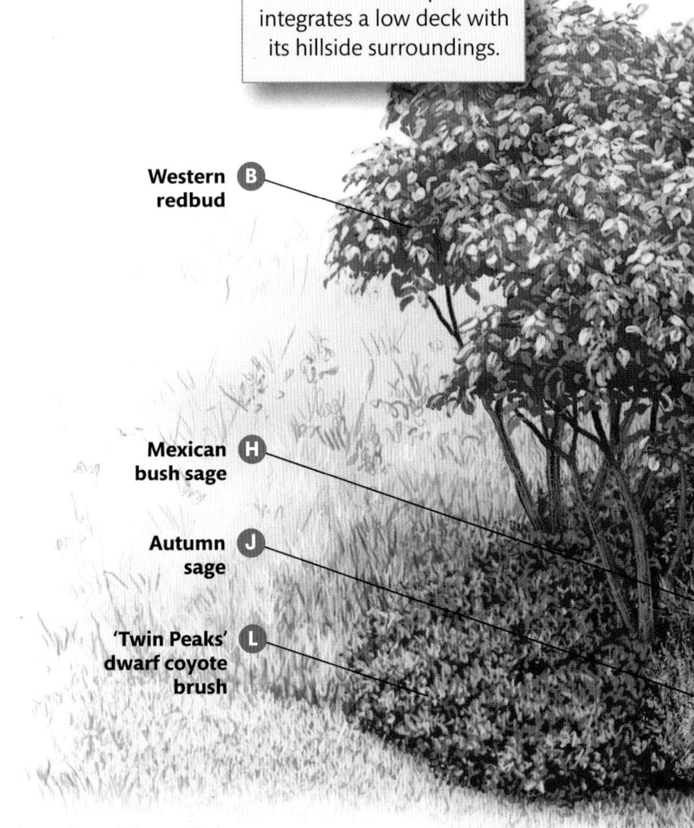

Plants & Projects

You'll need to water young plants to get them established. But after a year or two, these durable perennials, trees, and shrubs will require infrequent supplemental watering and a minimum of care. Prune the shrubs (particularly the hop bushes and the salvia) to keep them from overgrowing their neighbors. Shear the dwarf coyote brush each spring. Divide any perennials that become crowded.

A Chitalpa (use 1 plant)
This attractive deciduous tree has a wide crown of airy foliage and bears eye-catching clusters of ruffled pink or white flowers in early summer. See x *Chitalpa tashkentensis*, p. 128.

B Western redbud (use 3)
Tiny magenta flowers line the bare branches of this small multitrunked deciduous tree in spring. Bright-green summer foliage turns yellow in fall. See *Cercis occidentalis*, p. 128.

C Purple hop bush (use 3)
Native to the Southwest, this tough evergreen shrub has bronze-green foliage that turns purple in winter. See *Dodonaea viscosa* 'Purpurea', p. 131.

D 'Julia Phelps' ceanothus (use 4)
This popular evergreen shrub displays clusters of blue flowers against a backdrop of deep-green foliage in spring. See *Ceanothus*, p. 128.

E 'Howard McMinn' manzanita (use 7)
Lining the path, this evergreen shrub forms mounds of shiny dark-green foliage. Small white-to-pink spring flowers produce red berries. See *Arctostaphyllos densiflora*, p. 123.

F 'Indigo Spires' salvia (use 1)
This lush, vigorous perennial makes a bushy mound of triangular leaves topped all season with long spikes of blue-purple flowers. See *Salvia x 'Indigo Spires,'*, p. 147.

G Texas mountain laurel (use 1)
Clusters of purple flowers hang from this small glossy evergreen tree in early spring. Passersby on both sides of the fence will appreciate the delightful perfume. Bean pods with bright-red seeds follow the flowers. See *Sophora secundiflora*, p. 131.

H Mexican bush sage (use 8)
A shrubby perennial, its gray-green foliage contrasts nicely with the dark-evergreen leaves of nearby plants. Long spikes of purple-and-white flowers bloom from late spring to fall. See *Salvia leucantha*, p. 147.

I 'Tuscan Blue' rosemary (use 4)
The needlelike dark-green leaves of this evergreen shrub add interesting texture to the planting. Small deep-blue flowers appear in late winter and early spring. See *Rosmarinus officinalis*, p. 146.

J Autumn sage (use 11)
This bushy perennial's medium-green leaves are topped from spring to fall with airy spikes of red flowers. Place two plants in each of the planters on the wide steps leading up to the deck. See *Salvia greggii*, p. 147.

K 'Yellow Wave' New Zealand flax (use 4)
This evergreen perennial's colorful spray of swordlike leaves is topped in summer by tubular red flowers on tall stalks. See *Phormium tenax*, p. 141.

L 'Twin Peaks' dwarf coyote brush (use 10)
The dense foliage of this low, spreading evergreen shrub makes a fine ground cover. See *Baccharis pilularis*, p. 124.

M Path
A path mowed through the native grasses and wildflowers on the hillside will be easier to maintain than a path of wood chips or other loose material.

Chitalpa A
'Indigo Spires' salvia F
Texas mountain laurel G
'Yellow Wave' New Zealand flax K
Purple hop bush C
H Mexican bush sage
E 'Howard McMinn' manzanita
J Autumn sage
M Path
D 'Julia Phelps' ceanothus
'Tuscan Blue' rosemary I
'Howard McMinn' manzanita E
House
Planters
Deck
1 square = 1 ft.
Native grasses and wildflowers

A Green Screen

HIDE REFUSE AND RECYCLING BINS WITH A FENCE AND FOLIAGE

Sometimes the simplest landscaping project packs a surprisingly big punch. This design creates a multipurpose space for storing waste and recycling bins, bags of compost, or other items that don't quite fit in the garage, keeping them out of sight but easily accessible. The paving, screen, and plantings can be installed in a weekend. With this small investment of time and money you can turn a frequently visited part of your property into a more inviting feature.

A wooden screen angles around a paved area that is roomy enough to hold recycling bins, yard-waste containers, and even a lawnmower. Made of thin vertical slats, the screen obscures the area from view yet allows ventilation. It opens at the driveway, where the bins or the mower are most likely to be wheeled out. Against the screen, a simple planting of shrubs, vines, and perennials makes a bold year-round display.

Flowers, foliage, and fruit offer warm colors throughout the year. The planting stays cheery even in the winter months. Then, the autumn sage will be bright purple; dormant grasses will wave their plumes; and the rosemary will begin to offer blue flowers, while continuing to recycle fresh and fragrant greenery.

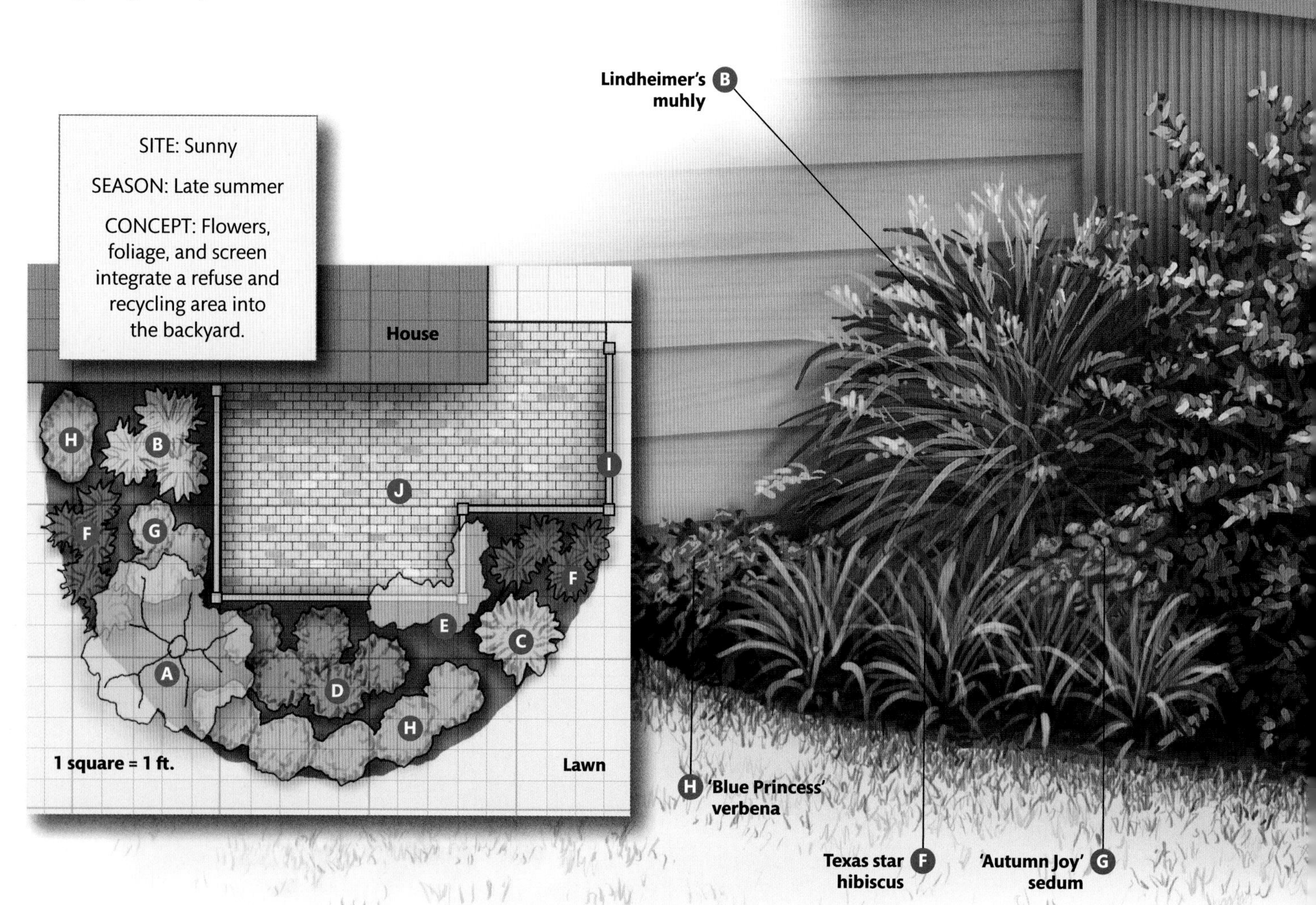

Spend a weekend installing this project. Then keep it looking good with no more than seasonal care.

A 'Wonderful' pomegranate (use 1 plant)
A very ornamental deciduous shrub, it decorates the space with graceful branches, glossy leaves, large orange flowers, and bright fruits as big and sweet as apples. See *Punica granatum* 'Wonderful', p. 143.

B Lindheimer's muhly (use 3)
A beautiful, fine-textured ornamental grass. Blue-green leaves and soft texture makes this grass popular for screening. See *Muhlenbergia lindheimeri*, p. 139.

C 'Hill's Hardy' rosemary (use 1)
This Mediterranean shrub is prized in the garden and the kitchen for its fine-textured fragrant evergeen foliage. Small blue flowers make a welcome appearance in late winter. See *Rosmarinus officinalis* 'Hill's Hardy', p. 146.

D 'Cherry Chief' autumn sage (use 5)
This bushy perennial's small oval leaves echo the holly's foliage, but are softer and paler. Small red flowers bloom heavily in spring and lightly in summer and fall. See *Salvia greggii 'Cherry Chief'*, p. 147.

E White passion vine (use 1)
This very striking deciduous vine grows in full sun to part shade, and it blooms from spring through fall. See P*assiflora incarnata 'Alba,'* page 141.

F Texas star hibiscus (use 9)
This perennial forms a large airy clump of slender, deeply divided, glossy leaves borne on red-tinged stems. Brilliant red five-petaled flowers open daily during the summer and fall. See *Hibiscus coccineus*, p. 134.

G 'Autumn Joy' sedum (use 3)
A great perennial partner for maiden grass, large succulent leaves and flat-topped flower heads create bold contrast. Blooms turn from pink to tan from late summer to fall. See *Sedum* 'Autumn Joy', p. 149.

H 'Blue Princess' verbena (use 6)
This perennial spreads to form a fine mat of leaves topped with lavender-blue flowers. Continuous bloom from spring to autumn if regularly deadheaded. See *Verbena* x *hybrida* 'Blue Princess', p. 151.

I Screen
A simple structure of louvered slats screens bins from sight while allowing air to circulate. See p. 192.

J Paving
Simple to install, precast pavers make a durable surface that is easy to sweep up when bags break or bins overflow. See p. 168.

See site plan for J.

White passion vine E

I Screen

C 'Hill's Hardy' rosemary

A 'Wonderful' pomegranate

D 'Cherry Chief' autumn sage

H 'Blue Princess' verbena

Screen for a shady site

The concept here is similar to that in the preceding design—create a storage area and screen it from view with just a weekend's work. The difference is that the plants in this design will do all the screening and thrive in dappled shade.

On the side facing the house, evergreen shrubs make an effective and attractive screen throughout the year. A small flowering tree and perennials taper off the screen around the back, creating a more open view from the backyard.

The tones and textures of the evergreen foliage will look cool and refreshing in the heat of summer. And the purples and greens will brighten up fall and winter months. Flowers add to the seasonal display, starting with redbud and columbine in early spring. Mexican petunia and 'Superbena purple' follow in summer, and pink camellias arrive in autumn.

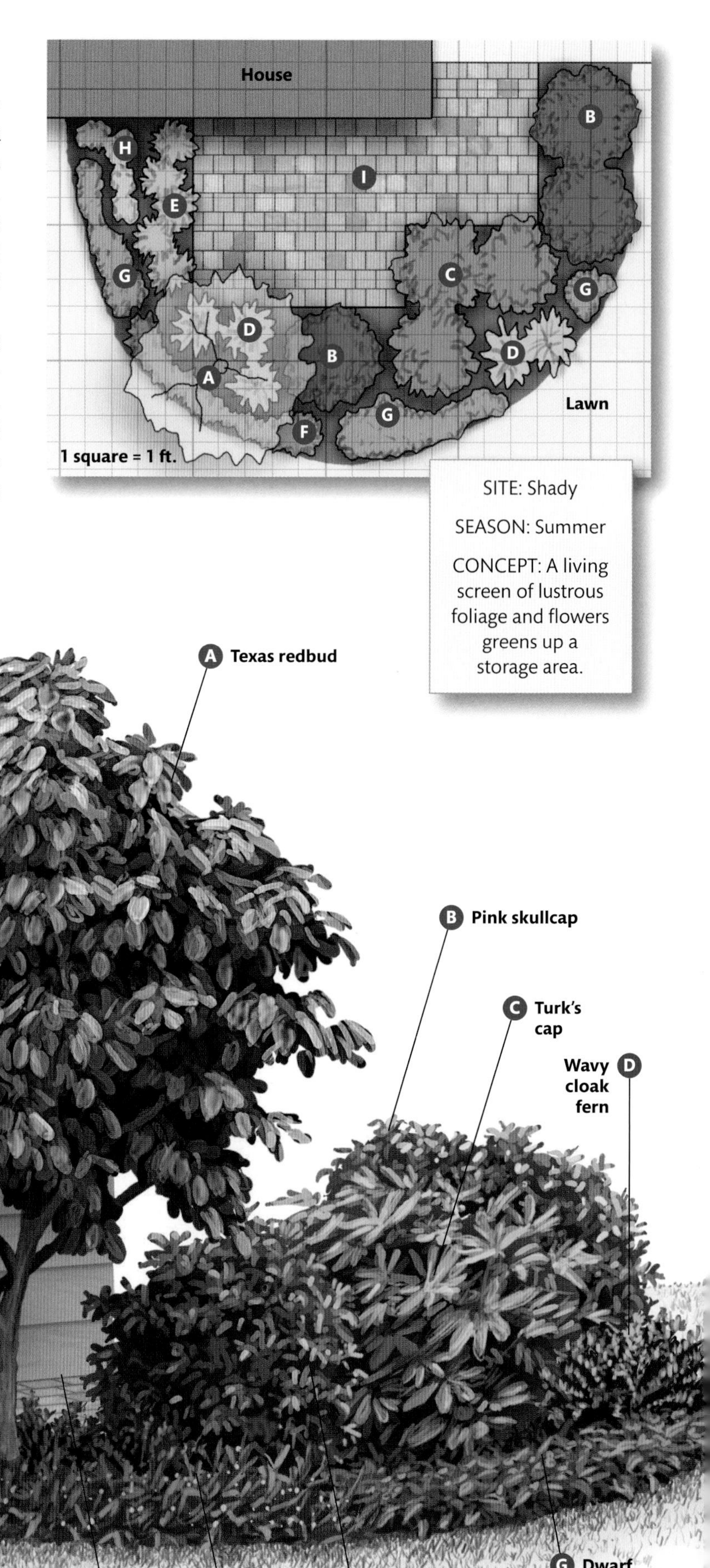

Plants & Projects

A Texas redbud (use 1 plant)
This lovely small tree provides a pleasant canopy for benchsitters in every season. Small pink blossoms line bare branches in early spring, giving way to shiny heart-shaped green leaves scattered with light-green bean pods in summer, and bright-yellow leaves in fall. Hints of violet-purple on the gray bark brighten up the branches in dull winter months. See *Cercis texensis*, p. 128.

B Pink skullcap (use 3)
A low-growing deciduous mound with pink flowers that requires full sun and low water. See *Scutellaria sufftutescens*, p. 149.

C Turk's cap (use 3)
A Texas favorite, this perennial forms a low bush of large leaves and red turbanlike flowers in summer. Hummingbirds attracted to the flowers will hover near the bench. Other birds may stop by for the cherrylike berries. See *Malvaviscus arboreus drummondii*, p. 139.

D Wavy cloak fern (use 5)
This semi-evergreen fern produces clumps of attractive rich green foliage, with a contrasting cinnamon underside. See *Astrolepsis sinuata*, p. 124.

E Inland sea oats (use 5)
This perennial grass creates an informal knee-high hedge; green in summer, russet in winter. In midsummer distinctive seed heads dangle among the foliage. See *Chasmanthium latifolium*, p. 128.

F 'Superbena purple' (use 3)
This spreading native blooms all summer, growing in full sun, it is heat and drought tolerant. See *Verbena hybrid*, p. 151.

G Dwarf Mexican petunia (use 19)
With its dark-green foliage and lavender-purple flowers this perennial makes an attractive informal border. See *Ruellia brittoniana* 'Katie', p. 148.

H Texas gold columbine (use 4)
Native to Texas, this perennial forms a neat mound behind the coarser ruellia. In spring it sends up slender stalks of golden flowers. See *Aquilegia chrysantha hinckleyana*, p. 123.

See p. 111 for the following:

I Paving

PLANT PORTRAITS

A mix of carefree plants creates or complements a colorful screen in all seasons.

● = First design, pp. 110-111

▲ = Second design, pp. 112-113

Pink skullcap
(*Scutellaria sufftutescens*, p. 149) ▲

White passion vine
(*Passiflora incarnata 'Alba'*, p. 141) ●

'Superbena purple'
(*Verbena x hybrid*, p. 151) ▲

Texas redbud (*Cercis texensis*, p. 128) ▲

Planting in the Pines

SURROUND YOUR WOODLAND DECK WITH FLOWERING SHRUBS

This simple patio planting is intended for a home (or home away from home) located on a wooded slope. Permanent residences and weekend retreats alike often feature backyard terraces or decks nestled in the pines, where fresh mountain air, cool evenings, and wildlife can be enjoyed year-round.

Numerous desirable ornamental plants thrive in dry mid-elevations. This design features drought-tolerant and fire-resistant trees and shrubs that look beautiful and natural in a setting of mature conifers.

Western redbuds that are planted around the deck create a leafy canopy among the bare trunks of taller pines. Beneath and around them are a selection of lower-growing shrubs displaying contrasting bold and fine-textured foliage and springtime flowers. The entire planting is edged in a foot-high swath of bright green foliage.

Like the surroundings, the planting will be in full bloom in spring, with masses of white, yellow, and pink flowers. The evergreen foliage looks fresh throughout the rest of the year.

Wildfires are always a concern in dry areas. To protect your home, keep areas near the house well irrigated and keep vegetation 15 to 20 feet from the house. For other tips on how to keep your home safe from wildfires, contact your local fire department or state Department of Forestry.

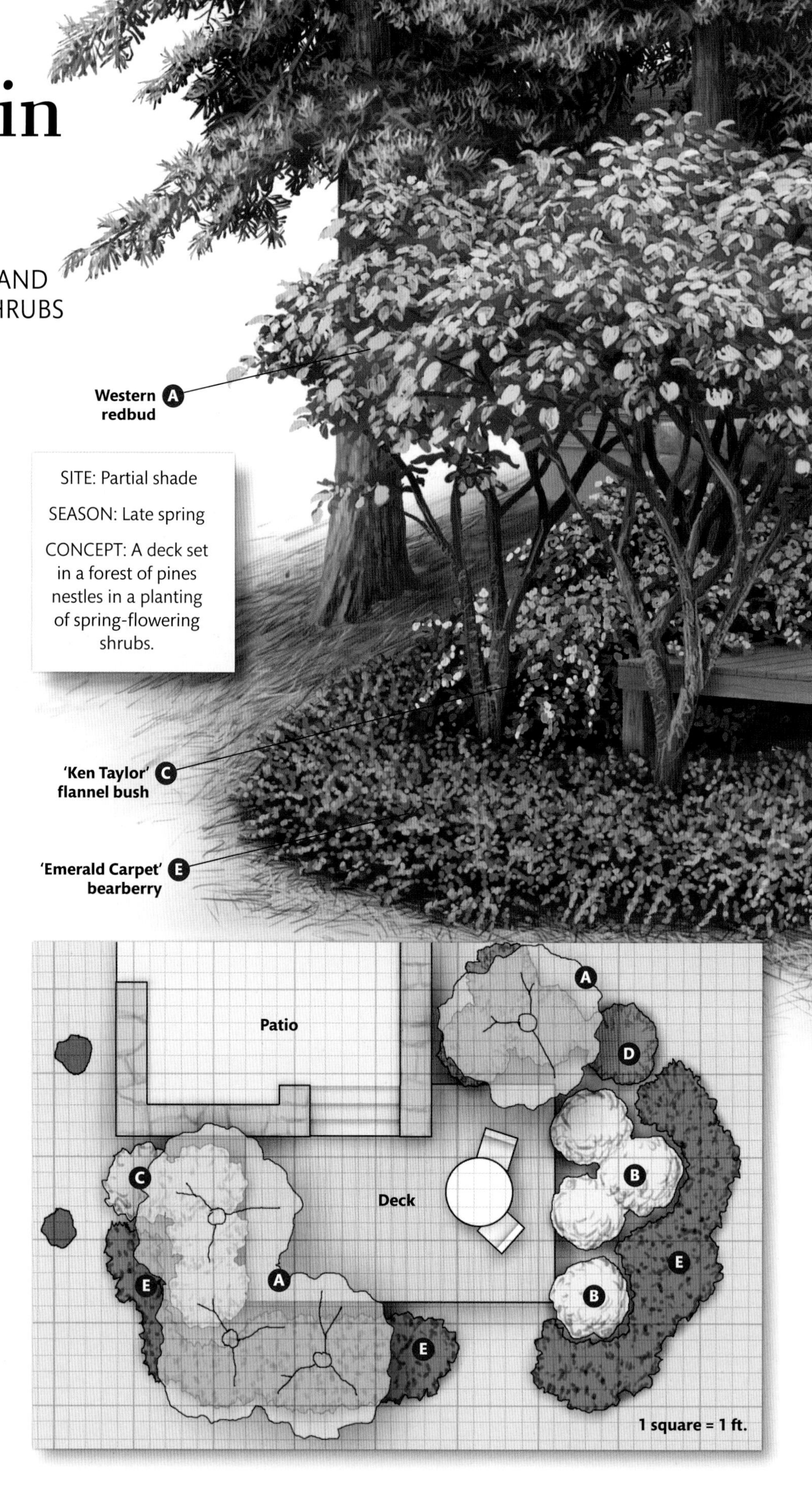

Plants & Projects

Preparing the planting beds and installing the shrubs can be done in a few weekends. Then sit back and enjoy the display. Once established, these plants require little care beyond seasonal pruning.

A Western redbud (use 4 plants)
Native to the foothills, this small tree is so vivid in bloom it stops drivers along the roads in spring. The purplish-pink flowers give way to bright green deciduous leaves that turn yellow in fall. Purplish seedpods decorate the bare branches in winter. See *Cercis occidentalis*, p. 128.

B Bush anemone (use 4)
One of the loveliest chaparral shrubs, its dark glossy leaves with whitish undersides create a beautiful backdrop in spring for masses of showy white flowers sporting bright-yellow centers. See *Carpenteria californica*, p. 127.

C 'Ken Taylor' flannel bush (use 4)
Cup-shaped golden yellow-to-orange flowers stand out brightly against this evergreen shrub's felty, dark-green leaves. See *Fremontodendron* 'Ken Taylor', p. 132.

D 'Majorca Pink' rosemary (use 4)
Lavender-pink flowers continuously adorn this tough, upright evergreen shrub during late winter into early spring. See *Rosemarinus* 'Majorca Pink', p. 146.

E 'Emerald Carpet' bearberry (use 12)
This low-spreading shrub forms a dense, slightly mounding carpet of small oval leaves that remain bright green throughout the year. It makes an exceptional choice for a ground cover. See *Arctostaphylos* 'Emerald Carpet', p. 123.

A Woodland Link

CREATE A SHRUB BORDER FOR NEARBY WOODS

SITE: Sunny

SEASON: Summer

CONCEPT: A small tree, shrubs, and perennials make a pleasing transition between lawn and adjacent woodland.

Mature woodlands are sometimes found in urban as well as rural areas in Texas. Some newer subdivisions incorporate woodland as communal space or have left it intact on individual properties. And in some older neighborhoods, mature trees on adjacent lots create almost the same woodland feeling.

The planting shown here integrates a domestic landscape with a woodland edge, making a pleasant transition between the open area of lawn and the woods beyond. The design takes inspiration from the buffer zone of small trees and shrubs nature provides at a sunny woodland edge, and it should provide the same attraction for wildlife and people as does the edge of a natural woodland.

Shrubs and perennials of various sizes mingle in the planting, larger ones toward the back, imitating natural layered growth. A small tree anchors one corner, its height echoing the taller trees in the woods behind. A path winds through a "meadow" of flowering shrubs and perennials before entering the woods.

Whether viewed from across the yard or up close, the planting is appealing all year. Spring ushers in nodding narcissus, redbud blossoms, scented viburnum, and stands of delicate, frilly irises; summer produces a rich assortment of red, pink, orange, and yellow flowers; and fall offers up pink-blushed camellias.

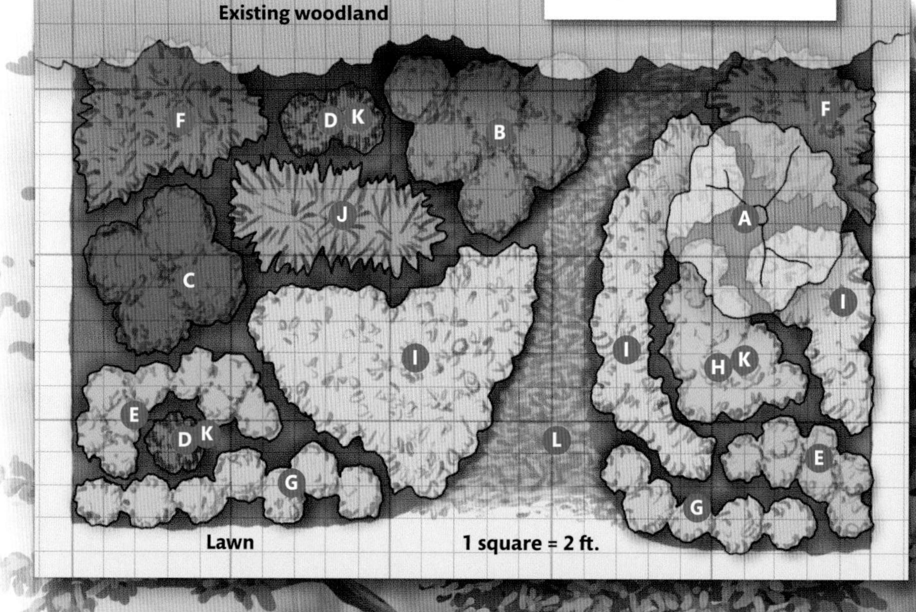

Plants & Projects

Before planting, dig and improve the soil throughout the entire area (except under the path) with organic matter. A mulch of compost or wood chips and regular watering the first summer will speed establishment. Other than seasonal maintenance, you'll need to divide the perennials when they become crowded in a few years.

A Redbud (use 1 plant)
A graceful native tree for the wood's edge, its branches are suffused in spring with pink-purple blossoms followed by heart-shaped leaves, green in summer, gold in fall. Its rounded shape is attractive even when branches are bare of blossoms and leaves. See *Cercis canadensis*, p. 128.

B Southern Arrowwood Little John (use 6)
This hybrid stays a manageable size growing 4–5 feet tall and wide and developing dark blue berries enjoyed by the birds. See *Viburnum dentatum*, p. 152.

C Magnolia 'Little Gem' (use 4) A dwarf southern magnolia with small, dark-green foliage and a compact form. Large, white blooms. See *Magnolia grandiflora*, p. 138.

D Texas star hibiscus (use 3)
This striking perennial will rise above neighboring plants in summer and fall, its leafy stalks showcasing large red flowers that attract butterflies and hummingbirds. See *Hibiscus coccineus*, p. 134.

E 'Goldflame' Japanese spirea (use 16)
For sunlit foliage, plant this gold-leafed shrub among the deeper greens. Large, flat clusters of tiny pink flowers give the shrub a lacy appearance from late spring through midsummer. See *Spiraea* x *bumalda* 'Goldflame', p. 149.

F Wood fern (use 35)
A vigorous spreading perennial fern. The fronds are bright green and deeply cut. Plant as many of them as needed on 2-ft. centers. See Ferns: *Thelypteris kunthii*, p. 132.

G 'Radiation' lantana (use 12)
This bushy perennial spreads to form a wide mound of fuzzy foliage covered from spring to fall with masses of tiny orange flowers. See *Lantana camara* 'Radiation', p. 137.

H Turk's cap (use 9)
Another perennial with striking red blooms sought by hummingbirds and butterflies. Deciduous leaves are heart-shaped and deep green. See *Malvaviscus arboreus drummondii*, p. 137.

I 'Goldsturm' black-eyed Susan (as needed)
Plant these black-eyed Susans in swaths—a hundred or more for an unbroken sweep of gold daisies the first season; half as many if you're willing to wait a year or so. These vigorous, bushy plants will soon fill the space. See *Rudbeckia fulgida* 'Goldsturm', p. 146.

J Louisiana iris (as needed)
This perennial forms an attractive clump of erect foliage. In early spring it sends up showy flowers on 3-ft. stalks. Colors range across the spectrum. For this planting we recommend a yellow-blooming variety. Plant on 2-ft. to 3-ft. centers. See *Iris* x *Louisiana* hybrids, p. 135.

K Narcissus (as needed)
Splashes of bright color can be had early in the season with these spring bulbs. Plant them around the Turk's cap and Texas star hibiscus; they'll be in bloom while the two shrubs are dormant. These bulbs come in yellows, whites, and oranges. Choose a yellow flower, as shown here, or your favorite mix of colors, and plant lots of them. See Bulbs: *Narcissus tazetta*, p. 126.

L Path
This wood-chip path nicely complements the woodland feeling. See p. 163.

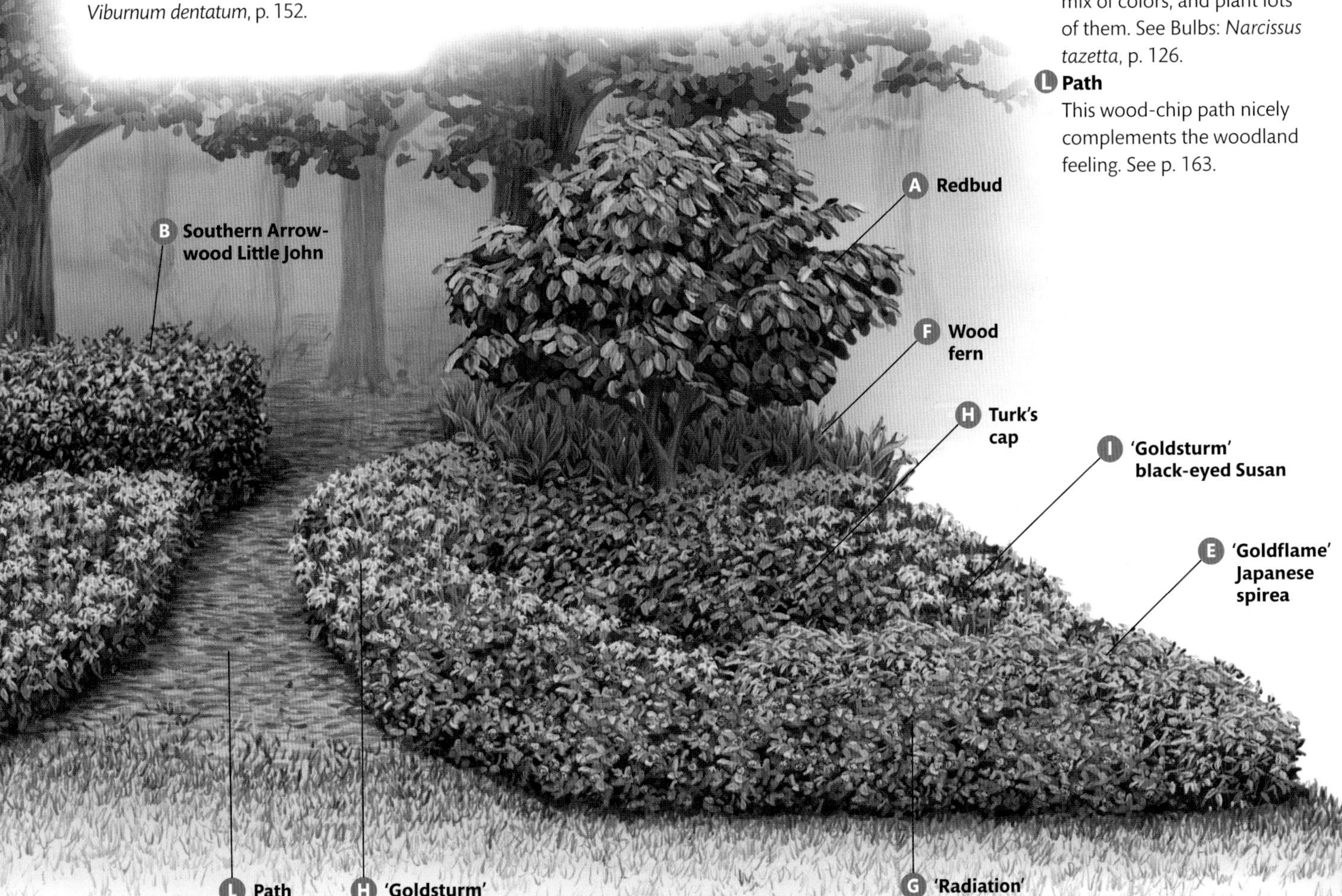

Link for a shadier edge

If an adjacent woodland shades your property, try this design, which features plants tolerant of shady conditions. The concept is the same as in the previous design—layers of plants increasing in height toward the woods—but the layout is somewhat different. A wider path ambles to the right; a flowering trellis marks the entry into the woods; and foliage textures and colors take the place of flowers, providing interest in all seasons.

The planting is at its most colorful in fall and winter, when masses of burnished autumn sage stand out against the light greens of ferns and the deeper greens of holly and euonymous. Fall is also emblazoned with the reds and purples of countless berries, fruits we fondly associate with woodland outings.

Plants & Projects

A Possumhaw holly (use 2 plants)
This native deciduous shrub has year-round appeal. In season, it wears a thick coat of glossy foliage. When shed, it exposes silver-gray twigs laden with long-lasting red berries. Birds love to eat them. See *Ilex decidua*, p. 135.

B Wax myrtle (use 12)
A graceful shrub that can be pruned into a shapely multitrunked tree. In most parts of Texas, foliage stays green through the winter. See *Myrica cerifera*, p. 139.

C American beautyberry (use 3)
A shrub with a somewhat open and arching habit. The inconspicuous flowers produce eye-popping purple berries that last long after the leaves drop. See *Callicarpa americana*, p. 127.

D Dwarf yaupon holly (use 14)
This shrub's olive-green foliage complements the other leaf colors. See *Ilex vomitoria* 'Nana', p. 135.

SITE: Shady

SEASON: Fall

CONCEPT: Attractive evergreen shrubs guarantee year-round color at this shady woodland edge.

Ⓔ **Coral honeysuckle** (use 1)
A native vine that blooms in shade. It bears showy whorls of red-orange flowers, followed by pretty red berries in fall and winter. Gray-blue leaves are attractive and usually evergreen. See *Lonicera sempervirens*, p. 138.

Ⓕ **'Cherry Chief' autumn sage** (use 3)
This bushy perennial's small oval leaves echo the holly's foliage, but are softer and paler. Small red flowers bloom heavily in spring and lightly in summer and fall. See *Salvia greggii* 'Cherry Chief', p. 147.

Ⓖ **Texas dwarf palmetto** (use 26)
This slow-growing shrub has pale-green fan-like leaves and spineless stems. See *Sabal minor*, p. 148.

Ⓗ **Wood fern** (as needed)
A vigorous spreading perennial fern. The fronds are bright green and deeply cut. Plant as many of them as needed on 2-ft. centers. See Ferns: *Thelypteris kunthii*, p. 132.

Ⓘ **Inland sea oats** (use 32)
This native grass makes a natural transition to the woods. Grows in ever-larger clumps and also spreads from seed. Long seed heads resemble oats and dangle and dance from arching stems in fall. See *Chasmanthium latifolium*, p. 128.

Ⓙ **Snowflake** (as needed)
White flowers planted among the ferns are lovely in early spring. Plant several hundred bulbs if possible. See Bulbs: *Leucojum aestivum*, p. 126.

Ⓚ **Arbor**
Placed at the entry to the woods, this simple cedar arbor invites visitors for a woodland stroll. See p. 189.

See p. 117 for the following:

Ⓛ **Path**

PLANT PORTRAITS

With handsome foliage and flowers, these plants are effective against a woodland backdrop.

● = First design, pp. 116-117
▲ = Second design, pp. 118-119

Magnolia 'Little Gem'
(*Magnolia grandiflora*, p. 138) ●

Louisiana iris
(*Iris* x *Louisiana* hybrids, p. 135) ●

'Goldflame' Japanese spirea
(*Spiraea* x *bumalda*, p. 149) ●

High-Allergen Plants

As climate and weather change, pollen production increases. Some areas of the U.S. are now experiencing a 20% increase in pollen. In particular, the Midwest and Southern U.S. have increased pollen rates. In addition to a long warm season, Texas is known for its mild and dry winters coupled with ever-present prevailing winds. This translates into year-round allergies for many Lone Star residents.

The seasonal timing of plant species pollen production varies. This means in mild and warm Texas there is nearly always something blooming to make you sneeze and itch your eyes. The winter months in Texas are known for allergens from elm and cedar (juniper) trees. Springtime brings tree pollen from ash, mulberry, sycamore, willow, oak, and pecan. In summer Texans can expect pollen from elm, marsh elder, pigweed, and sagebrush. Allergens from grasses can be expected to be at their height in summer. Come late summer and early fall the seasons are rounded out with pollen from ragweed.

Some plants contain both male and female flowers on the same plant, termed *monoecious*, meaning "one house." Other plants like holly are dioecious; each plant is either male or female, having their own flowers. In this case, both male and female plants must be present, within a certain range, for effective flower pollination to produce berries or fruit.

While some plants are desired for their colorful or decorative fruit, many plants in the nursery trade are male plants since they seem to be "neater," dropping less flowers, fruits, or seeds. However, only male plants produce pollen. This means that many of the ornamental plants in your landscape may be male, producing copious amounts of pollen.

In addition to flowering plants, molds are a prominent producer of allergies. Elements commonly used in the landscape can host mold such as composted materials, included leaves, plus bark mulches and other shredded organic products. Mold that causes allergies is highest during rainy periods.

It is projected that by the end of the 21st century, pollen season will begin 40 days earlier and extend about 20 days longer than it does now. It is also estimated that pollen levels may triple in some parts of the U.S. during this time.

To lessen the allergic effects of pollen and other plants, you can avoid being outside while pollen production is most active from pre-dawn through 8 a.m. and again from 5 p.m. through 9 p.m. Keep any lawn areas mowed to keep grass from going to seed and producing pollen. Ornamental grasses are a garden favorite, so try and select female grasses, which do not produce pollen.

By limiting your lawn areas, you can reduce the amount of potential pollen and replant with ground covers such as: partridgeberry (*Mitchella repens*), downy phlox (*Phlox pilosa*) or silver ponyfoot (*Dichondra argentea*).

Since pollen accumulates on surfaces including your clothes, hair, and skin, covering up and wearing a mask can reduce the pollen that you breathe in. This is particularly helpful on windy days or while mowing the lawn or gardening. After being outside during pollen season, nothing is as refreshing as taking a shower to wash off the pollen. If your allergies are particularly troublesome, you can consult your doctor or pharmacist for allergy remedies or medications.

While allergy season may seem endless in Texas, it is possible to live with it. Just remember many of the products and foods we depend on wouldn't be possible without pollen producing plants and their pollinators.

Reduce the amount of pollen in your garden by planting ground covers like downy phlox, shown here.

Plant Profiles

When you are ready to install your new landscape design, you will find this section a great reference for selecting the plants for your project. Plants are key, and here you'll find descriptions of all the ones used in all of the designs, along with helpful advice for planting and maintaining them. What's more, the trees, shrubs, perennials, grasses, bulbs, and vines that are included have all proven themselves as dependable performers in Texas. They offer a wide spectrum of lovely flowers and fruits and most add something special to your home's landscape for at least two seasons.

Using the plant profiles

All of these plants are proven performers in many of the soils, climates, microclimates, and other conditions commonly found in Texas. But they will perform best if planted and cared for as explained in the Guide to Installation, beginning on p. 154. In the following descriptions and recommendations, "full sun" means a site that gets at least eight hours a day of direct sun throughout the growing season. "Partial sun" and "partial shade" both refer to sites that get direct sun for part of the day but are shaded the rest of the time by a building, fence, or tree. Plants preferring partial sun or shade often do best with morning sun and afternoon shade. "Full shade" means sites that don't receive direct sunlight.

The plants are organized here alphabetically by their scientific name. If you are browsing, page references direct you to the designs in which the plants appear. Numbers in ***bold italic*** type indicate the page where you can find a photo of the plant.

In the writeups, we've noted plants that have been designated Texas Superstar® plants by the Texas Cooperative Extension and the Texas nursery industry because of their proven performance throughout the state.

Anisacanthus quadrifidus var. *wrightii*
FLAME ACANTHUS

Achillea millefolium

YARROW. This is a long-blooming, cool-season perennial with flat clusters of small flowers on 1 ft. stalks. The foliage is gray-green, growing in a dense mat about 6 in. tall. The species (p. 105) has white flowers and is very vigorous. 'Fire King' (pp. 84, ***86***) has hot-pink flowers. 'Apple Blossom' (pp. 36, ***36***) has light-pink flowers; if it isn't available, a good substitute is 'Rosea'. 'White Beauty' (p. 45) has pure-white flowers. Yarrow needs full sun and tolerates most soils. Cut off blooms when they fade, or before; they make good cut flowers.

Agapanthus

AGAPANTHUS, LILY-OF-THE-NILE. Flowering perennials with arching, straplike leaves and ball-shaped clusters of blue-and-white flowers in late spring and summer. *A. 'Peter Pan'* (p. 32) is a dwarf variety with leaves reaching only 12 in. tall and blue flowers on stalks up to 18 in. tall. Plant in full sun or light shade and well-drained soil. Evergreen in mild-winter climates; goes dormant in cold winters.

Agave

CENTURY PLANT. These are bold evergreen succulents with thick spiny leaves in fantastic architectural rosettes. (Be careful to avoid the sharp spines on the tips of the leaves.) A large native suited to xeric (drought) conditions. Rare flowering stalks occur after many years, giving rise to the popular name, century plant. Mother plants die upon flowering, followed by new suckers at their base. *A. americana* (pp. 45, ***47***) has striking blue-green foliage and grows 5 ft. tall and wide. Yellow variegated agave (*A. americana* 'Marginata', pp. 45, ***47***, 75, ***77***) has green and yellow leaves and is slightly smaller than the species. *A. victoriae-reginae* (pp. ***42,*** 43) has green-and-white leaves and grows only 1 ft. tall and wide. Agaves require full sun and good drainage. Twin-flower agave (*A. geminiflora*, p. 39) forms a tight rosette 2 to 3 ft. round of stiff, narrow green leaves with yellow bell-shaped flowers. Once plant is established, Century Plants may tolerate temperature of 15° Fahrenheit or lower while sustaining some winter damage and dieback. Newer plantings or plantings in exposed areas may die with sustained temperatures below 15° Fahrenheit.

Anisacanthus quadrifidus var. *wrightii*

FLAME ACANTHUS. This spreading deciduous shrub has red-orange tubular flowers and light-green leaves. It attracts hummingbirds and takes well to shearing. It is drought tolerant. Page: 58.

Anisodontea* x *hypomandarum

CAPE MALLOW. Fast-growing evergreen shrub with a long season of bloom. Small pink flowers with dark veins appear almost year-round in mild-winter areas. (Bloom time is shorter in inland and foothill areas.) Grows 6 ft. tall. Full sun. Page: 32.

Annuals

Gardeners in Texas use annuals generously to provide bright patches of colorful flowers throughout the year. They're fast-growing plants that bloom abundantly for months, and when they're finished, they are easy to uproot and replace with something else. One of the fun things about growing annuals is that you can try different kinds from year to year.

Annuals in Texas can be divided into three groups. Winter, or cool-season, annuals are planted when the weather starts to cool in the fall. They live through the winter, perhaps blooming off and on, and put on a good show in spring. This group includes pansies, snapdragons, violas, sweet alyssum, dusty miller, and dianthus.

Spring, or warm-season, annuals are planted in early spring and again in early fall. They grow best during the milder temperatures of spring and fall and only occasionally endure hot temperatures. This group includes petunias, begonias, verbena, ageratum, nicotiana, marigolds, and salvia.

Summer, or hot-season, annuals are the most useful during the scorching Texas summers. They are usually native to tropical climates and are planted during late spring and early summer. This group includes lantana, Mexican heather, purslane, vinca, ornamental sweet potato, Persian shield, blue daze, and purple fountain grass.

Antigonon leptopus

CORAL VINE. A vigorous vine that climbs by tendrils, it bears airy panicles of coral-pink heart-shaped flowers among apple-green foliage in summer and autumn. Grows best in full hot sun. Grow it as an annual in northern areas or substitute coral honeysuckle. Also known as queen's crown and Mexican love vine. Page: 101, ***101***).

Aquilegia chrysantha hinckleyana

TEXAS GOLD COLUMBINE. This native perennial bears fragrant golden flowers with long spurs. Blooms in early spring on 2-ft. stalks above neat clumps of blue-green leaves. The plant is relatively short-lived but self-seeds easily. Grows best in light shade and well-drained soil. Tends to go dormant in summer; cut it back when it does. Designated a **Texas Superstar®.** Pages: 35, 47, 58, 75, 87, 99, 107, 113.

Arctostaphylos

MANZANITA. Evergreen shrubs with shiny red bark, lustrous deep-green foliage, and small white-to-pink flowers in spring followed by red berries. *A. densiflora* 'Howard McMinn' (p. 109) grows 5 to 6 ft. tall and spreads a little wider. *A. 'Emerald Carpet'* (Bearberry, p. 115) grows 8 to 14 in. high by 5 ft. wide and has brilliant-green leaves. Best used in dry areas and on slopes where there is infrequent watering. Plant in fall in full sun to par tial shade.

Aquilegia chrysantha hinckleyana
TEXAS GOLD COLUMBINE

Astrolepis sinuata
WAVY CLOAK FERN

Artemisia x 'Powis Castle'
ARTEMISIA

Astrolepis sinuata

WAVY CLOAK FERN. This semi-evergreen fern produces clumps of attractive rich green foliage, with a contrasting cinnamon underside. It is uniquely drought tolerant and suited to poor rocky soils, preferring sun or part shade. It is clump forming and slowly spreads via rhizomes. Pages: 30-31, 35, 55, 58, 62, 87, 92-93, 94-95, 112.

***Artemisia* x 'Powis Castle'**

'POWIS CASTLE' ARTEMISIA. A beautiful accent plant, this shrubby perennial is grown for fragrant, silvery, finely divided foliage. Flowers rarely, if ever. It forms a dome-shaped mound 2 ft. tall and 3 ft. wide. Plant in full sun with good drainage. Tolerates dry soil but grows faster when watered during dry summers. Cut back lightly in early spring and fall to encourage new growth and to keep plant compact. Pest free. Pages: 27, 37, 43, 48, ***51***, 73, 80, 82, 105.

Arundinaria gigantea

RIVER CANE. Also known as giant cane, this is a species of bamboo native to Texas. It is non-invasive and well-suited for landscaping, providing a native and eco-friendly alternative to invasive bamboo varieties. River cane also supports local ecosystems and wildlife. Page 66.

Aster oblongifolius

FALL ASTER. This carefree native perennial bears showy lavender-purple daisylike flowers from early fall until the first hard freeze. The plant spreads to form a dense clump 2 ft. tall and 3 ft. wide. Fall aster thrives in full sun or partial shade with well-drained soil. It is drought tolerant and has no known pest problems. Prune to the ground after the first hard freeze. In late spring, cut new stems back by one-third to keep plants from getting floppy and to encourage more flowers in fall. Divide plants every few years in early spring. Pages: 25, 36, 48, ***51***, 56, 73, 79, 95.

***Baccharis pilularis* 'Twin Peaks'**

'TWIN PEAKS' DWARF COYOTE BRUSH. Evergreen shrub valuable as a ground cover for sunny, dry, low-maintenance areas. Grows 10 to 24 in. high and spreads 6 ft. wide, with a dense cover of small green leaves. It is a male selection that doesn't produce messy seeds. Needs little water near the coast, once a month in warmer areas. Page: 108.

Bergenia crassifolia

WINTER-BLOOMING BERGENIA. A low-growing perennial with large, dark-green, wavy-edged leaves that are evergreen except in cold-winter areas. In January and February, tall stems bear clusters of pink flowers. Plant in partial shade (or full sun where summers are cool). Will withstand poor conditions but looks best grown in good soil and with regular watering. Page: 103.

***Bignonia capreolata* 'Tangerine Beauty'**

'TANGERINE BEAUTY' CROSS VINE. This vigorous evergreen vine grows to a generous 15 ft. tall and wide. In spring, the entire plant turns into a mass of beautiful trumpetlike orange flowers with yellow throats. Scattered bloom continues through the growing season. Excellent for covering walls, trellises, and fences. Cross vine is a Texas native and requires little care or water. It is rarely plagued by insects or disease. Pages: 26, ***106***, 107.

Bulbs

The bulbs recommended in this book are perennials that come up year after year and bloom in late winter or early spring. Buy bulbs from a garden center or catalog in late summer or fall. Plant them promptly in a sunny or partly shaded bed in moderately well-drained soil. As a rule, plant at a depth two times the bulb's height. After bulbs flower in spring, their leaves continue growing until some time in May, when they gradually turn yellow and die down to the ground. In subsequent years, remove (or ignore, if you choose) the old leaves after they turn yellow. Most bulbs can be divided every four to five years if you want to grow them elsewhere. Dig them as the foliage is turning yellow; shake or pull them apart; and replant them right away. Perennial bulbs are great for naturalizing in meadows and borders, for edging flower beds and fences, and as pockets of color among shrubs and ground covers. See the box on p. 126 for information on specific bulbs.

Aster oblongifolius
FALL ASTER

Bignonia capreolata
'Tangerine Beauty'
CROSS VINE

Recommended Bulbs

***Narcissus tazetta*, Narcissus**
This enduring perennial bulb blooms between late fall and early spring. Extremely fragrant white flowers open in dense clusters on 1 to 1½ ft. stalks and make great cut flowers. The dark-green foliage occurs in clumps 1 ft. wide and tall, emerging in the fall and going dormant during the summer. 'Avalanche' (p. 107, ***107***) has creamy-white flowers with lemon yellow cups. 'Grand Primo' (p. 91) is a southern heirloom with creamy white flowers and pale-yellow cups; if unavailable, use 'Avalanche' as a substitute. Paperwhite (*N. tazetta papyraceous*) has pure-white flowers and can be used as a substitute in the milder areas below Interstate 10. Tazetta narcissus are pest free and require no irrigation. Pages: 85, 117.

Narcissus tazetta
NARCISSUS

Narcissus pseudonarcissus 'Ice Follies'
DAFFODIL

***N. pseudonarcissus* 'Ice Follies', 'Ice Follies' daffodil**
Along with the golden yellow cultivars 'Carlton' and 'Fortune', this is one of the few daffodils that does well in Texas. A spring-blooming perennial bulb, it has wide, ruffled, yellow trumpets fading to creamy white. The extremely showy blooms rise 1 ft. among blue-green foliage and make great cut flowers for display in the home. Daffodils require full sun and good drainage. Divide them every 5 to 10 years to keep them blooming. Pages: 35, 52, ***54***.

***N. jonquilla*, Jonquil**
This early spring bulb has heavenly scented small golden-yellow flowers above dark-green rushlike foliage. Goes dormant during the summer, re-emerging with fresh foliage in the winter. It has no pest problems and prefers dry summers. 'Trevithian' and 'Sweetness' are commonly available. Pages: 61, ***63***.

***Leucojum aestivum*, Snowflake**
This dependable perennial bulb delights with clusters of tiny white bells on 1 ft. stalks in early spring. The healthy green foliage emerges in early winter and goes dormant in summer. Snowflakes are great for introducing bright patches of early bloom among ground covers and landscaped beds. They grow in sun or shade and in moist or dry conditions. This foolproof bulb is pest free and requires no supplemental watering. Pages: 31, 119.

***Zephyranthes candida*, White rainlily**
This hardy little bulb produces dark- green grasslike foliage during the cool months of the year. In late summer the leaves often die back in exchange for showy white crocuslike flowers in the fall. White rainlily grows less than a foot tall and wide. It will grow in full sun or partial shade and tolerates dry or boggy soil. It has no serious insect or disease problems and can be used to naturalize in beds or as a border substitute. Pages: 75, ***77***.

Leucojum aestivum
SNOWFLAKE

Callicarpa americana
AMERICAN BEAUTYBERRY. This native deciduous shrub has a lax habit, spreading 4 ft. wide and tall. Tapered dull green leaves line the slightly arching branches. In fall, they give way to profuse clusters of vivid violet-purple berries. Beautyberry is pest free and drought tolerant. Irrigation may be needed during periods of drought to maintain attractive foliage. Thin one-third of the older branches to the ground each spring to promote a denser appearance. Pages: 25, 55, 58, 86, 118.

Campanula
BELLFLOWER. A large group of useful flowering perennials (a few are annuals) that vary in plant habit and flower form. Plant them in flower beds, rock gardens, or containers. Spreading types are useful as small-scale ground covers. All grow best in partial shade but can take full sun near the coast.

Campsis x *tagliabuana* 'Mme. Galen'
'MME. GALEN' TRUMPET CREEPER, OR VINE. This hummingbird favorite is a vigorous deciduous vine with a stout woody trunk, large compound leaves, and clusters of salmon-red flowers from summer until frost. Trumpet vine needs full sun, room to grow, and only occasional watering during summer droughts. Once established, it can climb and cover a trellis, fence, or wall with no further assistance or care. It grows at least 10 ft. tall and can reach 20 to 30 ft. Pages: 82, 92, ***94***.

Carex planostachys
CEDAR SEDGE.
This species evolved to grow in the shade of Cedar trees and as an understory plant in tall grass prairies and meadows. It is drought tolerant and can grow in a variety of soil types. It prefers well-draining humus-rich soil, it will also grow in clay, caliche and limestone-based soils. Pages: 42-43, 47, 52, 55, 63, 66-67, 83, 99.

Carex texenis
TEXAS SEDGE. A common sedge in Texas, this sedge is a good turf substitute with a tufted, grass-like appearance. It is a suitable option for a ground cover with a similar aesthetic to grass. Pages: 55, 58, 67.

Carpenteria californica
BUSH ANEMONE. This evergreen shrub is grown for its lovely, lightly fragrant white flowers with yellow centers, which are displayed in late spring and early summer against handsome, glossy, dark-green leaves. Grows upright 4 to 6 ft. high and equally as wide. Plant in full sun except in the hottest areas, where partial shade is best. Page: 115.

Callicarpa americana
AMERICAN BEAUTYBERRY

Carex planostachys
CEDAR SEDGE

Ceanothus americanus
New Jersey Tea

Ceanothus

Ceanothus, wild lilac. Evergreen shrubs useful in dry landscapes, especially on slopes. Blue or (rarely) white flowers appear in early spring. Leaves are deep green. 'Julia Phelps' (p. 104) reaches 4 to 7 ft. tall and up to 9 ft. wide and has deep-blue flowers. Plant ceanothus in full sun in fall. Do not water once established. New Jersey Tea (Ceanothus americanus): This charming shrub grows to form a 3' x 3' mound, covered in fragrant flowers in late spring to early summer. This small shrub establishes deep roots, growing in dry and rocky soils, it is not suited to wet soils. It is drought and fire tolerant, after a wildfire it grows back from its roots. The New Jersey Tea shrub is an environmentally beneficial nitrogen fixing plant, drawing nitrogen greenhouse gases from the atmosphere, and storing in its roots.

Cercis canadensis
Redbud

Cerastium tomentosum

Snow-in-summer. A perennial often used as a ground cover, with slivery evergreen foliage and masses of white flowers in early summer. Forms a low mat 6 to 8 in. high, with stems that trail 2 to 3 ft. wide. Requires full sun or partial shade and well-drained soil. Water regularly. Shear off the top of the plant, cutting it back by about one-half, right after it blooms. Page: 97.

Cercis

Redbud. This small, early-spring flowering, deciduous tree is native to East Texas and performs best in the piney woods region. It produces clusters of bright purple-pink flowers along bare twigs in early spring before the heart-shaped leaves unfold. Medium-green foliage turns gold in the fall. Texas redbud (*C. texensis*, pp. (46, ***47***, 113, ***113***) has thick shiny leaves. Native to central and north Texas, this redbud is adapted to the drier areas of Texas with alkaline soils but performs well throughout the state. Redbuds are generally available with single or multiple trunks and may reach 20 to 25 ft. tall and wide. They require well-drained soil and regular watering in the summer but have few pests. Western redbud (*C. occidentalis*, pp. 108, 115) is a good choice for dry or natural landscapes. It is often grown as a large multitrunked shrub. Magenta flowers are followed by seedpods some people find unsightly. Leaves turn yellow in fall. Grows 10 to 20 ft. tall. Thrives in poor, dry soils. Page: 35, 86, 106, 112, 117.

Chamaerops humilis

Mediterranean fan palm. A bushy palm with coarse, blue-green, palm-shaped leaves arising from the tops of multiple stalks. Yellow flowers are borne in long panicles in spring but are mostly hidden in the dense foliage. Grows 6 to 10 ft. tall and half as wide. The Mediterranean fan palm is an adaptable plant that does as well in full sun as it does in partial shade and in moderately fertile to poor soils. Page 68.

Chasmanthium latifolium

Inland sea oats. This is a native perennial grass that forms erect leafy clumps about 2 ft. tall, topped with loose clusters of flat seed heads that dance in the breeze from midsummer through winter. All parts are green in summer and russet or tan in the winter. Grows in sun or shade and

Chilopsis linearis
DESERT WILLOW

Chasmanthium latifolium
INLAND SEA OATS

adapts to almost any soil. Cut to the ground in spring before the new growth emerges. This vigorous, pest-free plant can reseed and naturalize quite prolifically. To reduce the number of seedlings, pull or hoe them as they appear, apply a heavy layer of mulch in the area, use a selective post or preemergent herbicide, or remove the seed heads before they shatter. The dainty seed heads are great for flower arrangments. Pages: 25, 86-87, 106-107, 113, 119.

Chilopsis linearis

DESERT WILLOW. This small native deciduous tree sports narrow willowlike leaves and showy tubular flowers from spring throughout the summer. Flower colors range from pure white to lavender to deeper purple. Desert willow can reach 15 ft. tall and wide and makes a good substitute for crapemyrtle in extremely dry areas. It performs well throughout the state in sunny, well-drained locations. The more compact 'Bubba' (pp. 92, ***94***) has greener leaves and dark wine-purple flowers. Desert willow has few pests and is very drought tolerant. Pages: 26, ***27***, 36, 38, 42, 61, ***63***, 74, 79, 84-85.

x *Chitalpa tashkentensis* 'Pink Dawn'

'PINK DAWN' CHITALPA. A hybrid of catalpa and chilopsis, this narrow-leaved deciduous tree quickly grows 20 to 30 ft. tall. Large clusters of ruffled, trumpet-shaped pink flowers bloom in early summer. Plant in full sun. Grows best with occasional water in hot-summer climates. Chitalpa may be defoliated by catalpa worms or fungal leaf spot but survives with little care. Pages: 32, 100, ***101***, 108.

Chyrsactinia mexicana

DAMIANITA. This tough little evergreen shrub stands up well to desert heat and is useful for lining walkways and borders. It forms a densely branched 2 ft. mound of highly aromatic, dark-green, needle-like leaves. Small, fragrant, golden yellow "daisies" are borne in spring and fall, and sometimes through the summer where temperatures are mild. Grows in full sun. Needs little water but will bloom more with occasional irrigation. Page: 35.

Chrysanthemum leucanthemum

OX-EYE DAISY. This vigorous cool-season perennial produces loads of white daisies on 2-ft. stems in spring; the flowers are a great addition to bouquets. Prefers full sun and adequate moisture and has few pest problems. Remove flowers after they finish blooming to encourage more of them. To produce more plants, divide the leafy clumps in fall. Ox-eye daisy is the best substitute for Shasta daisies in Texas. Pages: 37, 41.

Chrysanthemum x 'Country Girl'

'COUNTRY GIRL' DAISY MUM. This daisy mum is a cool-season perennial that produces a profusion of pink daisies on 2 ft. stems in the fall. It is one of the few chrysanthemums that performs as a reliable perennial in Texas. Requires full sun, good drainage, and regular watering in the summer. Plants may need staking when in bloom. After bloom, cut the spent stalks to their base. To promote heavier bloom in fall, shear the plant by half several times during the summer. Daisy mum has no pest problems. Page: 81, ***81***.

Chrysanthemum leucanthemum
OX-EYE DAISY

Coreopsis lanceolata
COREOPSIS

Cuphea
CUPHEA

Citrus

CITRUS. These evergreen trees offer handsome dark-green leaves, fragrant spring flowers, and colorful, edible fruits in winter. The many varieties vary in adaptation, tree height, and form. Check with local nurseries for the best varieties for your area. Good landcape varieties include 'Meyer' lemon (p. 97), which forms a compact tree seldom over 8 ft. tall. Plant in full sun and well-drained soil. Water and fertilize frequently for quality fruit. Prune to keep the center of the tree open or to maintain size. Protect trees if temperature drops below 30°F for prolonged periods.

Clethra alnifolia

SUMMERSWEET. This deciduous shrub bears long spikes of fragrant white or rose-pink flowers from midsummer through fall. Butterflies and hummingbirds love them. Tolerates full sun to partial shade. Requires regular watering. Grows to 4–6 ft. tall and 3–5 ft. wide. Page: 32.

Coreopsis lanceolata

COREOPSIS. A native Texas wildflower, coreopsis explodes each spring with masses of golden yellow daisylike flowers. Forms a clump 1 ft. tall and 1½ ft. wide of bright-green linear leaves and slender flower stalks. A warm-season perennial, coreopsis grows best in full sun with modest irrigation. Tolerates most soil types and has very few pest problems. Looks best if the spent blossoms are sheared off after bloom. Pages: 41, 95.

Cuphea

CUPHEA. These are showy plants from the tropics that are often grown as perennials or annuals in Texas gardens. Cigar plant (*C. micropetala*, pp. 70, 88) is a warm-season perennial that covers itself with yellow and orange tubular flowers each fall as the days grow short. It makes a bold clump 4 ft. tall and 3 ft. wide. The hybrid 'David Verity' (pp. 93, ***94***) grows a more compact 2½ ft. tall and wide and blooms all summer with smaller orange flowers. Both attract hummingbirds in profusion. Mexican heather (*C. hyssopifolia*, p. 27) is a tender perennial that is usually treated as an annual in the northern two-thirds of the state. It grows 1 ft. tall and wide and bears lavender-pink flowers all summer long. Cupheas are very tough plants that prefer full sun and tolerate most soil conditions. They are drought tolerant as well, requiring water only during periods of prolonged drought.

Dasylirion longissima

MEXICAN GRASS TREE. An evergreen shrub forming a grassy fountain of narrow, olive-green, succulent leaves. With age it bears spikes of tiny white flowers in early summer and develops a treelike trunk. Usually reaches 4 to 5 ft., but may get as tall as 10 ft. Grows best in full sun or light shade and needs good drainage. Its smooth tropical appearance is especially attractive in desert areas. Page: 39.

Dermatophyllum secundiflorum

TEXAS MOUNTAIN LAUREL. This native shrub or small tree boasts beautiful blossoms as well as shiny evergreen foliage. It generally grows 10 ft. tall or better and 7 ft. wide. The fragrant flowers hang like clusters of purple wisteria each spring. Requires full sun and good drainage. It may occasionally suffer attack from leaf-eating caterpillars but generally recovers. It requires little to no supplemental irrigation or pruning. Do not prune during the winter when flower buds are present. Pages: 41, 52, 105, 108.

***Dianthus* 'Bath's Pink'**

'BATH'S PINK' DIANTHUS. This low-growing perennial forms a dense, grassy mat of gray-green foliage 6 in. tall and 1 to 2 ft. wide. Fragrant flowers like tiny pink carnations carpet the plant during the spring. Needs full sun and well-drained soil. Water only when the soil is dry. After blooming, shear off the flower stalks and cut the plants back halfway. Fresh new foliage will soon develop. Divide every few years during the fall to keep the plants vigorous. Pages: 27, 35, 50, 61, 64, 73, 81, 91.

***Dodonaea viscosa* 'Purpurea'**

PURPLE HOP BUSH. A tough evergreen shrub that can withstand difficult conditions, including poor soil, heat, wind, and drought. Narrow leaves are bronzy green, picking up a stronger purplish tone in winter. Flowers are inconspicuous, but seedpods are interesting late in summer. Grows 10 to 15 ft. tall, about 8 ft. wide. Ideal hedge or screen. Best foliage color when planted in full sun. Page: 104.

***Euphorbia* hybrids**

Euphorbias are evergreen shrubs that come in a variety of sizes, shapes, and colors; some have the appearance of thorny palm trees; others are busy and thornless. Crown of thorns (*E. milii*) is a compact shrub growing 18 in. tall and wide. Evergreen leaves cluster at ends of thorny stems and are topped with red flower bracts all year. Page: 39.

Dianthus 'Bath's Pink'
DIANTHUS

Dermatophyllum secundiflorum
TEXAS MOUNTAIN LAUREL

Eustoma exaltum* ssp. *russellianum

TEXAS BLUEBELL. Showy, bell-shaped flowers with 1–3 ft stems. Waxy perennial bloom. Needs partial to full sunlight and moist soil. Cool blue, purple, pink, and white colors. Page: 32.

Felicia amelloides

BLUE MARGUERITE. Dependable perennial covered with small, blue, daisylike flowers for a long season, usually starting in late winter and spring. Some bloom year-round in warm-winter areas. Grows about 18 in. tall and 3 to 4 ft. wide. Plant in full sun and water regularly. Often grown as an annual. Great in pots. Remove spent flowers to promote more bloom. Cut back by half in late summer. Page: 83.

Thelypteris kunthii
WOOD FERN

Ferns

These are carefree long-lived perennials. Despite their delicate appearance, several are among the most durable plants you can grow. Most ferns prefer shade, but some do well in partial shade or even full sun. They grow best in well-drained soil that's been amended with extra organic matter. You can divide them every few years in early spring if you want more plants, or leave them alone for decades. If you want to keep the foliage fresh and green, you can cut all the fronds off at the crown each spring before the new fiddleheads start to unfurl.

Wood fern (*Thelypteris kunthii*, pp. 55, 87, 107, 119) is without a doubt the toughest, most versatile fern for Texas; it prefers some shade but will also perform fairly well in full sun. The lacy apple-green fronds grow in clumps 2 ft. tall and wide. Like most ferns, this one requires regular watering during the summer to look its best.

Fouquieria splendens

OCOTILLO. This distinctive desert shrub forms a wiry clump of upright, gray-green, thorned, and furrowed branches. Tubular orange-red flowers form quickly at branch tips after spring rains and attract humingbirds. The deciduous gray-green leaves are small and fleshy, and drop during dry spells. Ocotillo can reach 20 to 25 ft. tall. It makes an attractive silhouette in desert gardens or an impenetrable barrier. Grows in full sun and well-drained soil. Page: 39.

Fremontodendron 'Ken Taylor'

'KEN TAYLOR' FLANNEL BUSH. A smaller cultivar of a large showy evergreen shrub found in dry woodlands and mountain slopes. Golden yellow cup-shaped flowers bloom continuously from spring to fall among dark-green, lobed leaves, leathery above and downy below. Flowers are followed by bristly seedpods. Grows 4 to 6 ft. tall and about twice as wide. Requires full sun and excellent drainage, making it ideal for a hillside location. Page 115.

Gaura lindheimeri

GAURA. This native Texas perennial forms a loose clump of graceful arched stems bearing pale pink-and-white flowers from spring through fall. Gaura normally reaches about 3 ft. tall and wide. 'Whirling Butterflies' (pp. 94, ***95***) is slightly more compact. 'Dauphin' (pp. 48, ***51***) is slightly more upright. Gaura needs full sun, well-drained soil, and regular watering during droughts. Looks best if sheared occasionally after bloom cycles. Cut it to the ground after the first frost. Pages: 45, 79, 82, 85, 105.

Gaura lindheimeri
GAURA

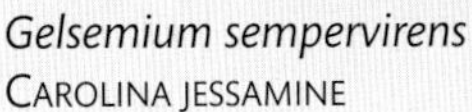

Gelsemium sempervirens
CAROLINA JESSAMINE

Hamelia patens
FIREBUSH

Gazania 'Burgundy'

'BURGUNDY' GAZANIA. Clumping evergreen perennials with daisylike flowers. 'Burgundy', with wine-colored flowers, is just one of many varieties that bloom in festive shades of yellow, orange, red, and purple. They make excellent small-scale ground covers. Upright blooms reaching 6 to 10 in. high appear mostly in spring and early summer. Can bloom year-round in mild-winter areas. Dark-green leaves have hairy, gray-green undersides. Tough plants that adapt to most soils but look best with occasional water in summer. Plant in full sun. Page: 83.

Gelsemium sempervirens

CAROLINA JESSAMINE. This is a Texas native evergreen vine beloved for its fragrant display of small bell-shaped yellow flowers in late winter and early spring. The small lancelike leaves are neat and green all year. This vine can climb trees but is usually trained to grow against a fence or trellis. Carolina jessamine can also be used as a ground cover but will need pruning yearly to keep it within bounds. This plant needs full or partial sun. Pages: 29, 58, 70, 105.

Hamelia patens

FIREBUSH. This colorful tropical shrub is normally grown in Texas as a tender perennial, usually reaching around 3 to 4 ft. tall and wide. In milder areas, it can grow even larger. Firebush bears red-orange trumpet-shaped flowers from summer to frost against red-tinged leaves that turn maroon as cool temperatures set in. Hummingbirds adore this plant. Extremely heat and drought tolerant. Cut to the ground after the first frost. In northern areas, mulch the crown heavily or grow it as a wonderful summer annual. Firebush has been designated a **Texas Superstar®**. Pages: 29, 70, 88, 92.

Helianthemum nummularium

SUNROSE. Flowering evergreen shrublets with small, bright-colored spring flowers in various shades of white, yellow, orange, pink, and red. Grows 6 to 8 in. high, 2 to 3 ft. wide. This small shrub needs full sun and well-drained soil. Good on dry banks. Page: 83.

Hesperaloe parviflora
RED YUCCA

Hesperaloe parviflora

RED YUCCA. This native Texas shrub grows in clumps of spiky gray-green succulent foliage. Attractive coral-pink trumpet flowers line graceful 3 ft. stalks from late spring to frost. Very heat and drought tolerant, red yucca is adapted to any well-drained soil in full sun. Generally requires no supplemental watering and attracts very few pests. Pages: 42, 45, 61, 79, 92.

Heuchera

CORABELLS, HEUCHERA. Perennials that form low clumps of almost-evergreen foliage and bloom spring into summer, bearing clouds of tiny red, coral, pink, or white flowers on slender stalks about 18 in. tall. They're fine accent plants or small-scale ground covers. Often sold as *H.* x *brizoides* or *H. sanguinea*; there are a number of other species and a variety of hybrids. All heucheras prefer full to partial sun, well-drained soil, and some summer water. Remove flower stalks as the blossoms fade. Divide every few years, replanting the divisions an inch or two deeper than the original planting. Page: 97.

Hibiscus coccineus

TEXAS STAR HIBISCUS. A tall, striking native perennial that bears large, brilliant red, star-shaped flowers above leafy stalks from early summer to frost. Foliage is medium green and deeply lobed. Plant can reach 6 ft. tall and 4 ft. wide with the right conditions. Prefers full sun and regular watering. Cut back after bloom cycle to promote bushy plants. It has no common insect or disease problems. Pages: 37, 64, **66**, 70, 81, 85, 88, 92, 103, 111, 117.

Hydrangea quercifolia

OAKLEAF HYDRANGEA. A medium-size shrub with lobed, oak-like leaves and leathery green foliage. Grows 4 to 8 ft. tall and equally wide. Hydrangeas are usually grown in partial shade but can be planted in full sun near the coast. Needs slightly acidic soil. Page: 103.

Hypericum calycinum

ST.-JOHN'S-WORT. A semievergreen mounding shrub that grows 2 ft. tall and wide. Its small oval leaves are green all year in mild climates and reddish purple to bronze where winters are cold. Bears five-petaled golden yellow flowers with long stamens in summer. Grows well in full sun to partial shade and prefers well-drained soils. It has few insect or disease problems and only requires watering during dry periods. Cut all stems by two-thirds in early spring. If you want to keep the plants shorter and more compact, prune all new shoots by half again in June. Pages: 50, 58, 75, 98.

Hibiscus coccineus
TEXAS STAR HIBISCUS

Hypericum calycinum
ST.-JOHN'S-WORT

Recommended Hollies

I. decidua, Possumhaw holly
A small Texas native deciduous tree with lustrous dark-green leaves. Berries are very showy after the leaves fall. They can be yellow, orange, or red depending on the cultivar. Designated a **Texas Superstar®**. Pages: 25, **27**, 118.

I. decidua 'Warren's Red'
This possumhaw cultivar has small, bright-red berries and an upright habit to 15 ft. tall and 6 ft. wide. Pages: 25, **27**.

I. vomitoria 'Nana', Dwarf yaupon holly
A dwarf version that reaches only 3 ft. tall and wide. Commonly used as a substitute for boxwood in Texas and the South. Pages: 25, 26, 35, 47, **47**, 48, 73, 74, 97, 118.

Ilex vomitoria 'Nana'
DWARF YAUPON HOLLY

Ilex decidua
POSSUMHAW HOLLY

Ilex

HOLLY. An extremely versatile group of shrubs and trees, hollies are used for foundation plantings, hedges, and specimens. The attractive leaves can be small or large, smooth or spiny, dull or glossy. Holly plants are either male or female. If a suitable male is planted within a few hundred yards, females bear heavy crops of small round berries that ripen in fall and last through the next spring. All tolerate sun and partial shade and almost any well-drained garden soil. Hollies are generally pest free. Prune or shear at any season to keep them at the desired size. See "Recommended hollies," left, for more information about specific hollies.

Iris x *germanica*

BEARDED IRIS. This popular perennial blooms in early spring, with large elegant flowers in shades of blue, lavender, pink, yellow, or white, on stalks 2 ft. tall. Flowers open above an attractive clump of stiff, bladelike, gray-green leaves. Bearded iris needs full sun and extremely well-drained soil and grows best with little to no irrigation. If you live close to the coast, plant heirloom and species types; they perform better because they are less likely to suffer root rot. Pages: 64, 73, 81.

Iris x Louisiana hybrids

LOUISIANA IRIS. This cool-season perennial forms a clump of straplike foliage 2 ft. tall and 3 ft. wide. Large delicate flowers rise on 3 ft. stalks in early spring. Cultivars come in almost every color of the rainbow. Tolerates wet soil or a well-drained soil with winter and spring moisture. Louisiana iris has few, if any, pests. Goes somewhat dormant in summer. Pages: 58, 99, 117, ***119***.

Ixora 'Thai Dwarf'

'THAI DWARF' IXORA. Ixoras are frost-tender evergreen shrubs grown for their showy clusters of brightly colored and highly perfumed flowers atop lustrous rounded leaves. Cultivars come in many sizes. 'Thai Dwarf' reaches 4 t. tall and wide and bears multicolored flower clusters in shades of red, orange, gold, pink, and yellow. Ixoras require full sun, acid soil, and regular watering. Page: 69.

Iris x *germanica*
BEARDED IRIS

Iris x Louisiana hybrids
LOUISIANA IRIS

Juncus effusus

SOFT RUSH. This native grass-like wetland perennial forms clumps 2 to 4 ft. tall with a 5 ft. wide spread. Yellow-green flowers appear in early summer on upright green stems. Spreads easily but can also be divided in mid-spring to early summer. Cut back in early spring. It grows well in moist soil and can tolerate water up to 4 inches deep. Good low-maintenance plant for ponds. Pages: 63, 99, 101.

Juniperus

JUNIPER. These needle-leafed evergreens are tough, hardy shrubs for exposed sites. 'Blue Pacific' shore juniper (*J. conferta* 'Blue Pacific', pp. 99, ***101***) makes a good ground cover, staying around 1 ft. tall and spreading 5 to 6 ft. wide. It has short, soft, blue-green needles. Dwarf Japanese garden juniper (*J. procumbens* 'Nana', p. 101, ***101***) grows 1 to 2 ft. high, spreads 5 to 6 ft. wide, and has blue-green foliage. Junipers prefer full sun and excellent drainage. They suffer blighted foliage from excess watering. Limit pruning to maintain a natural shape and to avoid brown-tipped foliage.

Lagerstroemia

CRAPEMYRTLE. An extremely popular deciduous shrub or small tree usually grown with multiple trunks. It blooms for several months in the heat of summer, with large clusters of papery red, pink, purple, lavender, or white flowers at the end of each stem. Leaves typically turn red, orange, or yellow in the fall. Exfoliating bark reveals wonderful, smooth mottled trunks in winter. There are many cultivars to choose from, ranging from dwarf types that grow 3 ft. tall to tree types that reach 30 ft. Look for the powdery mildew-resistant cultivars that are named for American Indian tribes. 'Twilight' (p. 29) has deep-purple flowers and grows to 10–15 ft. It is drought resistant, low maintenance, and blooms all summer long. 'Dynamite' (p. 52) flowers red in the spring and summertime, catching the eye of passers by. All crapemyrtles need full sun, well-drained soil, and a modest amount of irrigation during severe droughts. Prune them in late winter if at all, removing dead branches and basal suckers only. We discourage the common practice of topping crapemyrtles because it ruins their naturally beautiful shape, scars their trunks, causes them to flop over when blooming, and leads to basal suckering.

Lantana

LANTANA. These tough colorful plants are usually grown as tender perennials or summer annuals. Clusters of small flowers, each one a magnet for butterflies, top the plants from late spring until frost. Cultivars come in white, yellow, pink, orange, red, and purple flowers. Depending on the selection, they grow 1 to 3 ft. tall and spread 2 to 5 ft. wide. Lantanas make great bedding plants, container plants, or ground covers. They are exceptional choices for hot sites and poor soils, requiring full sun and little water. Shear after bloom cycles to keep them compact and encourage more flowers. See "Recommended lantanas" on p. 137 for information on specific kinds.

Lavandula

LAVENDER. Choice evergreen shrubs ideal for dry-summer climates. They form busy mounds of fragrant gray-green foliage topped in early summer with long-stalked spikes of very fragrant flowers. *L.* 'Goodwin Creek Gray' (pp. 32, 97) has gray foliage and deep-blue blooms from early summer into fall, or longer where summers are mild. Grows 2 to 3 ft. tall and wide. Lavenders need full sun, well-drained soil, and little water.

Recommended Lantanas

Lantana camara 'Dallas Red'
This bush-type cultivar has striking orange-red flowers. It grows 2 ft. tall and 3 ft. wide. Pages: 92, ***94***.

L. camara 'Confetti'
Another bush-type lantana, this one has eye-catching pink-and-yellow flowers and grows 2½ ft. tall and wide. Pages: 36, 80, 85.

L. camara 'Radiation'
This bush lantana has orange and yellow flowers and grows 2½ ft. tall and wide. Pages: 45, 70, 117.

_L._ x _hybrida_ 'Lemon Drop'
This vigorous cultivar of spreading lantana has creamy yellow flowers and grows 3 to 4 ft. wide. It sets little fruit, which contributes to increased flower production. Page: 93.

_L._ x _hybrida_ 'New Gold'
The most popular of all spreading lantanas, 'New Gold' has golden-yellow flowers on vigorous plants that reach 2 ft. tall and spread 3 to 4 ft. It sets little fruit so it doesn't need deadheading. It is designated a **Texas Superstar®**. Pages: 45, 61, 88.

L. montevidensis 'Trailing Lavender'
A low-growing, trailing species that stays under 1 ft. tall and spreads 5 ft. or more. It drapes a profusion of fragrant lavender flowers over steps and containers from spring through the first hard freeze. Not uncommon for it to bloom year-round in coastal areas and during mild winters. It sets no fruit, so it doesn't require deadheading. Designated a **Texas Superstar®**. Pages: 39, 41, **42**, 75, 95.

L. montevidensis 'Weeping White'
This vigorous trailing selection spreads 5 to 6 ft. wide and has pure white flowers. It blooms almost year-round and needs no deadheading. Designated a **Texas Superstar®**. Pages: 50, ***51***.

Lantana x *hybrida* 'Lemon Drop'

Lantana x *hybrida* 'New Gold'

Lantana camara 'Confetti'

Lantana camara 'Radiation'

Lantana montevidensis 'Trailing Lavender'

Leucophyllum frutescens 'Compactum'
COMPACT TEXAS SAGE

Lonicera sempervirens
CORAL HONEYSUCKLE

Leucophyllum frutescens 'Compactum'

COMPACT TEXAS SAGE. A dwarf cultivar of the striking, silver-leaved, drought-tolerant Texas native shrub. It has a dense, slightly irregular shape and reaches 3 to 4 ft. tall and wide. Following summer rains, it becomes flushed with orchid-pink flowers. Texas sage demands full sun and excellent drainage and requires little, if any, supplemental watering. Expect few if any insect or disease problems. Does not grow well in East Texas; 'Old Blush' China rose (*Rosa chinensis* 'Old Blush') makes a good flowering substitute there. Pages: 52, ***54***, 56, 61, 80, 95, 100, 102.

Lonicera sempervirens

CORAL HONEYSUCKLE. This native Texas evergreen vine twines around any support, climbing 10 to 15 ft. or higher. The smooth, oval, blue-green leaves are arranged in neat pairs on the stems. Blooms heavily in early summer and continues off and on until fall. The slender, tubular red-orange flowers are scentless but attractive to hummingbirds. Songbirds eat the bright-red berries that follow the flowers. Grows in shade but blooms best when planted in full or partial sun. Prune in winter if at all, thinning out some of the older stems. Unlike Japanese honeysuckle (*L. japonica*), this species is not aggressive or invasive. Pages: 39, 69, 70, 88, 119.

Lupinus texenis

BLUEBONNETS. Arrival of the Bluebonnets is a magical time in Texas. This cherished state flower is an annual; it grows from seed dispersed the previous season. Because of this, they can be a challenge to get established, requiring certain conditions and taking several seasons to establish. October and November are the best months to sow the seeds.

Magnolia grandiflora 'Little Gem'.

MAGNOLIA LITTLE GEM. A dwarf southern magnolia with small, dark-green foliage and a narrow form. Large, white blooms. Needs full sun. Once established, water deeply when dry. Reaches 20–25 ft tall. 10–15 ft wide. Page 30, 35, 103, 116, ***119***.

Malvaviscus arboreus drummondii
TURK'S CAP

Myrica cerifera
WAX MYRTLE

Malvaviscus arboreus drummondii

TURK'S CAP. One of the easiest perennials for Texas gardens, Turk's cap performs well in sun or shade, acidic or alkaline soils, and in wet or dry situations. Plants grow a bushy 2 ft. tall and 3 ft. wide in shade but can reach 5 ft. tall in full sun. The fairly coarse-textured foliage is medium green and slightly lobed. Small red Turk's turban flowers keep on coming from summer until frost, attracting a stream of sulfur butterflies and hummingbirds, especially in the fall. Turk's cap has few pest problems and requires little water. Shear throughout the growing season to keep tidy and cut to the ground after the first frost. Pages: 24-25, 30, 41, 42-43, 46, 55, 58, 63, 66, 86, 88, 92-93, 107, 113, 117.

Mitchella repens

PARTRIDGEBERRY. An evergreen creeping groundcover with small leaves, it produces small white flowers followed by scarlet berries enjoyed by birds and mammals. It can be utilized as a ground cover under acid-loving plants. Pages 42, 50.

Muhlenbergia

MUHLY. Gulf Coast Muhly (*Muhlenbergia capillaris*) is a 1–3 ft perennial grass with with fine, arching leaves that create an ornamental grass appeal. In fall, it takes on a feathery, deep-pink color (p. 27). Lindheimer's muhly (*Muhlenbergia lindheimeri*) features airy, pinkish-tan leaves, and providing a graceful, ornamental appeal of grass in landscape. Pages 28, 56, ***58***, 70, 88, 95, 98, 101, 111.

Myrica cerifera

WAX MYRTLE. A Texas native evergreen shrub that naturally maintains an upright and bushy profile. It can also be pruned into a small tree. The slender twigs are densely covered with glossy leaves that have a delicious spicy aroma. Historically, the leaves were used as a flavorful subtitute for bay leaf. In fall and winter, clusters of small gray berries line the stems of female plants. Wax myrtle needs full or partial sun and tolerates most soil conditions, including fairly wet ones. It has few pest problems. Water only during periods of drought. It grows quickly and can reach up to 20 ft. tall if left alone. Prune in winter if you want to keep it small or control its shape. Native Dwarf Wax Myrtle achieves a height and width of between 3 to 6 feet. This native creates great habitat for wildlife, it is useful for foundation plantings, it can be used for underplanting with larger woody plants or can create a midsized hedge. Dwarf Wax Myrtle is quite versatile, it can be grown in full sun to partial shade, it is suited to a range soil conditions from wet to dry. Pages: 16, ***30***, 31, 50, 55, 63, 66-67, 90, 98, 102, 118.

Nolina recurvata

BOTTLE PALM. A curious-looking small evergreen tree with a large swollen base, one or more tapering trunks, and drooping clusters of bright-green leaves. Bottle palm grows slowly and may eventually reach 12 to 15 ft. high. It needs full sun and well-drained soil. Does best where frosts are light or nonexistent. Page: 69.

Morella cerifera var. *pumila*
DWARF WAX MYRTLE

Opuntia lindheimeri
SPINELESS PRICKLY PEAR

Ophiopogon japonicus
MONDO GRASS

Ophiopogon japonicus

MONDO GRASS. This perennial ground cover resembles unmown grass. It grows in clumps of narrow, shiny, dark-green leaves 1 ft. tall and wide. Flowers are inconspicuous. The miniature 'Kyoto Dwarf' (pp. ***66***, 67) grows only 4 in. tall and 6 in. wide. Start with a number of small plants instead of a few large ones. They'll grow more quickly to fill a spot. Mow or shear off the top of old foliage in early spring before new growth appears. The new leaves will look fresh the rest of the year. Pages: 25, 63, ***66***, 67, 74.

Opuntia lindheimeri

SPINELESS PRICKLY PEAR. This popular cactus has smooth, succulent, gray-green leaf pads. Called "spineless," the leaves actually have tiny hidden spines, so wear gloves when handling them. The plant grows to 4 ft. tall and wide over time, on occasion producing showy yellow flowers in spring, followed by purple fruit in fall. Spineless prickly pear rarely needs water and has no major insect or disease problems. It makes a great living sculpture in the garden. Page: 61.

Panicum virgatum

SWITCHGRASS. Switchgrass is a native prairie grass or a warm season grass growing 3′–5′ tall, producing fine-textured lacey seedheads in late summer which persist throughout the winter. This grass is found in moist soil, lining the banks of streams. Switchgrass can handle dry conditions once established and is adaptable to a wide range of soil types. There are several switchgrass cultivars perfect for the home landscape with a variety of handsome traits. Pages: 25, 27, 76, 104-105.

Parthenocissus quinquefolia

VIRGINIA CREEPER. This native woody vine is a great climber, growing up to 30 ft. or more. The deciduous leaves are dark green in summer and vivid orange or red in autumn. The plant adapts to sun or shade and has few pest or disease problems. Water only in periods of drought. Once established, prune as needed to control its size. Page: 107, **107**.

Panicum virgatum
SWITCHGRASS

Passiflora incarnata 'Alba'

WHITE PASSION VINE. This very striking deciduous vine grows in full sun to part shade, and it blooms from spring through fall. Mentioned here is the eye-catching white flower, it also comes in shades of pink, blue, and purple. The passion vine has tendrils and happily climbs a trellis, It can just as easily trail along the ground. Either way, it provides berries for birds, nectar for bees, and attracts and hosts butterflies. It is heat and drought tolerant once established. 107, 111, ***113***.

Penstemon gloxinioides

GARDEN OR BORDER PENSTEMON. Late-spring- and summer-flowering perennial with showy tubular flowers spikes in shades of white, pink, red, and purple. Grown as an annual in cold-winter areas. Forms erect clumps about 3 ft. tall. Many varieties available. Needs full or partial sun. Looks best with regular water, but plants must have excellent drainage or they die quickly. Cut down spent flower stalks to encourage second bloom. In colder, high elevations, *P. barbatus* is a good substitute. It bears red flowers from spring into summer. Also check nurseries for locally native species. *P. serrulatus* (p. 97) is an 8 to 28 in. shade-tolerant Northwest native with dark blue and-purple flowers from June through August that can grow in moist soil. Cut back to encourage additional blooms and foliage growth. Page: 32.

Perovskia atriplicifolia

RUSSIAN SAGE. A shrubby perennial with an open, vase-shaped habit. Straight, fairly stiff stems are lined with sparse silver-gray foliage and tiny, but abundant, powdery blue flowers for many weeks in the summer. Grow in full sun and well-drained soil. It needs little water and is rarely bothered by insects or disease. Cut old stems down to the ground in spring. The plant will reach 3 ft. tall and 2 ft. wide by fall. To control its size, cut stems back by one-third in early summer. Pages: 41, 70, 79, 82, 104-105.

Phlox paniculata 'John Fanick'

'JOHN FANICK' GARDEN PHLOX. This is a beautiful and dependable pink-flowering perennial. It grows into a tidy 2-ft. clump of leafy flower stalks that produce dense clusters of fragrant pale-pink flowers with dark-pink eyes starting in early summer and continuing until frost. Garden phlox needs full or partial sun and adapts to most ordinary garden soil. Water regularly during dry conditions. To promote continuous bloom, cut off the flowers after they fade. Named for the late San Antonio nurseryman John Fanick. Designated a **Texas Superstar®.** Pages: 81, ***81***, 105.

Phormium tenax

NEW ZEALAND FLAX. A perennial prized for its bold evergreen foliage. Stiff, straplike leaves form a fan-like clump about 5 ft. tall and at least as wide. Stalks bearing red or yellow flowers rise high above the leaves. Many varieties with colorful foliage are available. 'Atropurpureum' (p. 82) has reddish purple leaves. A smaller variety, better suited to gardens, 'Yellow Wave' (p. 108) has yellow leaves. Plant New Zealand flax in full sun. Needs little water. Excellent accent plant, but large types need lots of room. In cold foothill areas, substitute an ornamental grass.

Perovskia atriplicifolia
RUSSIAN SAGE

Phlox paniculata 'John Fanick'
'JOHN FANICK' GARDEN PHLOX

Plumbago auriculata
TROPICAL PLUMBAGO

Plumbago auriculata

TROPICAL PLUMBAGO. A tropical ever-blooming shrub that is often grown as a tender perennial in Texas. Plumbago mounds to 2 ft. tall and 2 to 3 ft. wide or can be grown as a climber. It is smothered with baby-blue flowers from summer to frost. Rarely plagued by insects or disease. Only needs occasional watering during dry spells. Cut to the ground after the first hard freeze and mulch well. In northern areas, use it as a summer annual for a long season of blue flowers, or consider replacing it with a cold-hardy substitute such as hibiscus. Pages: 35, 52, 77, 91, 101. Polygala **x** dalmaisiana

SWEET-PEA SHRUB. Evergreen shrub with small narrow leaves and a long season of purplish pink, pea-shaped flowers. Grows 5 ft. tall, with a spreading habit, often bare near the ground. Plant in full sun or partial shade. Water regularly. Shear to keep full-foliaged.

Prunus caroliniana

CHERRY LAUREL. Laurel is an upright native evergreen shrub suited to screening or as a specimen. Its glossy foliage can be pruned into a naturalistic hedge. It does best with adequate soil moisture and some shade, reaching 15–30 ft. tall, and can be kept smaller with some pruning. This plant is mildly toxic if consumed in quantity, so keep children and pets away from consuming.

COMPACT CAROLINA CHERRY LAUREL (*Prunus caroliniana 'Compacta'*). A very useful shrub for hedge or screen. Glossy green leaves look fresh all year. Small spikes of lightly scented white flowers appear in spring, followed by black berries in summer. Berries can be messy if the shrub is planted near a patio or walk. Although cherry laurel will grow larger, it is often pruned to about 10 ft. tall and 8 ft. wide. It does best in full sun but can take partial shade. Prefers moist well-drained soil but tolerates dry sites. Shear anytime to desired size and shape. Pages: 74, 106.

Punica granatum

POMEGRANATE. This is a very ornamental deciduous fruiting shrub. Bronze new growth turns green in summer, and bright yellow in fall. Vibrant-orange flowers are held among the shiny leaves in spring. The widely grown cultivar 'Wonderful' (pp. 64, 111) has a fountainlike shape and reaches 6 to 8 ft. tall. Its flowers are followed by large, bright-red, edible fruit. Compact pomegranate (P. granatum'Nana', pp. 88, ***90***) makes an excellent container plant. It grows 3 ft. tall and 2 ft. wide and bears small inedible fruit. Plant pomegranates in full sun and well-drained soil. They need little water once established and are generally pest free. They can be sheared at any time to a desired shape.

Quercus

OAK. Among the most majestic and long-lived shade trees in Texas landscapes. The state is home to many deciduous and evergreen species.Shumard oak (Quercus shumardii p. 25), is a small oak with neat evergreen leaves and a show of fragrant yellow flowers in spring make this vigorous vine ideal for training up porch columns or along a railing.

Live oak (Q. virginiana, p. 94) is a slow-growing evergreen oak that achieves a height of 25 ft. and a width of 30 ft. in a person's lifetime but is capable of reaching immense proportions over the centuries. It has gnarled branches and small, hollylike deep olive-

Prunus caroliniana 'Compacta'
COMPACT CAROLINA CHERRY LAUREL

Quercus shumardii
SHUMARD OAK

green leaves that don't drop until the new leaves emerge in the spring. This oak casts dense shade, making it difficult to grow turfgrass underneath. Ground covers are a better option.

When buying oaks, ask where the trees were grown. Live oaks native to central Texas are smaller, more alkaline tolerant, and more drought tolerant than their cousins in east and southeast Texas.

All Texas oaks grow best in full sun and well-drained soils. They require supplemental watering only during periods of drought. They have few serious insect or disease problems. In areas of central Texas where oak wilt disease is a problem, prune the trees only during the dormant period of winter to avoid attracting disease-spreading insects to the fresh cut wounds. Applying a pruning paint is also recommended.

Rosa

Rose. Texans love roses. Most of the roses that do well in Texas are evergreen shrubs with glossy compound leaves, somewhat thorny stems or canes, and showy, sometimes fragrant, flowers. The classes that perform best include teas, Chinas, polyanthas, and the old-fashioned ramblers. All of these roses are often referred to as "antique roses" in the nursery. They are grown and sold in containers and can be planted year-round.

All roses grow best in full sun and well-drained soil topped with a few inches of mulch. Once established, the roses recommended in this book require no more care than many other shrubs. Prune them lightly once a year in early spring, before new growth starts. (See p. 213 for more on pruning.) Apply a light application of lawn fertilizer, manure, or compost after pruning. The roses we've selected (p. 145) have good resistance to various fungal diseases. They may have problems during years that are especially moist, but each has shown that it will survive and recover without chemical sprays. Aphids, soft-bodied insects the size of a pinhead, may attack new growth, especially in the spring. Wash them away with a blast from the water hose or shear off the infected new growth. Deer eat rosebushes, despite the thorns. Where deer are a problem, consider planting Turk's cap, Texas sage, or pomegranate instead of roses.

The Texas Cooperative Extension program (a branch of Texas A&M University) has conducted extensive research to identify the roses that perform best in Texas without pesticides. Those that pass the test are designated **Earth-Kind** roses.

Quercus virginiana
Live oak

Recommended Roses

***Rosa chinensis* 'Climbing Old Blush'**
The climbing form of the wonderful old China rose, 'Old Blush'. It has a heavy flush of loose double-pink blooms in spring and then a scattering of repeat blooms until fall. Grows vigorously up to 15 ft. tall and wide. There are legendary 'Old Blush' roses in front of the Admiral Nimitz Hotel in Fredericksburg. Pages: 72, **73**.

***R. chinensis* 'Martha Gonzales'**
This dwarf China rose has brilliant red semi-double blooms all season. It grows about 3 ft. tall and 2 ft. wide and occasionally larger. The new growth in spring is a brilliant plum color. Named for the late Martha Gonzales of Navasota. Page: 74, ***74***.

R. chinensis* 'Mutabilis', *Butterfly rose
This popular landscape rose produces showy single flowers all season in everchanging shades of yellow, orange, and pink. Flowers resemble a swarm of butterflies hovering about the bush. Grows to a generous 5 ft. tall and wide, and occasionally larger. New growth is plum colored. Designated an **Earth-Kind** rose. Pages: 76, 94.

Rosa chinensis 'Mutabilis' BUTTERFLY ROSE

Rosa x 'Belinda's Dream'

***R.* x 'Belinda's Dream'**
This showy shrub rose produces large, double, pink flowers all season. Generally grows around 4 ft. tall and 3 ft. wide. The fragrant flowers are great for floral arrangements. Designated a **Texas Superstar®** and an **Earth-Kind** rose. Pages: 36, 85, ***87***.

***R.* x 'Flower Carpet Pink'**
A low, spreading rose that forms a mat of dark-green leaves topped with pink flowers. Grows 2 ft. high by 3 ft. wide. Page 69.

***R.* x *odorata* 'Gilbert Nabonnand'**
This healthy tea rose makes a profusion of loosely double pink blooms all season, with the heaviest bloom in spring and fall. It grows 4 ft. tall and wide and has thornless stems. If you can't find it, try 'Belinda's Dream'. Pages: 72, **73**.

***R.* x *polyantha* 'Climbing Pinkie'**
This is the climbing form of the poly-antha, 'Pinkie'. It can be grown as a loose shrub or as a climber to 8 ft. Pink semidouble blooms smother the canes in spring and repeat the performance in fall. The stems are mostly thornless. Designated an **Earth-Kind** rose. Pages: 26, ***27***.

***R.* x *polyantha* 'Marie Daly'**
This is the pink sport of the popular polyantha, 'Marie Pavie'. It produces a profusion of very fragrant light-pink, semidouble flowers all season. Grows 3 ft. tall and 2 ft. wide, on mostly thornless stems. Named for the late Marie Daly of Longview. Designated both a **Texas Superstar®** and an **Earth-Kind** rose. Pages: 90, ***90.***

***R.* x *polyantha* 'Marie Pavie'**
This dwarf shrub rose produces small white blooms all season. It grows 3 ft. tall and 2 ft. wide. If you can't find it, another polyantha, such as 'White Pet' or 'Marie Daly', makes a good substitute. Pages: 74, ***77***, 91.

Rosa x *polyantha* 'Marie Pavie'

Rosmarinus officinalis

ROSEMARY. This classic Mediterranean evergreen is a tough and attractive herbal shrub. The gray-green needlelike leaves combine a lovely fragrance with a tasty flavor. Small blue flowers bloom in late winter and early spring and sporadically throughout the year. Most rosemary species grow upright to a dense 3 ft. tall and wide (pp. 29, 36). 'Tuscan Blue' (pp. 97, 108) is upright to 6 ft., has deep blue flowers, and can be grown as a low hedge. 'Majorca Pink' (p. 115) is upright to 2 to 4 ft. but has lavender-pink blooms. 'Hill's Hardy' (pp. 48, 61, 105, 111) is a cold-hardy selection named for Texas herb expert Madeline Hill. Trailing rosemary (the low-growing *R. officinalis* 'Prostratus') has curved stems and grows 1 ft. tall and 3 ft. wide (pp. 43, 79, 101). Rosemaries do best in full sun and very well-drained soil. They need little water once established and can be pruned or sheared lightly during any season, though they suffer if cut back hard.

Rudbeckia fulgida 'Goldsturm'

'GOLDSTURM' BLACK-EYED SUSAN. This is a popular perennial that bears daisylike flowers with bright-gold petals and prominent brown conical centers in early summer. It forms a robust clump 2 ft. tall and wide, with dark-green leaves at the base and stiff, erect, branching flower stalks. Plant in full sun or partial shade in a fairly well-drained soil. It looks best with regular watering. Remove spent flowers and cut down all the flower stalks in fall or early spring. Pages: 29, 47, 70, 85, 88, 117.

Rosmarinus officinalis ROSEMARY

Rosmarinus officinalis 'Hill's Hardy'

Rudbeckia fulgida 'Goldsturm' BLACK-EYED SUSAN

Rosmarinus officinalis 'Prostratus'

Recommended Salvias

Salvia chamaedryoides

GERMANDER SAGE. This shrubby perennial is grown for its long bloom season (late spring into fall) and tough constitution. It forms a spreading mound of silvery leaves about 2 ft. tall covered with short spikes of beautiful light-blue flowers. Prefers full sun but can take a little shade in inland areas. Lightly shear in late fall. Page: 82.

Salvia farinacea

MEALYCUP SAGE. A popular native Texas perennial. Clusters of medium-blue flower spikes are borne on upright plants that grow vigorously to 3 ft. tall and wide. Flowers top the gray-green foliage in spring and continue until frost. Improved cultivars are purple, blue, or white and grow to a compact 1½ ft. tall and wide. Requires little water and is generally pest free. Shear off old blooms to stimulate new ones and to keep the plants tidy. Pages: 41, 47, 61, 64, 71, 98.

Salvia greggii

AUTUMN SAGE. This shrubby perennial is native toTexas and Mexico. It produces small, oval, sage-scented leaves and a profusion of two-lipped flowers, especially in spring and fall. Flowers are white, pink, red, and other colors, depending on the cultivar. 'Alba' (pp. 56, ***58***) has pure white flowers. 'Pink' (pp. 52, ***54***, 61, 105) is a large and dependable vivid-pink cultivar, one of many pink ones available. 'Cherry Chief' (p. 48) offers bright-red flowers. Autumn sage generally grows 21⁄2 ft. tall and wide, has few pests, and is very tolerant of dry spells, requiring supplemental watering only during prolonged droughts. Plant autumn sage in full sun and well-drained soil and shear between flower cycles to keep the plants full and blooming. Pages: 25, 29, 46, 48, 50, 64, 78-79, 82, 92-93, 95, 101, 102, 108, 110-111, 119.

Salvia leucantha

MEXICAN BUSH SAGE. This perennial blooms in the fall with hundreds of spikes of purple and white flowers above handsome gray-green foliage. Grows upright to 4 ft. tall and wide. For a bushier plant with more flower spikes, cut the stems back by half several times during the growing season. Requires full sun and good drainage. It has very few pests and needs little watering. Cut to the ground after the first frost. Designated a **Texas Superstar®**. Pages: 25, 32, 44-45, **47**, 56, 61, 72, 82, 85, 108.

Salvia x 'Indigo Spires'

'INDIGO SPIRES' SALVIA. A vigorous perennial that grows a bushy 5 ft. tall and 3 ft. wide. It puts out a plethora of long, deep blue-purple spikes all season. See mealycup sage (S. *farinacea*, p. 46) for growing requirements and care. Pages: 80, 91.

Santolina chamaecyparissus
GRAY SANTOLINA

Salvia greggii 'Cherry Chief'
AUTUMN SAGE

Salvia leucantha
MEXICAN BUSH SAGE

Salvia farinacea
MEALYCUP SAGE

Salvia greggii
AUTUMN SAGE

Salvia x 'Indigo Spires'
'INDIGO SPIRES' SALVIA

Ruellia brittoniana 'Katie'
DWARF MEXICAN PETUNIA

Ruellia brittoniana 'Katie'

DWARF MEXICAN PETUNIA. An extremely durable and attractive perennial ground cover with narrow dark green leaves. Grows in low dense clumps 1 ft. tall and wide and offers a profusion of small light-purple petunialike flowers from spring until frost. Grows in full sun or partial shade and tolerates most soil types. It is also quite tolerant of both drought and excess moisture. It has few if any pest problems. It self-seeds; pull out unwanted seedlings. Cut to the ground after the first frost. Designated a **Texas Superstar**® because of its beauty and low-maintenance requirements. 'Violet wild petunia' (p. 97) resembles the popular garden center petunia. This variety stands 1-2 feet tall with large flowers, two inches wide, with pleasing gray-green foliage. This versatile wildflower has modest water needs, making it well suited to Texas' droughts once well established. It typically grows in sandy soil, from sun to shady conditions, readily spreading via seeds. Well suited to difficult sites where a vigorous ground cover is desired. It can be mowed or cut back to encourage season-long blooming. Pages: 31, 35, 58, 75, 87, 113.

Sabal minor

TEXAS DWARF PALMETTO. This slow growing evergreen shrub has pale-green fan-like leaves and spineless stems. It requires partial to full shade. Once established in a garden setting, it is drought tolerant. Pages: 55, 58, 63, 119.

Sabal palmetto

SABAL PALM. The Coastal Sabal Palm or Cabbage Palm is one of the most cold hardy of the native palms, to 15° Fahrenheit. The Sabal Palm produces fan shaped leaves 3-4 feet long, creating a rounded canopy measuring 10 to 20 feet in width. This robust palm generally grows to 30 to 40 feet tall. It sinks its roots deep, down to 15–20 feet and is drought tolerant once established. This palm is ecologically beneficial, providing needed habitat for local wildlife. Pages: 39, 62-63, 69, 76.

Santolina chamaecyparissus

GRAY SANTOLINA. A bushy little shrub grown for its soft, fragrant, fine-textured, silver-gray foliage. Often sheared to make an edging or a formal specimen, it is also useful as a ground cover. If left unsheared, it bears round yellow flowers in summer. Santolina needs full sun and well-drained, dry soil. Prune every year in early spring, before new growth starts, cutting the old stems back by half. It generally grows a little more than a foot tall and wide. Pages: 43, 48, 64, 77, 79, ***81***.

Ruellia nudiflora
VIOLET WILD PETUNIA

Scabiosa caucasica

PINCUSHION FLOWER. A perennial that forms a clump of gray-green leaves. Stalks about 2 ft. tall bear clusters of usually blue but sometimes white flowers from late spring through fall. Plant in full sun and water regularly. Remove spent flowers. Cut back in fall to promote additional bloom. Page: 32.

Scutellaria suffrutescens

PINK SKULLCAP. A low-growing deciduous mound with pink flowers that requires full sun and low water. Grows to 2 ft tall and equally as wide. Pages: 91, 113.

Sedum 'Autumn Joy'

'AUTUMN JOY' SEDUM. This hardy perennial forms clumps of succulent foliage on thick stems topped with flat clusters of tiny flowers in the fall. 'Autumn Joy' grows 18 in. tall and wide, with erect stems and gray-green foliage. The flowers change color from pale to deep salmon pink to rusty red over a span of many weeks in late summer and fall as they open, mature, and go to seed. Most sedums, including 'Autumn Joy', need full sun. They have few pest problems and only require occasional watering in periods of drought. Cut down the old stalks in winter or early spring. Pages: 29, 47, 111.

Sisyrinchium angustifolium

BLUE-EYED GRASS. This native perennial has narrow, grass-like light-green leaves with blue flowers. It behaves well in garden settings. Pages: 75, 77.

Sorghastrum nutans

INDIAN GRASS. This native ornamental perennial grass has tall clumps of upright blue-green foliage that turns orange and yellow in fall and keeps tones of those colors through winter. Can grow 3 to 7 ft. tall and 1 to 2 ft. wide. In late summer, light brown flowers rise above the foliage to 5 to 6 ft.tall and remain through winter. Drought tolerant and does best in poor, dry soil. Too much water or rich and wet soil will cause grass to flop over. In spring, you can cut back to the ground and divide. Pages: 12, 41, 79.

Sedum 'Autumn Joy'
'AUTUMN JOY' SEDUM

Spiraea x *bumalda*

JAPANESE SPIREA. A deciduous shrub, it creates a low mound of thin, graceful, arching stems that bear sharply toothed leaves and, from late spring into summer, round flat clusters of tiny flowers. 'Goldflame' (pp. 117, ***119***) has bright-gold leaves that are tinged with orange in spring and turn red in fall. Flowers are pink. Both cultivars grow about 2 to 3 ft. tall and wide. Plant them in full or partial sun. Prune every year after bloom, removing some of the older stems at ground level and cutting the others back partway. In summer, shear off faded flowers to promote possible reblooming. Water during periods of drought. Rarely suffers from insects or disease.

Sabal palmetto
SABAL PALM

Sterlitzia reginae

BIRD-OF-PARADISE. Beloved tropical-looking evergreen plant with large, eye-catching flowers that look like the head of a bird. Flowers, mostly orange but touched with blue and white, are concentrated in early spring, but some bloom year-round. Large leathery leaves form a dense clump about 5 ft. tall. Best adapted to frost-free areas. Needs protection elsewhere. Or plant in pots and move to a covered spot in winter. Best in full sun. Water and fertilize regularly. Remove spent flowers. Page: 69.

Tagetes lemmonii

COPPER CANYON DAISY. A shrublike perennial with small finely divided, dull-green aromatic leaves and bright orange-yellow, marigold-type flowers in fall. It grows 2 to 3 ft. tall and wide. Trim back by one-third several times during the growing season to maintain a compact habit and to prevent sprawling in bloom. Plant in full sun. Rarely needs water and has no pest problems. Late blooms can be damaged by a hard frost. Page: 41.

Tagetes lucida

MEXICAN MINT MARIGOLD. This Mexican perennial has aromatic foliage and clusters of small golden yellow marigold-like flowers in the fall. The scented foliage (tasting of licorice or anise) can be used as a culinary substitute for French tarragon. Generally grows 1½ ft. tall and wide and requires full to partial sun. Shear the plants back by one-third several times during the growing season to maintain a compact habit and to promote heavier bloom. It has few pests and requires watering only during dry periods. Pages: 56, 88, ***90***, 105.

Tecoma stans 'Gold Star'

'GOLD STAR' ESPERANZA. This showy Texas native can be grown as a deciduous shrub in the lower third of the state. In the middle section, it may be grown as a perennial, pruned to the ground after the first hard freeze. In the northern third, it may be grown as an annual. It bears shiny bright-green pecanlike leaves, extremely showy clusters of yellow bell-shaped flowers from summer until frost, and green bean pods after the flowers fade. Generally grows to a bushy 5 ft. tall and wide. Esperanza requires full hot sun and only occasional watering during the summer. It has no major insect or disease problems. Cut off bean pods or shear plants to encourage repeat bloom. Plant it in a protected area or

Tecoma stans 'Gold Star'
'GOLD STAR' ESPERANZA

Tagetes lemmonii
COPPER CANYON DAISY

mulch heavily to protect it from freezing. In the northern half of the state, consider using it as an annual or potted specimen, or use a more cold-hardy substitute like the butterfly rose. Designated a **Texas Superstar®.** Pages: 29, 39, 76, 85.

Thymus praecox ssp. *arcticus*

CREEPING THYME. A creeping perennial that forms low mats of wiry stems and tiny semievergreen leaves. Tolerates light foot traffic and smells good when you step on it. Clusters of pink, lavender, or white flowers bloom over a long season in midsummer. Grows 4 to 6 in. tall, 1 to 2 ft. wide. Look in the herb department of a nursery to find this plant. There are several other kinds of creeping thymes. 'Argenteus' and 'Aureus' varigated lemon thymes have lemon-scented, silver- and yellow-variegated leaves, respectively. All make attractive, fragrant, tough ground covers for sites with full sun and well-drained soil. They need little water once established. Shear old stems close to the ground in fall to early spring. Plants may self-sow and pop up in cracks of pavement, in gravel walks, or even in the lawn, but aren't weedy. Page: 97.

Tipuana tipu

TIPU TREE. This large semievergreen or deciduous tree makes a useful lawn or shade tree. It grows 25 to 35 ft. tall and spreads twice as wide. Light-green, finely divided leaves are topped with long clusters of yellow to apricot pealike flowers from late spring to early summer, followed by large seedpods. Best grown where summers are warm and winters are mild. Foliage is damaged at 25°F. Page: 68.

Verbena bonariensis

PURPLE VERBENA. This perennial forms a low mound of basal foliage topped by a thicket of stiff, erect, much-branched but almost leafless flower stalks. They bear countless little clusters of lavender-purple flowers throughout the season. The heaviest bloom comes before the heat of summer, beckoning butterflies and floral arrangers. Purple verbena needs full sun and tolerates most soil conditions. Shear as needed during the growing season to promote new bloom stalks. It may occasionally be attacked by flea hoppers. Generally self-sows but isn't weedy. Pages: 52, 75, 95.

Verbena x *hybrida*

VERBENA. These are sprawling perennials with evergreen leaves and round clusters of showy flowers. 'Blue Princess' (pp. 27, 29, 56, 91, 101, 110) has lightly fragrant lavender-blue flowers and is designated a **Texas Superstar®.** 'Homestead Purple' (pp. 36, 45, 49, 81, 85, 95, 99) has vibrant purple flowers. Plant them in full sun and they will bloom nonstop from early spring until hard frost if regularly deadheaded. Plants generally grow about 1 ft. tall and spread 3 ft. or wider. Prune any damaged or frosted shoots in early spring, and shear throughout the growing season to keep tidy. Water regularly during hot spells. Plants may suffer attack from flea hoppers during summer heat. 'Superbena purple' (pp. 31, 58, 76, 112, 113, ***113***) This spreading native blooms all summer, growing in full sun, it is heat and drought tolerant. This Verbena is cold hardy to 15° Fahrenheit, so it may be an annual and die back with lower temperatures.

Verbena x *hybrida* 'Blue Princess' VERBENA

Verbena bonariensis PURPLE VERBENA

Verbena x *hybrida* 'Homestead Purple' VERBENA

Viburnum dentatum
LITTLE JOHN

Viburnum dentatum

'KLM' LITTLE JOHN. This hybrid stays a manageable size growing 4–5 feet tall and wide. Growing in medium moisture and well-drained soil. Very showy flowers in May and June attracting birds and butterflies and developing dark-blue berries enjoyed by birds. Pages: 36, 90, 117.

Water plants

Many garden centers offer a limited selection of water plants. Specialty nurseries and mail-order water-garden specialists often offer dozens of kinds. Most water plants are fast-growing, sometimes even weedy, so you need only one of each to start. Some water plants are tender to frost, but you can overwinter them indoors in a pot or aquarium. There are three main groups of water plants: marginal, floating, and oxygenating. Choose one or more of each for an interesting and balanced effect.

Marginal plants grow well on the edge of the pond or in containers covered with 2 in. or more of water. Their leaves and flower stalks stand above the water surface while their roots stay submerged. Louisiana iris (see *Iris* x Louisiana hybrids, p. 99) is a common example.

Floating plants have leaves that rest on the water and roots that dangle into it. Water lettuce (*Pistia* species) is a floater that forms saucer-size rosettes of iridescent pale-green leaves.

Oxygenating, or submerged, plants grow completely under water. They help keep the water clear and provide oxygen, food, and shelter for fish. Anacharis (*Elodea* species) is a popular oxygenator with tiny, dark-green leaves.

Water lilies (*Nymphaea* species, pp. 99, ***101***) are the most popular plants for pools and ponds. There are two main groups of water lilies. Hardy water lilies survive outdoors from year to year and bloom in midsummer. They are usually the easiest to grow. Tropical water lilies, such as Dauben water lily (*N.* x *daubenyana*, p. 77, ***77***) need warm water and bloom over a longer season from summer through fall but are cold tender and often treated as annuals. Both kinds are available in dwarf-size plants, suitable for small pools, with fragrant or scentless flowers in shades of white, yellow, and pink. Tropicals also come in shades of blue and purple. All water lilies need full sun. Plant the roots in a container of heavy, rich, garden soil, and set the container in the pool, making sure that about 6 in. of water covers the soil. (See p. 203 for more on planting.)

Nymphaea x 'Charlene Strawn'
Charlene Strawn

Wisteria frutescens

American wisteria. A native deciduous woody vine with dense deep-green foliage full of dangling clusters of fragrant pea-like purple-and-blue flowers from early summer to early fall. It can be trained to climb a trellis, fence, or other vertical structures. Needs well-drained soil and prefers full sun but will tolerate partial shade. More sun results in more flower blooms. It typically grows 15 to 20 ft. tall but can get up to 40 ft. tall if left unchecked. This wisteria is not an aggressive spreader. Prune regularly to control the size and shape and heavily in spring to remove dead foliage and encourage new growth. Pages: 52, ***54***, 97.

Yucca

Yucca. These are bold architectural plants with pointed swordlike leaves and tall stalks of showy creamy white flowers. *Y. filamentosa* (pp. 41, ***42***) has narrow leaves with hairy filaments along the margins and generally grows 3 ft. tall and wide. Soft-tip yucca (*Y. gloriosa*, pp. 56, ***57***, 77, 79) has somewhat flexible gray-green leaves and grows 4 to 5 ft. tall and 3 ft. wide. Yuccas require full sun and good drainage and no supplemental irrigation. Maintenance is limited to removing dead leaves at their base and cutting down dead flower stalks. Yuccas have few if any pest problems.

Y. gloriosa
Soft-Tip Yucca

Guide *to* Installation

Landscaping is rewarding, but it does require hard work in order to reap its benefits. There are various necessary tasks that come with installing any of the designs in this book, and you will find all of those projects here. To keep things simple, we've organized the jobs in the order in which you'd most likely tackle them. In addition to the instructions, we've included numerous illustrations to help you learn how to plan the job; clear the site; construct paths, patios, ponds, fences, arbors, and trellises; prepare the planting beds; and install and maintain the plantings.

So, are you ready to roll up your sleeves and dig in? If you are, all it takes is just a few weekends to create a landscape feature that will provide years of enjoyment while adding outdoor appeal and value to your home.

Organizing Your Project

If your gardening experience is limited to mowing the lawn, pruning the bushes, and growing some flowers and vegetables, the thought of starting from scratch and installing a whole new landscape feature might be intimidating. But in fact, adding one of the designs in this book to your property is completely within reach, if you approach it the right way. The key is to divide the project into a series of steps and take them one at a time. This is how professional landscapers work. It's efficient and orderly, and it makes even big jobs seem manageable.

On this and the facing page, we'll explain how to think your way through a landscaping project and anticipate the various steps. Subsequent topics in this section describe how to do each part of the job. Detailed instructions and illustrations cover all the techniques you'll need to install any design from start to finish.

The step-by-step approach

Choose a design and adapt it to your site. The designs in this book address parts of the home landscape. In the most attractive and effective home landscapes, all the various parts work together. Don't be afraid to change the shape of beds; alter the number, kinds, and positions of plants; or revise paths and structures to bring them into harmony with their surroundings.

To see the relationships with your existing landscape, you can draw the design on a scaled plan of your property. Or you can work on the site itself, placing wooden stakes, pots, or whatever is handy to represent plants and structures.

Lay out the design on site. Once you've decided what you want to do, you'll need to lay out the paths and structures and outline the beds. Some people are comfortable pacing off distances and relying on their eye to judge sizes and relative positions. Others prefer to transfer the grid from the plan full size onto the site using garden lime (a white powder available at nurseries) or contractors marking spray paint (water based and temporary), as you would chalk on a blackboard, to draw a grid or outlines of planting beds.

Clear the site. (See pp. 158-159.) Sometimes you have to work around existing features—a nice big tree, a building or fence, a sidewalk—but it's usually easiest to start a new landscaping project by removing unwanted structures or

DIGGING POSTHOLES

AMENDING SOIL

pavement and killing, cutting down, or uprooting all the plants. This can generate a lot of debris for disposal, but it's worth the trouble to make a fresh start.

Make provisions for water. (See pp. 160-161.) In Texas, newly planted landscape plants may require more water than nature provides. Utilizing native plants adapted to the local climate helps reduce or eliminate the need for supplemental irrigation once plants are established. This is generally after the first 1–3 growing seasons. A well-planned irrigation strategy and system can help you make the most of this increasingly precious natural resource. Keep in mind that some permanent parts of most watering systems need to be installed before the other landscape features. Additional parts are installed after the soil is prepared. And the final components are normally placed after planting.

Be aware that soil expands and contracts as the moisture level of the soil fluctuates. These extremes seem to be increasing with causing extreme drought and extreme precipitation. Drought can cause soil to contract causing underground irrigation piping to shift and break creating leaks. The same can occur with extensive rainfall, causing the soil to expand cracking water pipes and irrigation. So, monitor your irrigation system for leaks during drought periods and during higher-than-normal rainfall.

Construct the "hardscape." (See pp. 163-197.) Hardscape includes landscape structures, such as fences, trellises, arbors, retaining walls, walkways, edging, and outdoor lighting. Install these elements before you start any planting.

Prepare the soil. (See pp. 198-201.) On most properties, it's uncommon to find soil that's as good as it should be for growing plants. Typically, the soil around a new house is shallow, compacted, and infertile. Some plants tolerate such poor conditions, but they don't thrive. To grow healthy, attractive plants, you need to improve the quality of the soil throughout the entire area that you're planning to plant.

Do the planting and add mulch. (See pp. 202-206.) Putting plants in the ground usually goes quite quickly and gives instant gratification. Mulching the soil makes the area look neat even while the plants are still small.

Maintain your plantings. (See pp. 202-212.) Most plantings need regular watering and occasional weeding for the first year or two. After that, depending on the design you've chosen, you'll have to do some routine maintenance—watering, pruning, shaping, cutting back, and cleaning up—to keep the plants looking their best. This may take as little as a few hours a year or as much as an hour or two every week throughout the growing season.

TRANSPLANTING

SETTING FLAGSTONES

Clearing the Site

The site you've chosen for a landscaping project may or may not need to be cleared of fences, old pavement, construction debris, and other objects. Unless your house is newly built, the site will almost certainly be covered with plants.

Before you start removing them, try to find someone to identify them for you. As you walk around together, make a sketch that shows what plants are where, and attach labels to them, too. Determine if there are any desirable plants worth saving—mature shade trees that you should work around, shapely shrubs that aren't too big to dig up and relocate or give away, worthwhile perennials and ground covers that you could divide and replant, or healthy sod that you could lay elsewhere. Likewise, decide which plants need to go—diseased or crooked trees, straggly or overgrown shrubs, weedy brush, invasive ground covers, or a tattered lawn.

You can clear small areas yourself, bundling the brush for pickup and tossing soft-stemmed plants on the compost pile. But if you have lots of woody brush or any trees to remove, you might want to hire someone else to do the job. A crew armed with power tools can turn a thicket into a pile of wood chips in just a few hours. Have them pull out the roots and grind the stumps, too. Save the chips; they're good for surfacing paths, or you can use them as mulch.

Working around a tree

If there are any large, healthy trees on your site, be careful as you work around them. It's okay to prune off some of a tree's limbs, as shown on the facing page, but respect its trunk and its roots. Keep heavy equipment from beneath the tree's canopy, and don't raise or lower the level of the soil there. Try never to cut or wound the bark on the trunk (don't nail things to a tree), because that exposes the tree to disease organisms. Planting beneath existing Texas natives such as post oaks can endanger their health. Consult a certified arborist on ways to integrate these handsome, but sensitive, trees into your landscape and care for them properly.

Killing perennial weeds

Some common weeds that sprout back from perennial roots or runners are bindweed, Bermuda grass, Johnson grass, nutsedge, smilax, and Carolina snailseed. Garden plants that can become weedy include bamboo, Mexican petunia, mint, and *Liriope spicata*. Once they get established, perennial weeds are hard to eliminate. You can't cut off just the tops, because the plants keep sprouting back. You need to dig out the weeds, smother them, or kill them with an herbicide.

Smothering weeds

Mow or cut the tops of the weeds close to the ground ❶. Then cover the area with overlapped sections of newspaper ❷ or flat cardboard and top with a layer of mulch spread several inches deep ❸.

Smothering works by excluding light, which stops photosynthesis. If any shoots reach up through the covering and produce green leaves, pull them out immediately. Wait a few months, until you're sure the weeds are dead, before you dig into the smothered area and plant there.

In Texas, you can also kill weeds through a process called "solarization." Till the weeds into the soil and moisten the area. Then cover the soil with a thick sheet of clear plastic, sealing its edges by burying them in a shallow trench. The heat generated underneath the plastic kills the weeds.

Digging. You can often remove a perennial weed if you dig carefully at the base of the stems, find the roots, and follow them through the soil, pulling out every bit of root that you find. Some plant roots go deeper than you can dig. Most plants will resprout from the bits that you miss, but these leftover sprouts are easy to pull.

Spraying. Herbicides are easy, fast, and effective weed killers when chosen and applied with care. Ask at the nursery for those that break down quickly into more benign substances, and make sure the weed you're trying to kill is listed on the product label. After spraying, you usually need to wait from one to four weeks for the weed to die completely. You may have to spray a second or third time. While herbicides may be convenient, they can be harmful to wildlife, to the environment, carcinogenic to pets and humans. Herbicides and pesticides can harm beneficial insects like pollinators. Before you use an herbicide or pesticide research if there is an organic or more environmentally friendly method.

Replacing turf

If the area where you're planning to add a landscape feature is currently part of the lawn, you have a fairly easy task ahead. How to proceed depends on the condition of the turf and on what you want to put in its place. If the turf is healthy, you can recycle it to replace, repair, or extend the lawn elsewhere.

The drawing below shows a technique for removing relatively small areas of strong healthy turf for replanting. First, using a sharp shovel, cut it into strips about 1- to 3 ft. square. (These small pieces are easy to lift) ❶. Then slice a few inches deep under each square and lift it, roots and all, the way you would lift brownies from a pan ❷. Quickly transplant the squares to a previously prepared site; water them well until the roots are established.

If you don't need the turf, or if it's straggly or weedy, leave it in place and kill the grass. Spraying with an herbicide kills most grasses within one to two weeks. Or cover it with a tarp or a sheet of black plastic for about four weeks during the heat of summer. Then dig or till the bed, shredding the turf, roots and all, and mixing it into the soil.

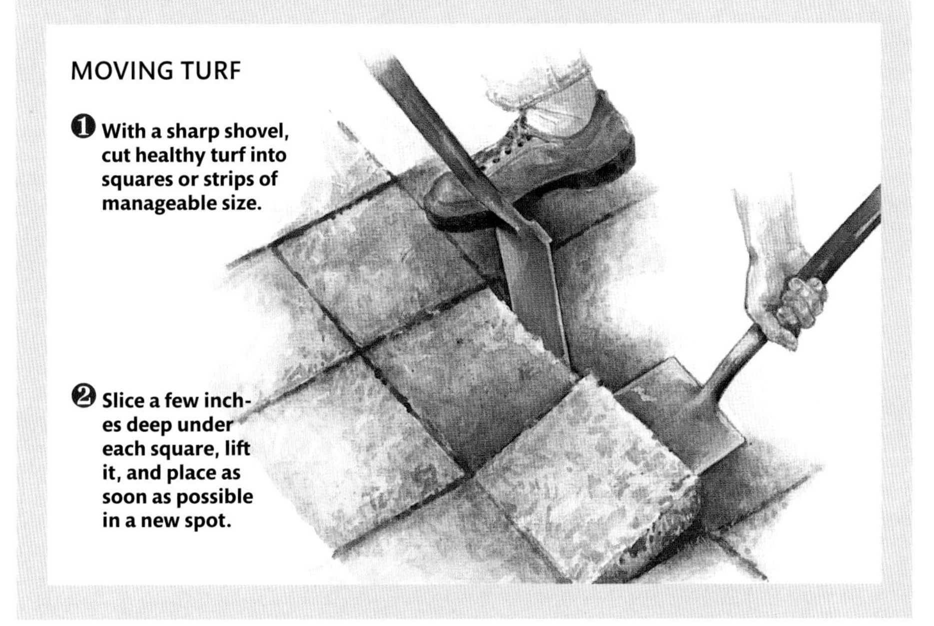

Removing large limbs

If there are large trees on your property now, you may want to remove some of the lower limbs so light can reach your plantings. Major pruning of large trees is a job for a professional arborist, but you can remove limbs smaller than 4 in. in diameter and less than 10 ft. above the ground yourself with a simple bow saw or pole saw.

Use the three-step procedure shown below to remove large limbs safely. First, saw partway through the bottom of the limb, approximately 1 ft. out from the trunk ❶. This keeps the bark from tearing down the trunk when the limb falls. Then make a corresponding cut through the top of the limb ❷ and be prepared to get out of the way when the limb drops. Finally, remove the stub ❸. Undercut it slightly or hold it as you finish the cut, so it doesn't fall away and peel bark off the trunk. Note that the cut is not flush with the trunk but is just outside the thick area at the limb's base, called the "branch collar." Leaving the branch collar helps the wound heal quickly and naturally. Wound dressing is considered unnecessary today.

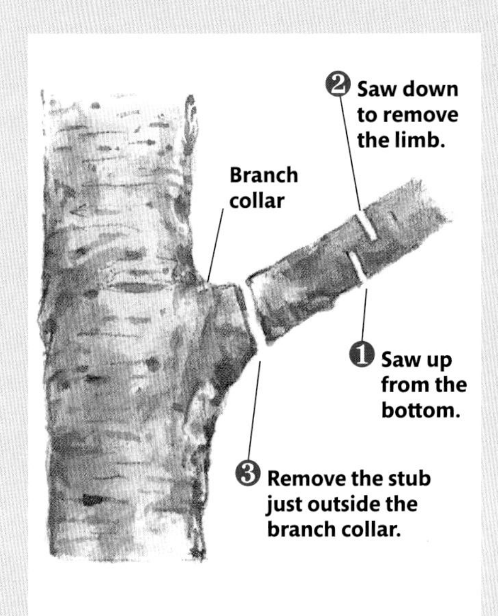

Water for Your Plants

Texas's long, dry summers and frequent droughts make watering a critical concern of gardeners here. Though some plants will survive long dry periods once established, almost all plants will need regular watering the first few years after planting. And most will need summer watering their entire life to look their best.

But there is more at stake than just the survival of plants. Water conservation is a daily obligation in Texas, where water is a valuable and limited resource. Outdoor landscapes use a large portion of urban water, so nothing should be wasted. During periods of drought, mandatory conservation is often strictly enforced.

So for the health of your plants and for the preservation of a valuable resource, make water conservation part of your landscape planning from the beginning. The box below outlines effective water-saving practices for home landscapes. (See p. 209 for more on when and how much to water.) You can also consult your local water department for advice about watering gardens and lawns.

In addition to extreme heat Texas also experiences extreme cold periodically. Below freezing temperatures can wreak havoc on an irrigation system. The solution is to empty irrigation lines and hoses of water before the chance of frost. This can be done by blowing compressed air through your irrigation system, expelling any excess moisture. A professional can assist with shutting your irrigation for the season. Just as important is disconnecting your hoses, draining, and storing for the winter. In addition, make sure to turn off water valves inside that send water to outside spigots as well as keeping outdoor spigots "open" so that any excess moisture can escape if it freezes and expands.

Watering systems

One of the best ways to conserve water is to use an efficient delivery system. The simplest watering systems—watering cans and handheld hoses—are also the most limited and inefficient. They can be adequate for watering new transplants or widely separated individual plants. But sprinkling plants in an entire bed with a hose and nozzle for even as long as an hour may provide less water than half an inch of rainfall. And wetting just the top few inches of soil this way encourages shallow root growth, making it necessary to water more frequently. To provide enough water to soak the soil to a depth of a foot or more, you need a system that can run untended for extended periods.

Hose-end sprinklers are easy to set up and leave to soak an area. But they're also inefficient: water is blown away by wind. It runs off sloped or paved areas. It is applied unevenly, or it falls too far away from individual plants to be of use to them. And because sprinklers soak leaves as well as soil, the damp foliage may breed fungal diseases.

Low-volume irrigation. For garden beds and landscape plantings such as those in this book, low-volume irrigation systems are the most efficient and offer the most flexibility and control. Frequently called "drip irrigation systems," they deliver water at low pressure through a network of plastic pipes, hoses, and tubing, and a variety of emitters and microsprinklers. Such systems are designed to apply water slowly and directly to the roots of targeted plants, so very little water is lost to runoff and evaporation or wasted on plants that don't need it. Because water is usually applied at soil level, the risk of foliar diseases is reduced, less soil is watered, and weeds are reduced.

Simple low-volume systems can be attached to ordinary outdoor faucets or garden hoses and controlled manually. You can set up such a system in less than an hour. Sophisticated systems include (1) their own attachment to your main water supply, (2) a network of valves and buried pipes that allow you to divide your property into zones, and (3) an electronic control device that can automatically water each zone at preset times for preset durations. Such systems often incorporate sprinklers.

A person with modest mechanical skills and basic tools can plan and install a low-volume irrigation system. Extensive multizoned systems (particularly those with their own attachment to the main water supply) are more difficult to design and install. If you tackle one, have a professional review your plans before you start. You can buy kits or individual system components from garden centers, nurseries, or specialty suppliers. Although most manufacturers provide helpful instructions, good criteria for choosing among different local suppliers are their knowledge of system design and installation and their ability to help you with both. A supplier may charge for this service, but good advice is worth it.

Low-volume-system components. Any irrigation system connected to a domestic water supply needs a ***backflow prevention device*** (also called an "antisiphon device") at the point of connection to the water supply to protect drinking water from contamination. Backflow devices are often mandated by city building codes, so check with local health or building officials to determine if a specific type of backflow prevention device is required.

Install a ***filter*** to prevent minerals and flakes that slough off metal water pipes from clogging the emitters. You'll need to clean the filter regularly. Between the filter and emitters, all

DRIP IRRIGATION SYSTEM

Basic components of a drip irrigation system are shown here. Individual systems will vary. Several common types of emitters are shown; systems can incorporate others.

Installing a drip irrigation system helps conserve water and keep your plants healthy.

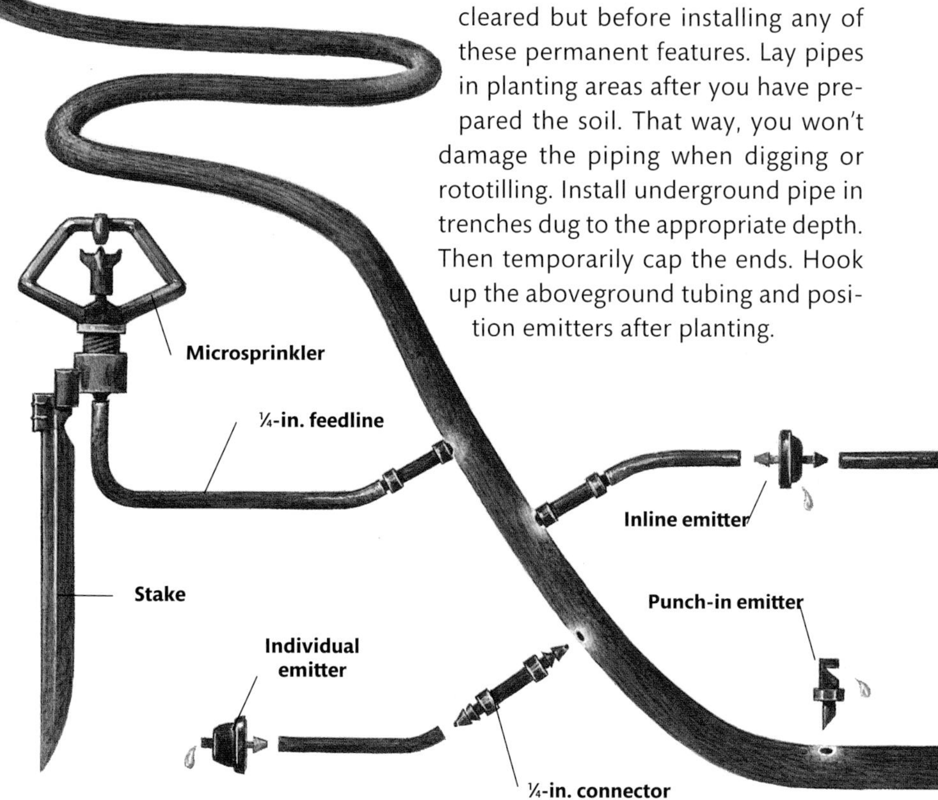

hoses and tubing should be plastic, not metal.

Pressure regulators reduce the mains' water pressure to levels required by the system's low-volume emitters.

Supply lines deliver water from the source to the emitters. Some systems incorporate buried lines of rigid plastic pipe to carry water to plantings anywhere on the property. For aboveground use, you'll need flexible tubing designed specifically for low-volume irrigation.

Emitters and ***soaker hoses*** deliver the water to the plants. A wide range of emitters are available for different kinds of plants and garden situations. Various drip fittings, bubblers, and microsprinklers can be plugged into the flexible plastic tubing. A single emitter or a group of emitters might serve individual or groups of plants. Soaker hoses and "ooze tubes" seep or drip water along their length. Consult with your supplier about which delivery systems best meet your plants' needs. (The high calcium and salt content of many water sources in Texas can clog drip emitters, so check emitters regularly to make sure they are watering properly.)

A ***timer*** or ***electronic controller*** helps ensure efficient water use. Used in conjunction with zoned plantings, these devices provide control and flexibility to deal with the specific water needs of groups of plants or even individual specimens.

With increased drought and water restrictions, smart ***irrigation controllers*** linked to the internet and live weather updates can maximize the efficiency of your irrigation system and reduce your water use. A smart controller can also reduce harmful overwatering. These smart systems can be accessed via an app to monitor and control from your smart phone. While this is convenient, errors and oversights can easily occur. So be sure to consult a professional or at least visually inspect your system as it cycles through to insure desired frequency.

Installation. Permanent irrigation equipment should be installed early in any project. Lay underground piping that crosses paths, patios, or similar landscape features after the site is cleared but before installing any of these permanent features. Lay pipes in planting areas after you have prepared the soil. That way, you won't damage the piping when digging or rototilling. Install underground pipe in trenches dug to the appropriate depth. Then temporarily cap the ends. Hook up the aboveground tubing and position emitters after planting.

Water-wise practices

Choose plants carefully. Many plants that require little water, including Texas natives, thrive in the state's dry summer climate and are increasingly available from local nurseries and garden centers.

Group plants with similar water needs. Position plants that require the most water near the house, where they can be more easily tended and watered. Use drought-tolerant plants farther from the house.

Plant in fall. This way, new plants will have the cooler, wetter winter and spring seasons to become established before facing the heat of summer.

Mulch plantings. A 2- to 3-in. layer of mulch reduces evaporation by keeping the soil cool and sheltering it from wind.

Create water-retaining basins. Use these to direct irrigation water to large plants. Make a low soil mound around the plant's perimeter, at its drip line. (Basins aren't necessary in drip-irrigated beds.)

Limit lawn size. Lawns demand lots of water. Reduce the size of your lawn by planting beds, borders, and less thirsty ground covers.

Water in the morning. Lower morning temperatures and less wind mean less water is lost to evaporation.

Adjust watering to conditions. Water less during cool weather in the spring and fall. Turn off automatic timers during the rainy season.

Install, monitor, and maintain an irrigation system. Even a simple drip system conserves water. Once it's installed, check and adjust the equipment on a regular basis. Be sure to inspect frequently for clogged emitters.

Installing a drip irrigation system helps conserve water and keep your plants healthy.

Making Paths and Walkways

Every landscape needs paths and walkways if for no other reason than to keep your feet dry as you move from one place to another. A path can also divide and define the spaces in the landscape, orchestrate the way the landscape is viewed, and even be a key element in enhancing its beauty.

Whether it is a graceful curving garden path or a utilitarian slab leading to the garage, a walk has two main functional requirements: durability and safety. It should hold up through seasonal changes and provide a well-drained surface that is easy to walk on and to maintain.

A path's function helps determine its surface and its character. In general, heavily trafficked walkways leading to a door, garage, or shed need hard, smooth (but not slick) surfaces and should take you where you want to go fairly directly. A path to a backyard play area could be a strip of soft wood bark, easy on the knees of impatient children. A relaxed stroll in the garden might require only a hopscotch collection of flat stones meandering from one prized plant to another.

Before laying out a walk or path, spend some time observing existing traffic patterns. If your path makes use of a route people already take (particularly children), it will be more likely to keep them on the path and off the lawn or flowers. Avoid areas that are slow to drain. When determining width, consider whether the path must accommodate rototillers or several strollers walking abreast, or just provide access for plant maintenance.

Dry-laid paths

You can make a path simply by laying bricks or spreading wood chips on top of bare earth. While quick and easy, this method has serious drawbacks. Laid on the surface, with no edging to contain them, loose materials are soon scattered, and solid materials are easily jostled out of place. If the earth base doesn't drain very well, the path will be a swamp after a rainstorm. In cold-winter areas of Texas, repeated expansion and contraction of the soil will heave bricks or flagstones out of alignment, making the path unsightly and dangerous.

The method we recommend—laying surface material on an excavated sand-and-gravel base—minimizes these problems. The sand and gravel improve drainage and provide a cushion against the freeze-thaw movement of the underlying soil. Excavation can place the path surface at ground level, where the surrounding soil or an installed edging can contain loose materials and prevent hard materials from shifting.

All styles, from a natural wood-bark path to a formal cut-stone entry walk, and all the materials discussed in this section, can be laid on an excavated base of gravel and sand.

Hard-surface walks

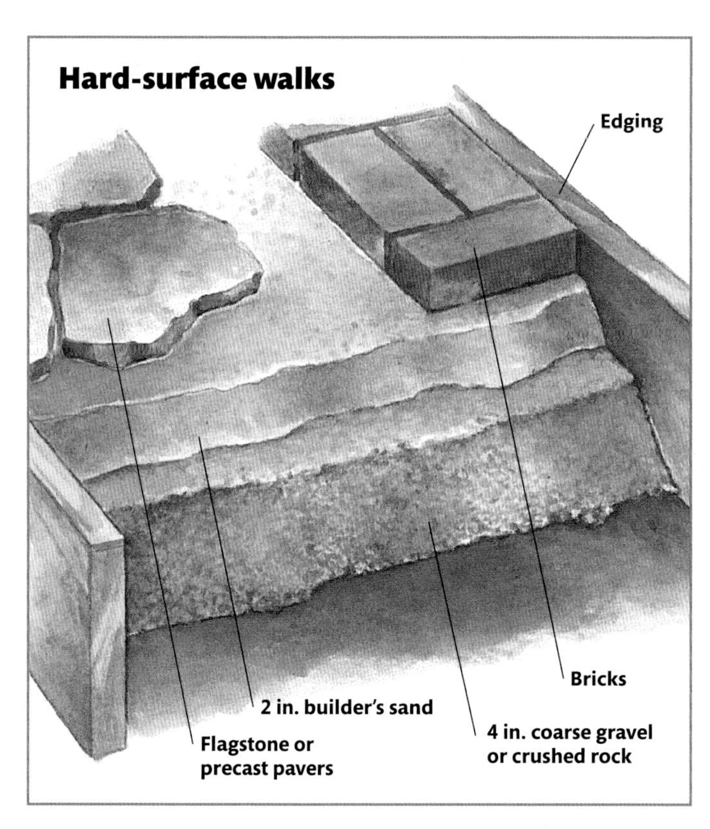

Loose-surface paths

Choosing a surface

Walkways and paths can be made of either hard or soft material. Your choice of material will depend on the walkway's function, your budget, and your personal preferences.

Soft materials, including bark, wood chips, pine needles, and loose gravel, are best for informal and low-traffic areas. Inexpensive and simple to install, they settle, scatter, or decompose and must be replenished or replaced every few years.

Hard materials, such as brick, flagstone, and concrete pavers, are more expensive and time-consuming to install, but they are permanent, requiring only occasional maintenance. (Compacted crushed stone can also make a hard-surface walk.) Durable and handsome, they're ideal for high-traffic, high-profile areas.

When choosing paving surfaces, consider utilizing local or regionally produced materials. This reduces the environmental impacts of long distance transportation. Plus, local materials contribute authenticity and the unique character of your region.

As extreme weather increases, so does erosion, flooding, and slippery conditions. Selection of paving materials is more important than ever. Consider that finer aggregates can wash away, other paving materials whether set in motor or dry laid can be undermined by extreme weather: freezing and thawing, increased runoff, and erosion.

Extreme Weather can increase the frequency of heaving, subsidence, and erosion. Carefully select and research construction methods and materials suited to your region and conditions to ensure success. Consider that finer aggregates can wash away and other paving materials whether set in motor or dry laid can be undermined by extreme weather: freezing and thawing, increased runoff, and erosion.

Bark, wood chips, and pine needles

Perfect for a natural look or a quick temporary path, these loose materials can be laid directly on the soil or, if drainage is poor, on a gravel bed. Bagged materials from a nursery or garden center will be cleaner, more uniform, and considerably more expensive than bulk supplies bought by the cubic yard. Check with local tree services to find the best prices on bulk material.

Gravel and crushed rock

Loose rounded gravel gives a bit underfoot, creating a soft but messy path. The angular facets of crushed stone eventually compact into a hard and tidier path that can be laid without an edging, if the surrounding soil is firm enough. Gravel and stone type and color vary from area to area. Buy materials by the ton or cubic yard.

Concrete pavers

Precast concrete pavers are versatile, readily available, and often the least expensive hard-surface material. They come in a range of colors and shapes, including interlocking patterns. Precast edgings are also available. Most home and garden centers carry a variety of precast pavers, which are sold by the piece.

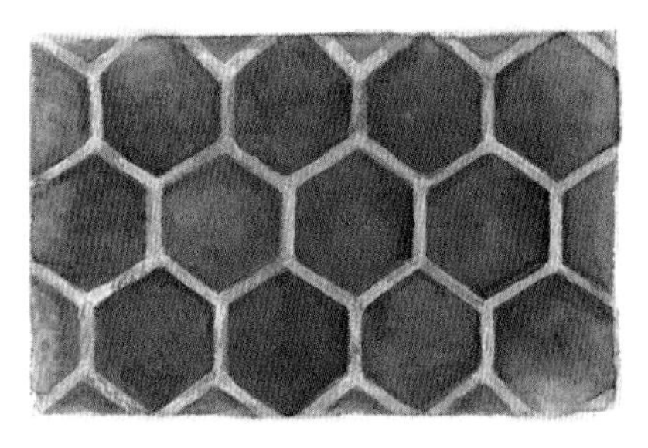

HEXAGONS

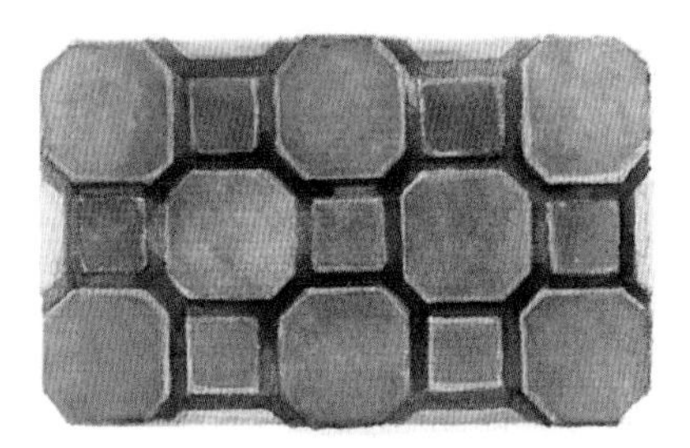

OCTAGONS AND SQUARES COMBINATION

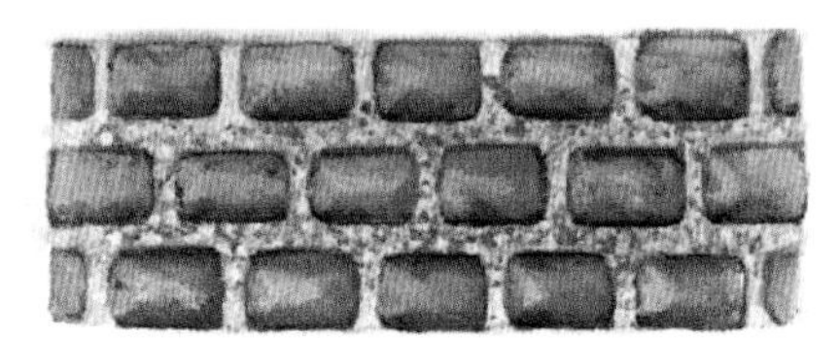

RUNNING BAND

Brick

Widely available in a range of sizes, colors, and textures, brick complements many design styles. When carefully laid on a well-prepared sand-and-gravel base, brick provides an even, safe, and long-lasting surface. When brick walks are wet or icy, they can become slick. In shady locations, brick walks can become slippery with moss or mold. Buy paving brick instead of the softer "facing" brick, which may break up after a few freeze-thaw cycles. (If you buy used brick, pick the hardest.) Avoid glazed types; the glaze traps moisture and salts, which will damage the brick.

RUNNING BOND

TWO-BRICK BASKET WEAVE

HERRINGBONE

DIAGONAL HERRINGBONE

Flagstone

"Flagstone" is a generic term for stratified stone that can be split to form pavers. Limestone and sandstone are common paving materials. The surfaces of marble and slate are usually too smooth to make safe paving. Cut into squares or rectangles, flagstone can be laid as individual stepping-stones or in interesting patterns. Flagstones come in a range of colors, textures, and sizes. Flags for walks should be at least 2 in. thick. Purchased by weight, surface area, or pallet load, flagstones are usually the most expensive paving choice. When Flagstone can become slick when wet or icy, it can become slippery with moss or mold in shady locations.

Reclaimed and Repurposed Materials

Only age can create a rich patina to stone, brick and other paving materials. These elements add a fine character to your landscape, bringing home a specialized texture and feel to your outdoor spaces. These antique elements can be interspersed with new materials or used exclusively. Reclaimed materials are available from specialized outlets. They may also be available from more traditional suppliers. Special know-how may be required to work with reclaimed materials.

CUT FLAGSTONE

CUT AND IRREGULAR FLAGSTONE

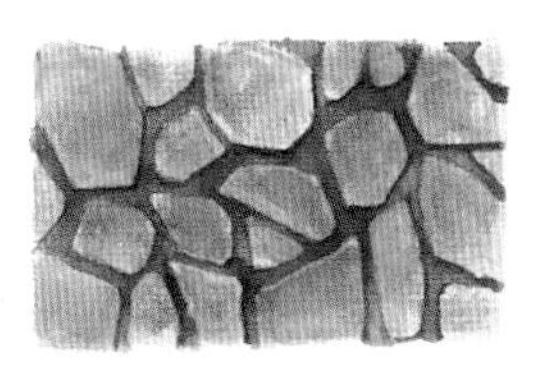

IRREGULAR FLAGSTONE

Drainage

Few things are worse than a path dotted with puddles or icy patches. To prevent these from forming, the soil around and beneath the path should drain well. The path's location and construction should ensure that rainwater does not collect on the surface. Before you locate a path, observe runoff and drainage on your property during and after heavy rains. Avoid routing a path through areas where water courses, collects, or is slow to drain.

While both loose and hard paving can be successfully laid directly on well-drained compacted soil, sometimes laying surface materials on a base of sand or gravel will help improve drainage and minimize frost heaving. Where rainfall is scant or drainage is good, a 4-in. base of either sand or gravel is usually sufficient. For most other situations, a 4-in. gravel bed topped with 2 in. of sand will work well. Very poorly drained soils may require more gravel, an additional layer of coarse rock beneath the gravel, or even drain tiles. If you suspect your site has serious drainage problems, consult a landscape architect or contractor.

Finally, keep water from pooling on a walk by making its surface higher in the center than at the edges. The center of a 4-ft.-wide walk should be at least ½ in. higher than its edges. If you're using a drag board to level the sand base, curve the lower edge to create this "crown." Otherwise, crown the surface by eye.

Edgings

All walk surfaces need to be contained in some fashion along their edges. Where soil is firm or tightly knit by turf, walls cut neatly out of the excavation can serve as edging. An installed edging often provides more effective containment, particularly if the walk surface is above grade. It also prevents damage to bricks or stones on the edges of paths. Walkway edgings are commonly made of 1- or 2-in.-thick lumber, thicker landscaping timbers, brick, or stone.

Wood edging

Wood should be rot-resistant redwood, cedar, or cypress, or pressure-treated for ground-contact use. If you're working in loose soils, fix a deep wooden edging to support stakes with double-headed nails. When the path is laid, pull the nails, and fill and tamp behind the edging. Then drive the stakes below grade. In firmer soils, or if the edging material is not wide enough, install it on top of the gravel base. Position the top at the height of the path. Dimensional lumber that is 1 in. thick is pliable enough to bend around gradual curves.

Treated dimensional lumber with support stakes

Landscape timbers with crossties laid on gravel base

Brick and stone edging

In firm soil, a row of bricks laid on edge and perpendicular to the length of the path adds stability. For a more substantial edging, stand bricks on end on the excavated soil surface; add the gravel base; and tamp the earth around the base of the bricks on the outside of the excavation. Stone edgings laid on end can be set in the same way. "End-up" brick or stone edgings are easy to install on curved walks.

Bricks on edge, laid on gravel base

Bricks on end, laid on soil

Preparing the base

Having decided on location and materials, you can get down to business. The initial steps of layout and base preparation are much the same for all surface materials.

Layout

Lay out straight sections with stakes and string, turning 90-degree corners with batter boards. (See illustration below.) You can plot curves with stakes and "fair" the curve with a garden hose, or outline the curve with hose alone, marking it with lime or sand ➊.

Excavation

The excavation depth depends on how much sand-and-gravel base your soil's drainage calls for, the thickness of the surface material, and its position above or below grade ➋. Mark the depth on a stake or stick, and use this to check depth as you dig. Walking surfaces are most comfortable if they are reasonably level across their width. Check the bottom of the excavation with a level as you dig. If the walk cuts across a slope, you'll need to remove soil from the high side and use it to fill the low side to produce a level surface. If you've added soil or if the subsoil is loose, compact it by tamping.

Edging installation

Some edgings can be installed immediately after excavation; others are placed on top of the gravel portion of the base ➌. (See the sidebar, "Edgings," on the previous page.) If the soil's drainage permits, you can now lay soft materials on the excavated, tamped, and edged soil base. To control weeds, and to keep bark, chips, or pine needles from mixing with the subsoil, spread water-permeable landscape fabric over the gravel or the excavated base.

Laying the base

Now add gravel (if required); rake it level; and compact it ➍. Use gravel up to 1 in. in diameter or ¼- to ¾-in. crushed stone, which drains and compacts well. You can rent a hand tamper (a heavy metal plate on the end of a pole) or a machine compactor if you have a large area to compact.

If you're making a loose-gravel or crushed-stone walk, add the surface material on top of the base gravel. (See "Choosing a surface" page 164.) For walks of brick, stone, or pavers, add a 2-in. layer of builder's sand, not the finer sand that masons use for mixing mortar.

Rake the sand smooth with the back of a level-head rake. You can level the sand with a wooden drag board, also known as a screed ➎. Nail together two 1x4s or notch a 1x6 to place the lower edge at the desired height of the sand, and run the board along the path edging. To settle the sand, dampen it thoroughly with a hose set on fine spray. Fill any low spots; rake or drag the surface level; then dampen it again.

PREPARING THE BASE

Laying the surface

Whether you're laying a loose or hard material, take time to plan your work. Provide access for delivery trucks, and have material deposited as close to the worksite as possible.

Loose materials

Install water-permeable landscape fabric over the gravel base to prevent gravel from mixing with the surface material. Spread bark or wood chips 2 to 4 in. deep. For a pine-needle surface, spread 2 in. of needles on top of several inches of bark or chips. Spread loose pea gravel about 2 in. deep. For a harder, more uniform surface, add ½ in. of fine crushed stone on top of the gravel. You can let traffic compact crushed-rock surfaces, or compact them by hand or with a machine.

Bricks and precast pavers

Take time to figure out the pattern and spacing of the bricks or pavers by laying them out on the lawn or driveway, rather than disturbing your carefully prepared sand base. When you're satisfied, begin in a corner, laying the bricks or pavers gently on the sand so the base remains even ➊. Lay full bricks first; then install cut bricks to fit as needed at the edges. To produce uniform joints, space bricks with a piece of wood cut to the exact joint width. You can also maintain alignment of the bricks with a straightedge or with a string stretched across the path between nails or stakes. Move the string as you proceed with the work.

As you complete a row or section, bed the bricks or pavers into the sand base with several firm raps of a rubber mallet or a hammer on a scrap 2x4. Check with a level or straightedge to make sure the surface is even ➋. (You'll have to do this by feel or eye across the width of a crowned path.) Lift low bricks or pavers carefully and fill beneath them with sand; then reset them. Don't stand on the walk until you've filled the joints.

When you've finished a section, sweep fine, dry mason's sand into the joints, working across the surface of the path in all directions ➌. Wet thoroughly with a fine spray, and let dry; then sweep in more sand if necessary. If you want a living walk, sweep a loam-sand mixture into the joints and plant small, tough, ground-hugging plants, such as dwarf mondo grass, in them.

Rare is the brick walk that can be laid without cutting something to fit. To cut brick, mark the line of the cut with a dark pencil all around the brick. With the brick resting firmly on sand or soil, score the entire line by rapping a wide mason's chisel called a "brickset" with a heavy wooden mallet or a soft-headed steel hammer as shown on the facing page. Place the brickset in the scored line across one face and give it a sharp blow with the hammer to cut the brick.

If you have a lot of bricks to cut, or if you want greater accuracy, consider renting a masonry saw. Whether you work by hand or machine, always wear safety glasses.

Stepping-stones

A stepping-stone walk set in turf creates a charming effect and is very simple to lay. You can use cut or irregular flagstones or fieldstone, which is irregular in thickness as well as in outline. Arrange the stones on the turf; then set them one by one. Cut into the turf around the stone with a sharp flat shovel or trowel, and remove the stone; then dig out the sod with the shovel. Placing stones at or below grade will keep them away from mower blades. Fill low spots beneath the stone with earth or sand so the stone doesn't move when stepped on.

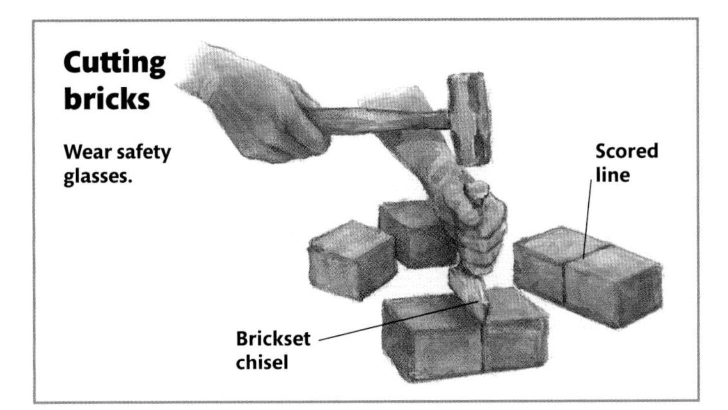

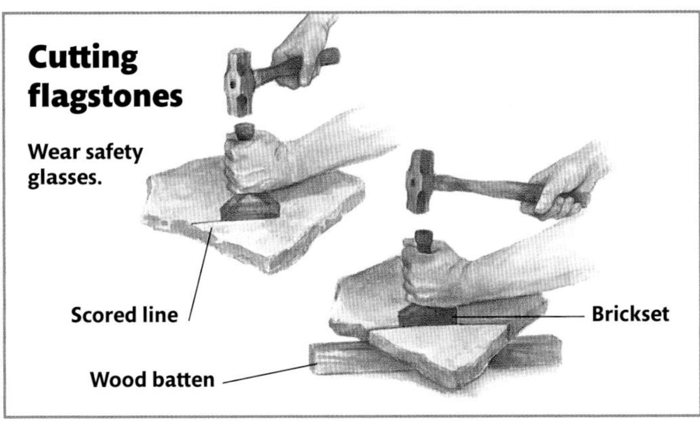

Flagstones

Install cut stones of uniform thickness as described for bricks and pavers. Working out patterns beforehand is particularly important—stones are too heavy to move around more than necessary. To produce a level surface with cut or irregular stones of varying thickness, you'll need to add or remove sand for each stone. Set the stone carefully on sand; then move it back and forth to work it into place ❶. Lay a level or straightedge over three or four stones to check the surface's evenness ❷. When a section is complete, fill the joints with sand or with sand and loam as described for bricks and pavers.

You can cut flagstone with a technique similar to that used for bricks. Score the line of the cut on the top surface with a brickset and hammer. Prop the stone on a piece of scrap wood, positioning the line of the cut slightly beyond the edge of the wood. Securing the bottom edge of the stone with your foot, place the brickset on the scored line, and strike sharply to make the cut.

FLAGSTONES

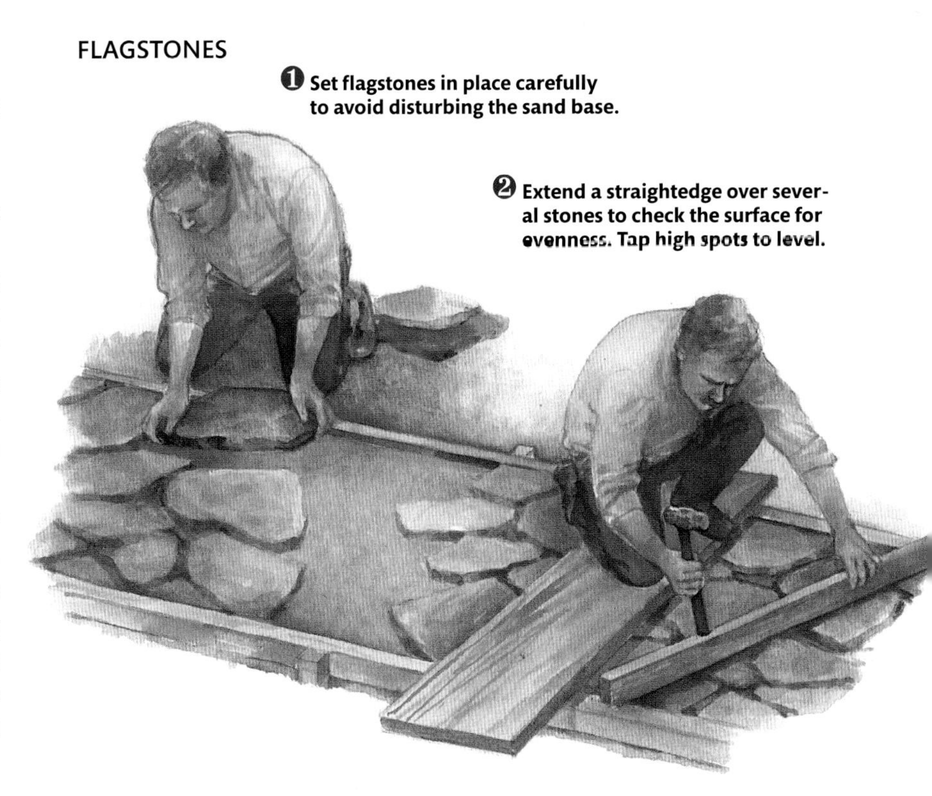

Laying a Patio

You can make a simple patio using the same techniques and materials we have discussed for paths. To ensure good drainage, an even surface, and durability, lay hard surfaces such as brick, flagstone, and pavers on a well-prepared base of gravel, sand, and compacted soil. (Crushed-rock and gravel surfaces likewise benefit from a sound base.) Make sure the surface drains away from any adjacent structure (house or garage); a drop-off of ¼ in. per foot is usually adequate. If the patio isn't near a structure, make it higher in the center to avoid puddles.

Establish the outline of the patio as described for paths; then excavate the area roughly to accommodate 4 in. of gravel, 2 in. of sand, and the thickness of the paving surface. (Check with a local nursery or landscape contractor to find out if local conditions require alterations in the type or amounts of base material.) Now grade the rough excavation to provide drainage, using a simple 4-ft. grid of wooden stakes as shown in the drawings.

Drive the first row of stakes next to the house (or in the center of a freestanding patio), leveling them with a 4-ft. builder's level or a smaller level resting on a straight 2x4. The tops of these stakes should be at the height of the top of the sand base (finish grade of the patio less the thickness of the surface material) ❶. Working from this row of stakes, establish another row about 4 to 5 ft. from the first. Make the tops of these stakes 1 in. lower than those of the first row, using a level and spacer block, as shown in the box below. Continue adding rows of stakes, making each 1 in. lower than the previous row, until the entire area is

LAYING A SIMPLE PATIO

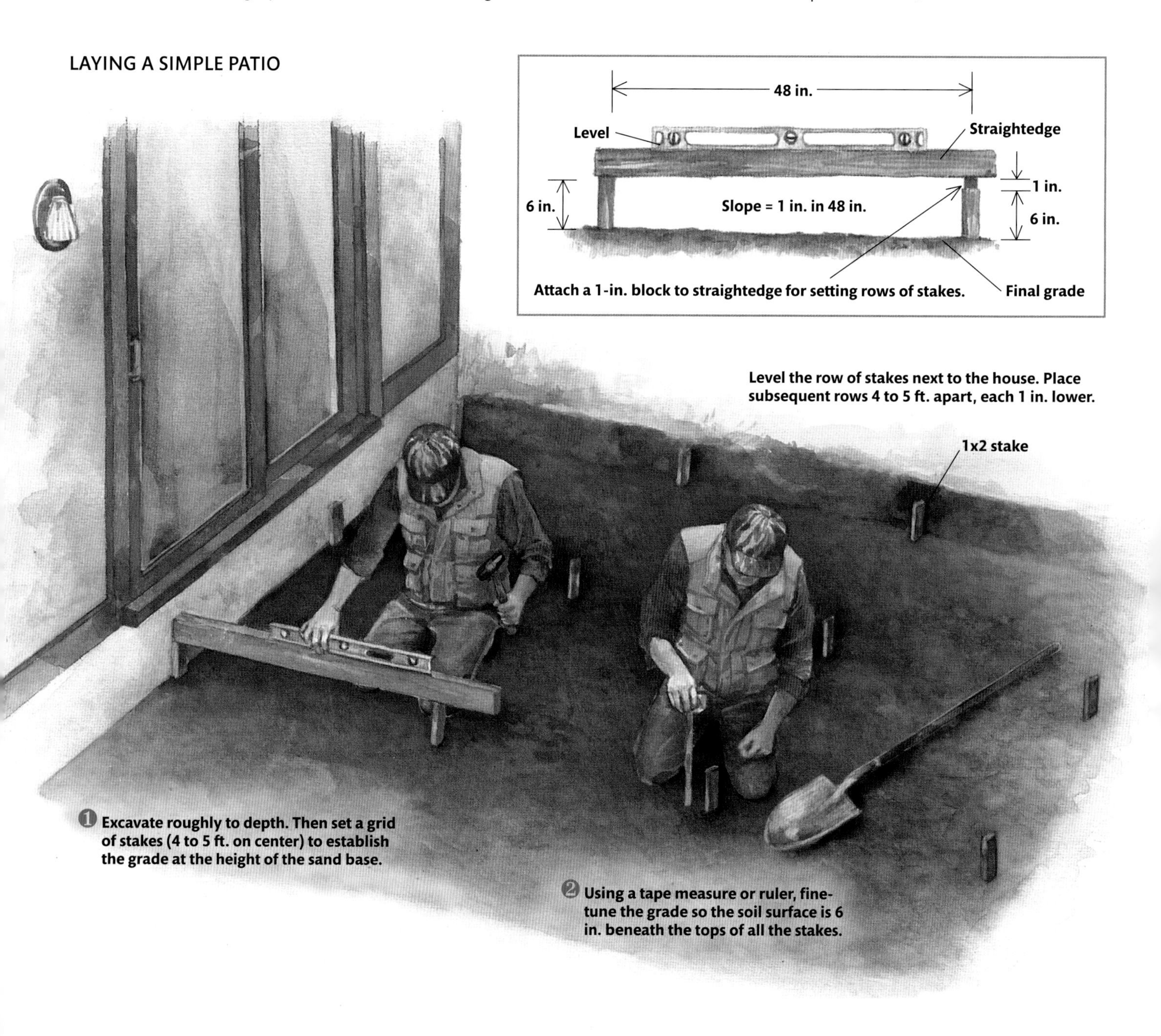

❶ Excavate roughly to depth. Then set a grid of stakes (4 to 5 ft. on center) to establish the grade at the height of the sand base.

❷ Using a tape measure or ruler, fine-tune the grade so the soil surface is 6 in. beneath the tops of all the stakes.

staked. Then, with a measuring tape or ruler and a shovel, fine-tune the grading by removing or adding soil until the excavated surface is 6 in. (the thickness of the gravel-sand base) below the tops of all the stakes ❷.

Use these stakes when installing the sand-and-gravel base, in order to maintain the drainage grade you've just established and produce an even surface for the paving material. If you have a good eye or a very small patio, you can do this by sight. Otherwise, you can use the stakes to install a series of 1x3 or 1x4 "leveling boards," as shown in the drawing below. (Before adding gravel, you may want to cover the soil with water-permeable landscape fabric to keep perennial weeds from growing; just cut slits to accommodate the stakes.)

Add a few inches of gravel ❸. Then set leveling boards along each row of stakes, making the boards' top edges even with the top of the stakes ❹. Drive additional stakes to sandwich the boards in place (don't use nails). Distribute the remaining inch or so of gravel and compact it by hand or machine; then add the 2 in. of sand. Dragging a straight 2x4 across two adjacent rows of leveling boards will produce a precise grade and an even surface ❺. Wet the sand and fill low spots that settle.

You can install the patio surface as previously described for paths, removing the leveling boards as the bricks or pavers reach them ❻. Disturbing the sand surface as little as possible, slide the boards out from between the stakes and drive the stakes an inch or so beneath the level of the sand. Cover the stakes and fill the gaps left by the boards with sand, tamped down carefully. Then continue laying the surface. Finally, sweep fine sand into the joints.

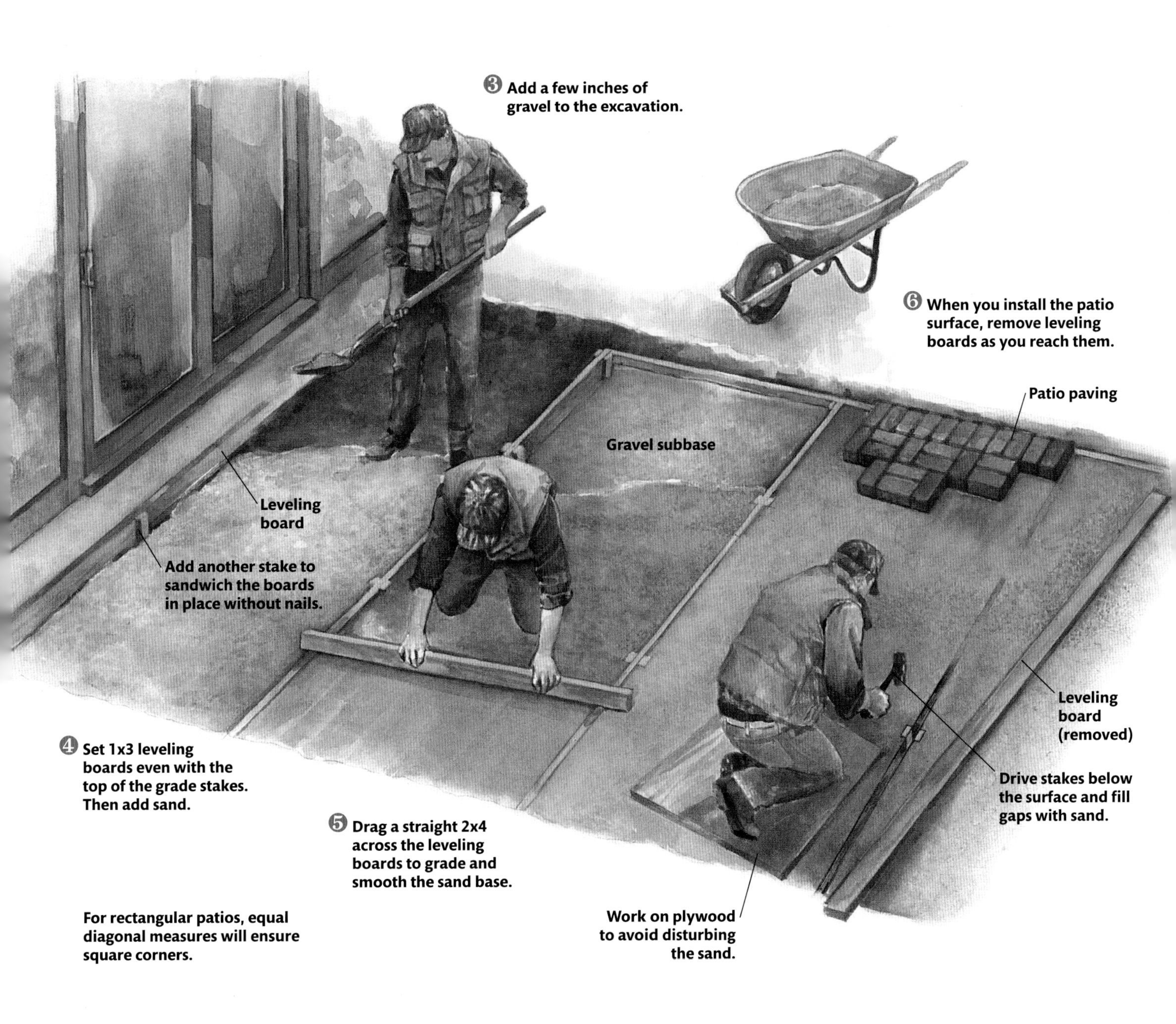

Installing a Pond

It wasn't so long ago that a garden pond required yards of concrete, an expert mason, and deep pockets. Today's strong, lightweight, and long-lasting synthetic liners and rigid fiberglass shells have put garden pools in reach of every do-it-yourselfer. Installation does require some hard labor, but little expertise: just dig a hole, spread the liner or seat the shell, install edging, and plant. We'll discuss installation of a lined pond in the main text; see below for installing a smaller, fiberglass pool.

Liner notes

More and more nurseries and garden centers are carrying flexible pond liners; you can also buy them from mail-order suppliers specializing in water gardens. Synthetic rubber liners are longer lasting but more expensive than PVC liners. (Both are much cheaper than rigid fiberglass shells.) Buy only liners specifically made for garden ponds—don't use ordinary plastic sheeting. Many people feel that black liners look best; blue liners tend to make the pond look like a swimming pool.

Before you dig

First, make sure you comply with any rules your town may have about water features. Then keep the following ideas in mind when locating your pond. Avoid areas with shady trees that keep sun-loving water plants from thriving. A tree's roots make digging a chore and its flowers, leaves, and seeds clog the water, making it unsightly and inhospitable to plants or fish. Avoid the low spot on your property; otherwise your pond will be a catch basin for runoff. Select a level spot; the immediate vicinity of the pond must

Small fiberglass pool

A fiberglass shell or half barrel 2 to 3 ft. in diameter and 2 to 3 ft. deep is ideal for the small pools on p. 96 and 72. Garden centers often stock pond shells in a variety of shapes. Dig a hole about 6 in. wider on all sides than the shell. Hole depth should equal that of the shell plus 1 in. for a sand base and an allowance for the mulch (p. 100) or bricks (p. 76) that surround the pool. Compact the bottom of the hole and spread the sand; then lower the shell into place. Add temporary wedges or props, if necessary, to orient and level the shell. Slowly fill the shell with water, backfilling around it with sand or sifted soil so that the fill keeps pace with the rising water level.

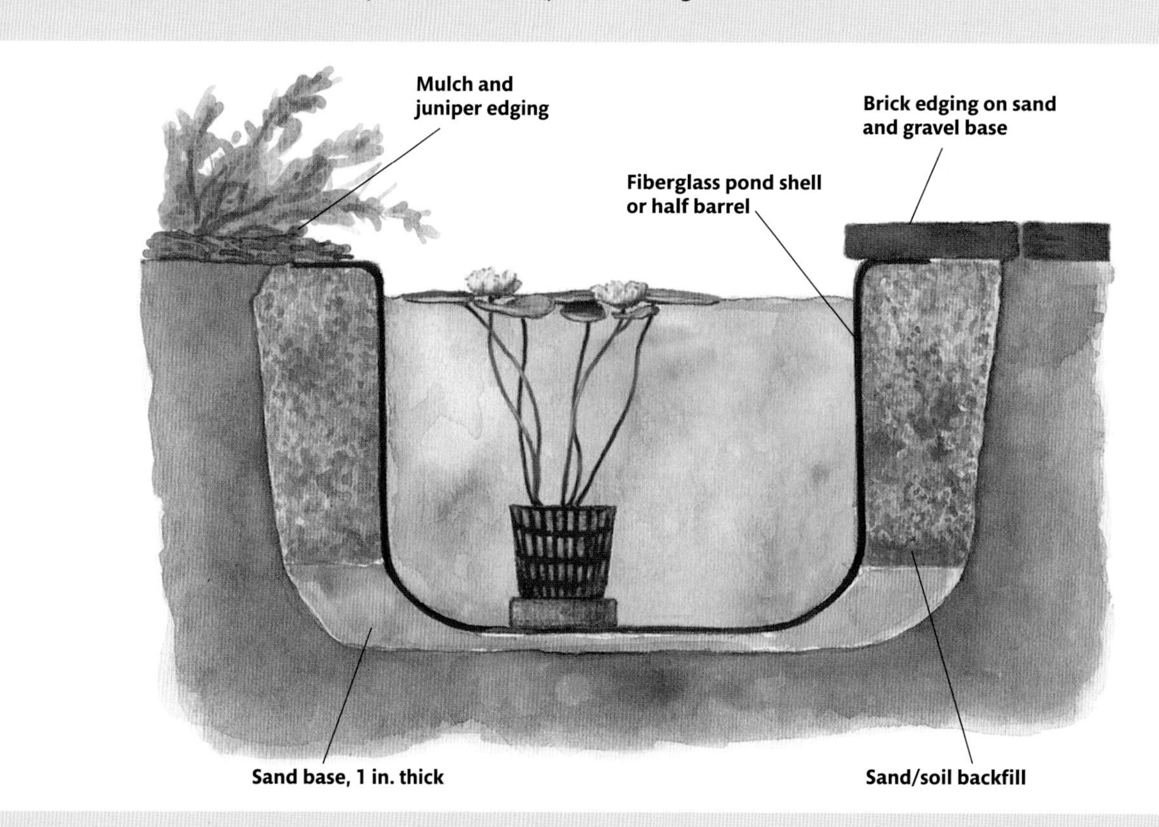

be level, and starting out that way saves a lot of work. (Remember that you can use excavated soil to help level the site.)

Using graph paper, enlarge the outline of the pond provided on the site plan on p. 98, altering it as you wish. If you change the size or depth of the pond, or are interested in growing a wider variety of water plants or in adding fish, remember that a healthy pond must achieve a balance between the plants and fish and the volume, depth, and temperature of the water. Even if you're not making changes, consult with a knowledgeable person at a nursery or pet store.

Calculate the liner width by adding twice the maximum depth of the pool plus an additional 2 ft. to the width. Use the same formula to calculate the length. So, for instance, for a pond 2 ft. deep, 7 ft. wide, and 12 ft. long, the liner width would be 4 ft. plus 7 ft. plus 2 ft. (or 13 ft.). The length would be 4 ft. plus 12 ft. plus 2 ft. (or 18 ft.).

Water work

Unless you are a very tidy builder, the water you used to fit the liner will be too dirty to leave in the pond. (Spilled mortar can also make the water too alkaline for plants or fish.) Siphon or pump out the water; clean the liner; and refill the pond. If you're adding fish to the pond, you'll need to let the water stand for a week or so to allow any chlorine (which is deadly to fish) to dissipate. Check with local pet stores to find out if your water contains chemicals that require commercial conditioners to make the water safe for fish.

Installing the pond and plants is only the first step in water gardening. It takes patience, experimentation, and usually some consultation with experienced water gardeners to achieve a balance between plants, fish, waterborne oxygen, nutrients, and waste that will sustain all happily while keeping algae, diseases, insects, and predators at acceptable levels.

Growing pond plants

One water lily, a few upright-growing plants, and a bundle of submerged plants (which help keep the water clean) are enough for a medium-size pond. An increasing number of nurseries and garden centers stock water lilies and other water plants. For a larger selection, your nursery or garden center may be able to recommend a specialist supplier.

These plants are grown in containers filled with heavy garden soil (not potting soil, which contains ingredients that float). You can buy special containers designed for aquatic plants, or simply use plastic pails or dishpans. Line basketlike containers with burlap to keep the soil from leaking out the holes. A water lily needs at least 2 to 3 gal. of soil; the more, the better. Most other water plants, such as dwarf papyrus, need 1 to 2 gal. of soil.

After planting, add a layer of gravel on the surface to keep soil from clouding the water and to protect roots from marauding fish. Soak the plant and soil thoroughly. Then set the container in the pond, positioning it so the water over the soil is 6 to 18 in. deep for water lilies, up to 6 in. for most other plants.

For maximum bloom, push a tablet of special water-lily fertilizer into the pots once or twice a month throughout the summer. Most water plants are easy to grow and carefree, although many are tropicals that die after hard frost, so you'll have to replace them each spring.

PLANTING WATER PLANTS

Set water plants in a container of heavy garden soil. Then cover soil surface with gravel to keep soil from floating away.

Excavation

If your soil isn't too compacted or rocky, a good-size pond can be excavated with a shovel or two in a weekend ❶. (Energetic teenagers are a marvelous pool-building resource.) If the site isn't level, you can grade it using a stake-and-level system such as the one described on pp. 170-171 for grading the patio.

Outline the pond's shape with garden lime, establishing the curves freehand with a garden hose or by staking out a large grid and plotting from the graph-paper plan. The pond has two levels. The broad end, at 2 ft. deep, accommodates water lilies and other plants requiring deeper water as well as fish. Make the narrow end 12 to 16 in. deep for plants requiring shallower submersion. (You can put plant pots on stacks of bricks or other platforms to vary heights as necessary.) The walls will be less likely to crumble as you dig and the liner will install more easily if you slope them inward about 3 to 4 in. for each foot of depth. Make the walls smooth, removing roots, rocks, and other sharp protrusions.

Excavate a shallow relief about 1 ft. wide around the perimeter to contain the liner overlap and stone edging. (The depth of the relief should accommodate the thickness of the edging stones.) Somewhere along the perimeter, create an overflow channel to take runoff after a heavy rain. This can simply be a 1- to 2-in. depression, 1 ft. or so wide, spanned by an edging stone. Lengths of PVC pipe placed side by side beneath the stone (as shown in the drawing opposite) will keep the liner in place. The overflow channel can open onto a lower area of lawn or garden adjacent to the pond or to a rock-filled dry well.

Fitting the liner

When the hole is complete, cushion the surfaces to protect the liner ❷. Here we show a 1-in.-thick layer of sand on the bottom

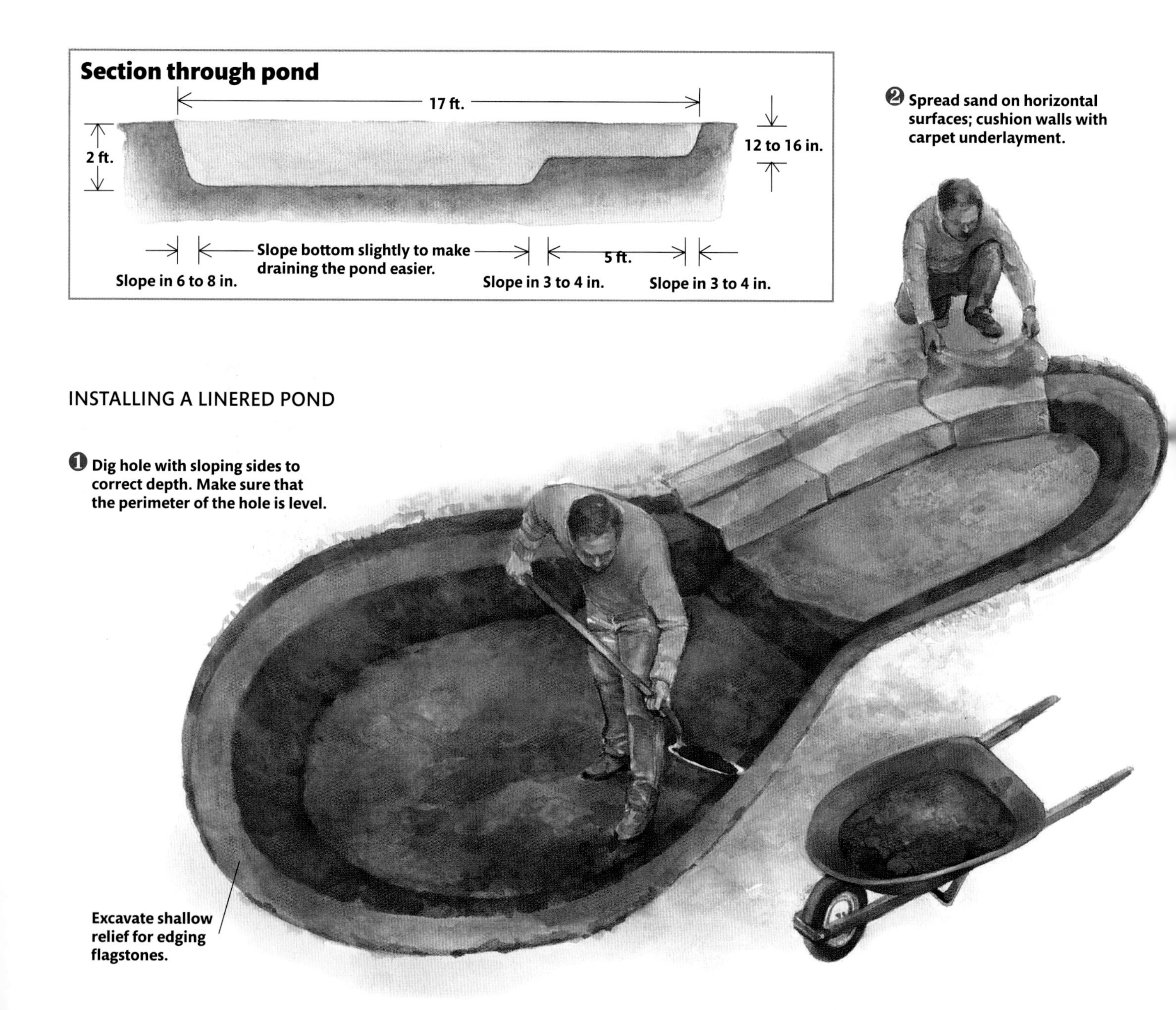

surfaces and carpet underlayment on the sloping walls. Fiberglass batting insulation also works well, as does heavy landscaping fabric.

Stretch the liner across the hole, letting it sag naturally to touch the walls and bottom but keeping it taut enough so it does not bunch up. Weight its edges with bricks or stones; then fill it with water ❸. The water's weight will push the liner against the walls; the stones will prevent it from blowing around. As it fills, tuck and smooth out as many creases as you can; the weight of the water makes this difficult to do after the pond is full. If you stand in the pond to do so, take care not to damage the liner. Don't be alarmed if you can't smooth all the creases. Stop filling when the water is 2 in. below the rim of the pond, and cut the liner to fit into the overlap relief ❹. Hold it in place with a few long nails or large "staples" made from coat hangers while you install the edging.

Edging the pond

Finding and fitting flagstones so there aren't wide gaps between them is the most time-consuming part of this task. Cantilevering the stones an inch or two over the water will hide the liner somewhat.

The stones can be laid directly on the liner, as shown ❺. Add sand under the liner to level the surface where necessary so that the stones don't rock. Such treatment will withstand the occasional careful traffic of pond and plant maintenance. If you anticipate heavier traffic, you can bed the stones in 2 to 3 in. of mortar. It's prudent to consult with a landscape contractor about whether your intended use and soil require some sort of footing for mortared stones.

Elevation detail of pond overflow

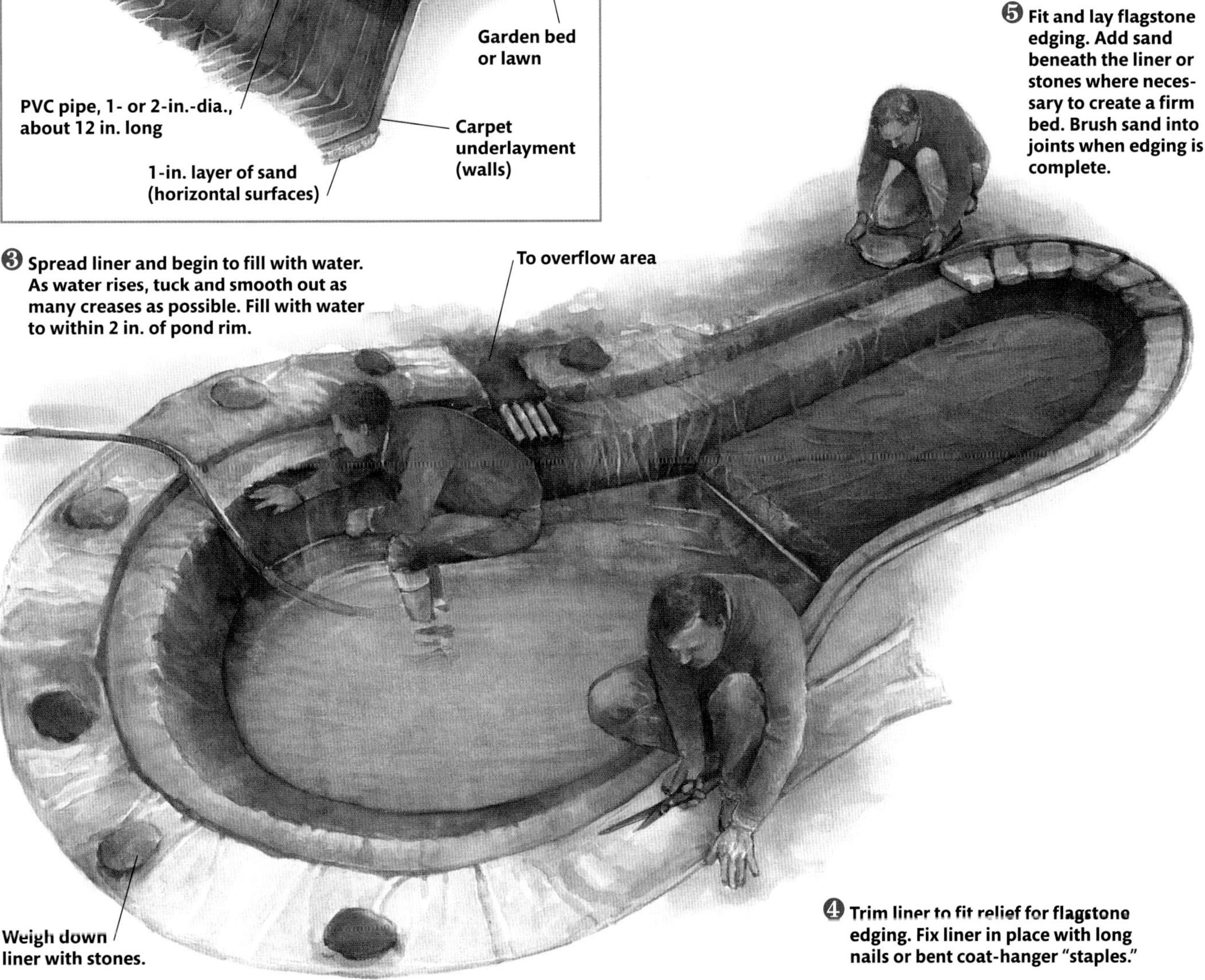

❸ **Spread liner and begin to fill with water. As water rises, tuck and smooth out as many creases as possible. Fill with water to within 2 in. of pond rim.**

❹ **Trim liner to fit relief for flagstone edging. Fix liner in place with long nails or bent coat-hanger "staples."**

❺ **Fit and lay flagstone edging. Add sand beneath the liner or stones where necessary to create a firm bed. Brush sand into joints when edging is complete.**

Building a Retaining Wall

Contours and sloping terrain can add considerable interest to a home landscape. But you can have too much of a good thing. Two designs in this book employ retaining walls to alter problem slopes. The wall shown on p. 53 eliminates a small but abrupt grade change, producing two almost level surfaces and the opportunity to install attractive plantings on them. On p. 40, two low retaining walls help turn a steep slope into an outdoor showpiece.

Retaining walls can be handsome landscape features in their own right. Made of cut stone, fieldstone, brick, landscape timbers, or concrete, they can complement the materials and style of your house or nearby structures. However, making a stable, long-lasting retaining wall of these materials can require tools and skills many homeowners do not possess.

For these reasons, we've chosen retaining-wall systems made of precast concrete for designs in this book. Readily available in a range of sizes, surface finishes, and colors, these systems require few tools and no special skills to install. They have been engineered to resist the forces that soil, water, freezing, and thawing bring to bear on a retaining wall. As extreme weather can bring increased flooding, prolonged drought, and even sub-freezing temperatures retaining walls can be subjected to additional stress. For best results, consult your local building department and use the latest materials and construction methods suited to your region and conditions. Install these walls according to the manufacturer's specifications, and you can be confident that they will do their job for many years.

A number of systems are available in Texas through nurseries, garden centers, and local contracting suppliers. (Check the Yellow Pages or online.) But they all share basic design principles. Similar to traditional dry-stone walls, these systems rely largely on weight and friction to contain the weight of the soil. In many systems, interlocking blocks or pegs help align the courses and increase the wall's strength. In all systems, blocks must rest on a solid, level base. A freely draining backfill of crushed stone is essential to avoid build-up of water pressure in the retained soil, which can buckle even a heavy wall.

The construction steps shown here are typical of those recommended by most system manufacturers for retaining walls up to 3 to 4 ft. tall; be sure to follow the manufacturer's instructions for the system you choose.

For higher walls, walls on loose soil or heavy clay soils, and walls retaining very steep slopes, it is prudent to consult with a landscape architect, engineer, or contractor. Also, check with your local building department for permits and codes.

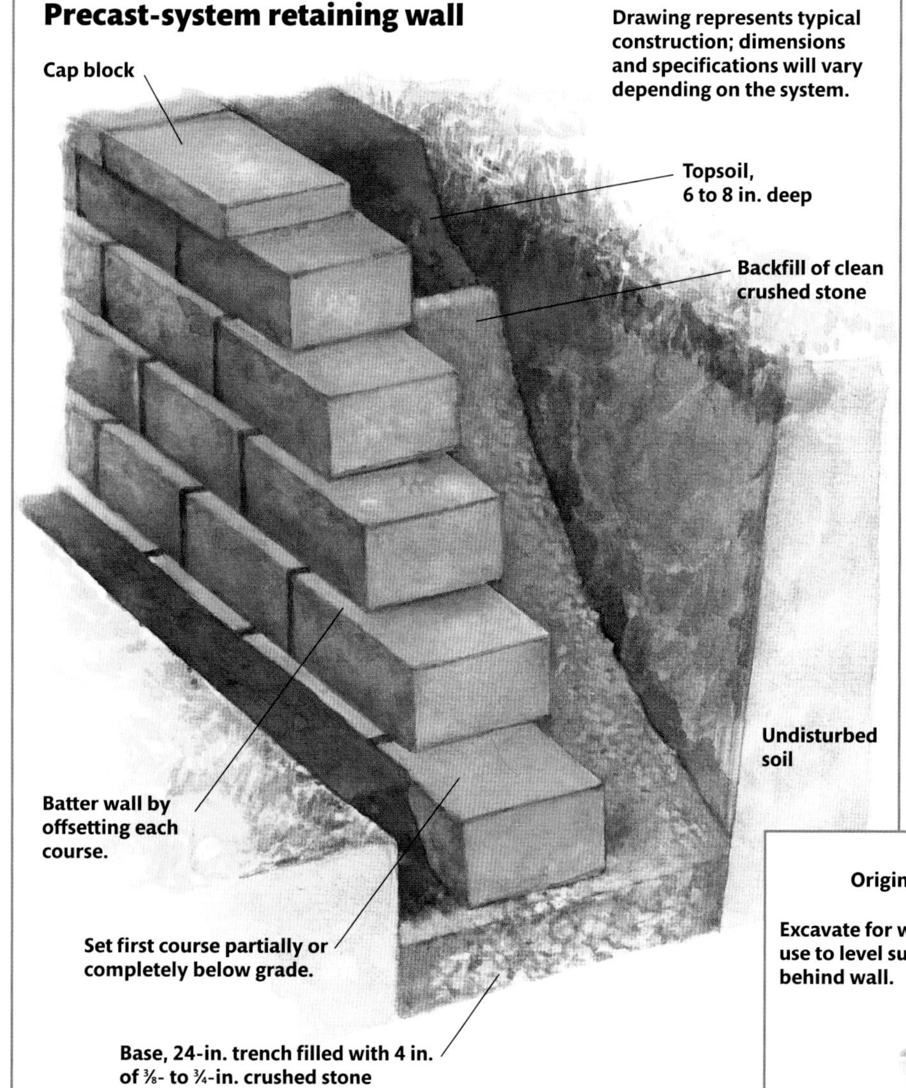

Building a wall

Installing a wall system is just about as simple as stacking up children's building blocks. The most important part of the job is establishing a firm, level base. Start by laying out the wall with string and hose (for curves) and excavating a base trench.

As the boxed drawing opposite shows, the position of the wall in relation to the base of the slope determines the height of the wall, how much soil you move, and the leveling effect on the slope. Unless the wall is very long, it is a good idea to excavate along the entire length and fine-tune the line of the wall before beginning the base trench. Remember to excavate back far enough to accommodate the stone backfill. Systems vary, but a foot of crushed-stone backfill behind the blocks is typical. (For the two-wall design, build the bottom wall first, then the top.)

Systems vary in the width and depth of trench and type of base material, but in all of them, the trench must be tamped firm and be level across its width and along its length. We've shown a 4-in. layer of ⅜- to ¾-in. crushed stone (blocks can slip sideways on rounded aggregate or pea gravel, which also don't compact as well). Depending on the system and the circumstances, a portion or all of the first course lies below grade, so the soil helps hold the blocks in place.

Add crushed stone to the trench; level it with a rake; and compact it with a hand tamper or mechanical compactor. Lay the first course of blocks carefully ❶. Check frequently to make sure the blocks are level across their width and along their length. Stagger vertical joints as you stack subsequent courses. Offset the faces of the blocks so the wall leans back into the retained soil. Some systems design this "batter" into their blocks; others allow you to choose from several possible setbacks.

As the wall rises, shovel backfill behind the blocks ❷. Clean crushed rock drains well; some systems suggest placing a barrier of landscaping fabric between the rock and the retained soil to keep soil from migrating into the fill and impeding drainage.

Thinner cap blocks finish the top of the wall ❸. Some wall systems recommend cementing these blocks in place with a weatherproof adhesive. The last 6 to 8 in. of the backfill should be topsoil, firmed into place and ready for planting.

BUILDING A WALL

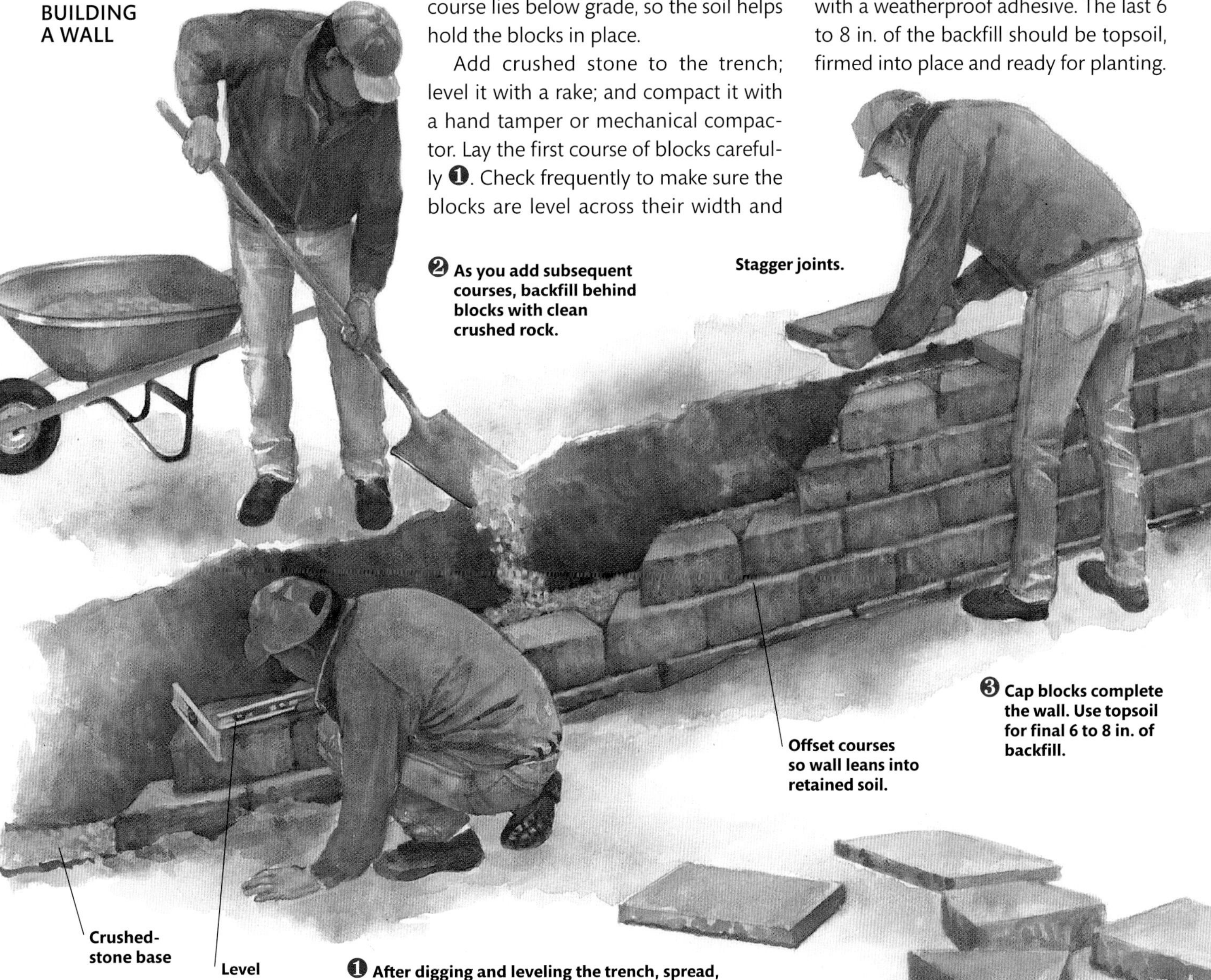

Wall parallel with a slope: Stepped base

Construct walls running parallel with a slope in steps, each with a level base.

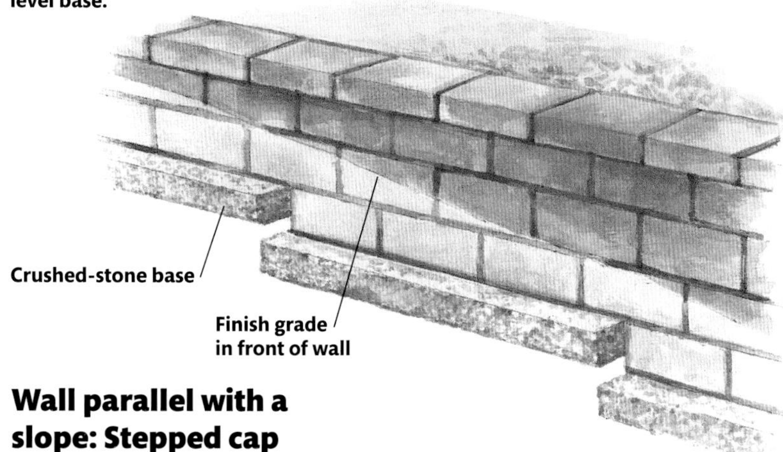

Wall parallel with a slope: Stepped cap

Sometimes the top of a wall needs to step up or down to accommodate grade changes in the slope behind.

A return corner

Where you want the slope to extend beyond the end of the wall, make a corner that cuts into the slope.

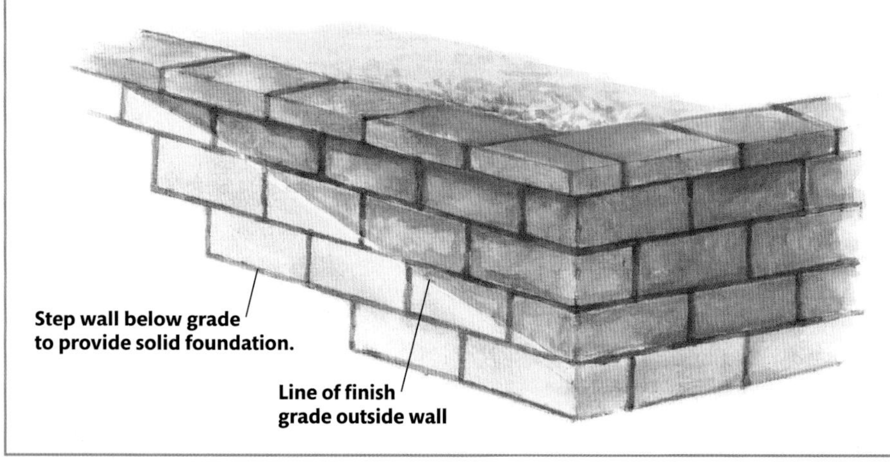

Sloped sites

If your site slopes along the wall's length, you'll need to step the bottom of the wall, as shown at top left. Create a length of level trench along the lowest portion of the site; then work up the slope, creating steps as necessary.

The top of the wall can also step if the slope dissipates at one end. These slopes are common on sites such as the one shown on p. 40, which slopes away from the house and toward the driveway. Here the base of the wall will rest on level ground, but the slope behind the wall decreases along the wall's length. The design on p. 40 shows one solution to this dilemma—a wall of uniform height with a return corner at the street end (see bottom left), backfilled to raise the grade behind to the top of the wall. Another solution, shown at center left, is to step the wall down as the slope decreases, which saves material, produces a different look, but still works with the planting design.

Curves and corners

Wall-system blocks are designed so that curves are no more difficult to lay than straight sections. Corners may require that you cut a few blocks or use specially designed blocks, but they are otherwise uncomplicated. If your wall must fit a prescribed length between corners, consider working from the corners toward the middle (after laying a base course). Masons use this technique, which also avoids exposing cut blocks at the corners.

You can cut blocks with a mason's chisel and mallet or rent a mason's saw. Chiseling works well when the faces of the blocks are rough textured, so the cut faces blend. A saw is best for smooth-faced blocks and projects requiring lots of cutting.

Where the wall doesn't run the full length of the slope, the best-looking and most structurally sound termination is a corner constructed to cut back into the slope, as shown at bottom left.

Steps

Steps in a low retaining wall are not difficult to build, but they require forethought and careful layout. Systems differ on construction details. The drawing below shows a typical design where the blocks and stone base rest on steps cut into firm subsoil. If your soil is less stable or is recent fill, you should excavate the entire area beneath the steps to the same depth as the wall base and build a foundation of blocks, as shown in the boxed drawing.

These steps are independent of the adjacent return walls, which are vertical, not battered (stepped back). In some systems, steps and return walls are interlocked. To match a path, you can face the treads with the same stone, brick, or pavers, or you can use the system's cap blocks or special treads.

SOLID FOUNDATION: CROSS SECTION

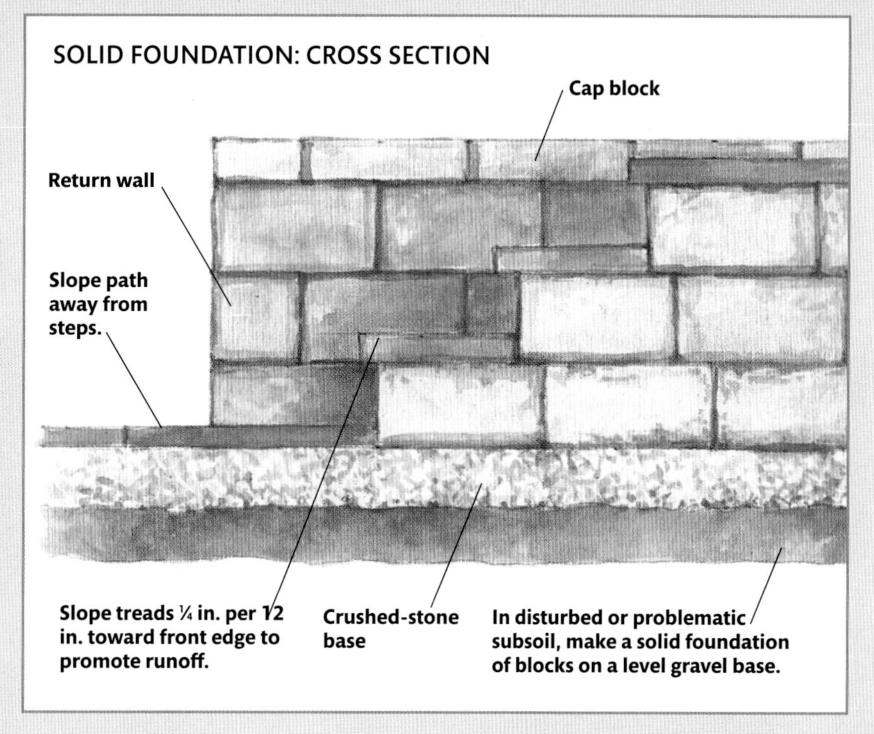

Stepped foundation

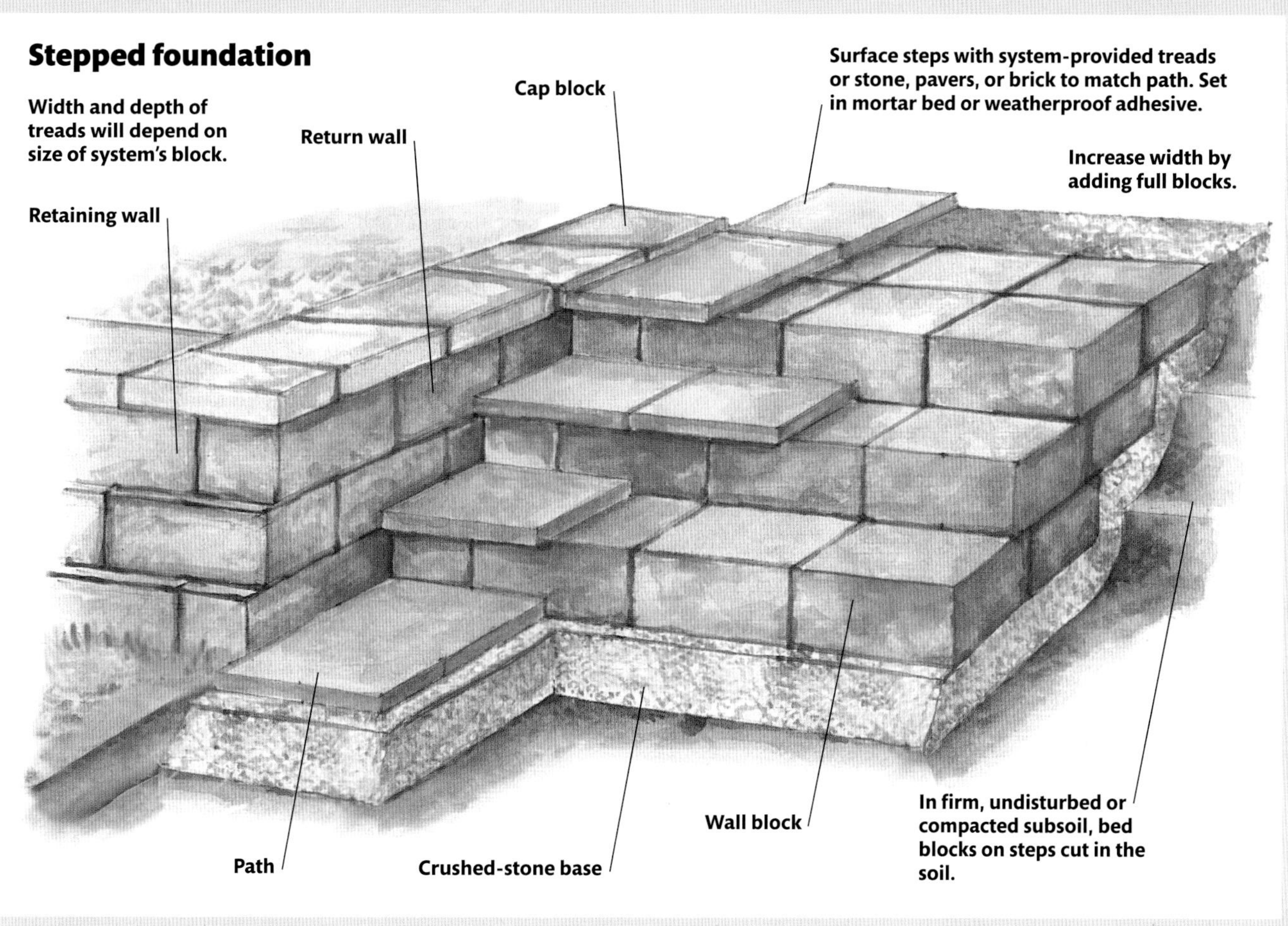

Fences, Arbors, and Trellises

Novices who have no trouble tackling a simple flagstone path often get nervous when it comes time to erect a fence, an arbor, or even a trellis. While such projects can require more skill and resources than others in the landscape, the ones in this book have been designed with less-than-confident do-it-yourself builders in mind. The designs are simple, the materials are readily available, and the tools and skills will be familiar to anyone accustomed to ordinary home maintenance.

As extended droughts become more common, so to do wildfires. When planning your outdoor wooden structures, assess the wildfire risk to your home and property. Fire-wise guidelines and info are available from the Texas A&M Forest Service .

First, we'll introduce you to the materials and tools needed for the projects. Then, we'll present the small number of basic operations you'll employ when building them. Finally, we'll provide drawings and comments on each of the projects.

Tools and materials

Even the least-handy homeowner is likely to have most of the tools needed for these projects: claw hammer, crosscut handsaw, brace-and-bit or electric drill, adjustable wrench, combination square, measuring tape, carpenter's level, and sawhorses. You may even have Grandpa's old posthole digger. Many will have a handheld power circular saw, which makes faster (though noisier) work of cutting parts to length. A cordless drill or screwdriver is invaluable if you're substituting screws for nails. If you have more than a few holes to dig, consider renting a gas-powered posthole digger. A 12-in.-diameter hole will serve for 4x4 posts; if possible, get a larger-diameter digger for 6x6 posts.

Materials

Of the materials offering strength, durability, and attractiveness in outdoor settings, wood is the easiest to work and affords the quickest results. While almost all commercially available lumber is strong enough for landscape structures, most decay quickly when in prolonged contact with soil and water. Cedar, cypress, and redwood, however, contain natural preservatives and are excellent for landscape use. Alternatively, a range of softwoods (such as pine, fir, and hemlock) are pressure-treated with preservatives and will last for many years. Parts of structures that do not come in contact with soil or are not continually wet can be made of ordinary construction-grade lumber, but unless they're regularly painted, they will not last as long as treated or naturally decay-resistant material.

In addition to dimensional lumber, several of the designs incorporate lattice, which is thin wooden strips crisscrossed to form patterns of diamonds or squares. Premade lattice is widely available in sheets 4 ft. by 8 ft. and smaller. Lattice comes in decay-resistant woods as well as in treated and untreated softwoods. Local supplies vary, and you may find lattice made of thicker or narrower material.

Fasteners

For millennia, even basic structures such as these would have been assembled with complicated joints. Today, with simple nailed, bolted, or screwed joints, a few hours' practice swinging a hammer or wielding a cordless electric screwdriver is all the training necessary.

All these structures can be assembled using nails. But screws are stronger and, if you have a cordless screwdriver, make assembly easier. Buy common or box nails that are galvanized to prevent rust. Self-tapping screws (deck screws) require no pilot holes. For rust resistance, buy galvanized screws or screws treated with zinc dichromate.

Galvanized metal connectors are available to reinforce the joints used in these projects. For novice builders, connectors are a great help in aligning parts and making assembly easier. (Correctly fastened with nails or screws, the joints are strong enough without connectors.)

Finishes

Cedar, cypress, and redwood are handsome when left unfinished to weather, when treated with clear or colored stains, or when painted. Pressure-treated lumber is best painted or stained.

Outdoor stains are becoming increasingly popular. Clear or lightly tinted stains can preserve or enhance the rich reddish browns of cedar, cypress, and redwood. Stains also come in a range of colors that can be used as you would paint. Because they penetrate the wood rather than coat the surface, stains won't peel or chip the way paint does, so they are easier to touch up and refinish.

When choosing a finish, take account of what plants are growing on or near the structure. It's a lot of work to remove yards of vines from a trellis or squeeze between a large shrub and a fence to repaint; consider an unfinished decay-resistant wood or an initial stain that you allow to weather.

Setting posts

All the projects are anchored by firmly set, vertical posts. In general, the taller the structure, the deeper the post should be set. For the arbors and the tallest fences, posts should be at least 3 ft. deep. Posts for fences up to 4 ft. tall can be set 2 ft. deep. To avoid post movement caused by expansion and contraction of the soil during freeze-thaw cycles, it's a good idea to set all arbor posts below the frost line. This depth is greater in colder climates; check with local building authorities.

The length of the posts you buy depends, of course, on the depth at which they will be set and their finished heights. When calculating lengths of arbor posts, remember that the tops of the posts must be level. The easiest method of achieving this is to cut the posts to length after installation. For example, buy 12-ft. posts for an arbor finishing at 8 ft. above grade and set 3 ft. in the ground. The convenience is worth the expense of the foot or so you cut off. The site and personal preference can determine whether you cut fence posts to length after installation or buy them cut to length and add or remove fill from the bottom of the hole to position them at the correct heights.

Arbor posts

Be sure to take extra care when positioning and installing arbor posts. The corners of the structure must be right angles, and the sides must be parallel with one another. Locating the corners with batter boards and string is fussy but accurate. Make the batter boards by nailing 1x2 stakes to scraps of 1x3 or 1x4, and position them about 1 ft. from the approximate location of each post as shown in the boxed drawing at right. Locate the exact post positions with string; adjust the string so the diagonal measurements are equal, which ensures that the corners of the structure will be at right angles.

At the intersections of the strings, locate the postholes by eye or with a plumb bob ❶. Remove the strings and dig the holes; then reattach the strings to position the posts exactly ❷. Plumb and brace the posts carefully. Check positions with the level and by measuring between adjacent posts and across diagonals. Diagonal braces between adjacent posts will stiffen them and help align their faces ❸. Then add concrete ❹ and let it cure for a day.

To establish the height of the posts, measure up from grade on one post; then use a level and straightedge to mark the heights of the other posts from the first one. Where joists will be bolted to the faces of the posts, you can install the joists and use their top edges as a handsaw guide for cutting the posts to length.

SETTING ARBOR POSTS

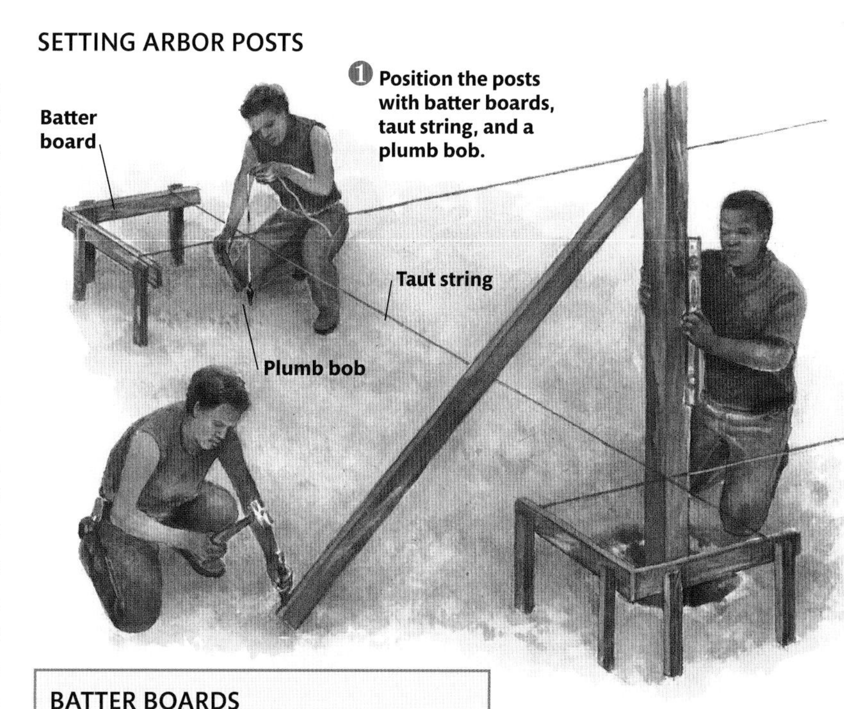

❶ **Position the posts with batter boards, taut string, and a plumb bob.**

BATTER BOARDS

Set L-shaped batter boards at each corner and stretch string to position the posts exactly.

1x2 stakes and 1x3 boards

Taut string

Taut string

18 to 24 in.

For square or rectangular post layout, diagonal measurements should be equal.

❷ **Remove the string to dig the holes; then reattach it and align the outer faces of the posts with the string while you plumb and brace them.**

❸ **Check distances between posts at top. Add diagonal bracing between posts to fix positions.**

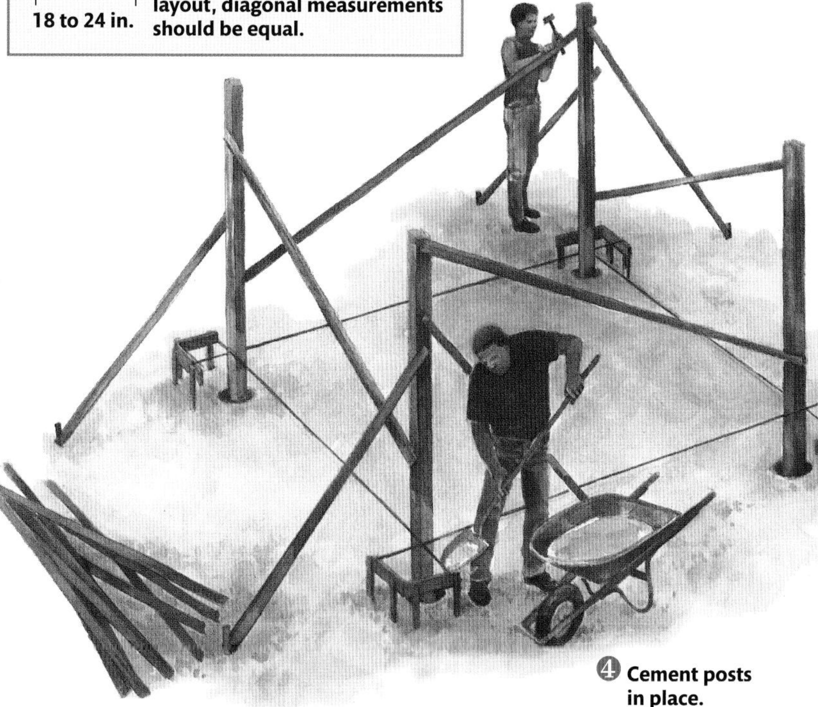

❹ **Cement posts in place.**

Fence posts

Lay out and set the end or corner posts of a fence first, then add the intermediate posts. Dig the holes by hand or with a power digger ❶. To promote drainage, place several inches of gravel at the bottom of the hole for resting the post. Checking with a carpenter's level, plumb the post vertically and brace it with scrap lumber nailed to stakes ❷. Then add a few more inches of gravel around the post's base.

If your native soil compacts well, you can fix posts in place with tamped earth. Add the soil gradually, tamping it continuously with a heavy iron bar or 2x4. Check regularly with a level to see that the post doesn't get knocked out of plumb. This technique suits rustic or informal fences, where misalignments caused by shifting posts aren't noticeable or damaging.

For more formal fences, or where soil is loose or fence panels are buffeted by winds or snow, it's prudent to fix posts in concrete ❸. Mix enough concrete to set the two end posts; as a rule of thumb, figure one 80-lb. bag of premixed concrete per post. As you shovel it in, prod the concrete with a stick to settle it, particularly if you've added rubble to extend the mix. Build the

SETTING A FENCE POST

❷ Plumb the post, checking on adjacent faces with a level. Hold it in position with stakes and braces.

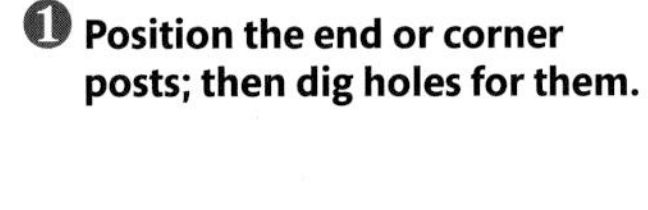
❶ Position the end or corner posts; then dig holes for them.

❸ Fill the hole with concrete and rubble.

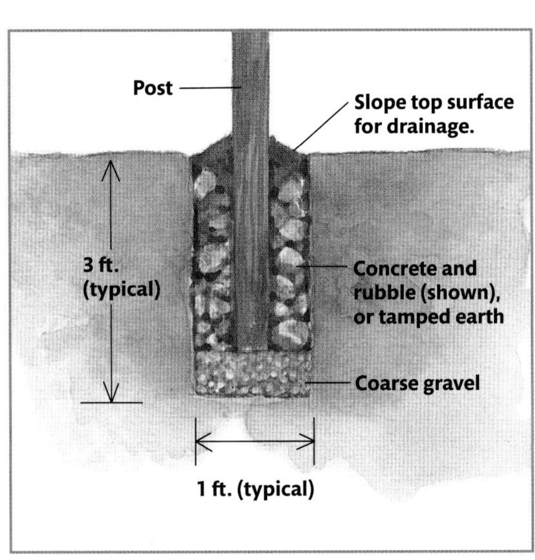

concrete slightly above grade and slope it away from the post to aid drainage.

Once the end posts are set, stretch a string between the posts. (The concrete should cure for 24 hours before you nail or screw rails and panels in place, but you can safely stretch string while the concrete is still wet.) Measure along the string to position the intermediate posts; drop a plumb bob from the string at each intermediate post position to gauge the center of the hole below ❹. Once all the holes have been dug, again stretch a string between the end posts, near the top. Set the intermediate posts as described previously; align one face with the string and plumb adjacent faces with the carpenter's level ❺. Make sure to check positions of intermediate posts a final time with a measuring tape.

If the fence is placed along a slope, the top of the slats or panels can step down the slope or mirror it (as shown in the drawings below). Either way, make sure that the posts are plumb, rather than leaning with the slope.

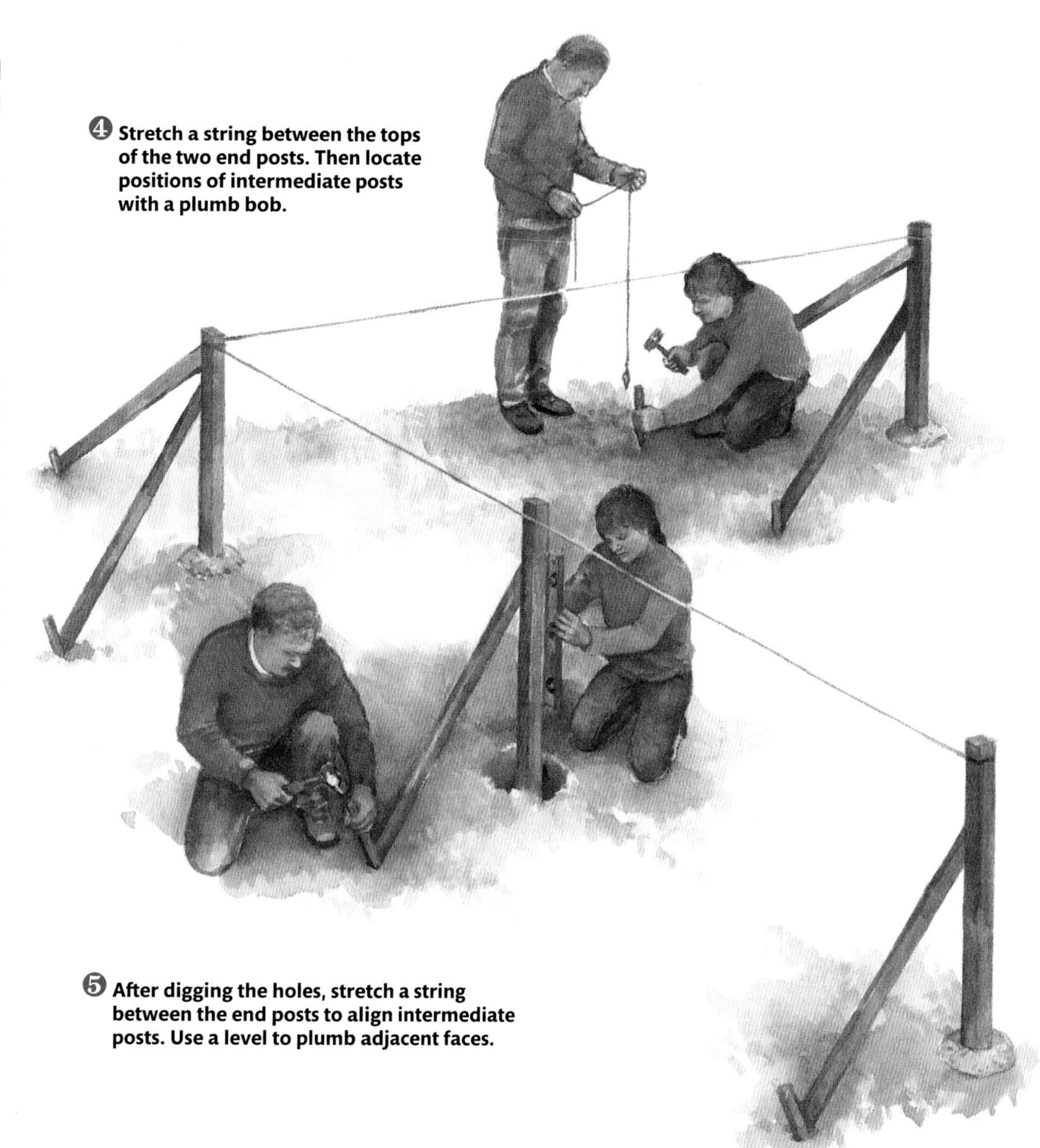

❹ Stretch a string between the tops of the two end posts. Then locate positions of intermediate posts with a plumb bob.

❺ After digging the holes, stretch a string between the end posts to align intermediate posts. Use a level to plumb adjacent faces.

Fencing a slope

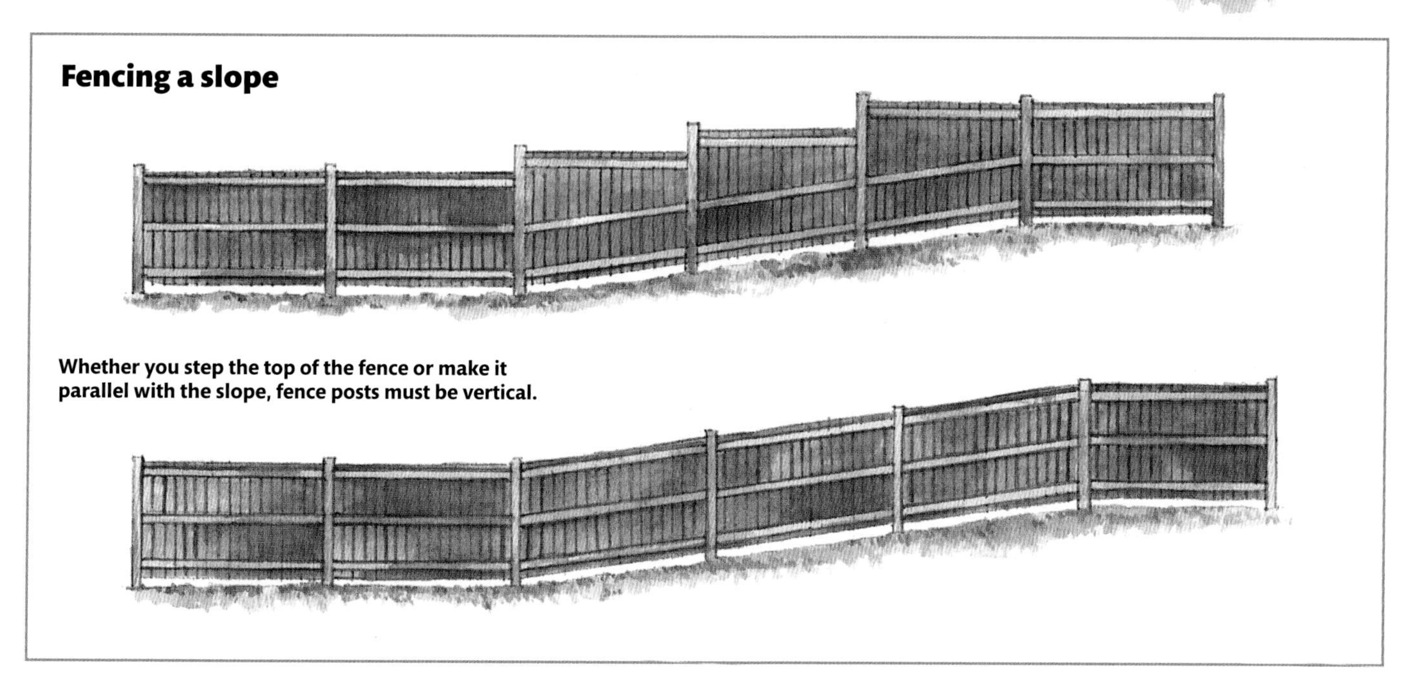

Whether you step the top of the fence or make it parallel with the slope, fence posts must be vertical.

Joints

The components of the fences, arbors, and trellises used in this book are attached to the posts and to each other with the simple joints shown below. Because all the parts are made of dimensioned lumber, the only cuts you'll need to make are to length. For strong joints, cut ends as square as you can, so the mating pieces make contact across their entire surfaces. If you have no confidence in your sawing, many lumberyards will cut pieces to length for a modest fee.

Novices often find it difficult to keep two pieces correctly positioned while trying to drive a nail into them, particularly when the nail must be driven at an angle, called "toenailing." If you have this problem, consider assembling the project using screws, which draw the pieces together, or with metal connectors, which can be nailed or screwed in place on one piece and then attached to the mating piece.

For several designs, you need to attach lattice panels to posts. The panels are made by sandwiching store-bought lattice

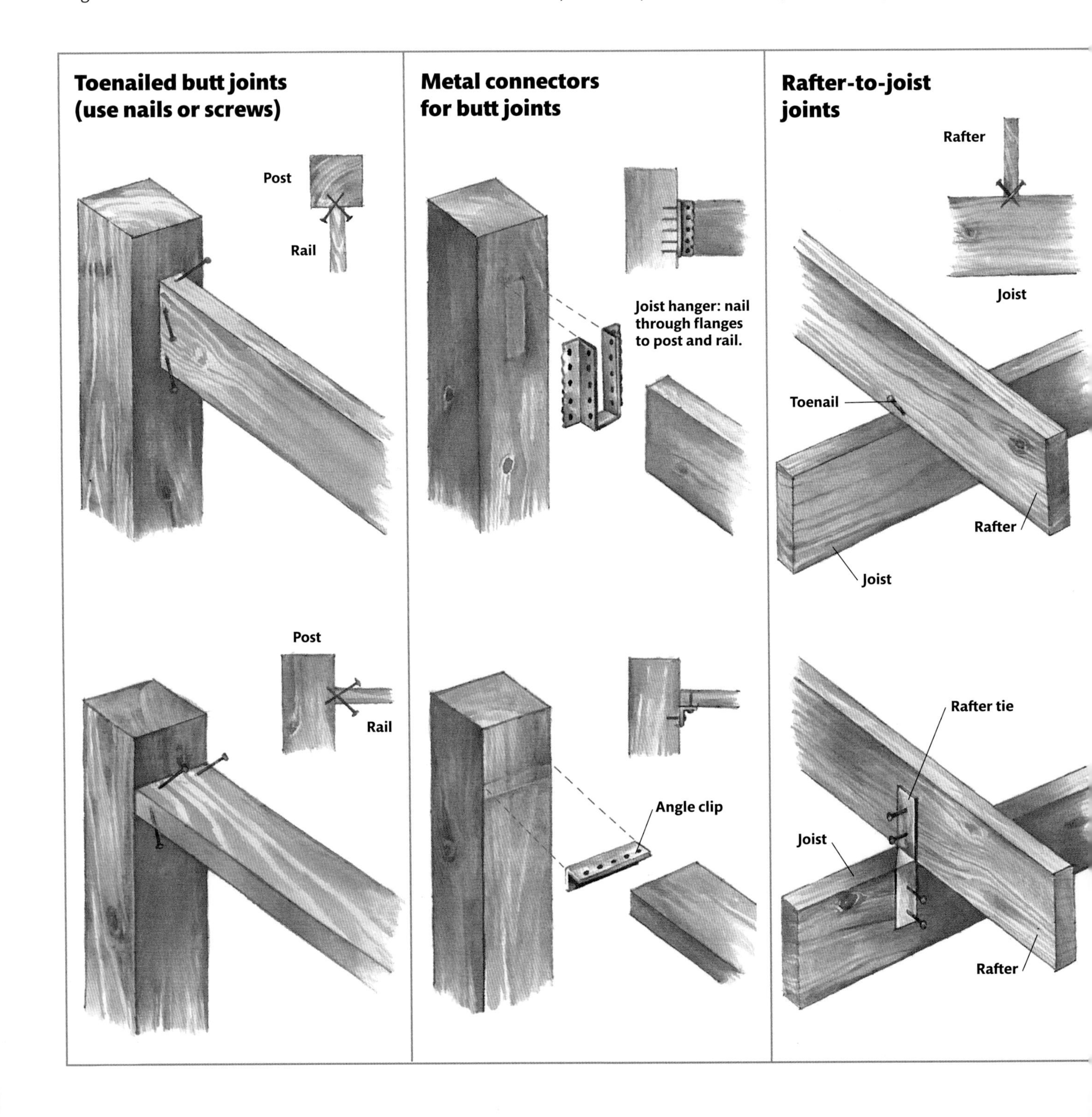

between frames of dimension lumber (construction details are given on the following pages). While the assembled panels can be toenailed to the posts, novices may find that the job goes easier using one or more types of metal connector, as shown in the drawings below. Attach the angle clips or angle brackets to the post; then position the lattice panel and fix it to the connectors. For greatest strength and ease of assembly, attach connectors using self-tapping screws driven by an electric screwdriver.

In the following pages, we'll show construction details of the fences, arbors, and trellises presented in the Portfolio of Designs. (The page number indicates the design.) Where the basic joints discussed here can be used, we have shown the parts but left the choice of fasteners to you. Typical fastenings are indicated for other joints. We have kept the constructions shown here simple and straightforward. They are not the only possibilities, and we encourage experienced builders to adapt and alter constructions as well as designs to suit differing situations and personal preferences.

Frame corner with metal connector

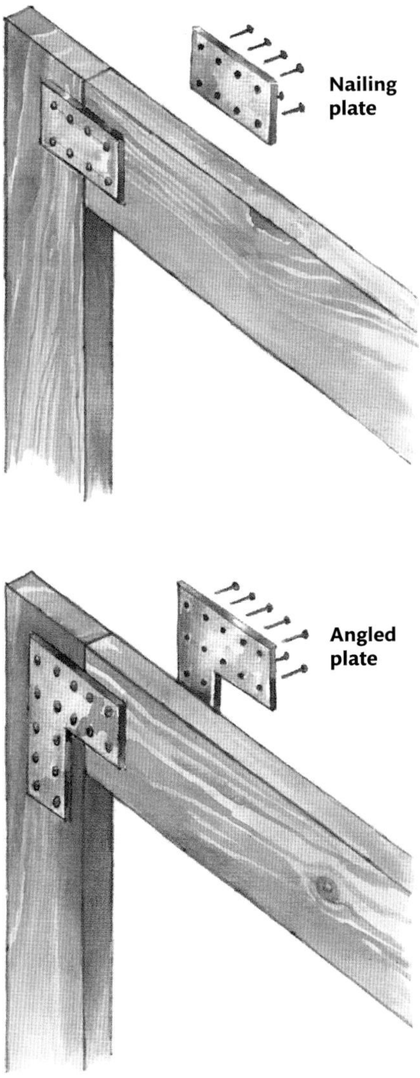

Nailing plate

Angled plate

Attaching framed lattice panels to posts

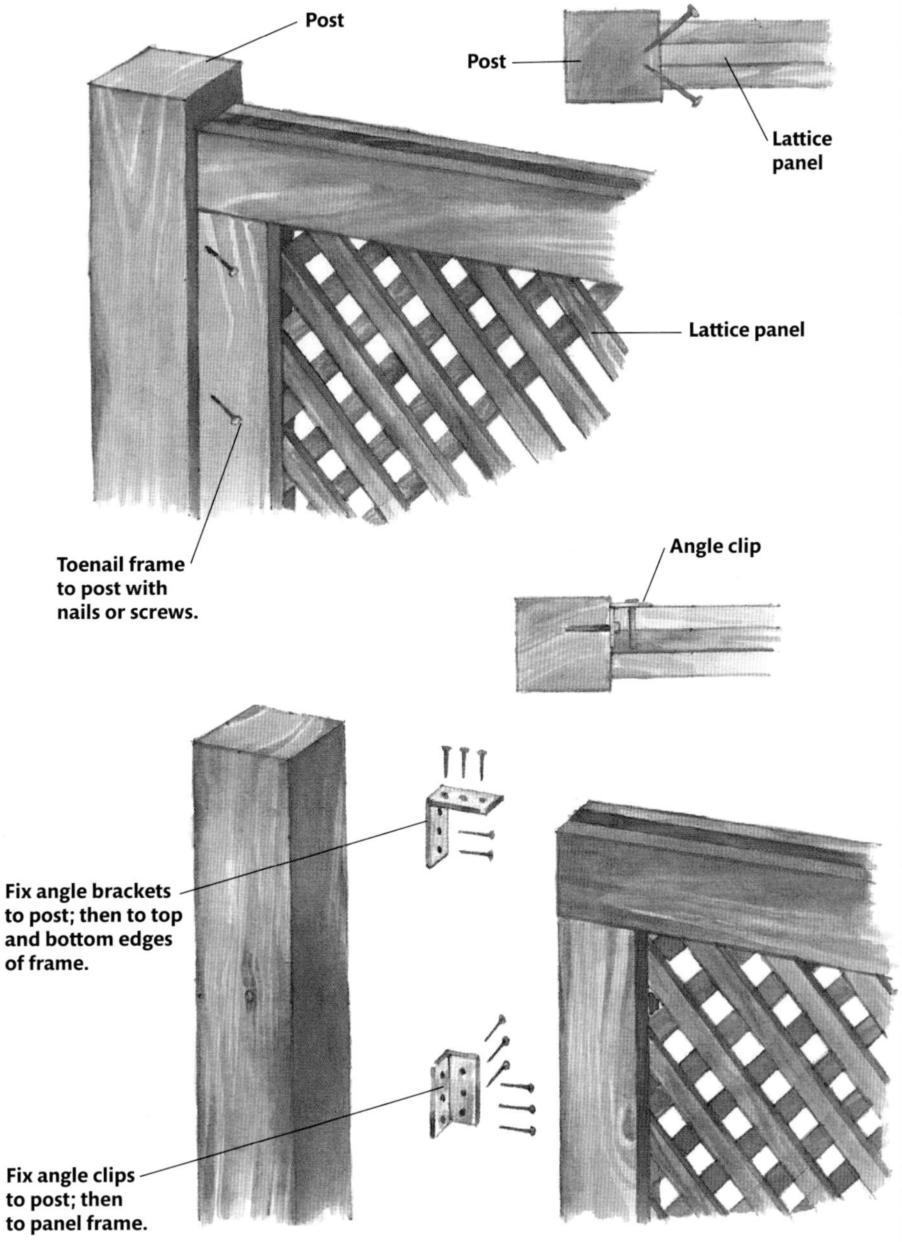

Post

Post

Lattice panel

Lattice panel

Toenail frame to post with nails or screws.

Angle clip

Fix angle brackets to post; then to top and bottom edges of frame.

Fix angle clips to post; then to panel frame.

Homemade lattice trellis (pp. 64-67)

The trellis shown here supports climbing plants to make a vertical garden of a blank wall. The design can be altered to fit walls of different sizes. The three 32-in.-wide modules, hung on L-hangers, are simpler to make than a single large trellis and easy to remove when you need to paint the wall. (If you're in a hurry, you can just attach ready-made lattice to 2x2 frameworks of the same dimensions as shown here.)

Start by cutting all the pieces to length. (Here we'll call the horizontal members "rails" and the vertical members "stiles.") Working on a large flat surface, nail or screw the two outer stiles to the top and bottom rails, checking the corners with a framing square. The 2x2 rails provide ample material to house the L-hangers.

Carefully attach the three intermediate stiles, then the 1x2 rails. Cut a piece of scrap 6 in. long to use as a spacer. Fix the L-shaped hangers to 2x4 studs inside the wall. Buy hangers long enough to hold the trellis several inches away from the wall.

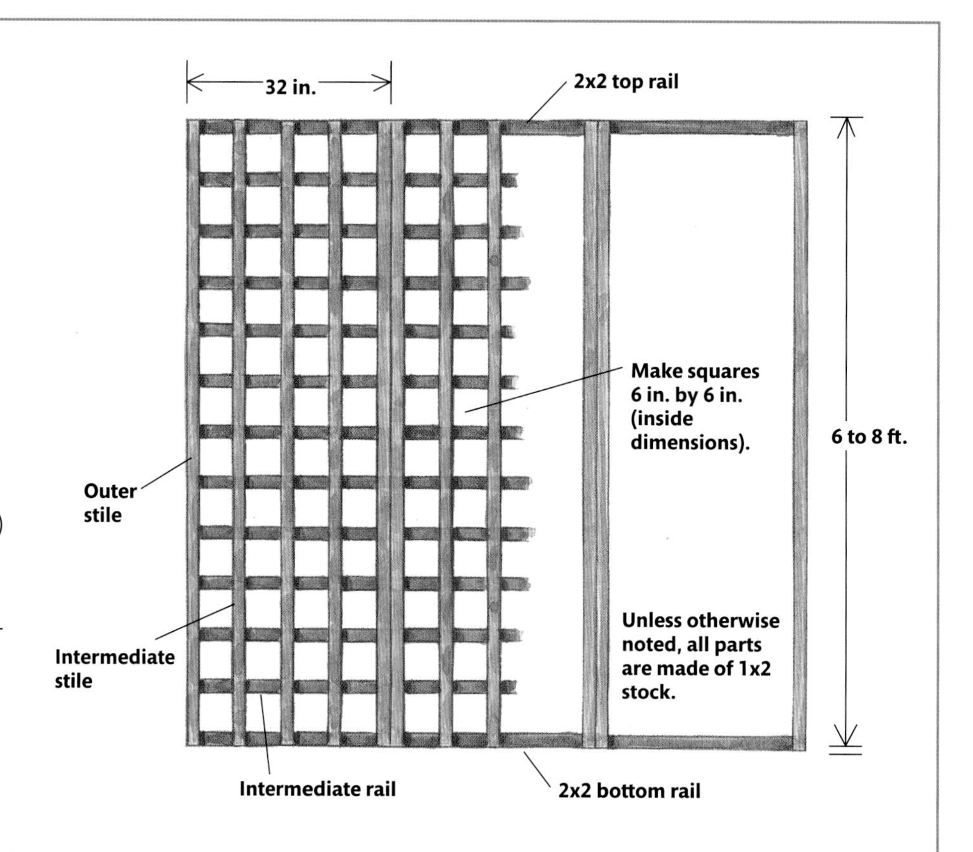

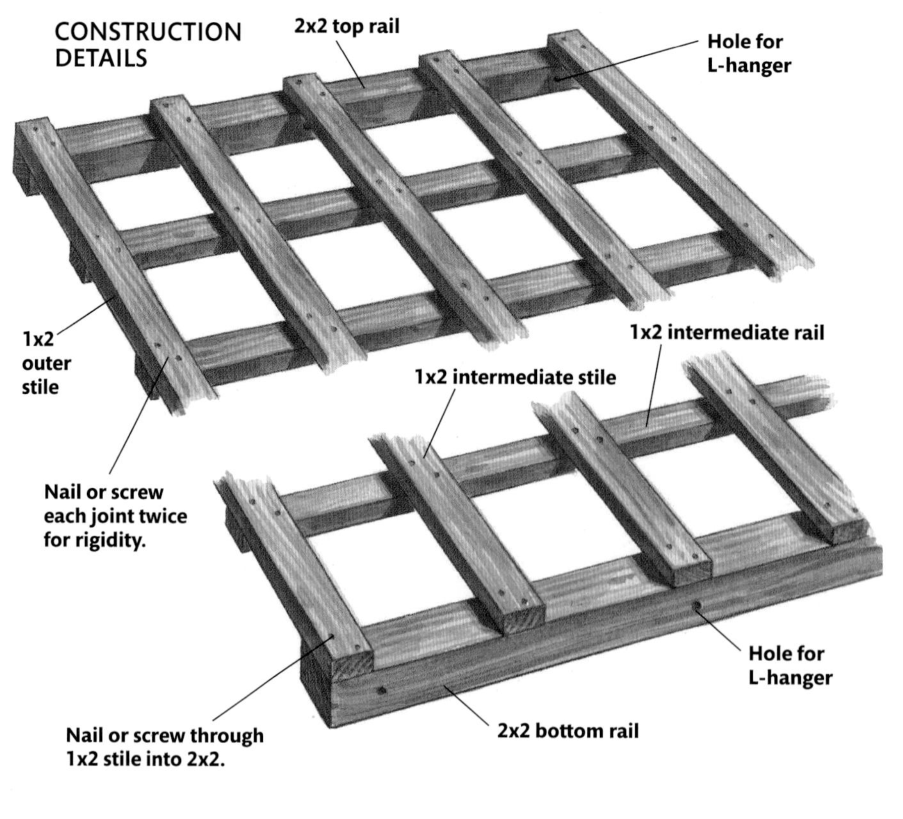

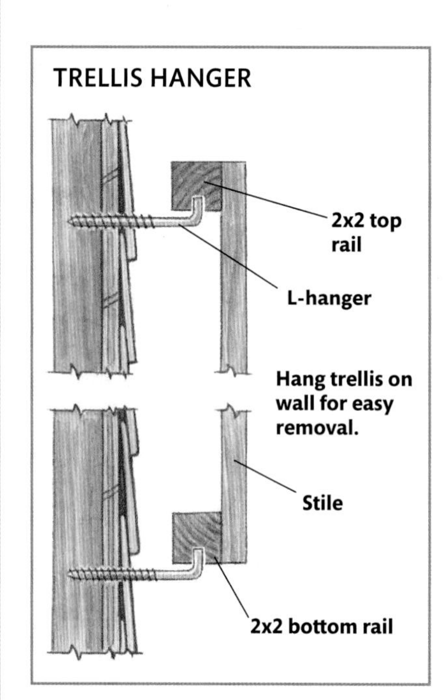

Lattice-panel screen
(pp. 24-27)

This screen serves as a decorative embellishment and vine support in the design on p. 22, but it can make an effective enclosure if you wish. The lattice is held in a frame made of 1x2s sandwiched between 1x3s and 1x4s. (The 1x4s add visual weight to the bottom of the screen.) Note how the parts overlap at the corners of the frame to form an interlocking joint.

Panels wider than 6 ft. are awkward to construct and to install. It is easiest to construct the panels on a large flat surface (a garage or basement floor). Lay out the 1x3s and 1x4 that form one face of the panel frame ❶. Then position and nail the 1x2s to them ❷. Add the lattice, then the other layer of 1x3s and 1x4 ❸. As you work, regularly check that the panel is square, its corners at right angles. (Use a framing square or measure across the diagonals to check that they are equal.) Lattice varies in thickness; if yours rattles in its groove, you can add ¾-in. quarter round as shown in the lower box to tighten the fit.

You can build the panels first and then use them to space the posts, or you can set the posts first (see pp. 181-183) and build the panels to fit. Either way, attach the panels to the posts by toe-nailing (using nails or screws) or with metal connectors along the lengths of the upright members. Add the 1x4 cap after attaching the panels to the posts. Finials in a variety of styles are available at home and garden stores.

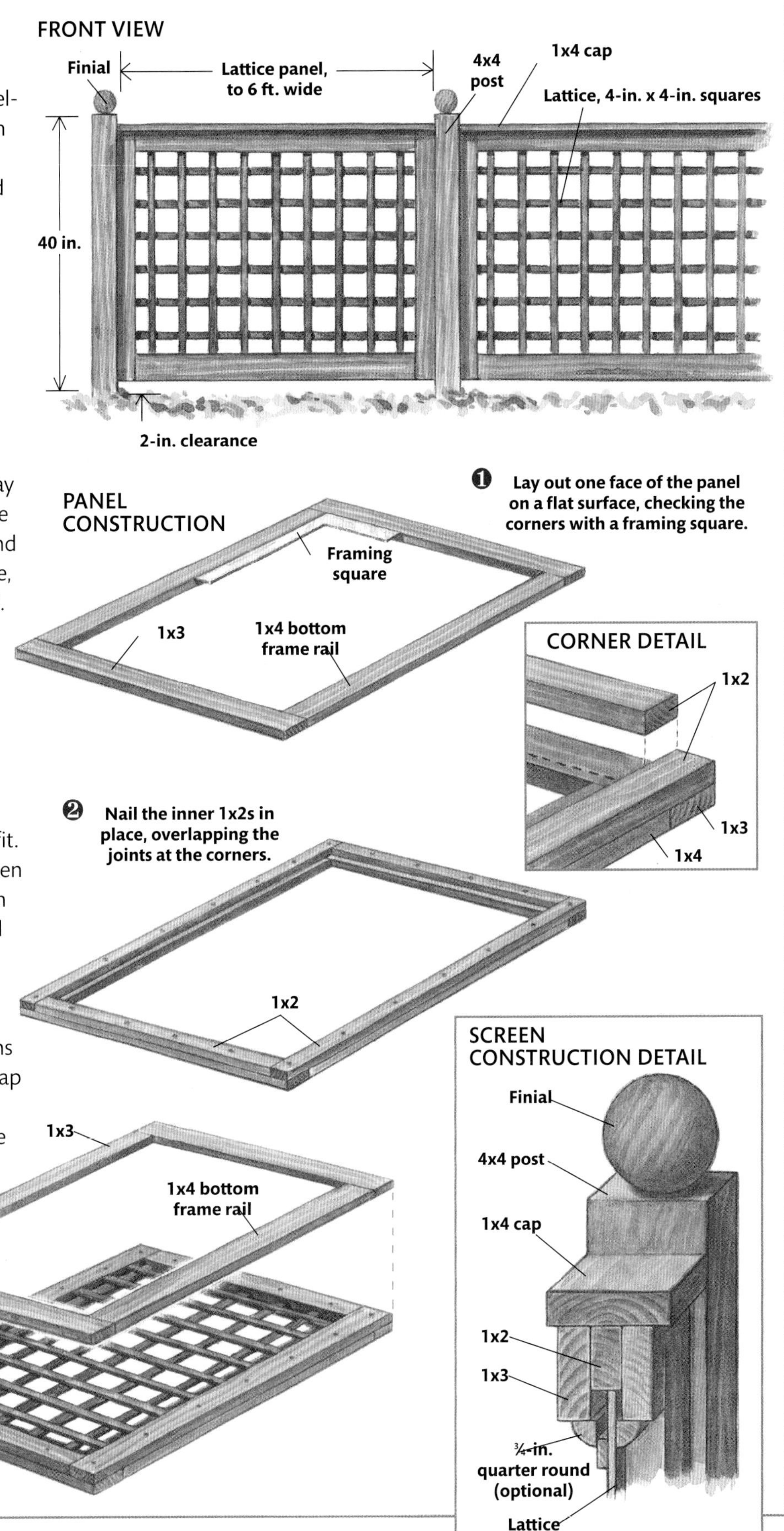

Patio arbor and sun screen
(pp. 96-97)

This simple structure offers relief from the sun on a portion of a backyard patio. The closely spaced 2x4 rafters form a sun screen, while allowing air circulation. Adapt rafter spacing and orientation to accommodate your site. In the design on pp. 88–89, the arbor supports a trumpet vine, which provides additional cooling shade as well as a pleasant leafy ambiance.

If you're building the patio and arbor at the same time, set the 6x6 posts (see pp. 181-183) before you lay the patio surface. If you're adding the arbor to an existing patio, you'll need to break through the paving to set the posts or pour footings to support surface attachments. Consult local building officials or a landscape contractor for advice on how best to proceed.

Once the posts are set, fix the 2x8 beams to pairs of posts using carriage bolts. Nail the 2x8s in place; then make the bolt holes by boring through the 2x8s and the post using a long electrician's bit. Fix the long 2x6 joists and the 2x4 rafters in place with metal connectors. Metal connectors fixed with screws will stand up best to the vigorous growth of the vine.

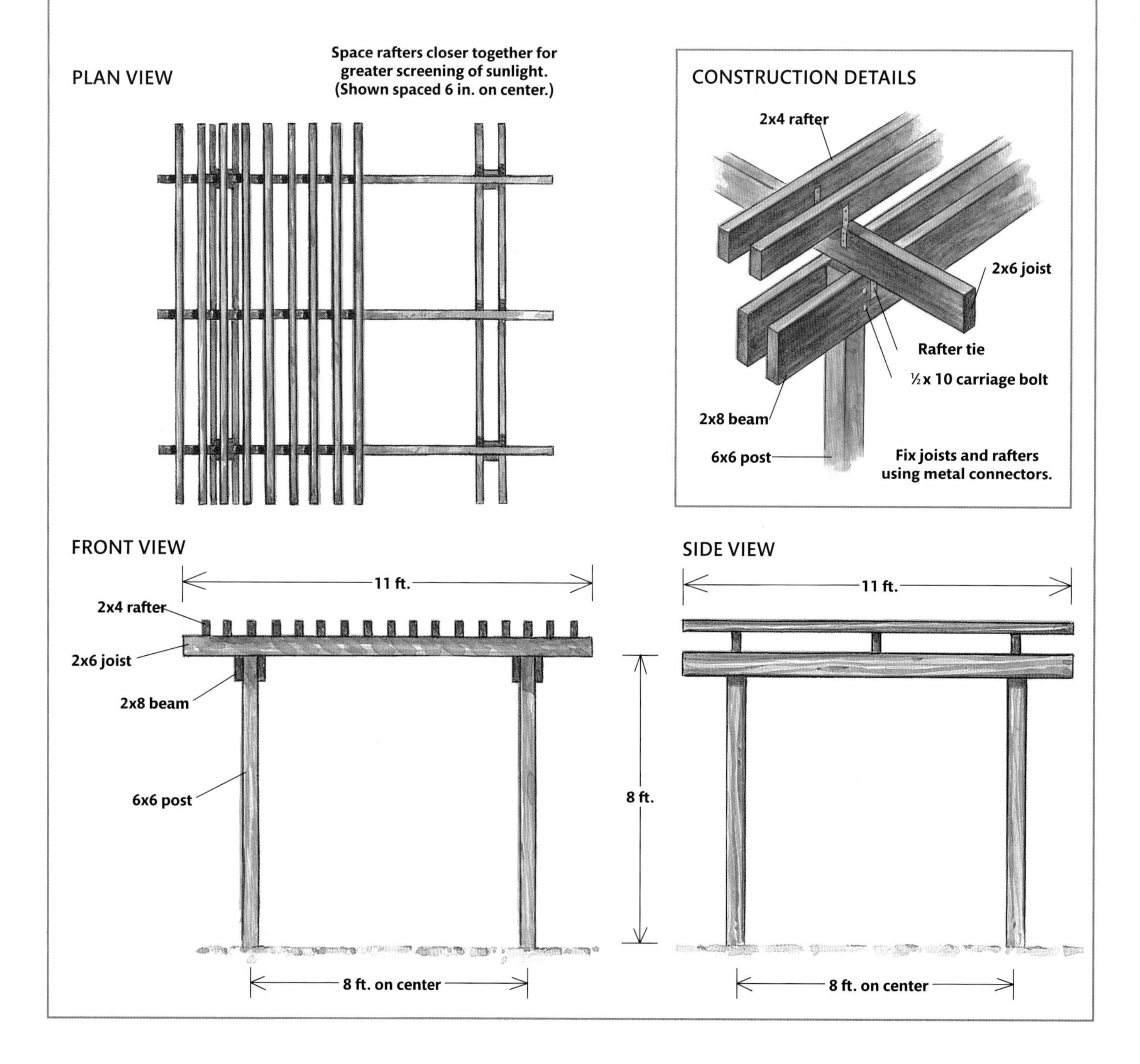

Woodland arbor
(pp. 118-119)

Draped with honeysuckle, this shallow arbor helps establish a connection between a mixed border and an adjacent woodland. Once you have gathered the materials, you should need no more than an afternoon to build the arbor.

Set the posts first, as described on pp. 181-183. The hefty 6x6 posts shown here add presence to the arbor, but cheaper, easier-to-handle 4x4s will make an equally sturdy structure. Cut the joists and rafters to length. The 60° angles on their ends can easily be cut using a handsaw. Bolt or nail the joists in place. Then toenail the short rafters to the joists or attach them with metal connectors.

In addition to the posts, you can provide other supports for the honeysuckle to twine around. Strands of coarse rope or cord work well when stretched between the large screw eyes fixed to the rafters and the base of the posts, as shown here. The vines soon hide the rope or cord from view.

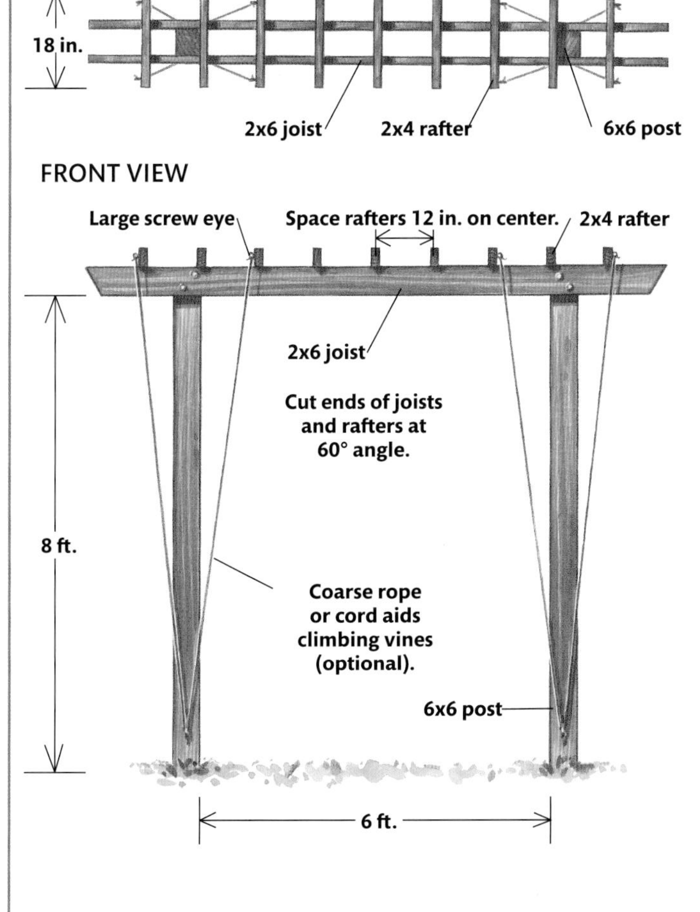

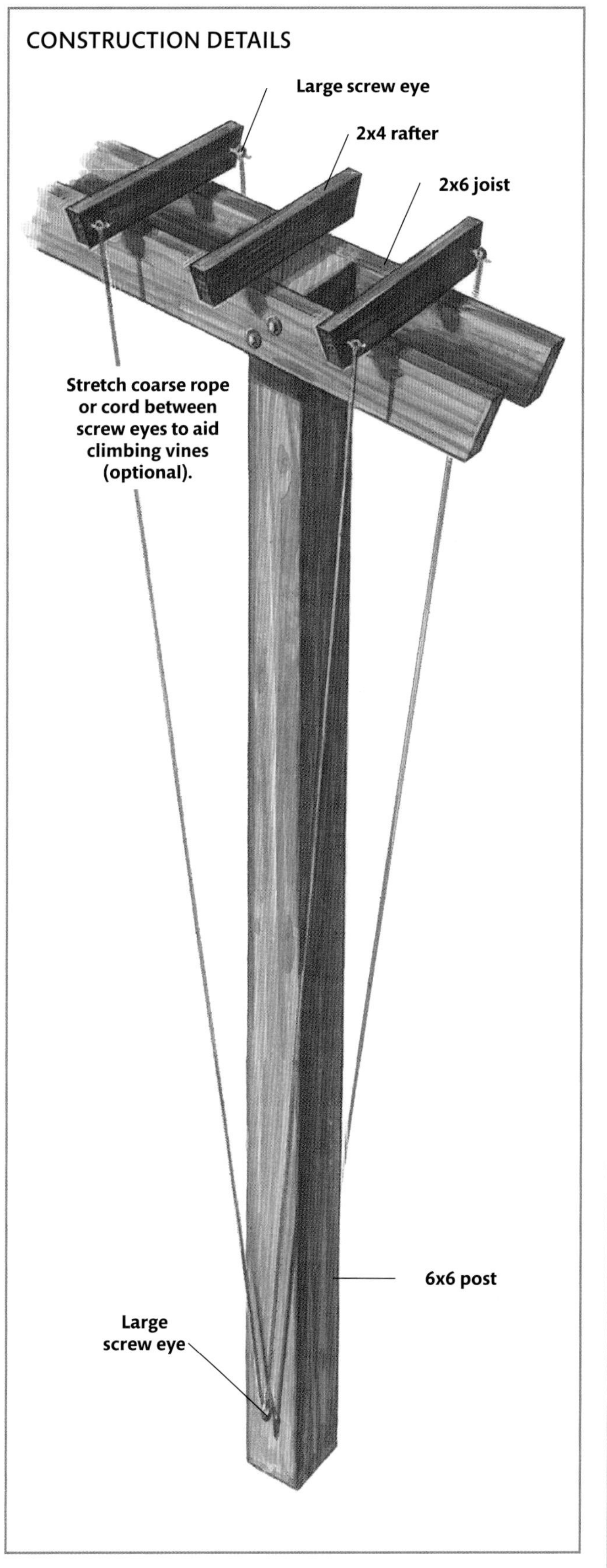

Entry arbor and fence (pp. 70-73)

This arbor makes an event of the passage from sidewalk to front door or from one part of your property to another. Two versions are shown in the Portfolio. One features the arbor alone; the other adds a picket fence.

Hefty 6x6 posts provide real presence here; the 12-footers you'll need are heavy, so engage a couple of helpers to save your back. You can toenail the 3x6 beams to the tops of the posts and the 2x4 rafters to the beams. (Or you can fix them using long spikes or lag screws, 10 in. and 8 in. long, respectively. This job is easier if you drill pilot holes, with bits slightly thinner than the spikes.) Use screws or nails to attach the 2x2 cross rafters. If you can't buy 3x6s, you can nail two 2x6s together face to face.

Sandwich lattice between 1x3s to make the side panels and fix them between posts using nails, screws, or metal connectors. Alternating the corner overlap, as shown on the drawing, makes a stronger frame.

The fence extends from both sides of the arbor. We've shown 6x6 fence posts to match the arbor. But 4x4s work just as well. Space posts farther apart than 8 ft. You can purchase ready-made lengths of picket fence, but it is easy enough to make yourself. Set the posts; then cut and fit 2x4 rails on edge between them. Space 1x3 picket slats 1½ in. apart. The drawing on the facing page shows large round wooden finials atop the fence posts; you can buy various types of ready-made finials, or you could work a heavy bevel around the top end of the posts themselves.

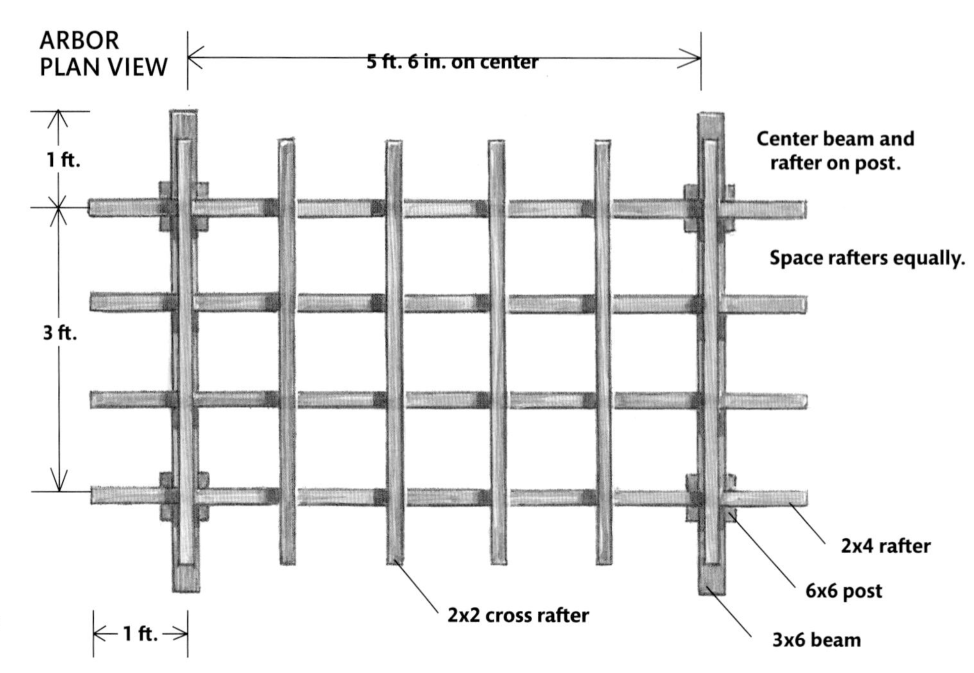

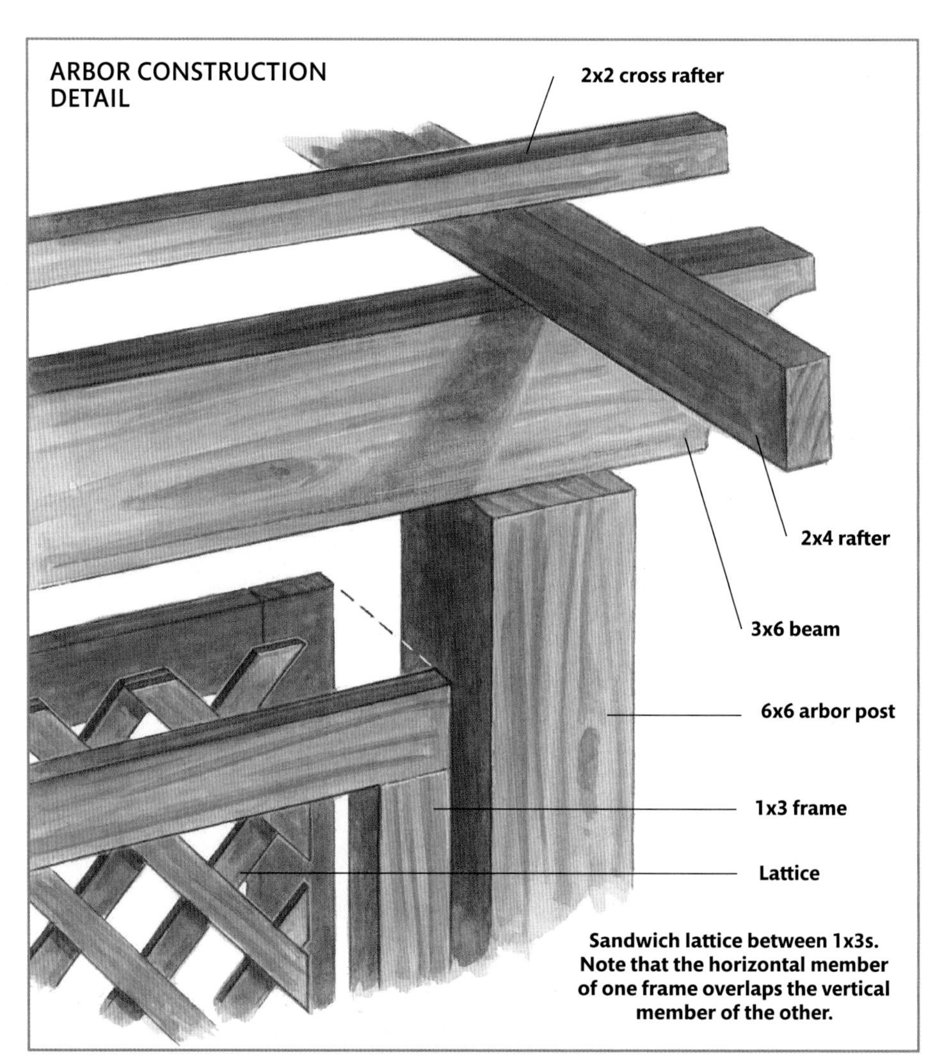

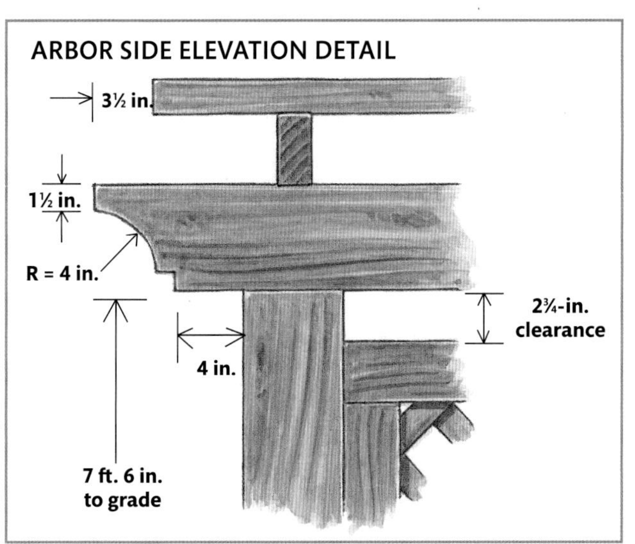

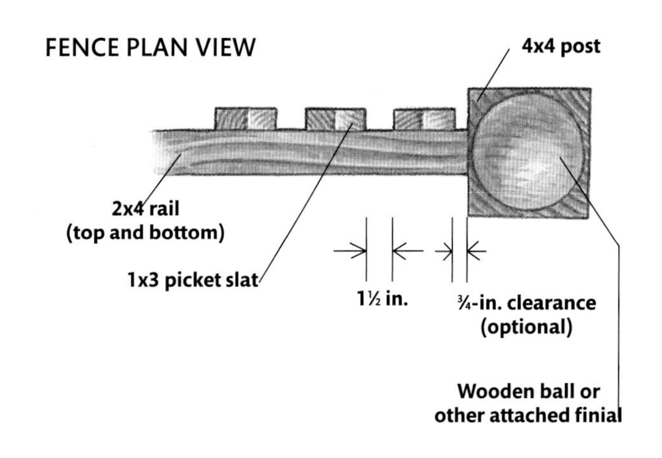

Entry arbor and fence

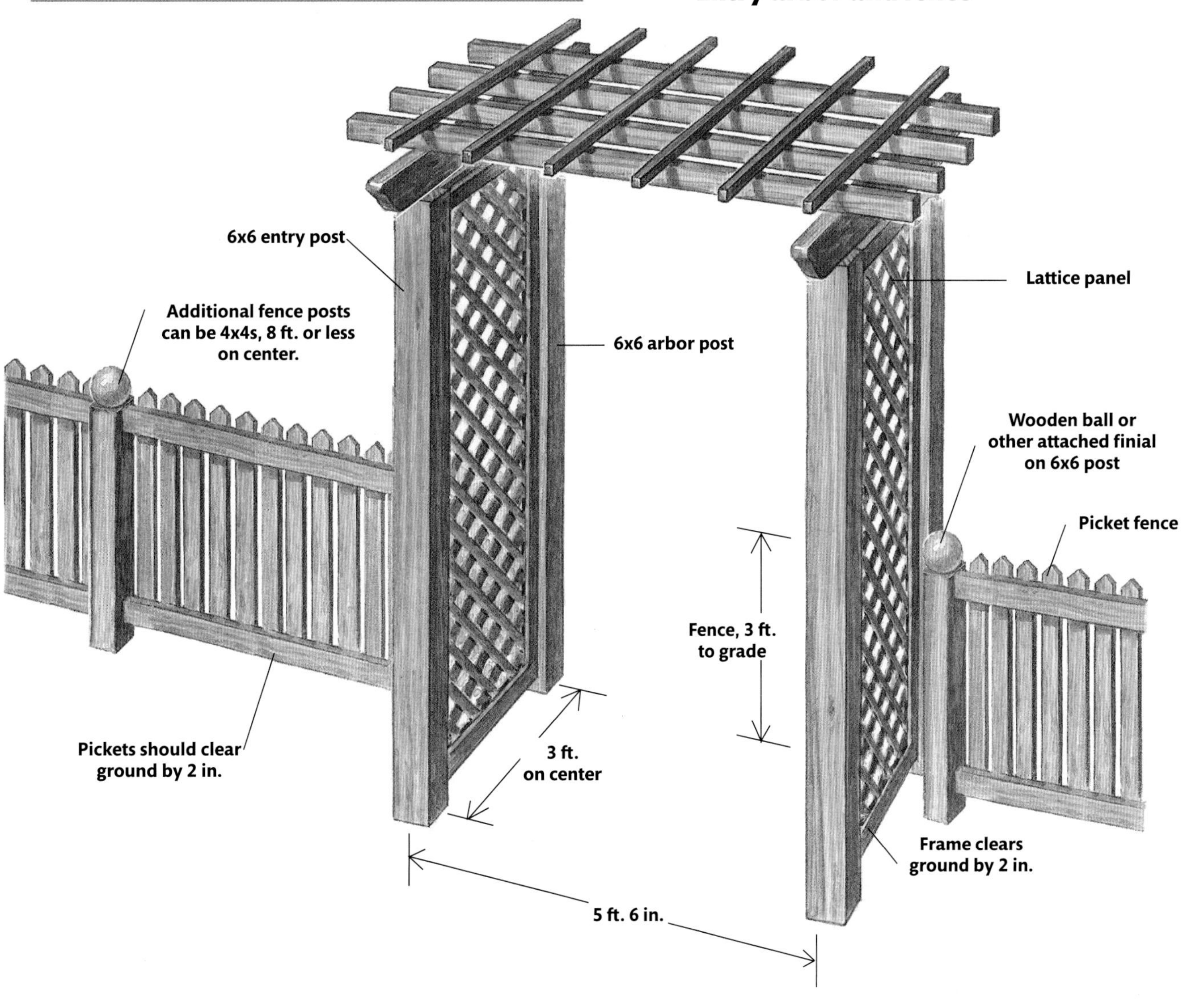

Louvered screen
(pp. 110-111)

Made of vertical slats set at an angle, this 6-ft.-tall fence allows air circulation to plants and people near the patio while providing a privacy screen. Be sure to check local codes about height and setback from property lines.

The slats are supported top and bottom by 2x4 rails; a 2x6 beneath the bottom rail stiffens the entire structure, keeps the slat assembly from sagging, and adds visual weight to the design. Set the posts; then cut the rails to fit between them. Toenailed nails or screws or metal connectors are strong enough, but you can add a 2x4 nailer between the rails (as shown in the drawing at bottom right) to make positioning and assembly easier.

Position the 1x6 slats with a spacer block 1½ in. wide and angled 45° at its ends. Nailing or screwing down through the top rail is easy. Nailing up through the bottom rail is more difficult; instead, you could toenail through the edges or faces of the slats into the bottom rail.

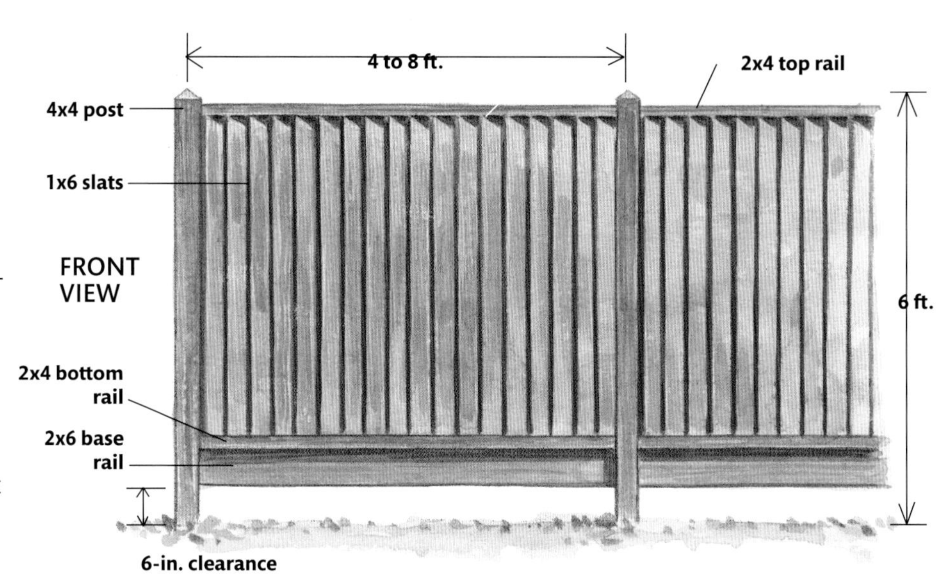

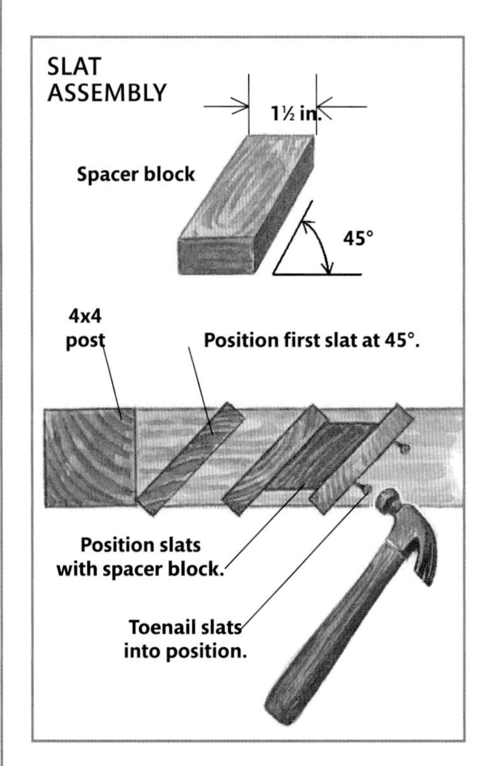

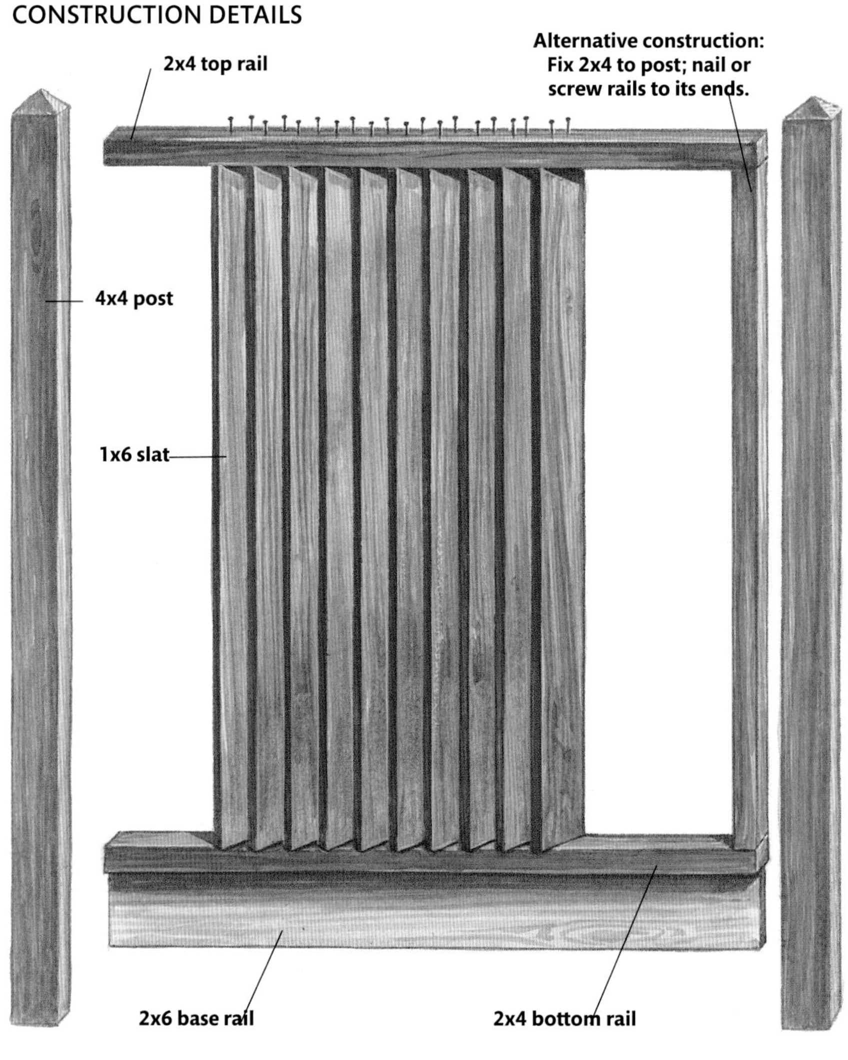

Hideaway arbor
(pp. 88-89)

This cozy enclosure shelters a bench and supports vines to shade the occupants. Once the posts are set in place, this project can be finished in a weekend.

Build the arbor before laying the pavers under it. After setting the posts (see pp. 181-183), attach the 2x10 joists using carriage bolts. (The sizes of posts and joists have been chosen for visual effect; 4x4 posts and 2x6 or 2x8 joists will work, too.) Use nails to tack the joists in place; then bore holes for the bolts through post and both joists using a long electrician's auger bit. Fix the rafters by toenailing or using rust-protected metal rafter ties. Nail or screw the rafters at each end to the posts for added stability. For more privacy, you can add lattice between the posts at each end. (See p. 187 for a method of lattice panel construction.)

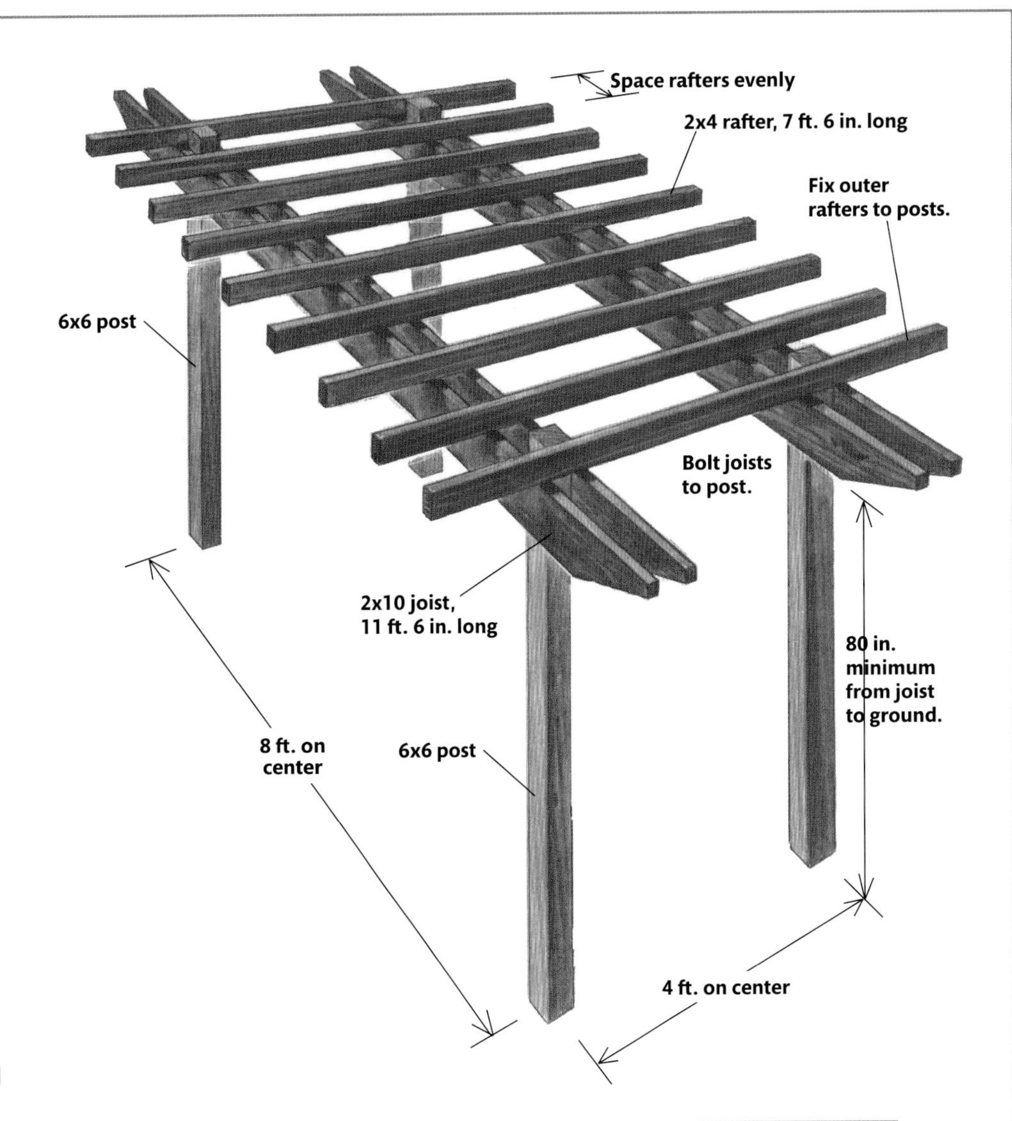

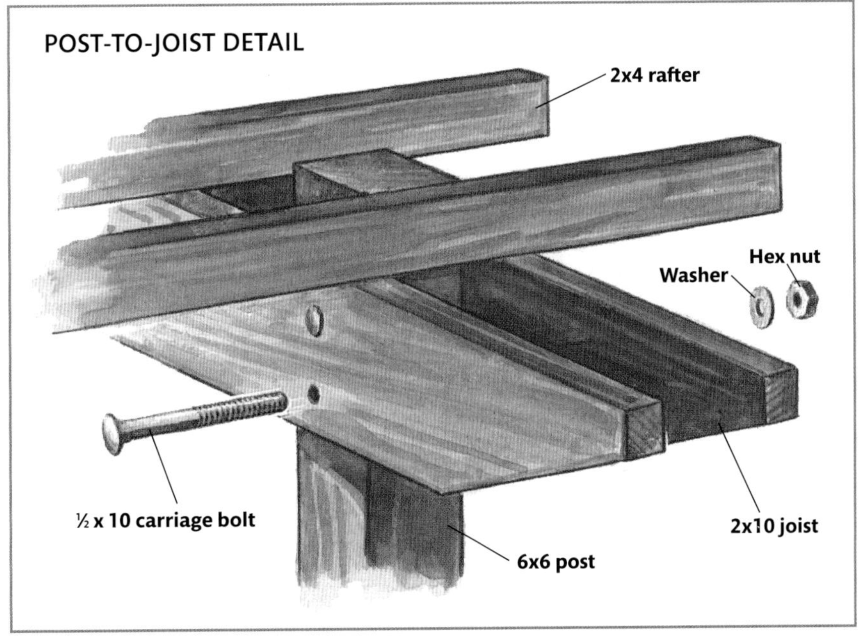

Good-neighbor fence
(pp. 78-79)

A variation on the traditional picket fence, this design provides privacy and good looks to neighbors on both sides, in addition to serving as a backdrop for a perennial border.

This is a simple fence to construct. Just set the posts; cut top and bottom rails to fit between them; and attach the slats. Note that the slats overlap roughly ½ in.; a 4½-in.-wide spacer block (1 in. narrower than the actual 5½-in. width of the 1x6s) makes positioning them a snap. Use two screws or nails positioned diagonally for each slat-to-rail connection.

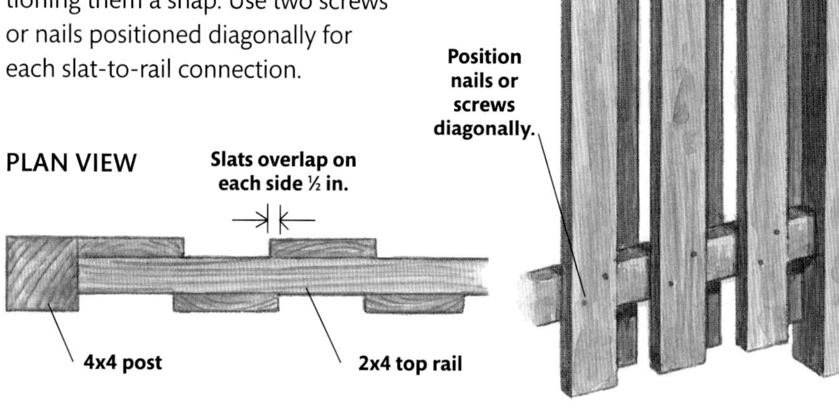

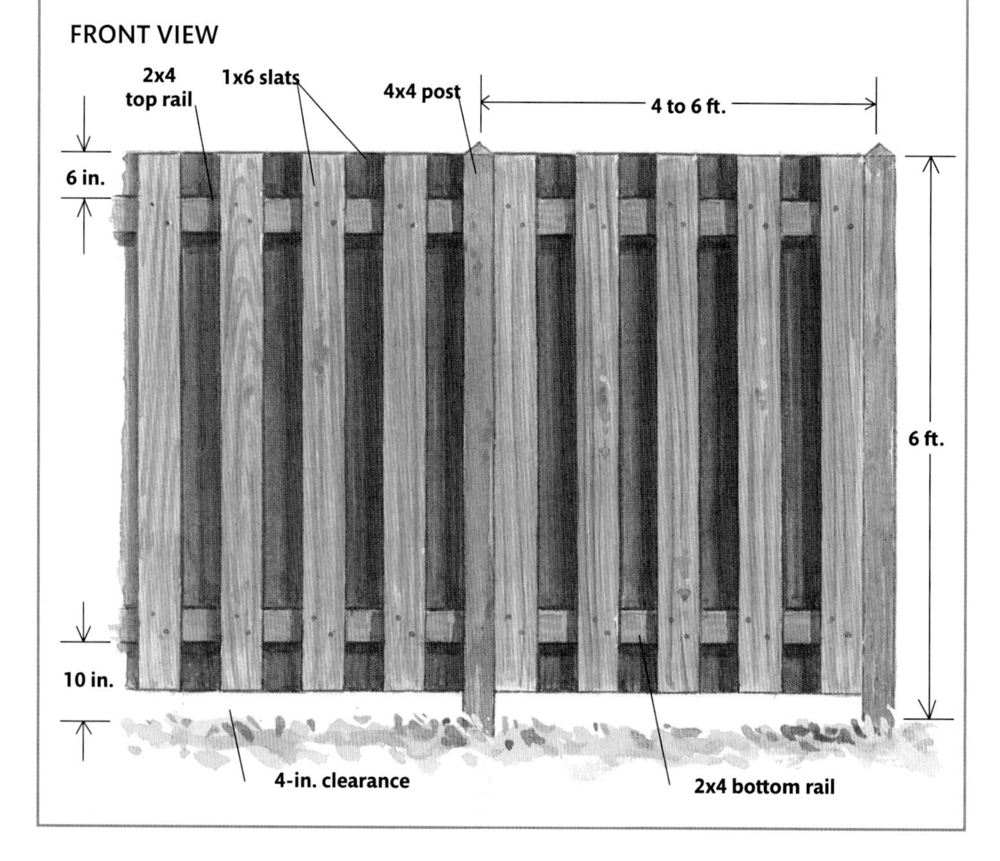

Picket fence
(pp. 100-101)

This fence, a variation of the traditional picket fence, supports a profusion of vining foliage and flowers and provides a sense of enclosure to a small pond and planting. The hefty 6x6 posts are used for their visual weight; 4x4 posts are strong enough if you prefer them.

To build the fence, you can set the posts first (see pp. 181-183) and make fence sections to fit between them. Or make the sections first and set posts accordingly. The pickets are sandwiched between two sets of rails top and bottom and are fixed in place using nails or screws. If you're making fence sections to fit a predetermined distance between

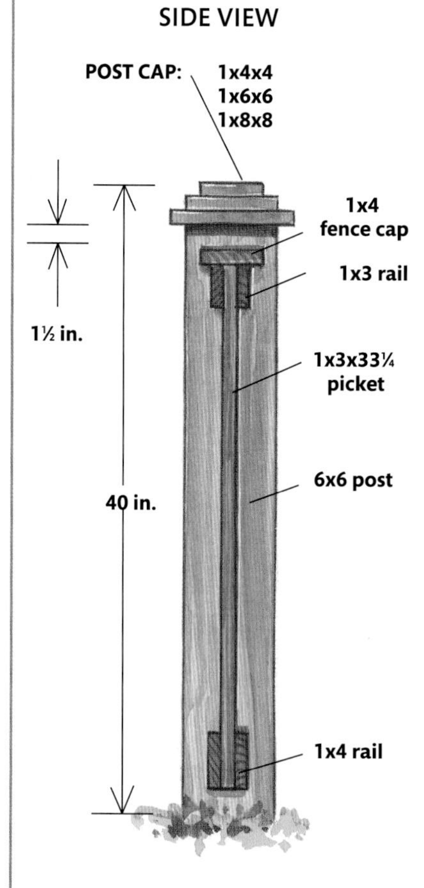

posts, adjust the gap between pickets to ensure uniform spacing. When you lay out the pickets, make sure that there is a space between each post and the end picket.

You can fasten the rails to the posts by toenailing or using metal fasteners. Adding a spacer between the ends of the rails, as shown in the detail drawing, may make attachment easier. After the fence sections are fixed to the posts, add the cap pieces to the top rails and to the posts.

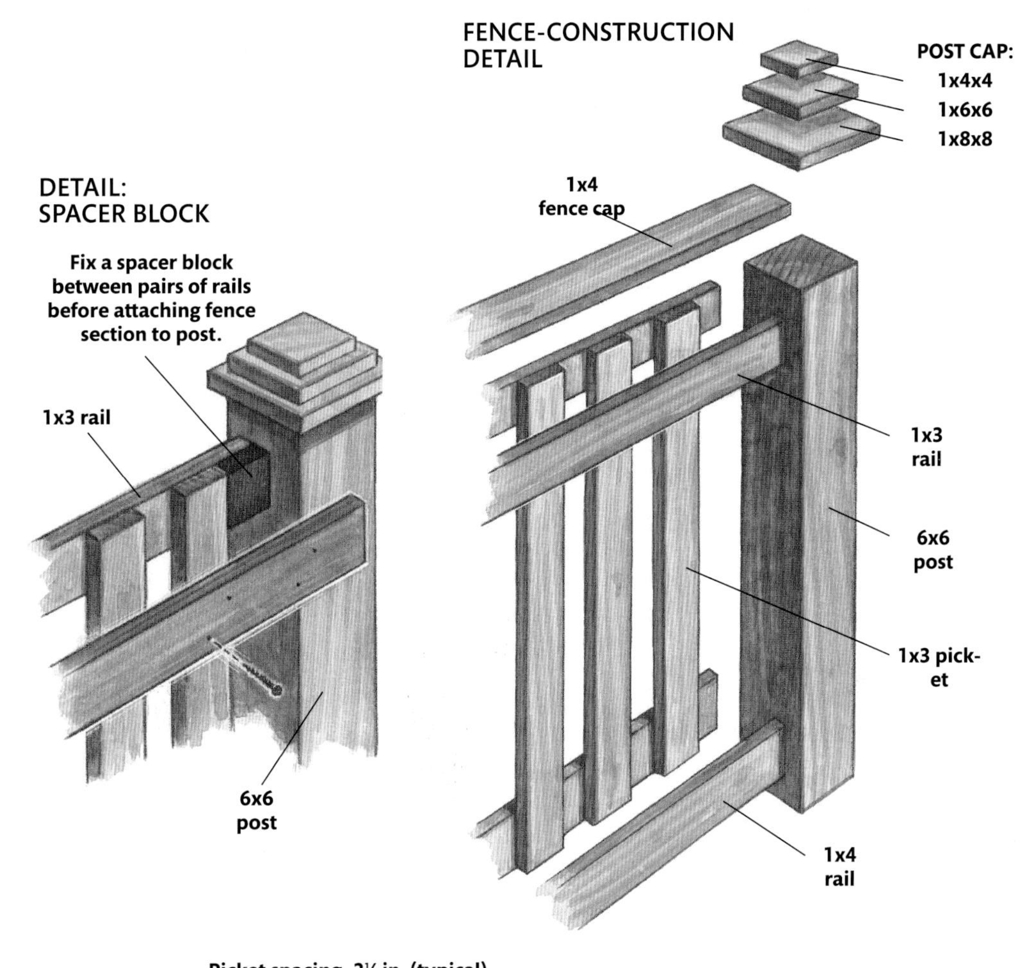

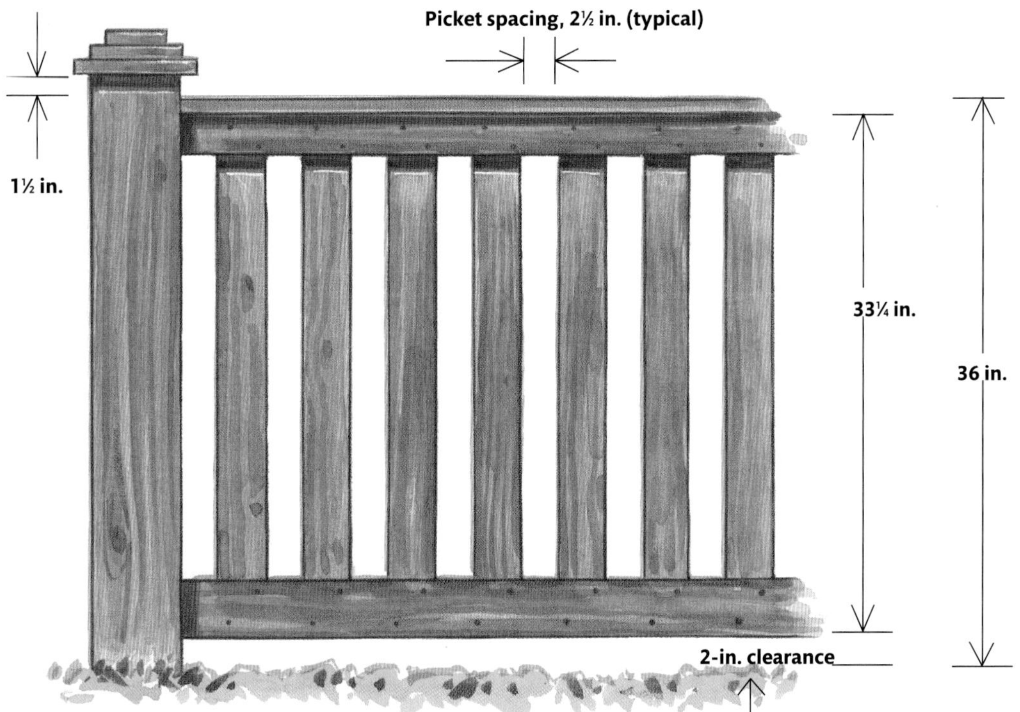

Patio screen
(pp. 92-95)

Draped with vines, this makes an attractive but unobtrusive privacy screen between your patio and an adjacent property.

The screen is a snap to build. After setting the posts (see pp. 181-183), add the top and bottom rails. Cut the ends of those for the angled corners at 45° and toenail or screw them to the posts. Trim the ends of the "pickets" at a 45° angle and fix them into each rail using a nail or a screw. Position the pickets before fastening them to ensure even spacing. If you want a more solid-looking screen, offset the pickets so that those on one side fill the gaps left by those on the other. You can vary the size of the screen and the materials shown here. Keep in mind that the proportions are what make this simple design look good.

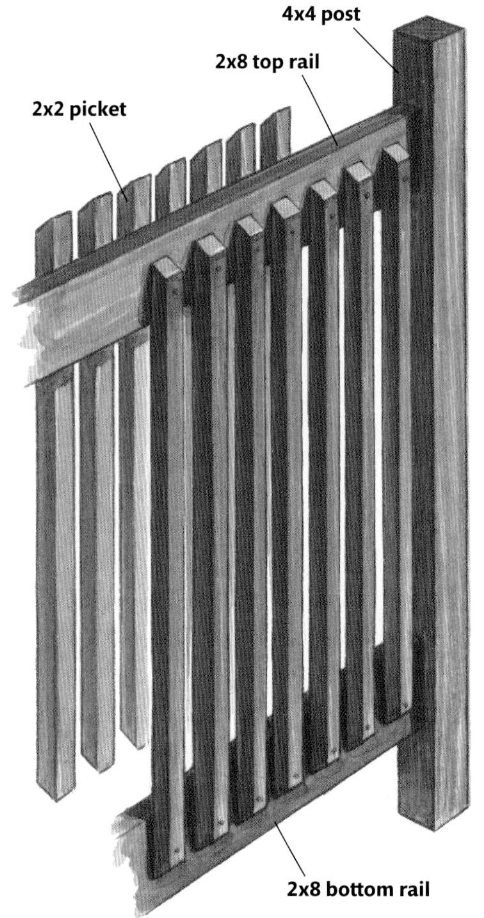

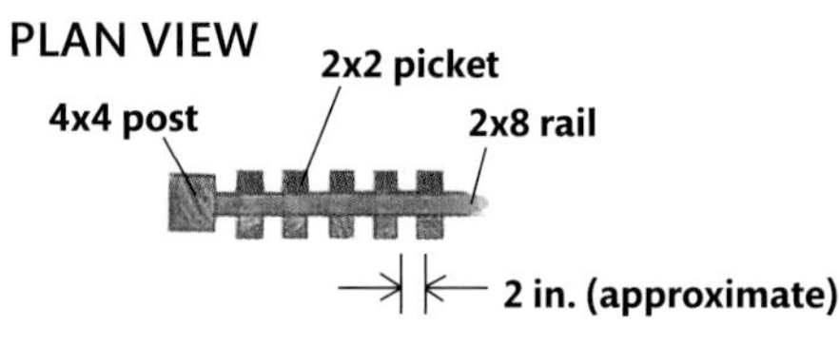

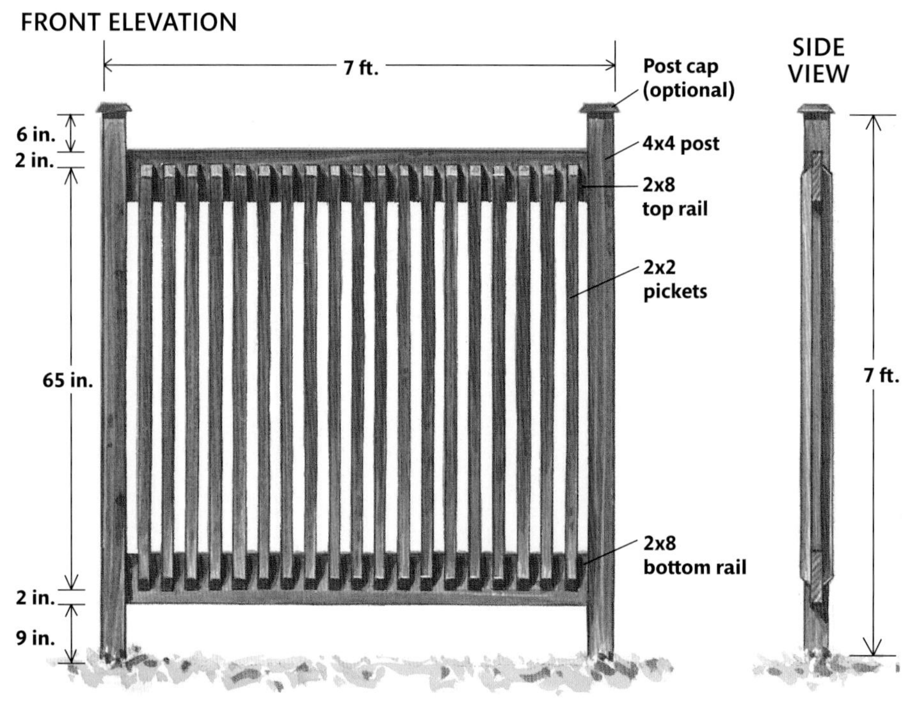

Privacy fence
(pp. 52-55)

This design provides privacy and an attractive backdrop for a planting. If the fence is used on a property line, be sure to check local codes for restrictions on placement and height.

This is a simple fence to construct. Assemble the panels on a flat surface, nailing or screwing the slats to the three 2x4 rails. You can lay out the arc at the top of each panel by "springing" a thin strip of wood, as shown on the facing page. Place the strip against a nail driven into a slat at the highest point of the arc in the center of the panel ❶. Enlist a couple of assistants to bend each end of the strip down to nails near each edge of the panel indicating the lowest points of the arc ∑. Pencil in the arc against the strip ∏; then cut to the line. (A handheld electric saber saw does the job quickly, but the curve is gentle enough to cut with a handsaw.)

Set the posts (see pp. 181-183)

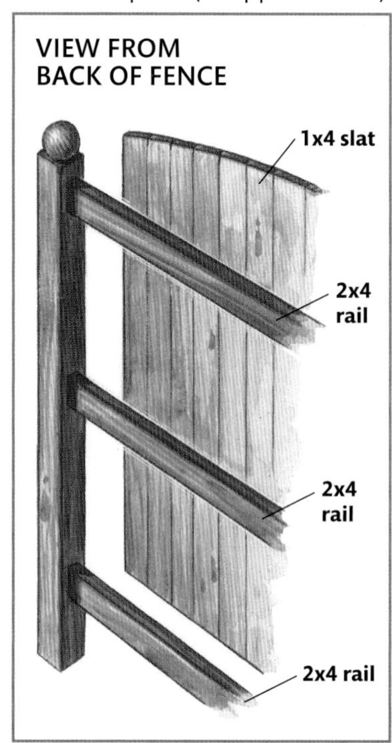

according to the widths of the finished panels. The 6x6 posts shown here add an eye-pleasing heft to the fence, an effect emphasized by setting the face of the panel 1 in. back from the faces of the posts. (Posts made of 4x4s will work just as well.) Metal connectors are the easiest means of attaching the completed panels to the posts. To allow yourself access to the rails when mounting the metal connectors, leave the last slats at each end off when you assemble the panels. We've shown a spherical finial attached to the end of each post; you can buy finials of various types at home centers.

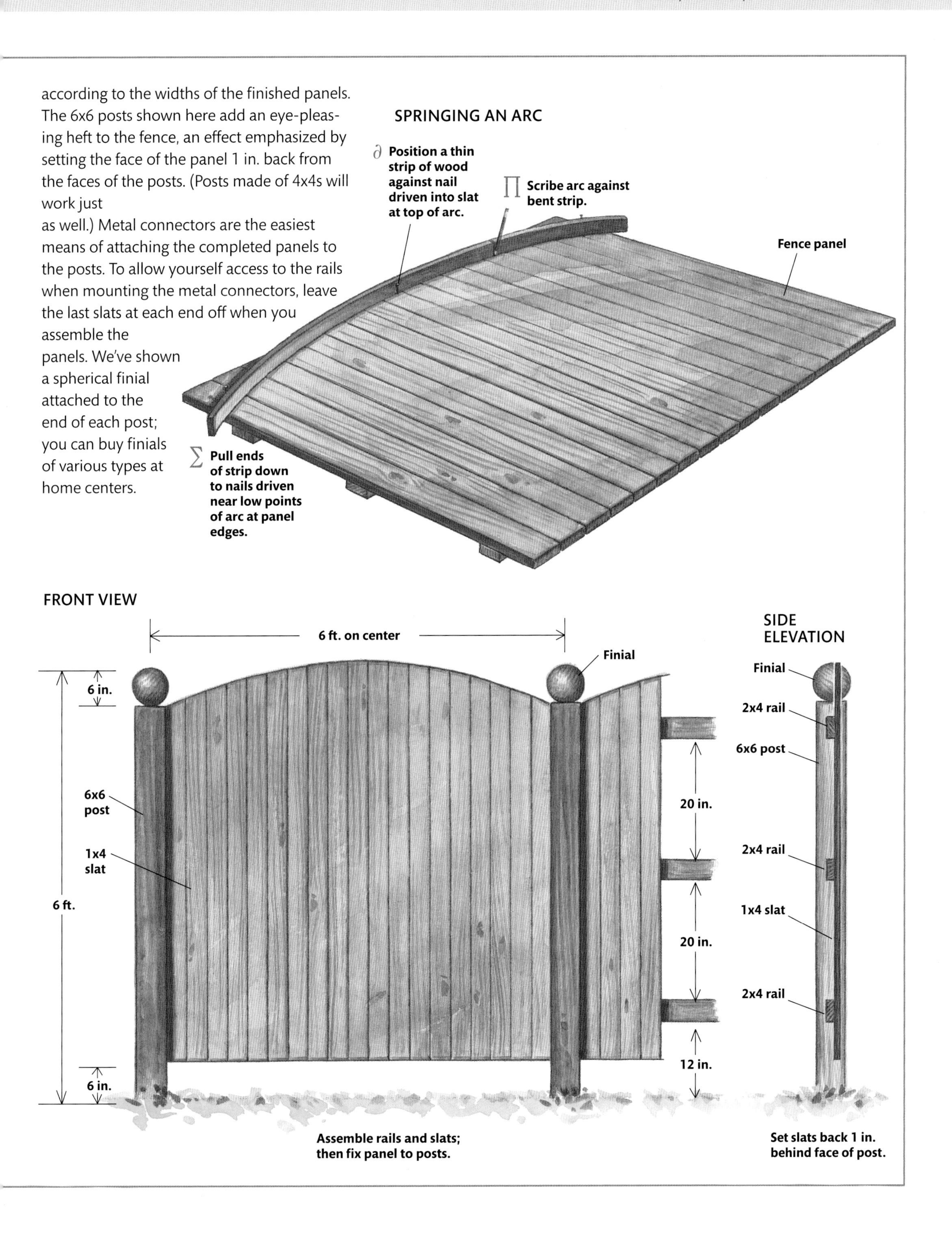

Preparing the Soil for Planting

The better the soil, the better the plants. Soil quality affects how fast plants grow, how big they get, how good they look, and how long they live. But on many residential lots, the soil is shallow and infertile. Unless you're lucky enough to have a better-than-average site where the soil has been cared for and amended over the years, perhaps for use as a vegetable garden or flower bed, you should plan to improve your soil before planting in it.

If you were planting just a few trees or shrubs, or planting a bed of perennials on a rocky hillside, you could prepare individual planting holes for the plants and leave the surrounding soil undisturbed. However, for nearly all the plantings in this book, digging individual holes is impractical, and it's much better for the plants if you prepare the soil throughout the entire area that will be planted. (The major exception is when you're planting under a tree, which is discussed on p. 200.)

For most of the situations shown in this book, you could prepare the soil using hand tools—a spade, digging fork, and rake. The job will go faster and mix in amendments better if you use a gas- powered rototiller. Unless you grow vegetables, you probably won't use a rototiller often enough to justify buying one yourself, but you can easily borrow or rent a rototiller or hire someone with a tiller to come and prepare your site.

Loosen the soil

After you've removed any sod or other vegetation from the designated area (see pp. 158-159), the first step is digging or tilling to loosen the soil ❶. Do this on a day when the soil is moist—not so wet that it sticks to your tools or so dry that it makes dust. Try to dig down at least 8 in., or deeper if possible. If the ground is very compacted, you'll need to make repeated passes with a tiller to reach 8 in. deep. Toss aside large rocks, roots, or debris. When you're working near a house or other building, be sure to locate buried wires, cables, and pipes. Most local governments and utility companies have a number you can call to request help locating buried utilities.

After this initial digging, the ground will likely be very rough and lumpy. Whump the clods with the back of a digging fork or make another tiller pass. Continue until you've reduced all the clumps to the size of apples.

Once you've loosened the existing soil and dug it as deeply as possible, you may need to add clean topsoil or a landscape mix to fill in low spots, refine the grade, or raise the planting area above the surrounding grade for better drainage or to make it easier to see a favorite plant. Unless you need just a small amount, order topsoil or landscape mix by the cubic yard. (Landscape mix is primarily composted pine bark, sometimes with sand, manure, and other composted materials.) Consult the staff at your local nursery to find a reputable supplier of bulk landscape materials.

In many areas of central Texas, only a thin layer of soil covers limestone bedrock, making digging or tilling impossible. In these areas, the best option is to bring in topsoil or landscape mix. Mound it to create a low berm or contain it in a raised soil bed enclosed in wood or stone.

Add organic matter

Common soil (and purchased topsoil, too) consists mainly of rock and mineral fragments of various size. One of the best things you can do to improve any

Common soil amendments and fertilizers

The following materials serve different purposes. Follow soil-test recommendations or the advice of an experienced gardener in choosing amendments that would be best for your soil. If so recommended, you can apply two or three of these amendments at the same time, using the stated rate for each one.

Material	Description	Amount for 100 sq. ft.
Compost	Amendment. Decomposed or aged plant parts and animal manures.	1 cubic yard
Wood by-products	Amendment. Finely ground bark or sawdust, composted or not. Add nitrogen to noncomposted material.	1 cubic yard
Organic fertilizer	Derived from a variety of organic materials. Provides nutrients in slow-release form.	According to label
Composted manure	Weak nitrogen fertilizers. Bagged steer manure is common.	6–8 lb.

kind of soil for landscape and garden plants is to add some organic matter.

Organic materials used in landscaping are derived from plants and animals and include ground bark, compost, and composted manures. Organic matter can be bought in bags or in bulk at nurseries, landscape supply companies, and many municipal recycling centers. If possible, buy only composted or aged material to amend your soil. Fresh manure can burn plant roots. Fresh bark and sawdust can steal nitrogen from the soil as they decay. If you buy uncomposted materials, ask at your nursery about how best to use them. (Some require supplemental nitrogen.)

How much organic matter should you use? Compost or aged material can be spread 2 to 3 in. thick across the entire work area ❷. At this thickness, a cubic yard (about one heaping pickup-truck load) of material will cover 100 to 150 sq. ft. Composted and aged manures, such as the bagged steer manure sold at nurseries, contain higher concentrations of nitrogen and should be applied at lower rates than other composts. They are more commonly used as slow-release fertilizers than as soil-improving amendments.

Add fertilizers and mineral amendments

Organic materials such as compost improves the soil's texture and helps it retain water and nutrients. It's most helpful if you mix materials into the soil before you do any planting ❸, working them into the root zone, but you can also sprinkle them on top of the soil to maintain an established planting.

Testing a sample of soil is the most accurate way to determine how much of each nutrient is needed. (To locate a soil-testing lab, consult the Internet, or your Cooperative Extension Service.) Less precise, but often adequate, is the advice of nursery staff. Test results or an adviser will point out any significant deficiencies. Most soil just needs a moderate, balanced dose of nutrients.

Avoid using too much of any fertilizer or mineral. Don't guess at this; measure and weigh carefully. Calculate your plot's area. Follow your soil-test results or instructions on a commercial product's package. If necessary, weigh out the appropriate amount, using a kitchen or bathroom scale. Apply the material evenly across the plot with a spreader or by hand.

PREPARING THE SOIL FOR PLANTING

❶ Use a spade, digging fork, or tiller to dig at least 8 in. deep and break the soil into rough clods. Discard rocks, roots, and debris. Watch out for underground utilities.

❷ Spread a 2- to 3-in. layer of organic matter on top of the soil.

❸ Sprinkle measured amounts of fertilizer and mineral amendments evenly across the entire area, and mix thoroughly into the soil.

Mix and smooth the soil

Finally, use a digging fork or tiller and go back and forth across the bed again until the added materials are mixed thoroughly into the soil and everything is broken into nut-size or smaller lumps ❹. Then use a rake to smooth the surface ❺.

At this point, the soil level may look too high compared with adjacent pavement or lawn, but don't worry. Once the soil gets wet, it will settle a few inches and end up close to its original level.

Working near trees

Plantings under the shade of old trees can be cool oasis, such as the one shown on pp. 76-77. But to establish the plants, you'll need to contend with the tree's roots. Contrary to popular belief, most tree roots are in the top few inches of the soil, and they extend at least as far away from the trunk as the limbs do. Always try to disturb as few roots as possible when planting beneath established trees. To do so, it's often best to dig individual planting holes, rather than tilling a bed. Avoid cutting large roots. To start ground covers and perennials, you can add up to 4 in. of loose soil or landscape mix under the canopy of many established trees. Keep the new soil and any mulch away from the trunk. Covering roots with too much soil can starve them of oxygen, damaging or killing them; soil or mulch next to the trunk can rot the adjacent bark.

Plantings beneath existing native post oaks are normally problematic because the additional water needed to maintain the planting may damage or kill these trees. If you're uncertain about whether or how to plant beneath any established tree, or if your landscape plans call for significant grade changes beneath them, consult with a certified arborist.

❹ **Use a tiller or digging fork to mix everything together, again working as deep as possible.**

❺ **Finish by smoothing the surface using a rake.**

Making neat edges

All but the most informal landscapes look best if you define and maintain neat edges between the lawn and any adjacent plantings. There are several ways to do this, varying in appearance, effectiveness, cost, and convenience. Attractive, easy-to-install edges include cut, brick or stone, and strip edgings of plastic, fiberglass, or steel. If you plan to install an edging, put it in after you prepare the soil but before you plant.

Cut edge

Lay a hose or rope on the ground to mark the line where you want to cut. Then cut along the line using a sharp spade or edging tool. Lift away any grass that was growing into the bed (or any plants that were running out into the lawn). Use a rake or hoe to smooth out a shallow trench on the bed side of the cut. Keep the trench empty; don't let it fill up with mulch.

Pros and cons: Free. Good for straight or curved edges, level or sloped sites. But you'll need to recut the edge every four to eight weeks during the growing season; you can cut 50 to 100 ft. in an hour or so. Don't cut the trench too deep; if a mower wheel slips down into it, you'll scalp the lawn. Crabgrass and other weeds may sprout in the exposed soil; if this happens, hoe or pull them out.

Brick mowing strip

Dig a trench about 8 in. wide and 4 in. deep around the edge of the bed. Fill it halfway with sand; then lay bricks on top, setting them level with the soil on the lawn side. You'll need three bricks per foot of edging. Sweep extra sand into any cracks between the bricks. In cold-winter areas, you'll probably need to reset a few frost-heaved bricks each spring. You can substitute cut stone blocks or concrete pavers for bricks.

Pros and cons: Good for straight or curved edges on level or gently sloped sites. Looks good in combination with brick walkways or brick house. Fairly easy to install and maintain. Some kinds of grass and plants will grow under, between, or over the bricks.

Metal Edging

This is available from suppliers of landscape goods in 8–10 foot lengths and 4–6 inch widths, in aluminum, coated steel, and unfinished weathering steel which will take on a stable rusted appearance. Metal edging is popular in formal garden settings where straight lines or definite curves are sought. Unfinished or weathering steel (naturally rusted appearance) is often a key component in a contemporary landscape in the form of edging, planters, and other decorative elements.

Pros and cons: Useful for straight or curved edges on relatively level sites. Requires some precision to successfully install. Achieves a handsome permanent appearance. Important to set edging height to avoid conflict with the lawn mower. Once set, metal edging is quite stable and not likely to shift. However, it will generally degrade sooner than brick or stone. Metal edging is also useful to contain gravel for a walkway or patio.

Plastic strip edging

Garden centers and home-improvement stores sell heavy-duty plastic edging in strips 5 or 6 in. wide and 20 or 50 ft. long. To install it, use a sharp tool to cut straight down through the sod around the edge of the bed. Hold the edging so the round lip sits right at soil level, and drive the stakes through the bottom of the edging and into the undisturbed soil under the lawn. Stakes, which are supplied with the edging, should be at least 8 in. long and set about 3 ft. apart. Similar strip edging in steel or fiberglass is installed in much the same way.

Pros and cons: Good for straight or curved edges, but only on relatively level sites. Neat and carefree when well installed, but installation is a two- or three-person job. If the lip isn't set right on the ground, you're likely to hit it with the mower blade. Liable to shift or heave unless it's very securely staked. Hard to drive stakes in rocky soil. Some kinds of grass and ground covers can grow across the top of this type of edging.

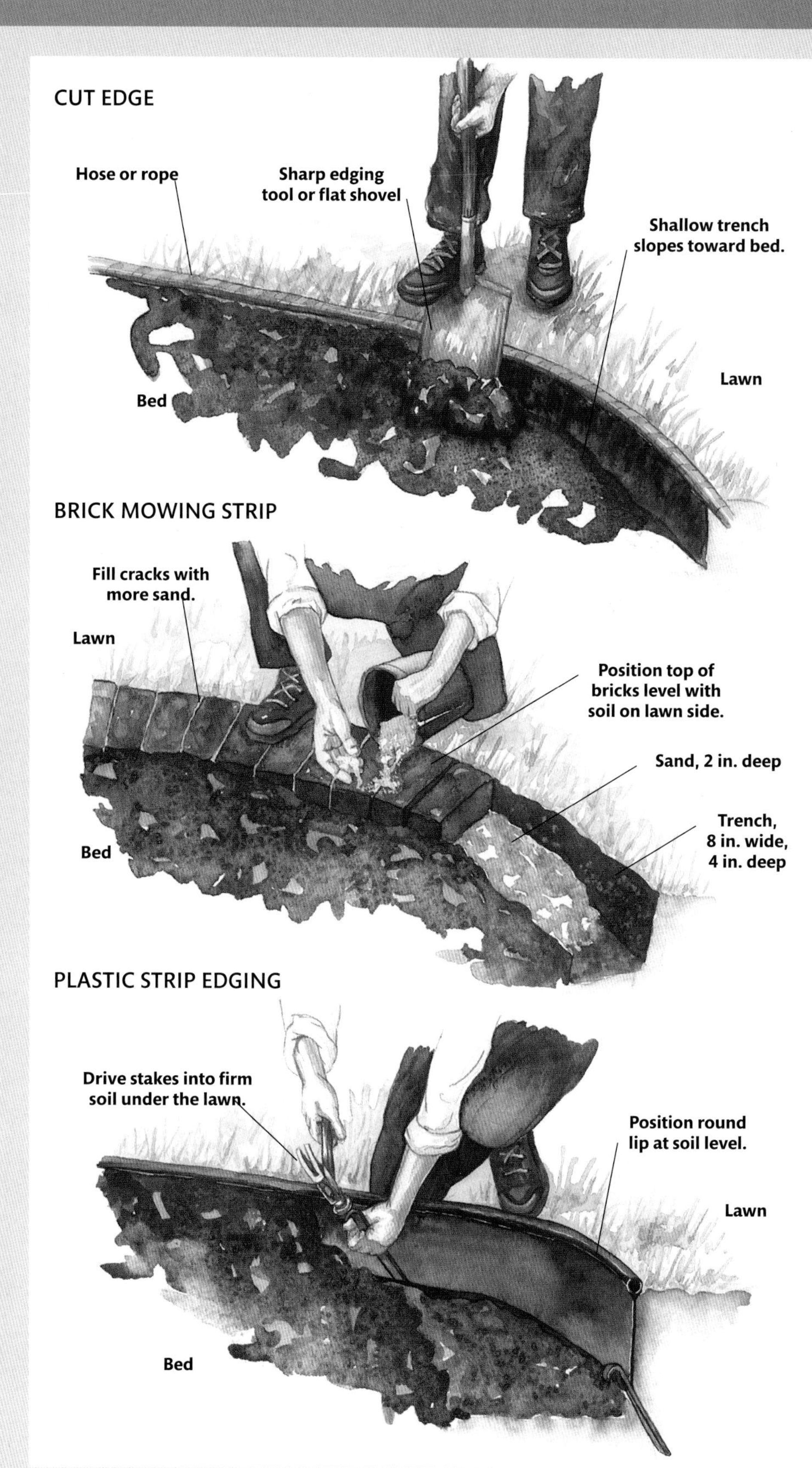

Buying Plants

Once you have chosen and planned a landscape project, make a list of the plants you want and start thinking about where to get them. You'll need to locate the kinds of plants you want, choose good-quality plants, and get enough of the plants to fill your design area.

Where and how to shop

A wide variety of sources offer plants for your landscape—some local, regional, and even mail-order sources. You may already have a favorite place to shop for plants. An online search for "Native Plant Suppliers," "Nurseries," and "Garden Centers" will list options for your plant needs. Suppliers outside of your area may offer shipping of seeds, bare root plants, and smaller potted plants. This can be helpful if your local suppliers do not offer native plants or other items you are seeking. Mail-order sources may offer a better value than local sources for some items. If shopping locally, takeyour shopping list, find a salesperson, and ask for help. The plants in this book are commonly available in most parts of Texas, but you may not find everything you want at one place. The salesperson may refer you to another nursery, offer to special-order plants, or recommend similar plants that you could use as substitutes.

Be aware that most plant suppliers offer non-native plants. Some of these may be invasive and others may not be suited to your local soil and climate conditions. So, do your research to ensure the plants you purchase are a good match for your landscape.

If you're buying too many plants to carry in your car or truck, ask about delivery—it's usually available and sometimes free. Some nurseries offer to replace plants that fail within a limited guarantee period, so ask about that, too.

The staff at a good nursery or garden center will normally be able to answer most of the questions you have about which plants to buy and how to care for them. If you can, go shopping on a rainy weekday when business is slow so staff will have time to answer your questions.

Don't be lured by the low prices of plants for sale at supermarkets or stores that sell plants for only a few months unless you're sure you know exactly what you want and how to identify it. The staff at these stores rarely have the time or knowledge to offer you much help, and the plants are often disorganized, unlabeled, and stressed by poor care.

If you can't find a plant locally or have a retailer order it for you, you can always order it yourself from a mail-order nursery. Most mail-order nurseries produce good plants and pack them well, but if you haven't dealt with a business before, be smart and place a minimum order first. Judge the quality of the plants that arrive; then decide whether or not to order larger quantities from that firm.

Timing

It's a good idea to plan ahead and start shopping for plants before you're ready to put them in the ground. That way, if you can't find everything on your list, you'll have time to keep shopping around, place special orders, or choose substitutes. Some nurseries will let you flag an order for later pickup or delivery, and they'll take care of the plants in the meantime. Or you can bring the plants home; just remember to check the soil in the containers every day and water if needed.

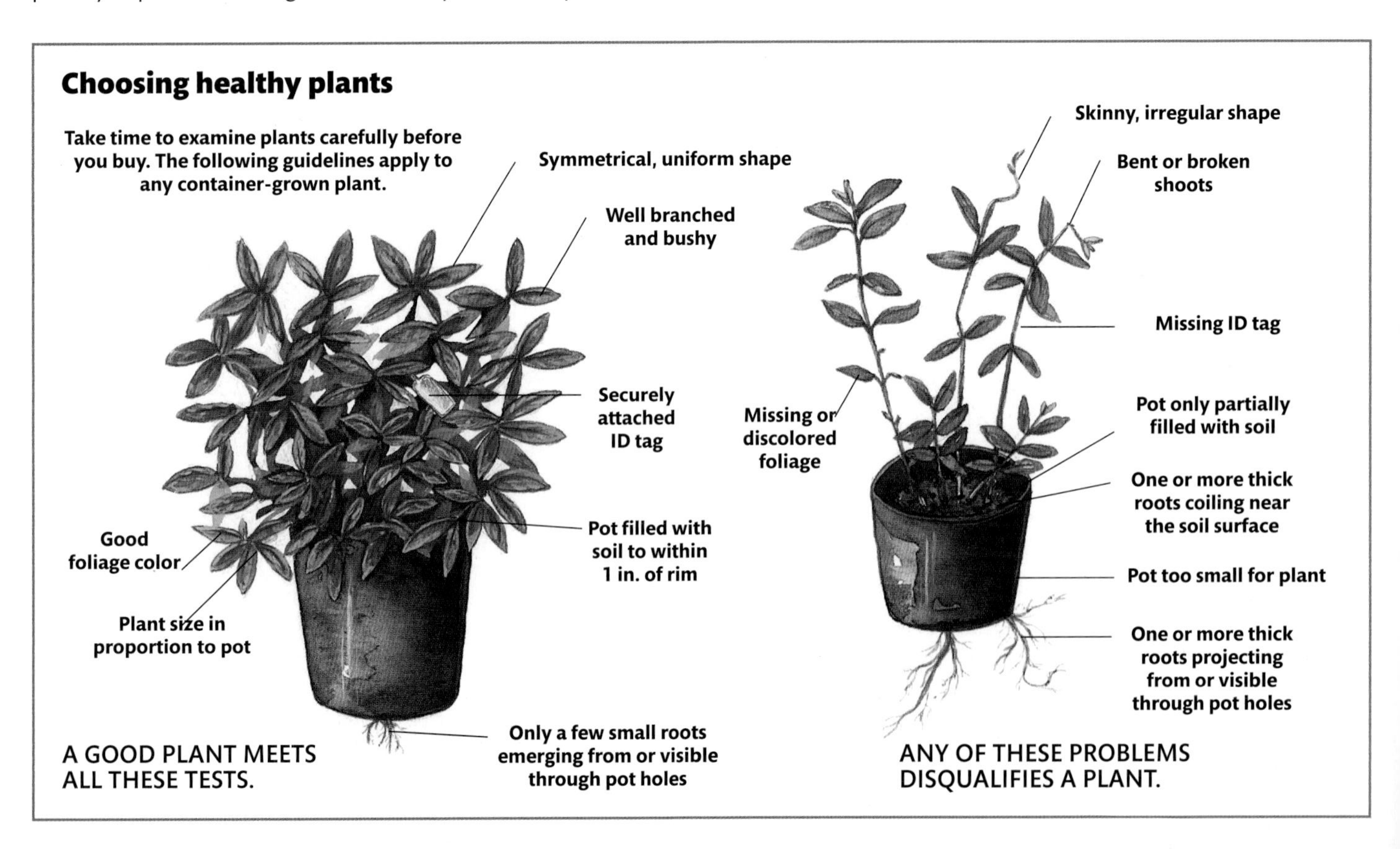

The Planting Process

Throughout most of Texas, the cooler weather of fall or early spring makes those times best for planting. In fall, new plants have the upcoming wet season to become established before the onset of hot summer weather. However, frost-tender plants such as tropical hibiscus are best planted in spring after the threat of cold temperatures has passed. Although it's handy to plant a whole bed at once, you can divide the job, setting out some plants in fall and adding the rest in spring, or vice versa. If possible, do the actual planting on a cloudy day or evening when rain is forecast. Compared with preparing the soil, putting plants in the ground goes quite quickly. If you're well prepared, you can plant a whole bed in just an hour or two. On the following pages, we'll give an overview of the process and discuss how to handle individual plants. If you're installing an irrigation system, remember that some of the components may need to be put in place after the soil is prepared but before planting.

Try to stay off the soil

Throughout the planting process, do all you can by reaching in from outside the bed. Stepping on the newly prepared bed compacts the soil and makes it harder to dig planting holes. Use short boards or scraps of plywood as temporary steppingstones if you do need to step on the soil. As soon as you can decide where to put them, lay permanent steppingstones.

Check placement and spacing

The first step in planting is to mark the position of each plant. It's easy to arrange most of the plants themselves on the bed; use empty pots or stakes to represent plants too heavy to move easily. Follow your site plan for the design, checking the spacing with a yardstick as you place the plants.

Then step back and take a look. Should any of the plants be adjusted a little? Don't worry if the planting looks a little sparse. It *should* look that way at first. Plants almost always get bigger than you can imagine when you're first setting them out. And it's almost always better to wait for them to fill in rather than having to prune and thin a crowded planting in a few years. You might fill in with low-growing annuals. (See p. 204)

PLANTING POINTERS

When working on top of prepared soil, kneel on a piece of plywood to distribute your weight.

Use empty pots or stakes to mark positions of plants not yet purchased or too heavy to move frequently.

Choosing particular plants

If you need, for example, five hollies and the nursery or garden center has a whole block of them, how do you choose which five to buy? Because the sales staff may be too busy to help you decide, you may need to choose yourself.

Most plants today are grown in containers, so it's possible to lift them one at a time and examine them from all sides. Following the guidelines shown in the drawings on the opposite page, evaluate each plant's shape, size, health and vigor, and root system.

Trees and shrubs are sometimes sold "balled-and-burlapped," that is, with a ball of soil and roots wrapped tightly in burlap. For these plants, look for strong limbs with no broken shoots, an attractive profile, and healthy foliage. Then press your hands against the burlap-covered root ball to make sure that it feels firm, solid, and damp, not loose or dry. (If the ball is buried within a bed of wood chips, carefully pull the chips aside; then push them back after inspecting the plant.)

To make the final choice when you're considering a group of plants, line them up side by side and select the ones that are most closely matched in height, bushiness, and foliage color. If your design includes a hedge or mass planting where uniformity is very important, it's a good idea to buy a few extra plants as potential replacements in case of damage or loss. It's easier to plan ahead than to find a match later. Plant the extras in a spare corner so you'll have them if you need them.

Sometimes a plant will be available in two or more sizes. Which is better? That depends on how patient you are. The main reason for buying bigger plants is to make a landscape look impressive right away. If you buy smaller plants and set them out at the same spacing, the planting will look sparse at first, but it will soon catch up. A year after planting, you can't tell if a perennial came from a quart or gallon pot: they will look the same. For shrubs, the difference between one size pot and the next usually represents one year's growth.

Moving through the job

When you're satisfied with the arrangement, mark the position of each plant using a stake or stone, and set the plants aside, out of the way, so you won't knock them over or step on them as you proceed. Start planting in order of size. Plant the biggest plants first; then move on to the medium-size and smaller plants. If all the plants are about the same size, start at the back of the bed and work toward the front, or start in the center and work to the edges.

Position trees and shrubs to show their best side

Most trees and shrubs are slightly asymmetric. There's usually enough irregularity in their branching or shape that one side looks a little fuller or more attractive than the other sides do. After you've set a tree or shrub into its hole, step back and take a look. Then turn it partway, or try tilting or tipping it a little to one side or the other. Once you've decided which side and position looks best, start filling in the hole with soil. Stop and check again before you firm the soil into place.

The fine points of spacing

When you're planting a group of the same kind of plants, it normally looks best if you space them in slightly curved or zigzag rows. Don't arrange plants in single file unless you want to emphasize a line, such as the edge of a bed. In that case, make the row perfectly straight by sight, adjusting any plants that are out of line. (Stretch a string for long rows.) After planting, step back and evaluate the effect. If you want to adjust the placement or position of any plant, now is the time to do so.

Rake, water, and mulch

Use a garden rake to level the bed after planting. Water enough to settle the soil into place around the roots. Water each plant individually, or you can set up a sprinkler to do the whole planting at once. Mulch the entire planting area with 1 to 3 in. of bark, wood chips, or other organic matter. Mulch is indispensable for controlling weeds and regulating the moisture and temperature of the soil. If you're running out of time, you don't have to spread the mulch right away, but try to get it done within a week or so.

Using annuals as fillers

The plants in our designs have been spaced so they will not be crowded at maturity. Buying more plants and spacing them closer may fill things out faster, but in several years (for perennials; longer for shrubs) you'll need to remove plants or prune them frequently.

If you want something to fill the gaps between young plants for that first year or two, use some annuals. The best annual fillers are those that stay fairly low to the ground. These plants will hide the soil or mulch and make a colorful carpet, but won't shade or smother your permanent plantings. And don't forget to feed them. Annuals generally require more nutrients than perennials.

The following annuals are all easy to grow, readily available, and inexpensive. In Texas, different annuals perform better at different times of the year. Here, those that do best in winter are indicated by **W**; spring and fall by **SF**; and summer by **Su**. For more on annuals, see p. 123.

Begonia (SF): Red, pink, or white flowers. Good for shady sites but takes sun if planted in early spring.

Blue daze (Su): Pure blue flowers on low-growing plant. Full sun or part shade.

Dianthus (W): Red, pink, or white flowers. Full sun.

Dusty miller (SF): Silvery foliage, often lacy-textured. No flowers Full sun or part shade.

Lantana (Su): Red, orange, yellow, pink, white, or bicolored flowers. Full sun.

Pansy and viola (W): Multicolored flowers. Full sun or part shade.

Persian shield (Su): Shrubby plant with pink and silver variegated foliage. Shade.

Petunia (SF): Red, pink, purple, or white flowers. Full sun or part shade.

Sweet alyssum (W): Fragrant white, pink, or purple flowers. Blooms for months. Full sun.

Vinca (Su): Red, pink, or white flowers. Full sun and hot, dry conditions.

Planting Basics

Most of the plants that you buy for a landscaping project today are grown and sold in individual plastic containers. A few large shrubs and trees may be balled-and-burlapped, and some deciduous plants are sold bare-root. Ground covers are sometimes sold in flats. In any case, be careful what you do to a plant's roots. Spread them out; don't fold, coil, or cram them into a tight hole. Keep them covered; don't let the sun or air get them dry. Don't bury them too deep; set the top of the root-ball level with the surrounding soil. Make sure to regularly water the young plant so that it doesn't get dry.

Planting container-grown plants

The steps are the same for any plant, no matter what size the container. Dig a hole that's a little wider than the container but not quite as deep ❶. Check by setting the container into the hole—the top of the soil in the container should be slightly higher than the surrounding soil. Dig several holes at a time, at the positions that you've already marked out.

Remove the container ❷. With one hand, grip the plant at the base of its stems or leaves, while you tug on the pot with the other hand. If the pot doesn't slide off easily, don't pull harder on the stems. Try whacking the pot with your trowel or use a strong knife to cut or pry it off the plant.

Examine the plant's roots ❸. If there are any thick, coiled roots, unwind them and cut them off close to the root-ball, leaving short stubs. If the root-ball is a mass of fine, hairlike roots, use the knife to cut three or four slits from top to bottom, about 1 in. deep. Pry the slits apart, and tease the cut roots to loosen them. This may seem drastic, but it's actually good for the plant because it forces new roots to grow into the surrounding soil.

Work quickly. Once you've taken a plant out of its container, get it in the ground as soon as possible. If you want to prepare several plants at a time, cover them to keep the roots from drying out.

Set the root-ball into the hole ❹. Make sure that the plant is positioned right, with its best side facing out, and that the top of the root-ball is level with or slightly higher than the surface of the bed. Then add enough soil to fill in the hole, and pat it down firmly.

PLANTING CONTAINER-GROWN PLANTS

Planting a balled-and-burlapped shrub or tree

Nurseries often grow shrubs and trees in fields, and then dig them with a ball of root-filled soil and wrap a layer of burlap snugly around the ball to keep it intact. The problem is that even a small ball of soil is very heavy. A root ball that is a foot wide is a two-person job. For larger root-balls, ask the nursery to deliver and plant it. Here's how to proceed with plants that are small enough that you can handle them.

Dig a hole several inches wider than the root-ball but not quite as deep as the root-ball is high. Firm the soil so the plant won't sink. Set the plant into the hole, and lay a stick across the top of the root-ball to make sure it's at or a little higher than grade level. Be sure to cut or untie any twine that wraps around the trunk. Fold the burlap down around the sides of the ball. Don't try to pull the burlap out altogether—roots can grow out through it, and it will eventually decompose. Fill soil all around the sides of the ball and pat it down firmly. Spread only an inch of soil over the top of the ball.

The top of the ball should be level with the surrounding soil. Cut twine that wraps around the trunk. Fold down the burlap, but don't remove it.

Planting bare-root plants

Mail-order nurseries sometimes dig perennials, roses, and other plants when the plants are dormant, cut back the tops, and wash all the soil off the roots, to save space and weight when storing and shipping them. If you receive a plant in bare-root condition, unwrap it, trim away any roots that are broken or damaged, and soak the roots in a pail of water for several hours.

To plant, dig a hole large enough that you can spread the roots across the bottom without folding them. Start covering the roots with soil, then lay a stick across the top of the hole and hold the plant against it to check the planting depth, as shown in the drawing. Raise or lower the plant if needed in order to bury just the roots, not the buds. Add more soil, firming it down around the roots, and continue until the hole is full.

Dig a hole wide enough that you can spread out the roots. A stick helps position the plant at the correct depth as you fill the hole with soil.

Planting ground covers from flats

Sometimes ground covers are sold in flats of 25 or more rooted cuttings. Start at one corner, reach underneath the soil, and lift out a portion of the flat's contents. Working quickly, because the roots are exposed, tease the cuttings apart, trying not to break off any roots, and plant them individually. Then lift out the next portion and continue planting.

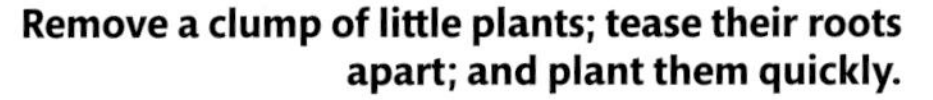

Remove a clump of little plants; tease their roots apart; and plant them quickly.

Planting bulbs

Plant spring-blooming bulbs in October and November. If the soil in the bed was well prepared, you can use a trowel to dig holes for planting individual bulbs; where you have room, you can dig a wider hole or trench for planting a group of bulbs all at once. The perennials, ground covers, shrubs, and trees you planted earlier in the fall or in the spring will still be small enough that you won't disturb their roots. As a rule of thumb, plant small (grape- or cherry-size) bulbs about 2 in. deep and 3 to 5 in. apart, and large (walnut- or egg-size) bulbs 4 to 6 in. deep and 6 to 10 in. apart.

Plant bulbs with the pointed end up, at a depth and spacing determined by the size of the bulb.

Basic Landscape Care

The landscape plantings in this book will grow increasingly carefree from year to year as the plants mature, but of course you'll always need to do some regular maintenance. This ongoing care may require as much as a few hours a week during the season or as little as a few hours a year. You'll need to control weeds, use mulch, water as needed, and do spring and fall cleanups. Trees, shrubs, and vines may need staking or training at first and occasional pruning or shearing afterward. Perennials, ground covers, and grasses may need to be cut back, staked, deadheaded, or divided. Performing these tasks, which are explained on the following pages, is sometimes hard work, but for many gardeners it is enjoyable labor, a chance to get outside in the fresh air. Also, spending time each week with your plants helps you identify and address problems before they become serious.

Mulches and fertilizers

Covering the soil in all planted areas with a layer of organic mulch does several jobs at once: it improves the appearance of your garden while you're waiting for the plants to grow, reduces the number of weeds that emerge, retards water loss from the soil during dry spells, moderates soil temperatures, and adds nutrients to the soil as it decomposes. Earthworms, which aerate the soil, also love it. Inorganic mulches such as landscape fabric and gravel also provide some of these benefits, but their conspicuous appearance and the difficulty of removing them if you ever want to change the landscape are serious drawbacks.

Many materials are used as mulches; the box on p. 208 presents the most common ones, with comments on their advantages and disadvantages. Consider appearance, availability, cost, and convenience when you're comparing products. Most garden centers have a few kinds of bagged mulch materials, but for mulching large areas, it's easier and cheaper to have a supplier deliver a truckload of bulk mulch. A landscape looks best if you see the same mulch throughout the entire planting area, rather than a patchwork of different mulches. You can achieve a uniform look by spreading a base layer of homemade compost, hay, or other inexpensive material and topping that with a neater-looking material such as bark chips or shredded bark.

It takes at least a 1-in. layer of mulch to suppress weeds, but there's no need to spread it more than 3 in. deep. As you're spreading it, don't put any mulch against the stems of any plants, because that can lead to disease or insect problems. Put most of the mulch between plants, not right around them. Check the mulch during your spring and fall cleanups. Be sure it's pulled back away from the plant stems. Rake the surface lightly to loosen it, and top it up with a fresh layer if the old material has decomposed.

Fertilizer

Decomposing mulch frequently supplies enough nutrients to grow healthy plants, but using fertilizer helps if you want to boost the plants—to make them grow faster, get larger, or produce more flowers. Young plants or those growing in poor soils also benefit from occasional applications of fertilizer. There are dozens of fertilizer products on the market—liquid and granular, fast-acting and slow-release, organic and synthetic. All give good results if applied as directed. And observe the following precautions: don't overfertilize, don't fertilize when the soil is dry, and don't fertilize tender plants after late summer, because they need to slow down and finish the season's growth before cold weather comes.

Planting on a hillside

Successful planting on a hillside depends on keeping the bare soil and young plants from blowing or washing away while they establish themselves. Here are some tips: rather than digging and amending all the soil, prepare individual planting holes. Work from the top of the slope to the bottom. Push one or more wooden shingles into the slope just below a plant to help hold it in place. Mulch with heavier materials, such as wood chips, that won't wash or blow away. If the soil is loose, spread water-permeable landscape fabric over it to help hold it in place; slit the fabric and insert plants through the openings. Water with drip irrigation, which erode less soil than sprinklers.

Confining perennials

Mexican petunia, obedient plant, mint, bee balm, and various other perennials, grasses, and ferns are described as invasive because they spread by underground runners. To confine these plants to a limited area, cut off the bottom of a 5-gal. or larger plastic pot; bury the pot so its rim is above the soil; and plant the perennial inside. You'll need to lift, divide, and replant part of the perennial every second or third year.

Mulch materials

Bark products

Bark nuggets, chipped bark, shredded bark, ground bark, and composted bark, usually from conifers, are available in bags or in bulk. All are attractive, long-lasting, medium-price mulches.

Chipped tree trimmings

The chips available from utility companies and tree services are a mixture of wood, bark, twigs, and leaves. Chips such as these cost less than pure bark products. In fact, you may be able to get a load for free. But they don't look very attractive, and you have to replace them more often because they decompose quickly.

Sawdust and shavings

These are cheap or free at sawmills and woodshops. They make good path coverings, but they aren't ideal mulches, because they tend to pack down into a dense, water-resistant surface. Sawdust can also blow around.

Hulls and shells

Ground coconut hulls, cocoa hulls, and nut shells can be picked up at food-processing plants and are sometimes sold at garden centers. They're all attractive, long-lasting mulches. Price varies from free to quite expensive, depending on where you get them.

Tree leaves

A few big trees may supply all the mulch you need, year after year. You can just rake the leaves onto a bed in fall, but it's better to chop them up with the lawn mower, pile them in compost bins for the winter, and spread them where needed in late spring. Pine needles, likewise, make good mulch, especially for camellias, azaleas, gardenias, and other acid-loving shrubs. Also, they are not messy; you can spread pine needles in fall, because they cling together and don't blow around.

Gravel

A mulch of pea gravel or crushed rock, spread 1 to 2 in. thick, helps keep the soil cool and moist. Many plants grow very well with a gravel mulch, especially succulents that thrive in dry conditions and Mediterranean herbs. However, gravel mulch is much more tiring to apply than organic materials, such as bark or leaves. It's harder to remove leaves and litter from gravel or weeds that sprout up through it. It's annoying to dig through the gravel if you want to replace or add plants later. And it's tedious to remove the gravel itself, should you ever change your mind about having it there.

Grass clippings

A 1- to 2-in. layer of dried grass clippings makes an acceptable mulch that decomposes within a single growing season. Don't pile clippings too thick, though. If you do, the top surface dries and packs into a water-resistant crust, and the bottom layer turns into nasty slime.

Hay and straw

Farmers sell hay that's unsuitable for fodder as "mulch" hay. Hay is cheap but likely to include weed seeds. Straw and coastal Bermuda grass hay are both more expensive than mulch hay but are usually free of seeds. Both hay and straw are more suitable for mulching vegetable gardens than landscape plantings because they decompose quickly and must be renewed each year. They also tend to attract rodents.

Landscape fabrics

Various types of synthetic fabrics, usually sold in rolls 3 to 4 ft. wide and 20, 50, or 100 ft. long, can be spread over the ground as a weed barrier. Unlike plastic, these fabrics allow water and air to penetrate into the soil. A topping of gravel, bark chips, or other mulch can anchor the fabric and hide it from view. If you're planting small plants, you can spread the fabric and insert the plants through X-shaped slits cut in the fabric where needed. You can plant larger plants first; then cut and snug the fabric around them. Drip irrigation is best laid on top of the fabric to make it easier to see clogs and leaks. It's also useful to lay fabric under paths, although it can be difficult to secure the fabric neatly and invisibly along the edges of adjacent planting beds. Removing fabric—if you change your mind—is a messy job. However, there are newer biodegradable fabrics that break down after a few years.

Clear or black plastic

Don't even think about using any kind of plastic sheeting as a landscape mulch. The soil underneath a sheet of plastic gets bone-dry, while water accumulates on top. Any loose mulch you spread on plastic won't stay in an even layer. No matter how you try to secure them, the edges of plastic sheeting always pull loose, appear at the surface, degrade in the sun, and shred into tatters.

Watering

Watering, as we've discussed previously (see pp. 160-162), is a necessity for most residential landscapes in Texas. To use water efficiently and effectively, it is helpful to know how to gauge when your plants need water, how much water they need, and how to ensure that your system supplies the desired amounts.

Deciding whether water is needed

Many experienced gardeners can judge whether a plant needs water simply by looking at its leaves. But drooping or dull leaves can also be caused by pests, disease, and overwatering. A surer way to decide whether you need to water is to examine the soil. If the top 3 to 4 in. is dry, most annuals, perennials, and shallow-rooted shrubs such as azaleas will need to be watered. Most trees and larger shrubs need water if the top 6 to 8 in. is dry. To check soil moisture, you can get down on your hands and knees and dig. But digging in an established planting can be awkward as well as harmful to crowded roots.

To better assess soil moisture, a simple moisture meter can be purchased at a garden center or online. For best results, sample several areas to ensure a proper moisture reading. Another method of checking moisture is to use a paint stirrer or similar piece of unfinished, light-colored wood as a dipstick. Push it down through the mulch and 6 to 8 in. into the soil. Leave it there for an hour or so, and pull it out to see whether moisture has discolored the wood. If so, the soil is moist enough for plants. If not, it's time to water. Let the stick dry out before you use it again; it's handy to have several of these sticks around the garden shed.

It is also helpful to make a habit of monitoring rainfall. Set up your own rain gauge and listen to the weather reports, marking a calendar to keep track of rainfall amounts.

Pay attention to soil moisture or rainfall amounts all year long, because plants can suffer from dryness in any season, not the heat of summer. Water whenever the soil is dry. As for time of day, it's best to water early in the morning when the wind is calm, evaporation is low, and plant foliage will have plenty of time to dry off before nightfall. (Wet leaves at night can promote some foliar diseases.) Early morning (before 5 a.m.) is also when most urban and suburban neighborhoods have plenty of water pressure.

How much to water

Determining how much water to apply and how often to apply it is one of gardening's greatest challenges. Water too often, and plants drown. Water too little, and they dry out and die. For most gardeners, gauging how much water a plant or bed needs is an art more than a science. The key to watering enough but not too much is to be a good observer. Examine your soil often; keep an eye on your plants; and make adjustments with the weather.

New plantings, even those of drought-tolerant plants, require frequent watering during the first year until the plants are established. In the heat of summer, new plantings may require water twice a week or more. Established landscape plants vary in their water needs.

It is always best to water deeply, wetting a large portion of the plant's root zone. Shallow watering encourages shallow rooting, and shallow-rooted plants dry out fast and need watering more frequently. Furthermore, a water-stressed plant is also more susceptible to disease and insect damage. As a rule of thumb, water most perennials to a depth of 12 to 18 in.; water most shrubs 2 to 3 ft. deep and most trees 3 to 4 ft. deep. (Lawns, in contrast, should be watered 6 to 8 in. deep, but they require frequent watering.)

Determining how much water will be required to penetrate to these depths depends on your soil. Water moves through different soils at different speeds. In general, 1 in. of water will soak about 4 to 5 in. deep in clay soil, 6 to 7 in. deep in loam, and 10 to 12 in. in sandy soil.

Different systems deliver water at different rates. Manufacturers often provide these rates in the product descriptions. You can determine the delivery rate for a sprinkler by setting tuna-fish cans in the area it covers and timing how long it takes to deposit an inch of water in one or more cans.

Whatever your system, you'll need to know how long it has to run for water to penetrate to the desired depth. To gauge penetration, use a wooden "dipstick," see below, after you've watered. For a rough gauge of deeper penetration, you can push a ¼- to ½-in.-diameter iron bar into the soil. The bar will move easily through wet soil. When it encounters dry soil, the bar will become harder to push. Run your system, and time it as you check penetration depths.

CHECKING SOIL MOISTURE

Stick a paint stirrer or similar piece of light- colored, unfinished wood down through the mulch and into the soil. Pull it up after an hour. If the bottom of the stick looks and feels damp, the soil is moist enough for plants.

Defensible Space

A prolonged drought can create dry fire-prone landscapes. In addition, during a drought the ground can contract or subside, affecting buildings and other structures, underground piping including irrigation, walks, patios, and roads. Your home landscape and region may become at risk to fire, even if this has not occurred historically before.

Of course, you want your landscape to succeed, be beautiful, green, and as low-maintenance as possible. There are some gardeners who enjoy regularly working in their gardens, but even non-gardeners enjoy the beauty of their home landscape. Planting smart means utilizing the latest landscape research to find plants best suited to your environment, site conditions, goals, and a changing climate.

Climate change is altering the rules of what will thrive in your region, as well as increasing the risk of wildfire. As climate change progresses, regions of Texas are projected to have reduced rainfall, higher temperatures, and more chances of wildfires. This means some marginally hardy plants may not survive the coming environmental changes; even large well-established plants can succumb. Some of these changes are already here. Research and experience have shown that non-native or exotic species are particularly susceptible to failure due to climate change.

In some regions of the U.S. and especially in Texas, climate change often means longer periods between rainfall. When it does rain, it can be concentrated causing flooding and erosion. These extreme downpours often run-off parched soil and fail to percolate into the soil to water plantings.

Research shows the western half of Texas is part of the growing desertification of the U.S. Desertification is the loss of productive land. This desertification begins in parts of the Mid-West and extends to encompass much of the Western U.S. all the way to the Pacific Ocean. So, what's the solution? The goal should be selecting plants that can thrive despite

Use drought-resilient plants near your home to be fire wise.

the challenges of extreme weather and a changing climate. We already know many resilient native plants suited to drought and weather extremes. These species are ideal for our more challenging weather and growing conditions. Some of these are super species, up to the challenges of extreme weather. These plants may be less well known and not be as widely available at all retail locations yet. As consumer demand continues to increase for resilient native and adapted species, growers and suppliers will continue to widen and increase their selection of these super species.

With dryer conditions, fire-wise plantings and guidelines become important, and if followed, can save lives and save properties. To create a defensible space around our home, an assessment is needed. You can do this yourself following Texas A&M Forest Service Firewise Guidelines or reach out to a Texas A&M Forest Service WUI Coordinator for a wildfire risk assessment.

In order foe the area (zone 1) immediately around your home to be fire wise, it can have some low plantings that are green and healthy, with plenty of air circulation between plantings and your home. Plants and materials in zone 1 should be ember resistant. It's important to check your gutters regularly and remove any dead leaves, pine needles, or debris. Gravel mulches can be used in this area, but no large shrubs and no trees.

The next area (zone 2) extends from 10–30 feet (3-9 meters) from your home. Within this area it's important to maintain lawn areas, trimming grass low and keeping the lawn watered to remain green. Individual deciduous trees with larger leaves can be planted. Lower limbs should be removed to prevent ladder fuels. Groupings of shrubs can be planted if separated from trees. Smaller deciduous trees are preferable in this zone. Be sure to remove dead leaves and pine needles from the ground in this area.

Getting further from your home now is zone 3, extending from 30–100 feet (9-30.5 meters). The theme in this zone is to reduce fuels. This means keeping the lawn trimmed to a maximum of 4 inches (10.2 centimeters) and maintaining plenty of horizontal area between individual trees and shrub groups. Create vertical space between grasses, perennials, shrubs, and trees to prevent ladder fuel. Be sure to remove dead plants and any fallen limbs, leaf litter or debris more than 3 inches (7.6 centimeters) deep.

Crape myrtle (*Lagerstroemia indica*) and other popular non-native landscape staples in the Southern U.S. is prone to leaf drop and failure during prolonged droughts, which now occur regularly. As crape myrtles die or new trees are planted, they can be replaced with the more resilient and drought tolerant desert willow (*Chilopsis linearis*). This marvelous tree holds its blooms for a prolonged period and stays a manageable size for the home landscape. The ubiquitous Knock Our Rose (non-native) can be replaced with the Mexican bush sage (*Salvia leucantha*) native to Mexico and South America. The Mexican bush sage flourishes despite prolonged droughts, displaying its exuberant purple blooms and soft-to-the-touch foliage. The Mexican bush sage is lower maintenance than roses, not needing specialized pruning, irrigation, or pesticides to succeed.

Where you plant your resilient species is equally as important as what you plant. For instance, your home landscape has microclimates, areas that are hotter, cooler, windier, drier, or wetter than others. You can discover this by observing your outdoor areas at a variety of times of day and throughout the seasons. When it rains observe if there are areas where water pools up or erodes the soil. Does your home or existing plantings create pockets of shade? If in full sun, the southern and western exposures of your home landscape are often the hottest and driest.

Next, with a small garden tool dig down about 12 inches (30.5 centimeters), creating small holes in a variety of areas (microclimates) on your property. Observe the soil texture and soil moisture level. Once you have equal sized holes dug, you can fill each with water and wait about an hour. If the various holes do not appear to drain at all, you likely have heavy clay soil. If the hole drains completely, you likely have sandy soil. If the hole partially drains, you likely have a mix of sand, clay, and hummus which are suitable to a range of plants. With all this data, you can begin to match appropriate superspecies to the range of conditions you have observed. Research which plants are suited to your area and soil type, see the Plant Profiles section of this book for more info.

A multitude of excellent resilient native plantings are listed in this book. To observe them in person, you can visit local, state, and federal parks and preserves, botanical gardens, campuses, and arboretums. The Lady Bird Johnson Wildflower Center in Austin is also a good resource both in person and online.

Be aware that some drought-resilient species are not tolerant of wet soil conditions. These species grow in drier soils, but may rot or fail if conditions stay wet. So, when selecting drought-resilient species check if they can handle temporary wet conditions. If they can't, then make sure to site them in a well-drained area or a drier upland location.

Some areas of Central Texas experience a phenomenon of drought and deluge, a period of prolonged drought followed by very heavy rainfall. This heavy rainfall can cause washouts, erosion, and flooding. If you experience these conditions, confirm that the plants you select are suited to your rainfall. Plants native to your area are generally uniquely suited to this challenge.

Controlling weeds

Weeds are not much of a problem in established landscapes. Once the "good" plants have grown big enough to merge together, they tend to crowd or shade out all but the most persistent undesirable plants. But weeds can be troublesome in a new landscape unless you take steps to prevent and control them.

There are two main types of weeds: those that mostly sprout as seedlings and those that keep coming back from perennial roots or runners. Try to identify and eliminate any perennial weeds before you start a landscaping project (see p. 159). Then you'll only have to deal with new seedlings later, which is a much easier job.

Annual and perennial weeds that commonly grow from seeds include Bermuda grass, bindweed, dandelions, oxalis, plantain, purslane, and spurge. Trees and shrubs such as cherry laurel, Chinese tallow, privet, cedar elm, mimosa, hackberry, and Chinaberry produce weedy seedlings, too. For any of the weeds that grow from seeds, the strategy is twofold: try to keep the weed seeds from sprouting, and eliminate any seedlings that do sprout as soon as you see them, while they are still small.

Almost any patch of soil includes weed seeds that are ready to sprout whenever that soil is disturbed. Preparing the soil for planting will probably cause an initial flush of weeds, but you won't see as many weeds again if you leave the soil undisturbed in subsequent years. You don't need to hoe, rake, or cultivate around perennial plantings. Leave the soil alone, and fewer weeds will appear. Using mulch helps even more; by shading the soil, it prevents weed seeds from sprouting. And if weed seeds blow in and land on top of the mulch, they'll be less likely to germinate there than they would on bare soil.

Pull or cut off any weeds that appear while they're young and small, just a few inches tall. Don't let them mature and go to seed. Most weed seedlings emerge in late spring and early summer. If you get rid of them then, you won't see many more seedlings for the rest of the growing season.

Using herbicides

Two kinds of herbicides can be very useful and effective in maintaining home landscapes, but only if used correctly. Choose the right product for the job and follow the directions on the label regarding dosage and timing of application exactly. Some commonly available herbicides (such as Glyphosate) have been shown to be cancer causing (carcinogenic). Research your weeds and removal options before purchasing an herbicide. These same herbicides can easily come into contact with children and pets, so it's best to research and read labels before purchasing and applying.

Preemergent herbicides. Sold in granular or liquid form, these herbicides are designed to prevent weed seeds, particularly crabgrass and other annual weeds, from sprouting. For annual winter weeds such as chickweed and henbit, make the first application in early fall

WEEDS THAT SPROUT FROM SEEDS

Simple root systems can be easily pulled while still small.

WEEDS THAT SPROUT BACK FROM PERENNIAL ROOTS OR RUNNERS

Connected by underground runners, the shoots of these weeds need to be pulled repeatedly, smothered with a thick mulch, or killed with an herbicide.

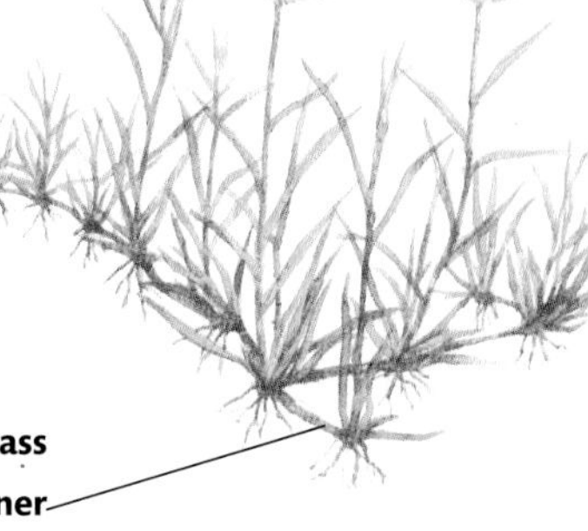

Use a disposable, sponge-type paintbrush to apply the herbicide selectively, painting only the weeds. Prepare the solution as directed for spray application. Use only enough to wet the leaves, so none drips off.

USING HERBICIDES ON PERENNIAL WEEDS

Ready-to-use spot-weeder sprays are convenient, but you must aim carefully. Try using a sheet of cardboard as a backdrop to protect desirable plants from herbicide drift.

before the first signs of rain and cooler weather. For annual summer weeds such as crabgrass and spurge, you'll need to make another application in spring. Follow package directions to determine how long to wait between each application.

Read the label carefully, and make sure the herbicide you buy is registered for use around the kinds of plants you have. Granular forms are often used in smaller areas, liquid in larger areas. Apply them exactly as described on the product label. Wear heavy rubber gloves that are rated for use with farm chemicals, not common household rubber gloves, and follow the safety precautions on the label.

Postemergent herbicides. These chemicals are used to kill growing plants. Some kill only the aboveground parts of a plant; others are absorbed into the plant and kill it, roots and all. Postemergent herbicides are typically applied as sprays, which you can buy ready-to-use or prepare by mixing a concentrate with water. Look for those that break down quickly, and read the label carefully.

Postemergent herbicides work best if applied when the weeds are growing vigorously and the weather is dry. You usually need to apply enough to thoroughly wet the plant's leaves. Herbicides can be effective at getting rid of perennial weeds that you can't dig or pull up, but it's really better to do this before you plant a bed, as it's hard to spray herbicides in an established planting without getting some on your good plants. (Some postemergent herbicides are more selective, affecting only certain types of plants.) Aim carefully, shielding nearby plants as shown in the drawing at left, and don't spray on windy days. You can brush or sponge the herbicide on the leaves to avoid damaging adjacent plants. Using postemergent herbicides in an established planting may be the only way to get rid of a persistent perennial weed.

Caring for Woody Plants

A well-chosen garden tree, such as those recommended in this book, grows naturally into a pleasing shape, won't get too large for its site, is resistant to pests and diseases, and doesn't drop messy pods or other litter. Once established, these trees need very little care from year to year.

Regular watering is the most important concern in getting a tree off to a good start. Don't let it suffer from drought for the first few years. To reduce competition, don't plant ground covers or other plants within 2 ft. of the tree's trunk. Arborists now dismiss other care ideas that once were common practice. According to current thinking, you don't need to fertilize a tree when you plant it (in fact, unless they show obvious signs of deficiency or grow poorly, most landscape trees never need fertilizing). Keep pruning to a minimum at planting time; remove only dead or damaged twigs, not healthy shoots. Finally, research has shown that tree trunks grow stronger when they're not staked rigidly. However, taller trees and shrubs need some support, usually for no more than a year. It is very important that the supported trunk be allowed to flex in the wind. Be sure to ask an arborist or nursery staff about proper staking for the trees you buy.

Pruning basics

Proper pruning keeps plants healthy and looking their best. There are two basic types of pruning cuts: heading and thinning. Heading cuts are made along the length of a branch or stem, between its tip and its base. These cuts induce vigorous growth in the dormant buds below the cut. Such growth is useful for filling in hedges and rejuvenating shrubs and perennials. But heading can drastically change the appearance of a plant, even destroying its natural shape. Heading can also produce weakly attached branches in trees and shrubs.

Thinning cuts remove stems and branches at their origin (the plant's crown or where the branch attaches to the trunk or a larger limb). Unlike heading, thinning does not produce vigorous growth. Instead, thinning opens the plant's interior to light and air, which improves its health. And, by reducing congested growth, thinning often enhances the natural appearance of the plant. In most cases, thinning is the preferred pruning technique, especially for trees and shrubs.

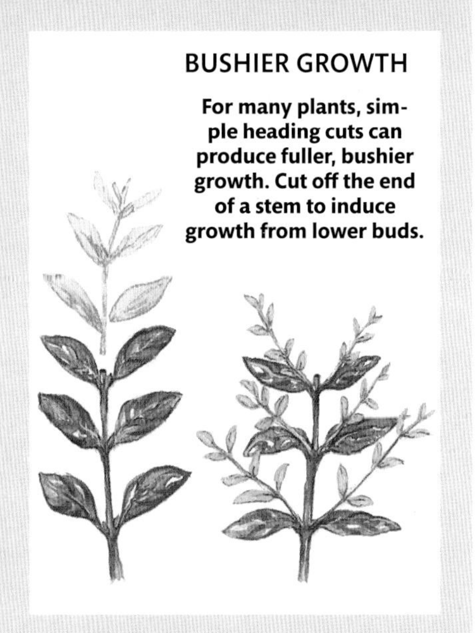

BUSHIER GROWTH

For many plants, simple heading cuts can produce fuller, bushier growth. Cut off the end of a stem to induce growth from lower buds.

Pruning roses

Roses are vigorous, fast-growing shrubs that need regular pruning to keep them shapely and attractive. Most of this pruning is done in winter to early spring, just as the buds start to swell but before the new leaves start to unfold. Right after pruning is a good time to add fresh mulch around the plant.

Prune hybrid tea roses to keep them neat, compact, and continuously producing long-stemmed flowers. Remove skinny or weak stems, plus a few of the oldest stems (their bark is tan or gray instead of green) by cutting them off at their base. Prune off any shoots that got broken or were blackened by freezing during the winter, remove old or weak shoots and crossing or crowded stems, and trim back any asymmetric or unbalanced shoots. If you cut old stems near the graft union (the swelling at the base of the plant where the top growth was grafted to the root stock), new ones will replace them.

Hybrid tea roses bloom on new growth, so if you prune in early spring you aren't cutting off any flower buds. During the growing season, remove flowers as soon as they fade. This keeps the plant neat and makes it bloom longer and more abundantly. At least once a week, locate each faded flower, follow down its stem to the first or second five-leaflet leaf, and prune just above one of those leaves. (Follow the same steps to cut roses for a bouquet.)

Climbing roses are pruned differently than hybrid teas. In late winter, remove weak, dead, or damaged shoots by cutting them back to the ground or to healthy wood. Select the healthiest stems for a main framework, and tie them securely to a support. Shorten all side shoots on these stems to two buds. Shoots growing from these buds will produce flowers.

Climbing roses need regular attention throughout the summer because their stems (also called canes) can grow a foot or more in a month. Check regularly and tie this new growth to the trellis while it's still supple and manageable. When the canes grow long enough to reach the top of the trellis or arbor, cut off their tips and tie the canes horizontally to induce production of flowering side shoots. Remove spent roses by cutting the stems back to the nearest healthy five-leaflet leaf.

Tea, China, polyantha, and other shrub roses can be pruned with hedge shears. Simply cut back one-third to one-half the growth in winter and remove diseased or damaged canes.

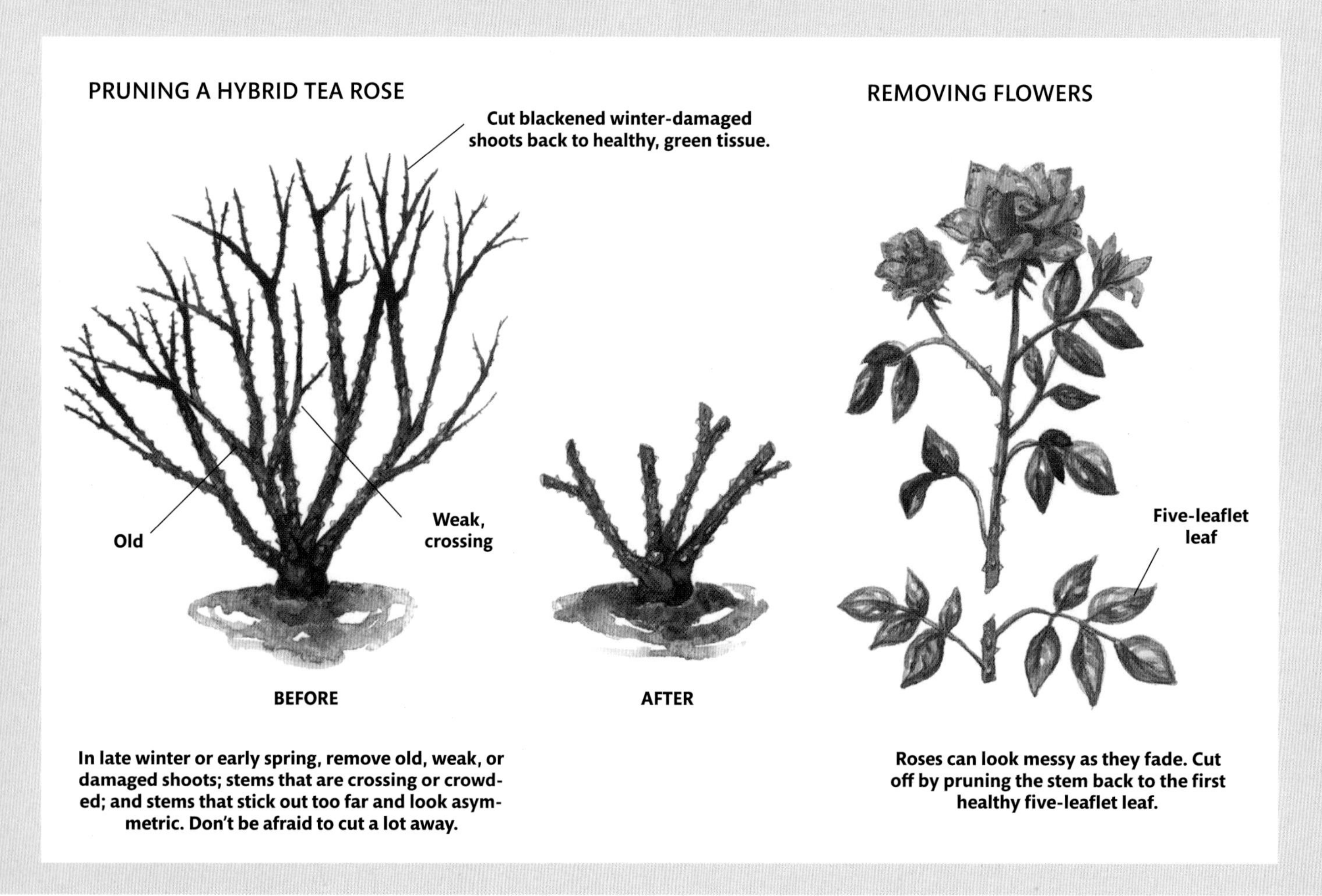

In late winter or early spring, remove old, weak, or damaged shoots; stems that are crossing or crowded; and stems that stick out too far and look asymmetric. Don't be afraid to cut a lot away.

Roses can look messy as they fade. Cut off by pruning the stem back to the first healthy five-leaflet leaf.

Shaping young trees

As a tree grows, you can affect its shape by pruning once a year, usually in winter. Take it easy, though. Don't prune just for the sake of pruning; that does more harm than good. If you don't have a good reason for making a cut, don't do it. Follow these guidelines:

- **Use sharp pruning shears, loppers, or saws,** which make clean cuts without tearing the wood or bark.
- **Cut branches back** to a healthy shoot, leaf, or bud, or cut back to the branch collar at the base of the branch, as shown far right. Don't leave any stubs; they're ugly and prone to decay.
- **Remove any dead or damaged branches** and any twigs or limbs that are very spindly or weak.
- **Where two limbs cross over or rub** against each other, save one limb—usually the thicker, stronger one—and prune off the other one.
- **Prune or widen narrow crotches.** Places where a branch and trunk or two branches form a narrow V are weak spots, liable to split apart as the tree grows. Where the trunk of a young tree exhibits such a crotch or where either of two shoots could continue the growth of a branch, prune off the weaker of the two. Where you wish to keep the branch, insert a piece of wood as a spacer to widen the angle, as shown in the drawings below. Leave the spacer in place for a year or so.

WHERE TO CUT

When removing the end of a branch, cut back to a healthy leaf, bud, or side shoot. Don't leave a stub. Use sharp pruning shears to make a neat cut that slices the stem rather than tears it.

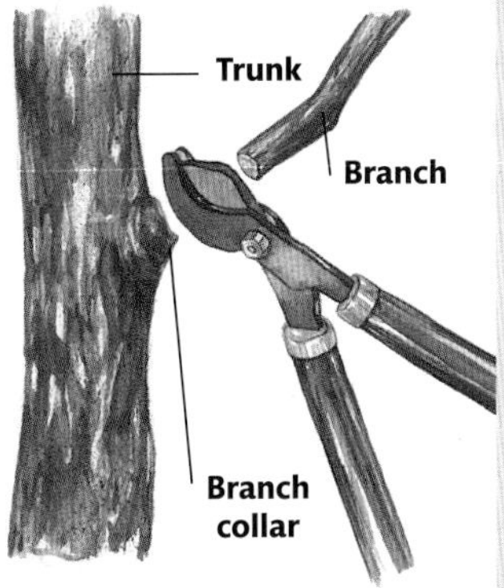

When removing an entire branch, cut just outside the slightly thickened area, called the branch collar, where the branch grows into the trunk.

One trunk or several?

If you want a young tree to have a single trunk, identify the leader or central shoot and let it grow straight up, unpruned. The trunk will grow thicker faster if you leave the lower limbs in place for the first few years, but if they're in the way, you can remove them. At whatever height you choose, select the shoots that will become the main limbs of the tree. Be sure they are evenly spaced around the trunk, pointing outward at wide angles. Remove any lower or weaker shoots. As the tree matures, the only further pruning required will be an annual checkup to remove dead, damaged, or crossing shoots.

Several of the trees in this book, including redbud and Texas mountain laurel, are often grown with multiple trunks, for a graceful, clumplike appearance. When buying a multiple-trunk tree, choose one with trunks that diverge at the base. The more space between them, the better. Prune multiple-trunk trees as previously described for single-trunk trees. Remove some of the branches growing toward the center of the clump, so that it doesn't get too dense and tangled, reducing ventilation.

AVOIDING NARROW CROTCHES

A tree's limbs should spread wide, like outstretched arms. If limbs angle too close to the trunk or to each other, there isn't room for them to grow properly and they may split apart after a few years, ruining the tree.

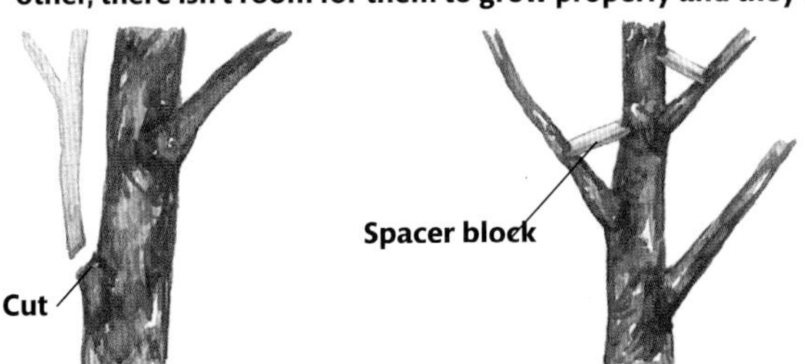

SINGLE-TRUNK TREES: Correct narrow crotches on a young tree by removing the less desirable limb or by widening the angle with a wooden spacer block. Choose well-spaced shoots to become the main limbs of a shade tree.

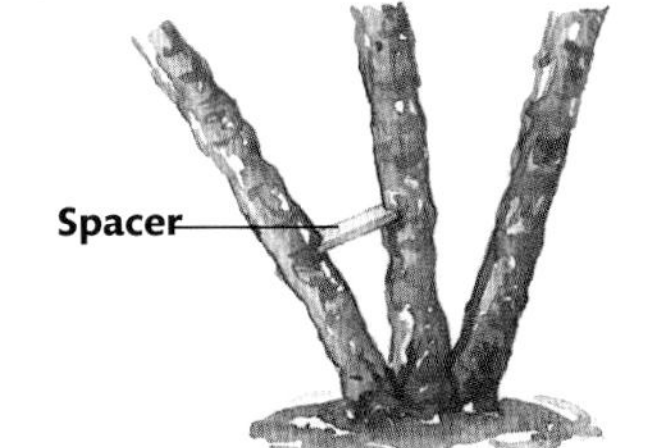

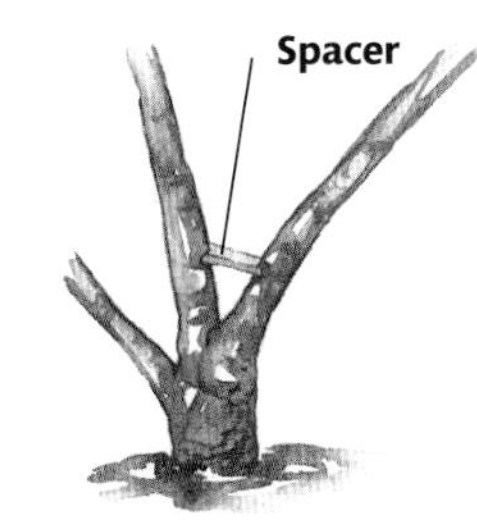

MULTIPLE-TRUNK TREES: Whether the stems of a multiple-trunk tree emerge from the ground or from a single trunk near the ground, widen angles if necessary to keep the trunks from touching.

Pruning shrubs

Shrubs are generally carefree plants, but they almost always look better if you do some pruning at least every other year. As a minimum, remove dead twigs from time to time, and if any branches are broken by storms or accidents, remove them as soon as convenient, cutting back to a healthy bud or branch or to the plant's crown. Also, unless the shrub produces attractive seedpods or berries, it's a good idea to trim off the flowers after they fade.

Beyond this routine pruning, some shrubs require more attention. (The entries in Plant Profiles, pp. 120-153, give more information on when and how to prune particular shrubs.) Basically, shrub pruning falls into three categories: selective pruning, severe pruning, and shearing.

Selective pruning means using pruning shears to head back or thin individual shoots in order to refine the shape of the bush and maintain its vigor, as well as limit its size. (See the drawing at right.) This job takes time but produces a very graceful and natural-looking bush. Cut away weak or spindly twigs and any limbs that cross or rub against each other, and head all the longest shoots back to a healthy, outward-facing bud or to a pair of buds. You can do selective pruning on any shrub, deciduous or evergreen, at any time of year.

Severe pruning means using pruning shears or loppers to cut away most of a shrub's top growth, leaving just short stubs or a gnarly trunk. This kind of cutting back is usually done once a year in late winter or early spring. Although it seems drastic, severe pruning is appropriate in several situations.

It makes certain fast-growing shrubs, such as vitex and Mexican bush sage, flower more profusely. It keeps others, such as salvia, artemisia, and verbena, compact and bushy.

One or two severe prunings done when a shrub is young can make it branch out at the base, producing a bushier specimen or a fuller hedge plant. Nurseries often do this pruning as part of producing a good plant, and if you buy a shrub that's already bushy, you don't need to cut it back yourself. Older shrubs that have gotten tall and straggly sometimes respond to a severe pruning by sprouting out with renewed vigor, sending up lots of new shoots that bear plenty of foliage and flowers. This strategy doesn't work for all shrubs, though—sometimes severe pruning kills a plant. Don't try it unless you know it will work. Check with a pruning specialist, such as an arborist, or a knowledgeable person at a nursery.

Shearing means using hedge shears or an electric hedge trimmer to trim the surface of a shrub, hedge, or tree to a neat, uniform profile, producing a solid mass of greenery. Both deciduous and evergreen shrubs and trees can be sheared; those with small, closely spaced leaves and a naturally compact growth habit usually look best. A good time for shearing most shrubs is late spring, after the new shoots have elongated but before the wood has hardened, but you can shear at other times of year. You may have to shear some plants more than once a year.

If you're planning to shear a plant, start when it is young and establish the shape—cone, pyramid, flat-topped hedge, or whatever. Looking at the profile, always make the shrub wider at the bottom than on top; otherwise the lower limbs will be shaded and won't be as leafy. Shear off as little as needed to maintain the shape. Once it gets as big as you want it, shear to maintain its size.

SELECTIVE PRUNING. Remove weak, spindly, bent, or broken shoots (red). Where two branches rub on each other, remove the weakest or the one that's pointing inward (orange). Cut back long shoots to a healthy, outward-facing bud (blue).

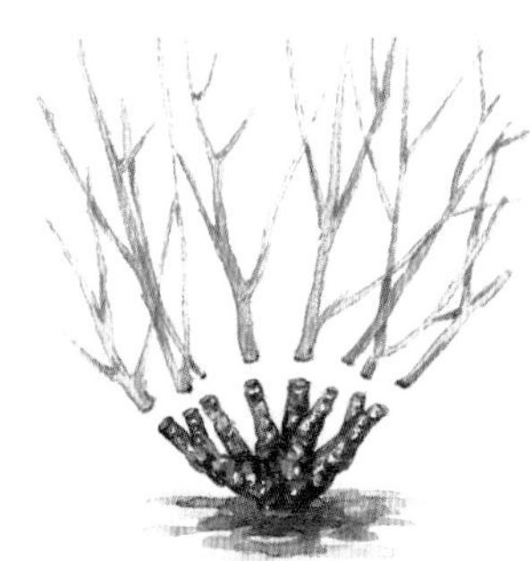

SEVERE PRUNING. In late winter or early spring, before new growth starts, cut back all the stems close to the ground.

SHEARING. Trim with hedge clippers to a neat profile.

Making a hedge

To make a hedge that's dense enough that you can't see through it, choose shrubs that have many shoots at the base. If you can find only skinny shrubs, prune them severely the first spring after planting to stimulate bushier growth.

Hedge plants are set in the ground as described on pp. 205-206 but are spaced closer together than they would be if planted as individual specimens. We took that into account in creating the designs and plant lists for this book; just follow the spacings recommended in the designs. If you're impatient for the hedge to fill in, you can space the plants closer together.

A hedge can be sheared, pruned selectively, or left alone, depending on how you want it to look. Slow-growing, small-leaved plants, such as dwarf yaupon holly, make rounded but natural-looking hedges with no pruning at all, or you can shear them into any profile you choose and make them neat. Choose one style and stick with it. Once a hedge is established, you cannot start or stop shearing it without creating an awkward transition phase that may last a few years before the hedge looks good again.

Getting a vine off to a good start

Nurseries often sell climbing vines as young plants attached to stakes or trellises. To plant the vine, simply tie the plant and stake with string or twine to the base of a permanent support they are to climb ❶. The original stake can be removed after the plant becomes attached to its new home ❷.

Once they're started, twining vines, such as wisteria and Carolina jessamine, can scramble up a lattice trellis, although it helps if you tuck in any stray ends. The plants can't climb a smooth surface, however. To help them cover a fence with wide vertical slats or a porch post, you have to provide something the vine can encircle. Screw a few eyebolts to the top and bottom of such a support and stretch wire, nylon cord, or polypropylene rope between them. (The wires or cords should be a few inches out from the fence, not flush against it.) Clinging vines, such as trumpet creeper and cross vine, can climb any surface by means of their adhesive rootlets and need no further assistance or care.

So-called "climbing roses" don't really climb at all by themselves—you have to fasten them to a support. Loosely fixed twist-ties or twine are handy for this job. Roses grow fast, so you'll have to tie-in the new shoots every few weeks from spring to fall.

After the first year, most vines need annual spring pruning to remove any dead, damaged, or straggly stems. If vines grow too long, you can cut them back anytime and they will branch out from below the cut.

STARTING A VINE

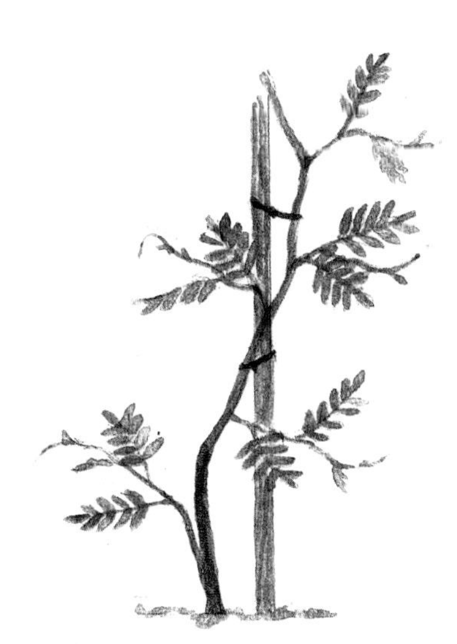

❶ **At planting, loosely tie stem and shoots to a stake.**

❷ **When the vine is established on its permanent support, you can remove the planting stake.**

Caring for Perennials

Perennials are simply plants that send up new growth year after year. A large group, perennials include flowering plants, such as daylilies and purple coneflower, as well as ornamental grasses, ferns, and hardy bulbs. Ornamental grasses are a very useful and striking garden element planted in conjunction with perennials. Native ornamental grasses are suited to a wide range of conditions. Taller grasses add a kinetic element to your garden, illustrating the movement of wind. In addition to their beauty, ornamental grasses attract birds, providing food and habitat.

Although some perennials need special conditions and care, most of those in this book are adaptable and easy to grow. Get them off to a good start by planting them in well-prepared soil, adding a layer of mulch, watering as often as needed throughout the first year, and keeping away weeds. After that, keeping perennials attractive and healthy typically requires just a few minutes per plant each month.

Routine annual care

Some of the perennials that are used as ground covers, such as cedar sedge, mondo grass, and vinca, need virtually no care. On a suitable site, they'll thrive for decades even if you pay them almost no attention at all.

Most garden perennials, though, look and grow better if you clean away the old leaves and stems at least once a year. When to do this depends on the type of plant. Perennials such as firebush, cigar plant, and Turk's cap have leaves and stalks that turn tan or brown after they're frosted in fall. Cut these down to the ground in late fall or early spring; either time is okay.

Some perennials, such as oxeye daisy, columbine, yarrow, verbena, and dianthus, have foliage that is more or less evergreen, depending on the severity of the winter. For those plants, wait until after they've bloomed or until the fall; then cut back leaves or stems that are discolored or shabby looking. Don't leave cuttings lying on the soil, because they may contain disease spores. To avoid contaminating your compost, send diseased stems or leaves to the dump.

Right after you've cleared away the dead material is a good time to renew the mulch on the bed. Use a fork, rake, or cultivator to loosen the existing mulch, and add some fresh mulch if needed. Also, if you want to sprinkle some granular fertilizer on the bed, do that now, when it's easy to avoid getting any on the plants' leaves. Fertilizing perennials is optional, but it does make them grow bigger and bloom more than they would otherwise.

Remove faded flowers

Removing flowers as they fade (called "deadheading") makes a garden bed look neater, prevents unwanted self-sown seedlings, and often stimulates a plant to continue blooming longer than it would if you left it alone, or to bloom a second time later in the season. (The same is true for shrubs and annuals as well as for perennials.)

Pick large flowers, such as daisies, daylilies, irises, and hibiscus, one at a time, snapping them off by hand. Use pruning shears on perennials such as salvia, gaura, phlox, and yarrow that produce tall stalks crowded with lots of small flowers, cutting the stalks back to the height of the foliage. Use hedge shears on bushy plants that are covered with lots of small flowers on short stalks, such as lantana, Turk's cap, and verbena, cutting the stems back by about one-half their length.

Instead of removing them in the late fall, you may want to let the faded flowers remain on black-eyed Susans, 'Autumn Joy' sedum, and the various ornamental grasses. These plants all bear conspicuous seedpods or seed heads that are on stiff stalks, which remain standing and look interesting throughout the fall and winter months.

Pruning and shearing perennials

Some perennials that bloom in summer or fall respond well to being pruned earlier in the growing season. Aster, chrysanthemum, Mexican sage, garden phlox, and 'Autumn Joy' sedum all form tall clumps of stems topped with lots of little flowers. Unfortunately, tall stems are liable to flop over in stormy weather, and even if they don't, too-tall clumps can look leggy or top-heavy. To prevent floppiness, prune these plants when the stems are about 1 ft. tall. Remove the weakest stems from each clump by cutting them off at the ground; then cut all the remaining, strong stems back by about one-third. Pruning in this way keeps these plants shorter, stronger, and bushier, so you don't have to bother with stakes to keep them upright.

'Superbena purple' and 'Powis Castle' artemisia are grown more for their foliage than for their flowers. You can use hedge shears to keep them neat, compact, and bushy, shearing off the tops of the stems once or twice in spring and summer.

PRUNING A PERENNIAL

Prune to create neater, bushier clumps of some summer- and fall-blooming perennials such as garden phlox, chrysanthemums, and 'Autumn Joy' sedum. When the stalks are about 1 ft. tall, cut them all back by one-third. Remove the weakest stalks at ground level.

Dividing perennials

Most perennials send up more stems each year, forming denser clumps or wider patches. Dividing is the process of cutting or breaking apart these clumps or patches. This is an easy way to make more plants to expand your garden, to control a plant that might otherwise spread out of bounds, or to renew an old specimen that doesn't look good or bloom well anymore.

Most perennials can be divided as often as every year or two if you're in a hurry to make more plants, or they can go for years if you don't have any reason to disturb them. Fall is the best time to divide most summer- and fall-blooming perennials, but you can also do it in early spring.

There are two main approaches to dividing a perennial, as shown in the drawings at right. You can leave the plant in the ground and use a sharp spade to cut it apart, and then lift out one chunk at a time. Or you can dig around and underneath the plant and lift it out all at once; shake off the extra soil; and lay the plant on the ground or a tarp where you can work with it.

Some plants, such as yarrow and some ferns, are easy to divide. They almost fall apart when you dig them up. Others, such as daylilies and most grasses, have very tough or tangled roots and you'll have to wrestle with them, chop them with a sharp butcher knife, pry them apart with a sharp spade, or even cut through the roots with a hatchet or pruning saw. However you approach the job, before you insert any tool, take a close look at the plant at ground level, and be careful to divide between, not through, the biggest and healthiest buds or shoots. Using a hose to wash away loose mulch and soil will also make it easier to see what you're doing.

Don't make the divisions too small; they should be the size of a plant that you'd want to buy, not just little scraps. If you have more than you need or want, choose the best-looking ones to replant and discard or give away the others. Replant new divisions as soon as possible in freshly prepared soil. Water them right away, and water again whenever the soil dries out over the next few weeks or months, until the plants are growing again.

Hardy bulbs, such as narcissus and snowflakes, can be divided every few years. Dig clumps after bloom when the foliage turns yellow. Shake the soil off the roots; pull the bulbs apart; and replant them promptly, setting them as deep in the soil as they were buried before.

DIVIDING PERENNIALS

You can divide a clump or patch of perennials by cutting down into the patch with a sharp spade, then lifting out the separate chunks.

Or you can dig up the whole clump, shake the extra soil off the roots, and then pull or pry it apart into separate plantlets.

Problem Solving

Some plants are much more susceptible than others to damage by severe weather, pests, or diseases. In this book, we've recommended plants that are generally trouble free, especially after they have had a few years to get established in your garden. But even these plants are subject to various mishaps and problems. The challenge is learning how to distinguish the problems that are really serious from those that are merely cosmetic, and then deciding how to solve—or, better yet, prevent—the problems that are serious from occuring.

Identify, then treat

Don't jump to conclusions and start spraying chemicals on a supposedly sick plant before you know what (if anything) is actually wrong with it. That's wasteful and irresponsible, and you're likely to do the plant as much harm as good. Pinpointing the exact cause of a problem is difficult even for experienced gardeners, so save yourself frustration and seek out expert help from the beginning.

If it seems that there's something wrong with one of your plants—for example, if the leaves are discolored, have holes in them, or have spots or marks on them—cut off a sample branch, wrap it in damp paper towels, and put it in a plastic bag (so it won't wilt). Take the sample to the nursery or garden center where you bought the plant, and ask for help. If the nursery can't help, contact the nearest office of the state's Cooperative Extension Service or a public garden in your area and ask if they have a staff member who can diagnose plant problems.

Meanwhile, look around your property and around the neighborhood, too, to see if any other plants (of the same or different kinds) show similar symptoms. If a problem is widespread, you shouldn't have much trouble finding someone who can identify it and tell you what, if anything, to do. If only one plant is affected, it's often harder to diagnose the problem, and you may just need to wait and see what happens to it. Keep an eye on the plant, continue with watering and other regular maintenance, and see whether the problem gets worse or goes away. If nothing more has happened after a few weeks, stop worrying. If the problem continues, intensify your search for expert advice.

Plant problems stem from a number of causes: insect and animal pests, diseases, and poor care, particularly in winter. Remember that plant problems are often caused by a combination of these; all the more reason to consult with experts about their diagnosis and treatment.

Pests, large and small

Deer and rabbits are liable to be a problem if your property is surrounded by or adjacent to fields or woods. You may not see them, but you can't miss the damage they do—they bite off the tops or eat whole plants of cannas, daylilies, and many other perennials. Deer also eat the leaves and stems of roses, azaleas, and many other trees and shrubs. Commercial or homemade repellents that you spray on the foliage may be helpful if the animals aren't too hungry and you use them often. (See the box, below right, for thoughts on deer-proof plants.) But in the long run, the only solution is to fence out deer and to trap and remove smaller animals. In addition to browsing your landscape plants, deer can carry ticks. These can carry serious diseases such as Lyme disease. These can be transmitted to humans and outdoor pets. A plant healthcare technician can assess your property for ticks and treat if needed. Precautions to reduce the risk of tick-borne diseases include keeping the lawn mown in areas you spend time in outdoors, spraying the perimeter of the property for ticks, wearing long pants outdoors, avoid walking in tall grasses, and checking for ticks after being outside.

Squirrels are cute but naughty. They normally don't eat much foliage, but they do eat some kinds of flowers and several kinds of bulbs. They also dig up new transplants, and they plant nuts in your flower beds and lawns. Field mice can kill trees and shrubs by stripping the bark off the trunk, usually near the ground. Gophers eat the roots of shrubs, trees, and perennials. Moles don't eat plants, but their digging makes a mess of a lawn or flower bed. Persistent trapping is the most effective way to control these little critters. (You can protect the roots of some plants from gophers by planting the plants in wire cages sold at many nurseries.)

Deer-proof plants?

Planting from lists of deer-proof plants often results in disappointment. What's deer-proof in one area may not be in another. And if deer are really hungry, they'll eat almost anything. If you live in an area where deer are common, check with local nurseries, public gardens in your region, or the nearest Cooperative Extension Service office for advice and planting solutions.

DEER-CONTROL FENCING
If your property borders a woodland, deer can be a real problem. Deer have been known to jump very tall fences. Cattle guards can be used in conjunction with fencing at road entrances to deter deer. To be effective, cattle guards can be place side by side forming a 10–15 foot barrier in the direction of travel. A single cattle guard may not be enough to deter deer. Experience shows that a wide midheight fence is one of the best ways to keep out deer. This fence is suitable for a larger property. It is about 6 ft. wide and 5 ft. high and consists of angled poles fixed to posts spaced about 10 ft. apart. Attach wires at 12-in. intervals to the poles. For advice on deer fences that work best in your area, consult your Cooperative Extension Service.

Aphids, beetles, caterpillars, grubs, grasshoppers, spider mites, white flies, scale insects, slugs, snails, and countless other pests can cause minor or devastating damage in a home landscape. Most plants can afford to lose part of their foliage or sap without suffering much of a setback, so don't panic if you see a few holes chewed in a leaf. However, whenever you suspect that insects or related pests are attacking one of your plants, try to catch one of them in a glass jar and have it identified, so you can decide what to do about it.

There are several new kinds of insecticides that are quite effective but much safer to use than the older products. For example, insecticidal soap, a special kind of detergent, quickly kills aphids and other soft-bodied insects, but it's nontoxic to mammals and birds and it breaks down quickly, leaving no harmful residue. Horticultural oil, a highly refined mineral oil, is a good control for scale insects, which frequently infest gardenias, camellias, and other broad-leaved evergreens. Most garden centers stock these and other relatively safe insecticides.

Before using any insecticide, study the fine print on the label to make sure that the product is registered to control your particular pest. Carefully follow the directions for how to apply the product, or it may not work.

Diseases

Several types of fungal, bacterial, and viral diseases can attack garden plants, causing a wide range of symptoms such as disfigured or discolored leaves or petals, powdery or moldy-looking films or spots, mushy or rotten stems or roots, and overall wilting. If you suspect that a plant is infected with a disease, treat it as you would an insect problem. Gather a sample of the plant and show it to someone who can identify the problem before you do any spraying.

In general, plant diseases are hard to treat, so it's important to prevent problems. Choose plants adapted to your area and are disease-resistant plants. Space plants far enough apart so that air can circulate between them, and remove dead stems.

Perennials that would otherwise be healthy are prone to fungal infections during humid weather, especially if plants are crowded or if they have flopped over and are lying on top of each other or on the ground. If your garden has turned into a jungle, look closely for moldy foliage and if you find any, prune it off and discard (don't compost) it. It's better to cut the plants back severely than to let the disease spread. After each pruning cut, dip the blades into a 1:10 solution of bleach and water to avoid spreading the disease. Avoid repeated problems by dividing the perennials, replanting them farther apart, and pruning them early in the season so they don't grow tall and floppy again. Crowded shrubs are also subject to fungal problems in the summer and should be pruned so that air can flow around them.

Winter damage

Historically, much of Texas has been known for relatively mild winters. That has changed with the common occurrence of extreme cold spells. With this comes complete dieback of tropical plants and other marginally hardy plants, plus partial dieback of normally hardy plants. After a particularly hard winter, wait until at least midspring to assess the severity of the freeze damage. At that time, new growth will tell you just how far back a plant has been killed. You can then prune out limbs that are brown and dead.

Oak Wilt Disease

Oak Wilt is a virulent disease caused by the fungus *Bretziella fagacearum*. It can affect all types of oak trees. However, it tends to quickly kill trees in the red oak group more than the white oak group. This vascular disease is prevalent in Central Texas, extending Southeast to Houston and North to Dallas Fort Worth, as well other fragmented areas in Texas.

Oak Wilt can be spread underground via interconnecting tree roots (root grafts), or over longer distances via sap-feeding beetles that transport the fungal spores from one tree to another. Pruning or other tree wounds can also be a point of entry for the disease. Freshly cut firewood can host the fungus and spread the disease if wood is transported. Remember not to transport firewood at any time, since it can spread a range of diseases and insects. The burning of infected wood does not spread the fungus.

It is estimated that this devastating disease has already killed more than one million oak trees in Texas, with a concentration in Central Texas. Oak Wilt can also be found in the Midwest, the Great Lakes Region, the South, and it is spreading to the East Coast.

As mentioned, there are two groups of oaks: the red oak group and the white oak group. Oaks in the red oak group are particularly susceptible to Oak Wilt. This includes Texas red oak or Spanish oak, Shumard oak, blackjack oak, and water oak. If a tree in the red oak group is infected the mortality rate is often 85-100%.

Oaks in the white oak group are a bit more resistant but still susceptible. This includes white oak, post oak, bur Oak, Mexican white oak or Monterrey oak, Lacey oak, and Chinquapin oak. Live oaks are in the white oak group, however when growing in groups live oaks roots often graft forming interconnected roots which can quickly spread the disease. Some white oaks can hang on for a couple of years after being infected.

Infected trees in the red oak group can succumb and die within 2-4 weeks. This is quite shocking to witness. Oak Wilt prevention is more practical than treatment. Trees in the white oak group when infected may show foliage infection (browning of the leaves) and partial canopy dieback may occur over a period of time.

In spring, Oak Wilt fungus creates spores via fungal mats on trees in the red oak group. Sap-feeding beetles are attracted to the sweet fruity smell of the mats. These mats occur under the bark. As the mats expand, they cause small cracks in the bark to form. While feeding on the sap, the beetles pick up the spores and transfer to the next oak they visit.

To reduce the risk of Oak Wilt spread, abstain from pruning or wounding your oaks from February through early July.

Browning of the leaves are a symptom of Oak Wilt.

The leaves of a healthy Texas red oak.

This can include utility line clearing of Oaks on your property boundaries. Wounds include pruning, a freshly cut tree stump, and damage to roots. Trunk and root wounds can occur from lawn mowers, trimmers, and heavy equipment, creating a point of entry for Oak Wilt.

When pruning oaks, make sure tools are sanitized before pruning and between pruning of each tree, use isopropyl alcohol (at least 70% alcohol) or a household disinfectant. After pruning, promptly paint all pruning cuts or wounds with a tree wound dressing or paint with latex paint. Painting of wounds is only appropriate when protecting from Oak Wilt. Do not paint wounds of other species—this can trap moisture, causing harm.

To prevent the spread of Oak Wilt from infected other nearby oaks, the roots of the infected tree can be severed by mechanically trenching to a depth up to 4 feet (1 meter), depending on soil type. Once trenched, infected trees and adjacent trees ought to be removed to reduce the risk of the fungus spreading.

In addition to trenching, fungicide can be applied prophylactically to oaks via injection by a professional. Fungicides have limited effect if applied after symptoms of Oak Wilt appear. An ISA Certified Arborist or other Plant Care Professional with Oak Wilt treatment experience can offer options appropriate to your situation.

Oaks are beloved in Texas for their shade, beauty, wildlife habitat, and the many ecological benefits they provide, but they can perish from disease. To reduce the risk of tree loss, diversify and plant other species in your landscape, as well as closely monitoring your [aks. Additional information on Oak Wilt can be found at Texas A&M Forest Service, *https://tfsweb.tamu.edu.*

Glossary

Amendments. Organic materials or minerals used to improve the soil. Peat moss, pinebark, and compost are commonly used.

Annual. A plant that grows from seed, flowers, produces new seeds, and dies during a single growing season; a tropical plant treated as an annual in that it is grown for only a single season's display and then removed after it freezes.

Balled-and-burlapped. Describes a tree or shrub dug out of the ground with a ball of soil intact around the roots; the ball is then wrapped in burlap and tied for transport.

Bare-root. Describes a plant dug out of the ground and then shaken or washed to remove the soil from the roots.

Chlorosis. Yellowing of the foliage usually due to a lack of iron uptake in alkaline soils.

Compound leaf. A leaf consisting of two or more leaflets branching from the same stalk.

Container grown. Describes a plant raised in a pot that is removed before planting.

Crown. The part of a plant where the roots and stem meet, usually at soil level.

Cultivar. A cultivated variety of a plant, often bred or selected for some special trait such as double flowers, compact growth, cold hardiness, or disease resistance.

Deadheading. Removing spent flowers during the growing season to improve a plant's appearance, prevent seed formation, and stimulate the development of new flowers.

Deciduous. Describes a tree, shrub, or vine that drops all its leaves in winter.

Division. Propagation of a plant by separating it into two or more pieces, each piece possessing at least one bud and some roots. Plants commonly divided include perennials, bulbs, grasses, and ferns.

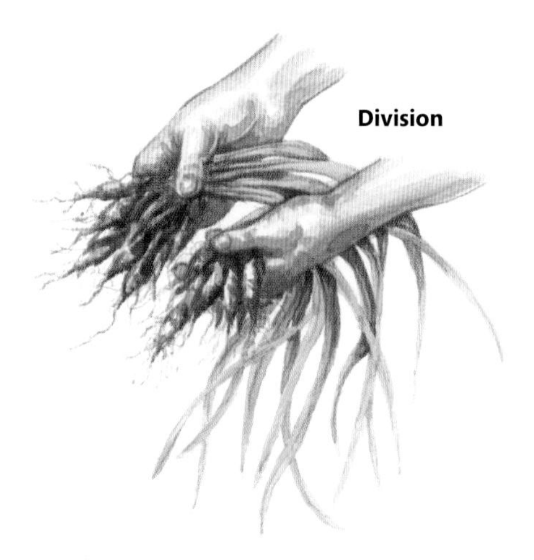

Drainage. Movement of water through soil. If water poured into a foot-deep hole drains completely in a few hours, the drainage is good.

Drip line. An imaginary line beneath a tree that marks the perimeter of the tree's canopy. This area benefits from direct rainfall and "drip" from leaves. Because many of the tree's feeder roots are found along the drip line and beyond, this area is the best for fertilizing and watering.

Dry-laid. Describes a masonry path or wall that is installed without mortar.

Edging. A barrier that serves as the border between lawn and a planting bed. Edgings may be shallow trenches or barriers of plastic, brick, or metal.

Exposure. The characterization of a site according to the sun, wind, and temperature acting upon it.

Formal. Describes a style of landscaping that features symmetrical layouts, with beds and walks related to adjacent buildings, and often with plants sheared to geometric or other shapes.

Foundation planting. Traditionally, a narrow border of evergreen shrubs planted around the foundation of a house. Contemporary foundation plantings often include deciduous shrubs, grasses, perennials, and other plants as well.

Full shade. Describes a site that receives no direct sun during the growing season.

Full sun. Describes a site that receives at least eight hours of direct sun each day during the growing season.

Garden soil. Soil specially prepared for planting to make it loose enough for roots and water to penetrate easily. Usually requires digging or tilling and the addition of some organic matter.

Grade. The angle and direction of the ground's slope in a given area.

Ground cover. A plant providing continuous cover for an area of soil. Commonly a low, spreading foliage plant such as Carolina jessamine, vinca, or cedar sedge.

Habit. The characteristic shape of a plant, such as upright, mounded, columnar, or vase-shaped.

Hardiness. A plant's ability to survive the winter temperatures in a given region without protection.

Hardscape. Parts of a landscape, such as walks, walls, and trellises, made of wood, stone, or other materials.

Herbicide. A chemical used to kill plants. Preemergent herbicides are used to kill weed seeds as they sprout, and thus to prevent weed growth. Postemergent herbicides kill plants that are already growing.

Hybrid. A plant with two parents that belong to different species or genera.

Interplant. To use plants with different bloom times or growth habits in the same bed to increase the variety and appeal of the planting.

Invasive. Describes a plant that spreads quickly, usually by runners or seeds, and mixes with or dominates the adjacent plantings.

Landscape fabric. A synthetic fabric, sometimes water permeable, spread under paths or mulch to serve as a weed barrier.

Loam. Soil rich in organic matter and with mineral particles in a range of sizes. Excellent for many garden plants.

Microclimate. A small-scale system of factors affecting plant growth on a particular site, including shade, temperature, rainfall, and so on.

Mowing strip. A row of bricks or paving stones set flush with the soil around the edge of a bed, and wide enough to support one wheel of the lawn mower.

Mulch. A layer of organic or other materials spread several inches thick around the base of plants and over open soil in a bed. Mulch conserves soil moisture, smothers weeds, and moderates soil temperatures. Where winters are cold, mulches help protect plants from freezing. Common mulches include compost, shredded leaves, pine straw, lawn clippings, gravel, cotton-seed hulls, and landscape fabric.

Native. Describes a plant that is or once was found in the wild in a particular region and was not imported from another area.

Nutrients. Elements needed by plants. Found in the soil and supplied by organic matter and fertilizers, nutrients include nitrogen, phosphorus, potassium, calcium, magnesium, sulfur, iron, and other elements, in various forms and compounds.

Organic matter. Partially or fully decomposed plant and animal matter. Includes leaves, trimmings, and manure.

Peat moss. Partially decomposed mosses and sedges. Dug from boggy areas, peat moss is often used as an organic amendment for garden soil.

Perennial. An herbaceous plant with a life span of more than two years, usually much longer. Cool-season perennials usually go dormant during the summer. Warm-season perennials go dormant during the winter.

Pressure-treated lumber. Softwood lumber treated with chemicals that protect it from decay.

Propagate. To produce new plants from seeds or by vegetative means such as dividing plant parts, taking cuttings, and grafting stems onto other plants.

Retaining wall. A wall built to stabilize a slope and keep soil from sliding or eroding downhill.

Rhizome. A horizontal underground stem from which roots and shoots emerge. Some swell to store food. Branched rhizomes (those of iris, for instance) can be divided to produce new plants.

Root-ball. The mass of soil and roots dug with a plant when it is removed from the ground; the soil and roots of a plant grown in a container.

Selective pruning. Using pruning shears to remove or cut back individual shoots in order to refine the shape of a shrub, maintain its vigor, or limit its size.

Severe pruning. Using pruning shears or loppers to cut away most of a shrub's top growth, leaving just short stubs or a trunk.

Selective pruning

Severe pruning

Shearing. Using hedge shears or an electric hedge trimmer to shape the surface of a shrub or hedge, or to deadhead annuals or perennials.

Soil pH. The alkalinity or acidity of the soil, which affects plant growth and nutrient uptake. Alkaline soils in the western two thirds of Texas are often amended with sulfur and iron products.

Specimen plant. A striking plant, often providing year-round interest, placed for individual display.

Spike. An elongated flower cluster on which individual flowers are attached directly to the main stem or are on very short stalks attached to the main stem.

Tender. Describes a plant that is damaged by cold weather in a particular region.

Underplanting. Growing short plants, such as ground covers, under a taller plant, such as a shrub.

Variegated. Describes foliage with color patterns in stripes, specks, or blotches.

Index

NOTE: Page numbers in ***bold italic*** *refer to illustrations.*

Q

R

S

Photo Credits

Front Cover: *(main image)* Charles Mann, Antique Rose Emporium; *top left & top right* Richard Shiell

Back Cover: Richard Shiell

page 1: happykamill

page 8: RjMjR

page 18: Wisakaka

page 19: The Jungle Explorer

page 20: Anelo

page 21: Bild-Wasser

pages 22–23: Le-thuy Do/Dreamstime.com

page 27: *top* Saxon Holt; *middle* Nikolay Kurzenko; *bottom* Greg Grant

page 30: *top* Beekeepx; *bottom right* Judy M Darby; *bottom left* rueba

page 36: *top* Rita Buchanan; *middle* Albin Raj; *bottom* Masini

page 42: *top* Traveller70; *middle left* Rick Mastelli; *middle right* Saxon Holt; *bottom left* NOPPARAT718; *bottom right* Richard Shiell

page 47: *top* Richard Shiell; *middle left & middle right* Greg Grant; *bottom left* Jerry Pavia

page 51: *top & bottom right* Greg Grant; *middle left* Richard Shiell; *middle right* aniana; *bottom middle* Charles Mann; *bottom left* Galen Gates

page 54: *top left* Jerry Pavia; *top right* Tienuskin; *middle left* Charles Mann; *bottom right* Sundry Photography; *bottom left* P. OCHASANOND

page 58: *top* MaryAnne Campbell; *middle* Greg Grant; *bottom* Jerry Pavia

page 63: *top* Saxon Holt; *middle & bottom* Charles Mann

page 66: *top* Dusan UHRIN; *middle* Asifur_Rahman36; *bottom* Greg Grant

page 73: *top left & bottom left* Greg Grant; *top right* Charles Mann

page 77: *top* Jerry Pavia; *middle left* Greg Grant; *bottom right* Saxon Holt; *bottom left* Charles Mann

page 81: *top & middle right* Greg Grant; *middle left* foto-molka; *bottom* Charles Mann

page 87: *top* Richard Shiell; *middle* Greg Grant

page 90: *top* Thomas Eltzroth; *middle left, middle right & bottom* Greg Grant

page 94: *top left* Jerry Pavia; *top right* Richard Shiell; *middle right* Greg Grant; *bottom right* Charles Mann; *bottom left* Thomas Eltzroth

page 101: *top left & bottom left* Jerry Pavia; *top right & middle right* Rita Buchanan; *bottom right* Richard Shiell

page 107: *top left* Charles Mann; *top right & bottom left* Jerry Pavia

page 113: *top left* TuktaBaby; *top right* Matt Howard; *middle right* Gonzalo de Miceu; *bottom* Andrea Quintero Olivas

page 119: *top left* William Cushman; *top right & bottom* Jerry Pavia

page 120: Brian Woolman

page 121: Zhou Minyun/Dreams-time.com

page 122: Marianne Pfeil

page 123: Charles Mann

page 124: *top* Sunshower Shots; *middle* Charles Mann

page 125: *top* Greg Grant; *bottom* Charles Mann

page 126: *top middle & bottom right* Jerry Pavia; *bottom left* Greg Grant

page 127: *top* Charles Mann; *bottom* Knelson20

page 128: *top* Svetlana Mahovskaya; *bottom* Saxon Holt

page 129: *top left* Bakusova; *top right* Jerry Pavia; *bottom* Charles Mann

page 130: *top* Charles Mann; *bottom* Saxon Holt

page 131: *top* Galen Gates; *bottom* Charles Mann

page 132: *top* Greg Grant; *bottom* Charles Mann

page 133: *both* Jerry Pavia

page 134: *top* Charles Mann; *bottom left* Carole Ottesen; *bottom right* Saxon Holt

page 135: *top* Rita Buchanan; *bottom* John Elsley

page 136: *left* Cheryl Richter; *right* Jerry Pavia

page 137: *bottom left* Richard Shiell; *bottom middle & middle right* Jerry Pavia; *top right & bottom right* Greg Grant

page 138: *top left & top right* Richard Shiell; *bottom* mizy

page 139: *top* Galen Gates; *bottom* Skyprayer2005

page 140: *top left* Greg Grant; *top right* Charles Mann; *bottom* Kabar

page 141: *top* Charles Mann; *bottom* Greg Grant

page 142: Richard Shiell

page 143: *right* Richard Shiell; *left* Jose Luis Vega

page 144: Greg Grant

page 145: *top middle & bottom left* Richard Shiell; *bottom right* Greg Grant

page 146: *top right & bottom left* Charles Mann; *middle* Greg Grant; *bottom right* Saxon Holt

page 147: *top left & top center* Charles Mann; *top right* sasimoto; *bottom left* Richard Shiell; *bottom center* Jerry Pavia; *bottom right* Richard Shiell

page 148: *top* Greg Grant; *bottom* AAPgrad

page 149: *top* Charles Mann; *bottom* Antoshka_Gartz

page 150: *top* Greg Grant; *bottom* Saxon Holt

page 151: *top* Greg Grant; *middle* Jerry Pavia; *bottom* Charles Mann

page 152: Nancy J. Ondra

page 153: *top* Brian Vanden Brink; *bottom* Sergey Denisenko

pages 154–155: Nytumbleweeds/Dreamstime.com

page 162: AleMasche72

page 210: merkulan

page 222: Hope Dorman

page 223: KeriG

page 229: Saxon Holt

page 230: Ruth Rogers Clausen

Check out More Creative Homeowner Books!

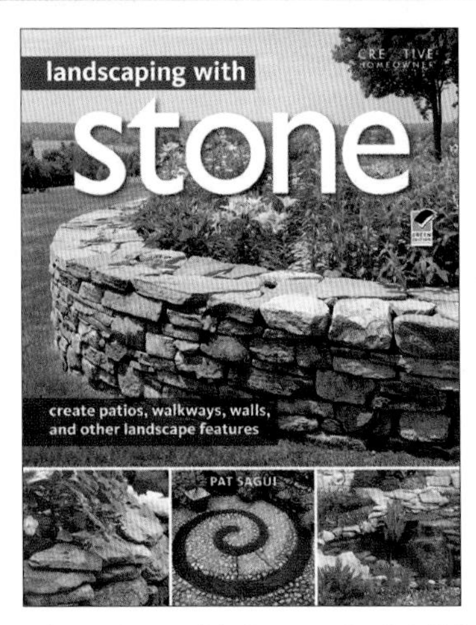

Landscaping with Stone, 2nd Edition
Paperback • 224 pages • 8.5 x 11
978-1-58011-446-2 • Code #4462L
$19.95 US / $21.95 CAD

Pocket Guide to Houseplants
Paperback • 312 pages • 5 x 7
978-1-58011-846-0 • Code #8460
$14.99 US / $18.99 CAD

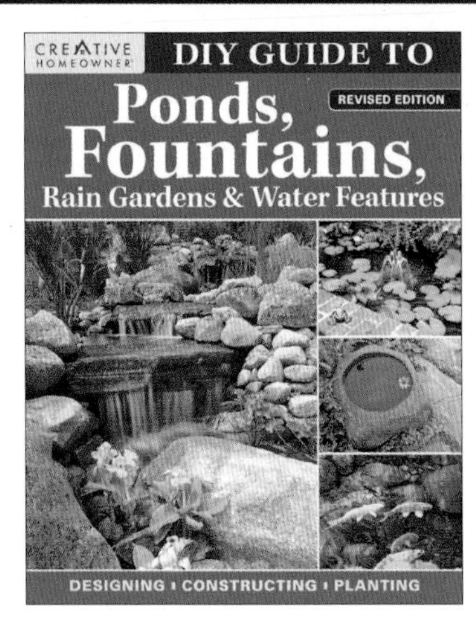

DIY Guide to Ponds, Fountains, Rain Gardens & Water Features, Revised Edition
Paperback • 256 pages • 8.5 x 11
978-1-58011-584-1 • Code #5841D
$24.99 US / $31.99 CAD

Beginner's Guide to Gardening
Paperback • 176 pages • 8.5 x 11
978-1-58011-563-6 • Code #5636
$14.95 US / $16.95 CAD

Trees, Shrubs & Hedges for Your Home, 4th Edition
Paperback • 256 pages • 8.5 x 11
978-1-58011-571-1 • Code #5711
$24.99 US / $31.99 CAD

Succulents for Your Home and Garden
Paperback • 216 pages • 8 x 10
978-1-58011-572-8 • Code #5728C
$22.99 US / $28.99 CAD

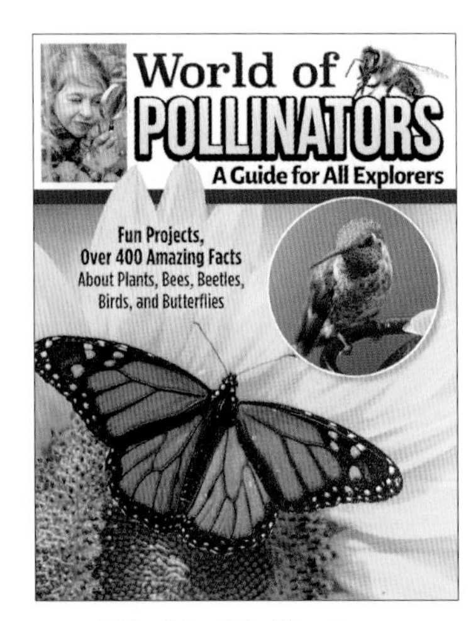

World of Pollinators: A Guide for Explorers of All Ages
Paperback • 144 pages • 8 x 10
978-1-58011-596-4 • Code #5964K
$14.99 US / $18.99 CAD

Ultimate Guide: Decks, Updated 6th Edition
Paperback • 320 pages • 8.5 x 11
978-1-58011-862-0 • Code #8620
$24.99 US / $33.99 CAD

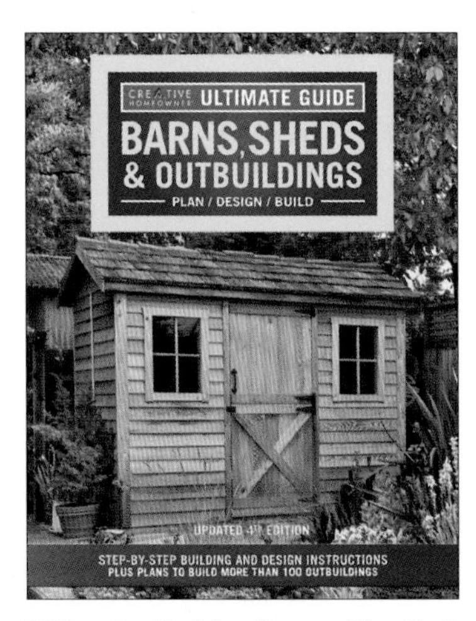

Ultimate Guide: Barns, Sheds & Outbuildings, Updated 4th Edition
Paperback • 304 pages • 8.5 x 11
978-1-58011-799-9 • Code #7999U
$24.99 US / $33.99 CAD

Shop Online at www.FoxChapelPublishing.com